RUGS & CARPETS
OF THE
WORLD

The Salting carpet. Wool and metal thread; this superbly woven piece is now known to be an outstanding example of the carpets in the Persian taste produced at the Imperial Ottoman factories. This piece, usually assigned to Hereke, probably dates from the first half of the 19th century. 7 ft. 5 in. × 5 ft. 5 in. (223 × 163 cm.). Victoria and Albert Museum, London.

RUGS & CARPETS
OF THE
WORLD

Edited by Ian Bennett

NEW
BURLINGTON
BOOKS

A QUARTO BOOK

This edition published by
New Burlington Books, London W1

Copyright © 1977 Quarto Limited

Reprinted 1985

ISBN 0 906286 19 0

This book was designed and produced by
Quarto Publishing Limited
32 Kingly Court, London W1
Picture research: Anne-Marie Ehrlich

Phototypeset in England by
Filmtype Services Limited, Scarborough
Printed in Hong Kong

Contents

Introduction 7
by Ian Bennett

**Techniques and Materials
of Oriental Carpet Weaving** 9
by John Siudmak

Oriental and African Rugs and Carpets 23
by Ian Bennett
Historical Introduction 27
Early Weaving 38
Safavid Weaving 44
Early Ottoman Weaving 90
Mamluk and Ottoman Weaving in Egypt 112
Rugs and Carpets of Moghul India 122
Caucasian Weaving 138
Weaving of the Turkoman and Baluchi Tribes 158
Far Eastern Weaving 180
Later Ottoman Weaving 197
Moroccan and Tunisian Rugs and Carpets 218
Later Persian Weaving 221
Flat Weaving 251

European Rugs and Carpets 259
by Isabelle Anscombe

North American Rugs and Carpets 321
by Harmer Johnson
Navajo Rugs 323
Handmade American Rugs 332

Buying and Maintenance of Rugs and Carpets 335
Glossary 339
Bibliography 344
Index 346
Acknowledgements 351
Picture Credits 352

Maps
Major Weaving Areas of Asia and Africa 24
The Navajo Weaving Centres 322

Page numbers in inner margins refer to illustrations

Spanish carpet from
Alcaraz. Early
16th century.
Approximately
8 ft. 6 in. × 5 ft. 4 in.
(259 × 162.5 cm.).

Introduction

THIS BOOK sets out to be a discussion of the carpets and other woven products of the major weaving areas of the world from the earliest times to the present day. Naturally, a subject of such vast proportions cannot be dealt with in depth in a one-volume study, but we have tried to give the reader a greater coverage than is normally found in carpet books, the great majority of which deal with Oriental carpets alone. Indeed, it is surprising how very little up-to-date and in-print literature there is on European and American weaving, or on specific aspects such as Navajo or Moroccan and Tunisian weavings. More than this, compared to the many books available on Persian carpets and, more recently, Turkoman pieces, the reader might well think that the rest of Oriental weaving had been treated somewhat perfunctorily by scholars. We still await, for instance, a major study of Turkish and Moghul carpets.

My principal aim in the chapter on Oriental weaving has been an attempt to steer a path for the reader through the world of carpet scholarship, a world which has an unfortunate tendency to become a morass of conflicting opinions, more likely to confuse the layman than enlighten him. Indeed, carpet books, more than any other form of art history, apparently incline to the view that not only should they be written exclusively by scholars, but read exclusively by them also. The principal difficulty is that there is very little factual evidence of a documentary nature to help us in our search for the origins and derivations of Oriental carpet styles. As far as we can judge, weaving in the Near and Middle East was considered a manufacturing industry (much the same is true, of course, of the European aristocracy's attitude toward its artists and craftsmen in the Middle Ages, the Renaissance and, most significantly, in the 18th century) and there was no reason, therefore, why details of designs and designers, weavers and manufactories should be recorded. Thus, the scholar, working with a minimum of hard facts, must perforce erect a hypothetical structure. This is particularly true of Safavid weaving. The trouble is that carpet scholars, with little justification, often consider that their hypotheses are proved, and proceed therefrom with calm assurance and dogmatism. Such scholarship is, in reality, built upon an edifice of shifting sand.

In many respects, our knowledge of carpets has progressed little since the early days of scholarship around the turn of this century. Advances have been made in ethnology, archaeology, and linguistics, which have increased what we know of the life and culture of Eastern kingdoms and empires. Similarly, a concentration on European sources – old master paintings, documents such as wills, etc. – has given new insights into early weaving styles, which are not known from extant carpets. Also much study has been done in the last twenty years or so on the techniques of knotting in order to arrive at a more accurate chronology and provenance. This comparatively new science of technical exegesis is still in its infancy, but nevertheless has been responsible for a number of important ideas – the Turkoman 'S-group', for instance, and a critical reassessment of Persian vase carpets.

If there is any area in which modern scholars differ from their predecessors, it is in the moving forward of dates. Many carpets once thought sixteenth- or seventeenth-century are now considered to be eighteenth- or nineteenth-century. The German scholar R. G. Hübel, one of the pioneers of technical analysis, dropped a considerable bomb in 1970 in his study *The Book of Oriental Carpets* (published in English in 1971) when he suggested that even the most 'sacred' of early weavings, the Berlin dragon and phoenix carpet and the Stockholm Marby rug were not, in fact, the fifteenth-century lone survivors of a once great and widespread style, but late seventeenth- or early eighteenth-century copies. As we can see from this and other examples mentioned throughout this book, very little can be taken on trust in the field of Oriental carpet scholarship; and it has to be said that although scholars in fifty or a hundred years time may differ in degree on stylistic attributions or chronology, it is unlikely, without any major archaeological discoveries on a par with that of the Altai Mountains, that they will have any more hard evidence than the scholar of today.

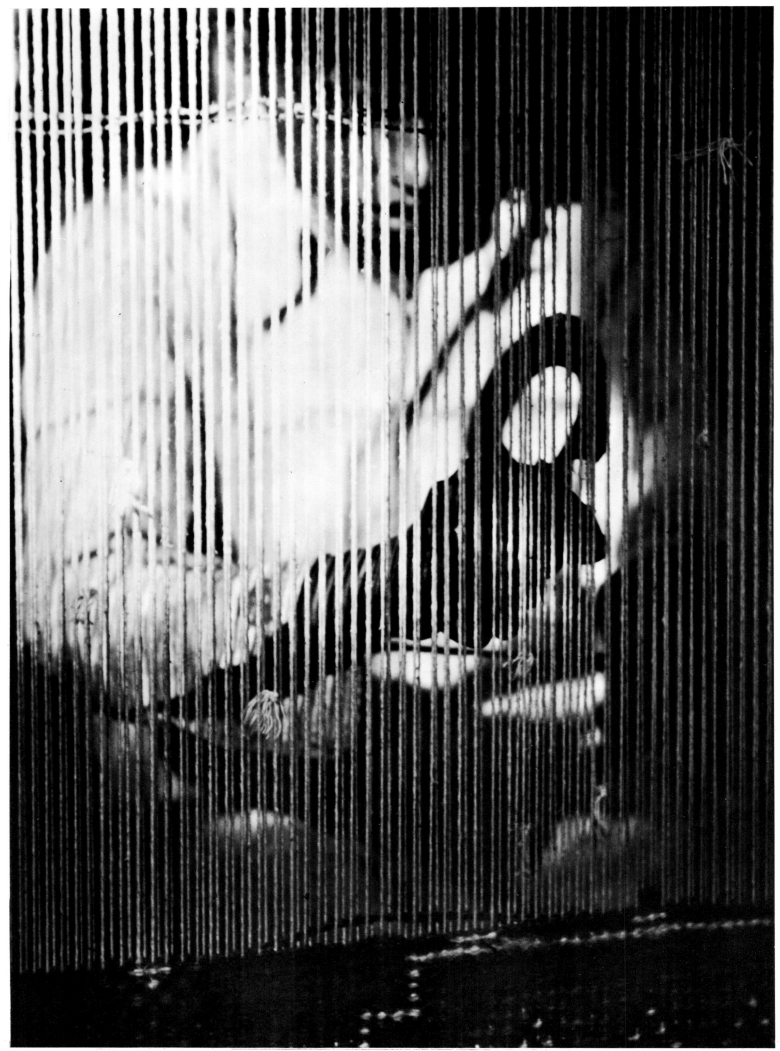

Carpet weaving in a Jaipur workshop.

TECHNIQUES AND MATERIALS OF ORIENTAL CARPET WEAVING

Shirazi weavers working on a fixed horizontal loom copying a design from the reverse side of a finished rug.

Rugs left in strong sunlight to age them artificially.

Techniques and Materials
of Oriental Carpet Weaving

THE TECHNIQUES OF WEAVING knotted rugs are very varied. These techniques have developed in the course of time under the influence of physical and historical circumstances. Many of them date from after the early 16th century, when the character of weaving in Persia underwent a great change and a major proliferation of techniques took place. Carpet weaving began as a nomadic craft and it still continues today basically unchanged amongst nomadic people in Persia and Turkey. Although it may already have been established in the Near East prior to the invasion of the Seljuk Turks in 1037, it took firm root in Turkey and Persia during Seljuk times. It seems to have been organized on a commercial basis in at least one centre in Turkey, and Seljuk carpets enjoyed a considerable reputation in the time of Marco Polo.

Technically there is little to distinguish the surviving Seljuk rugs from some Turkish village types woven up to the 19th century. They use warps of undyed two-ply wool and wefts of red wool in multiples of two and three on an even foundation and are loosely knotted with a Turkish knot. Although design is very diversified in later Turkish rugs, there is strong conservatism and general homogeneity in technique.

In Timurid times, design in Persia closely resembled that in Turkey: predominantly geometrical patterns arranged in a universal repeat. However, towards the end of the 15th century, design gradually became more curvilinear and floral motifs began to appear. In the early Safavid period, weaving was elevated to the level of court taste and the vast repertoire of book illumination and miniature painting became a major source of design.

To meet these new demands many technical innovations were required, including the use of very fine quality material. The new designs could not be reproduced from memory or sight, but required complex cartoons. The Persian knot was used exclusively, as this was more suited to rendering fine details. Silk was extensively used as a warp material, as it is much stronger than wool in relation to its thickness. The looms producing these carpets relied on court patronage and many were directly organized by the court. The royal looms of Isfahan during the reign of Shah Abbas the Great (1587–1629) were organized on an export basis and during his reign royal looms were also established in other centres including Shirvan and Karabagh in the Caucasus.

Meanwhile, in Ottoman Turkey royal looms were established in Ushak, Bursa and Istanbul. Large-scale weaving declined in Persia after the collapse of the Safavid dynasty in the early 18th century, but was revived by merchants in the second half of the 19th century.

Weaving in India has closely paralleled that of Persia; although certain rugs of the early period are difficult to distinguish from some Persian ones, notably those of Herat, and have still not been firmly attributed to a single place.

Despite the growth of sophisticated royal looms, weaving continued as a nomadic craft and also developed as a cottage industry in villages and towns in the Near East. As a cottage industry it developed its own local techniques and designs. In Persia, design generally reflected the taste of the court, whereas in Turkey and the Caucasus geometrical designs continued to be used. West Turkestan, virtually inaccessible until the 19th century, continued weaving designs unchanged for centuries. Spain and Egypt on the other hand constitute a totally separate development and technically both areas remain influenced by developments further east.

Construction

Rows of knots are tied on a foundation of warp and weft and become the pile, which consists of upright yarn. The warp runs along the length of the carpet and the fineness of the weave depends on its thickness and the proximity of the warps to one another. It is always tightly spun for strength. When the rug is completed, the ends form the fringes which may be weft-faced, braided, tasselled or secured in some other manner.

The warps on the side of the rug are normally combined into one or more cables of varying thickness which are overcast to form the selvedge. The warps must be kept at an even tension throughout the weaving process. The wefts pass under and over the warps from one side of the rug to the other. They are loosely plied or sometimes unplied to allow them to be tightly packed to secure each row of knots.

Weaving normally begins by passing a number of wefts to form a base to work on. The knots are then tied around consecutive sets of adjacent warps. Between each row of knots, one or more shots of weft are passed. The fineness of the weave depends on the density of the knots. The knot count can be determined in a specific area by multiplying the horizontal count by the vertical count. Knot counts vary from sixteen to 500 and more per square inch.

Design

Village and nomadic rugs generally use traditional inherited designs which are usually reproduced from memory. These often have totemic or symbolic associations, but in most instances they are mutated forms whose original significance has long since been forgotten. More sophisticated town rugs use curvilinear designs reproduced from cartoons and the designs are called by the head weaver. As cartoons are costly, the design of some rugs is sometimes copied from other rugs.

Looms

These do not vary greatly in essential details, although they vary greatly in size and sophistication. There is no direct correlation between fineness of weave and sophistication of loom. The main technical requirement of a loom is to provide the correct tension and a means of dividing the warps into alternate sets of leaves. A shedding device allows the weaver to pass wefts through crossed and uncrossed warps, instead of laboriously threading the weft in and out of the warps.

The simplest form of loom is a horizontal one which can be staked to the ground or supported by side pieces on the ground. The necessary tension can be obtained through the use of wedges. This is ideal for nomadic people as it can easily be assembled or dismantled. Rugs produced on horizontal looms are generally fairly small and cannot be wider than the beams, which must be small enough to be transported. Vertical looms are undoubtedly more comfortable to operate, although they are not portable and thus only found amongst sedentary people. There is no limit to the size of the carpet to be woven, as there is no restriction on the width of the beam, and in India especially very large looms have been recorded.

There are three broad groups of vertical loom which, however, may be locally modified in many ways: the fixed village loom, the Tabriz or Bunyan loom and the roller beam loom.

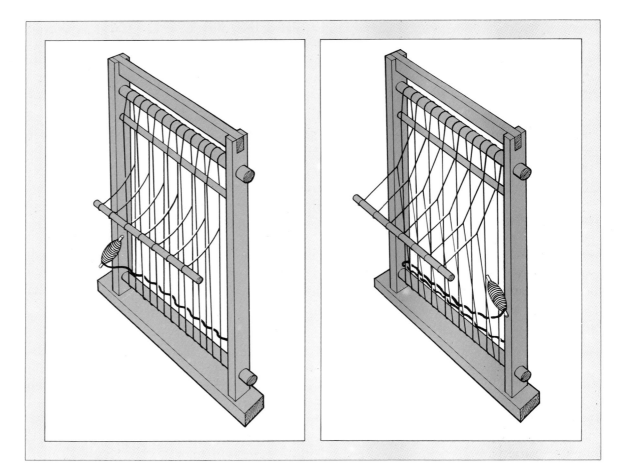

A vertical loom showing a crossed and uncrossed shed of warps, using a simple shedding device.

Weavers packing down wefts with steel combs. Below: a Kerman village weaver working at a simple horizontal loom, which is staked in position.

The first loom is used mainly in Persia and consists of a fixed upper beam and a movable lower beam or cloth beam, which slots into two side pieces. The correct tension is obtained through driving wedges into the slots. The weaver or weavers work on an adjustable plank which is raised as the work progresses.

The Tabriz loom is used in north-east Persia and in commercial centres in Turkey. On this type of loom, the warps are continuous and pass around behind the loom. Tension is again obtained through the use of wedges. The weavers sit on a fixed seat and when a portion of the carpet has been completed, the tension is released and the carpet is pulled down around the back of the loom. This process continues until completion of the carpet, when the warps are severed and the carpet taken off the loom.

The roller beam loom is the traditional village loom of Turkey, but is also found in Persia and India. It consists of two movable beams to which the warps are attached. Both beams are fitted with rachets or similar locking devices and completed work is rolled on to the lower beam. It is possible to weave very long rugs by this means, and in some areas of Turkey rugs are woven in series.

Tools

In order to operate the loom, the weaver needs a number of essential tools: a knife for cutting the yarn as the knots are tied; a comb-like instrument for packing down the wefts and a pair of shears for trimming the yarn. In Tabriz the knife is combined with a hook with which the knots are tied; normally the fingers alone are used. A small steel comb is sometimes used for combing out the yarn after each row of knots, which both tightens the weave and clarifies the design. A variety of instruments are used for packing the weft.

15

Far left: a weaver preparing a knot and cutting the yarn. Left: a weaver packing down wefts with a comb.

Some weaving areas in Persia renowned for compact weaves use additional equipment to the beating comb. In Kerman, a sabre-like instrument is used horizontally inside the shed, and in Bijar a heavy nail-like tool is used. A number of different shears are used, but the type depends on the method of trimming the rug. It may be trimmed as the work progresses, or the trimming may be performed after completion of the rug. In Chinese rugs, the yarn is trimmed after completion and is slanted where the colour changes, giving an embossed effect.

The Knots

Two basic knots are used: the Turkish or Ghiordes knot and the Persian or Senneh knot. As these terms are often confusing, the terms 'symmetrical' and 'asymmetrical' are often used. The Turkish knot is found in Turkey, the Caucasus, Turkestan and in Persia amongst people of Turkish or Kurdish race. The Persian knot is found in Persia, India, Turkestan, Egypt and in Turkey in the case of some court rugs. Turkish and Persian knots are normally tied around two adjacent warps, although sometimes they may be tied around more.

The Turkish knot is executed in the following manner: the yarn is passed between two adjacent warps, brought back under one, wrapped around both forming a collar, then pulled through the centre so that both ends emerge from between the same warps.

The Persian knot is wrapped around one warp only, then the yarn is passed open behind the adjacent warp so that the two ends are divided by a single warp. It may be open on the left or the right.

The Spanish knot is looped around single alternate warps so the ends are brought out on either side.

The Jufti knot, frequently encountered in Khorassan, is tied around four warps instead of two. (See diagrams overleaf.)

Materials and Preparation

Dyed wool is customarily used for the pile. This can vary enormously in quality. Early Safavid rugs use soft fleecy wool of the highest quality, while Turkish and Caucasian village rugs generally use fairly coarse, harsh wool. Silk is used for more sumptuous rugs and is rarely encountered in village rugs, although it is used in small quantities to embellish Turkoman, Caucasian and Turkish rugs.

Cotton is frequently used for details in early Safavid and Indian rugs, in later Ghiordes rugs, Turkoman Saryk rugs and in Ottoman Bursa rugs. Usually it is undyed, but a blue-dyed cotton is used in Bursa rugs. Silver and silver-gilt thread wrapped on a silk core is found brocaded in some Safavid rugs and in later Turkish court rugs like Hereke and Koum Kapou. In later Persian rugs a cruder technique of plain wire woven on directly is found.

Foundation

In Turkish and nomadic rugs, including those from West Turkestan, wool is used almost exclusively for the warp, which is undyed. It is tightly spun and often of dark colours which are unsuitable for dyeing. In some Transylvanian and Ushak rugs, a technique known as

Opposite: a Baluchi weaver working on a simple fixed vertical loom.

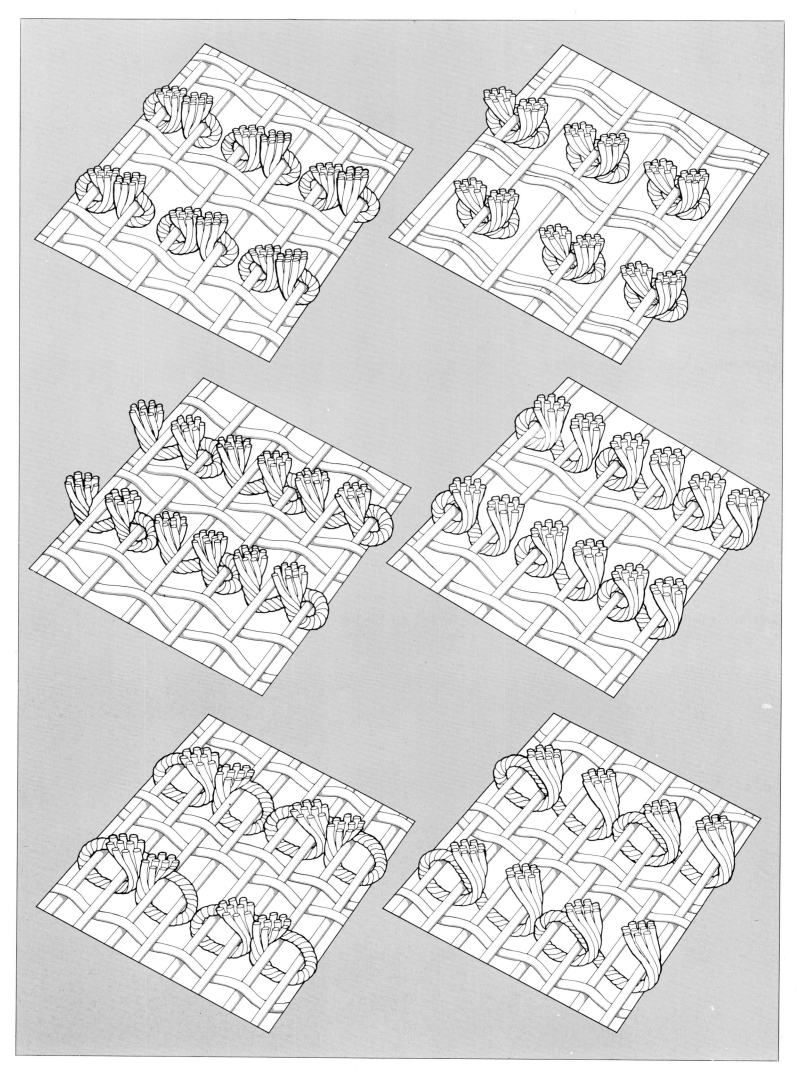

end-dip is used, whereby the ends of the warp, which will later become the fringe, are dyed in colours usually taken from the yellows and reds of the spectrum.

The weft is generally loosely plied wool, but cotton is sometimes used, especially in Caucasian rugs. In Turkey and related areas the weft is usually dyed, red being the most common colour. Persian rugs of the early Safavid period use a tightly spun silk warp and loosely spun silk weft. In Persia and India silk warps were gradually replaced by mill-spun cotton warps. As many later Safavid and Indian rugs have a complex weft structure, more than one material is often used. Wool and/or cotton and silk may be found in rugs of the vase groups and in Moghul court rugs.

Coarse late Indian rugs often use jute as a weft material. Generally, there has been an increasing use of cotton, often dyed except for silk rugs like Tabriz, Herez and Kashan which use a silk foundation. Coarse town rugs of Persia, like Hamadan, use a home-spun cotton. Spanish and Egyptian rugs use a wool foundation which is usually dyed. Central Asian rugs use wool, silk and cotton as foundation material.

Twist and Ply

In most weaving areas, yarns of whatever material are spun in an anti-clockwise direction and plied in a clockwise direction. The symbols S and Z are used to designate clockwise and anti-clockwise twist respectively: when the yarn is twisted tight, the diagonal ribs formed will correspond to the diagonal of an S and Z. Cairo and Bursa (which includes Ottoman and later nineteenth-century silk rugs), use an S spin and a Z twist.

Dyes

Dyeing was carried out in most Oriental weaving areas by the village dyer who was often Jewish and the craft was kept a closely guarded secret. Although similar dyestuffs were used throughout the Near East, enormous variation in colour resulted, as the colour is not determined by the ingredients alone, but by the type of wool used and primarily by the quality of the water. This is a convenient guide for classification since particular areas can be associated with particular tones of colour after some experience.

Until the introduction of chemical colours in the second half of the 19th century, only natural dyestuffs were used, such as the madder and indigo plant, to produce shades of red and blue. These primary colours could be mixed with other primary colours to produce a wide range of secondary colours. One can find between six and twelve different colours in most antique rugs. Other dyestuffs include berries, plants, fruit, bark and fungi. The agents used in the production of some colours, primarily brown, produce a corrosive effect,

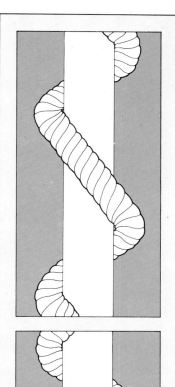

Opposite: types of knot. Top left: Turkish, Ghiordes or symmetrical knot. Top right: Spanish or single warp symmetrical knot. Centre left: Persian, Senneh or asymmetrical knot open on the left. Centre right: Persian knot open on the right. Bottom left: Turkish Jufti knot tied on four warps. Bottom right: Persian Jufti knot open on the right.

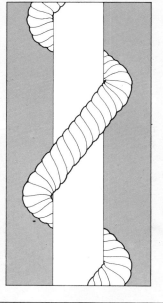

Above: yarn twisted tight in a clockwise direction will form the diagonal of an S; yarn twisted in an anti-clockwise direction will form the diagonal of a Z. Left: materials used for the preparation of dyes at the Shiraz weaving school, where only natural dyes are used. Dyes are prepared from a variety of materials, including madder (red), yellow larkspur (yellow), walnut husks (light brown) and pomegranate rind (dark brown).

Dyeing and yarn preparation in a carpet factory in Jaipur, India. Above: preparing yarn for dyeing. Opposite: yarn about to be immersed in a vat of indigo dye (above left); operating the immersion mechanism (top right); balls of dyed yarn ready for the weavers (bottom).

and wool dyed in these colours is liable to wear away more quickly than wool dyed in other colours. Ferrous oxide, in particular, tends to weaken the pile very quickly.

Although natural colours are fast, they do fade slightly in the course of time when exposed to light and alkalis, but this produces a pleasing, harmonious effect which cannot be equalled with chemical colours. Before wool is dyed, it is specially prepared by first scouring in hot water, then steeped in a mordant. It is then placed in the vat with the prepared dye and boiled. Afterwards it is washed in water, running if possible.

Most dyestuffs, with the exception of indigo and cochineal, were locally cultivated or gathered. Indigo was imported from India in concentrated form and prepared in a fermentation vat. Cochineal was used extensively in nineteenth-century rugs in Khorassan and Kerman, and makes its appearance in Turkoman rugs in the late 19th century.

Chemical colours fall into two groups both of which are completely inferior to natural dyes. One is the acid or aniline dye which is completely fugitive to light and alkalis; the second is more sophisticated and known as chrome dye, but its main disadvantage is that it is too fast and tends to lack subtlety.

Structure

Each weaving district or atelier has a characteristic weave by which it may be recognized. The main structural feature of a rug is the way in which the warp and weft are combined and in what factors, and the type of knot used. Additionally, minor features such as treatment of selvedge, ends or presence of diagonal lines in the ground weave help to identify types. Differentiation can also be made in terms of colour and design, but these criteria should never be isolated from structural considerations. Familiarity of all techniques is essential in attributing and dating a rug and also in determining its authenticity. Many sixteenth- and seventeenth-century groups have been skilfully copied.

Positioning of warps varies considerably, ranging from a single-plane to a two-plane system. A particular warp system is maintained by a complementary weft system. If a weft is

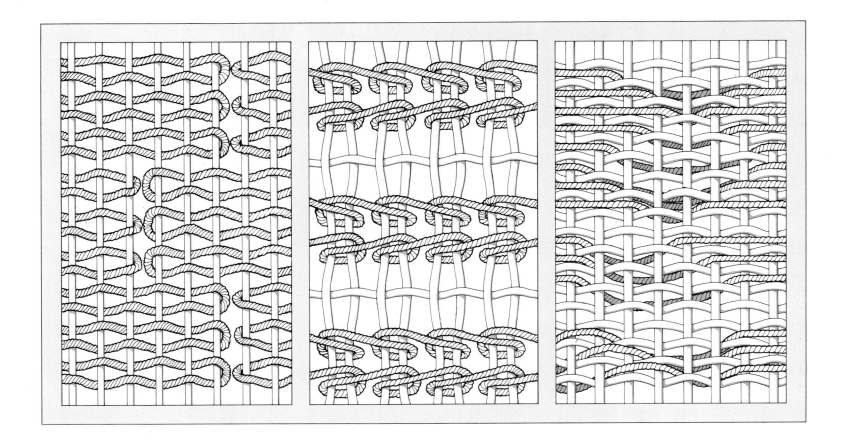

stretched taut across alternate warps, it will have the effect of displacing them, but if it is loosely applied the warps will remain in an even position. Thus, depending on how the wefts are used in the rug, one may have an even or depressed foundation, as is the case with most Turkish village rugs. A two-plane system is not found and would not seem to be adapted to the Turkish knot.

Many rugs with an even foundation are multi-wefted, having an irregular distribution of wefts with anything from one to six shots between each row of knots. Rugs with depressed foundations, like Ushak, Ladik, Kula and Ghiordes, are usually double-wefted, in which the first weft is taut and the second weft sinuous.

Discontinuous wefts are found in some Turkish rugs such as Ghiordes, Transylvanian and Ushak and these produce diagonal lines or lazy lines visible on the back of the rug. These indicate that a weaver has been unwilling to change her position and has returned the wefts along the area which she has been working on, moving in one warp at a time. Copies of Transylvanian and Ushak rugs have a selvedge of two to five cables of weft-faced warps. The ground weft may only loop over the first cable or may be woven around the whole selvedge. Usually ends are finished with a broad kelim strip.

Ottoman court rugs from Bursa, Hereke and Koum Kapou are woven on a silk foundation with a depressed structure. Caucasian rugs are constructed with a depressed warp and are usually double- or triple-wefted, with the exception of Kazak rugs which are multi-wefted and use an even foundation. Wool is generally used for warps, although some types use a silk warp. A cotton weft is frequently used. The ends are usually braided.

Persian rugs of the 16th century are usually triple-wefted with a depressed warp and use the Persian knot open on the left. The foundation is generally silk. In the 17th century there was a tendency for the double weft to be used, and the Turkish knot became increasingly prevalent in the north-east.

While most Safavid rugs use the depressed warp system, the Kerman vase group and the related Sanguszko group use a two-plane warp system. This is combined with a triple weft, the first and third being taut and generally of wool, and the second of thin cotton or silk which is sinuous. Although it creates a firm foundation, it has an inherent weakness in that, when the carpet is worn, the connecting second weft is exposed and releases the top level of warps if broken. The same system is used for nineteenth-century Kerman carpets.

Later Persian rugs are generally much more heterogeneous than Turkish rugs. The Persian knot is normally used, although both knots are used in Tabriz and Baluchi and

Kashgai weaves. The Turkish knot is used exclusively in the Kurdish weave of Senneh. Hamadan and Malayer, which are all single-wefted. Most town rugs are double-wefted with depressed warps. Generally, selvedge consists of a single cord, with the exception of Baluchi rugs and Tabriz and Herez rugs which use multiple cording.

Indian rugs are technically similar to Persian rugs. Moghul court rugs have a two-plane warp system similar to the vase group. The first and third weft is generally of dyed cotton and the second a sinuous silk red thread.

Egyptian rugs are usually woven on a wool foundation with a Persian knot. They are triple-wefted, each shot comprising two or three unplied yarns. Spanish rugs on the other hand are single-wefted.

Turkoman rugs use a remarkably wide range of techniques. Turkish and Persian knots open on the left and right are used sometimes in the same rug and an even foundation ranging through a two-plane system can be found. Generally, these rugs are compact and finely woven. Selvedge consists of a single overcast cable and older rugs generally have a wide kelim strip at both ends. They are usually woven exclusively of wool, although cotton is found in rugs of the Saryk. A number of tribes also use silk.

Related Techniques

The term *kelim* applies to tapestry-woven fabrics in the Near East. The technique produces a weft-faced textile in which the warps are concealed. The wefts are discontinuous and return as the design/colour changes. Unless the wefts of two adjacent colour areas pass around the same warp a slit is produced, and this is the technique used in most areas. This is referred to as slit tapestry weave. If the areas are connected, it is known as linked tapestry weave.

The *Soumak* technique also produces a weft-faced fabric. Here the wefts are passed over two warps and back under one. The weave may be plain or countered. The technique can be either structural or supplementary. The first type uses no ground weave and is usually referred to as Soumak wrapping. The second type uses a ground weft, and Soumak wefts are supplementary and discontinuous in different colour zones. This type is referred to as Soumak brocading.

Brocading is similar to Soumak brocade, where a ground weave is patterned by supplementary discontinuous wefts consisting of floats of different lengths.

Ottoman Cairene floral court carpet with central medallion. Erdmann suggests that the motifs within the central medallion of carpets of this type are of Mamluk origin. Traditionally attributed to Cairo, but probably Anatolian. Late 16th or early 17th century. 8 ft. 10 in. × 5 ft. 5 in. (269 × 165 cm.). Victoria and Albert Museum, London.

ORIENTAL AND AFRICAN RUGS AND CARPETS

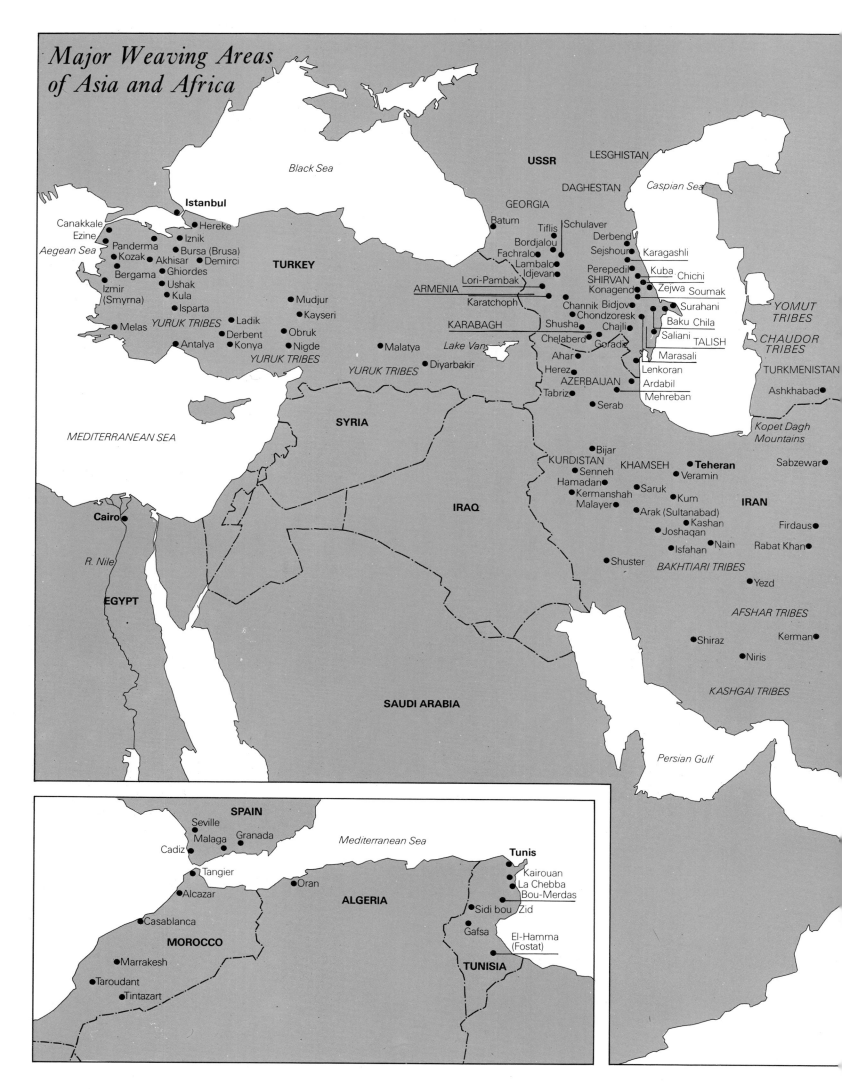

Major Weaving Areas of Asia and Africa

USSR

LESGHISTAN

Black Sea

DAGHESTAN

GEORGIA

Caspian Sea

Istanbul

Batum

Tiflis · Schulaver

Derbend

Canakkale
Ezine

· Hereke

Bordjalou

Sejshour

Karagashli

· Iznik

Fachralo

Aegean Sea

Panderma
Kozak

· Bursa (Brusa)
Akhisar · Demirci

Lambalo

Perepedil

SHIRVAN

Kuba · Chichi

TURKEY

Idjevan

Konagend

Zejwa Soumak

Bergama
Ghiordes

Lori-Pambak

*YOMUT
TRIBES*

Izmir
(Smyrna)

Ushak

ARMENIA

Surahani

Kula

Channik Bidjov

Baku Chila

*CHAUDOR
TRIBES*

Isparta

Karatchoph

Chondzoresk

Saliani

TALISH

· Melas

Mudjur

KARABAGH

Shusha

Chajli

TURKMENISTAN

YURUK TRIBES · Ladik

· Kayseri

Chelaberd

Goradiz

Marasali

Derbent

Obruk

Ahar

Lenkoran

Ashkhabad

· Antalya

Konya

· Nigde

YURUK TRIBES

Herez

Ardabil

AZERBAIJAN

· Malatya

Lake Van

Tabriz

Mehreban

*Kopet Dagh
Mountains*

YURUK TRIBES · Diyarbakir

· Serab

SYRIA

Bijar

KURDISTAN

KHAMSEH

Teheran

Sabzewar

· Senneh

Veramin

MEDITERRANEAN SEA

Hamadan

Saruk

IRAN

· Kermanshah
Malayer

· Kum

Firdaus

Cairo ·

IRAQ

Arak (Sultanabad)

R. Nile

Kashan

Rabat Khan

Joshaqan

EGYPT

Isfahan Nain

· Shuster

BAKHTIARI TRIBES

· Yezd

AFSHAR TRIBES

· Shiraz

Kerman

· Niris

SAUDI ARABIA

KASHGAI TRIBES

Persian Gulf

SPAIN

Seville

Mediterranean Sea

Malaga
Granada

Cadiz

Tunis

Tangier

Kairouan

· Oran

La Chebba

Alcazar

ALGERIA

Bou-Merdas

· Sidi bou Zid

Casablanca

· Gafsa

El-Hamma
(Fostat)

MOROCCO

· Marrakesh

TUNISIA

· Taroudant

· Tintazart

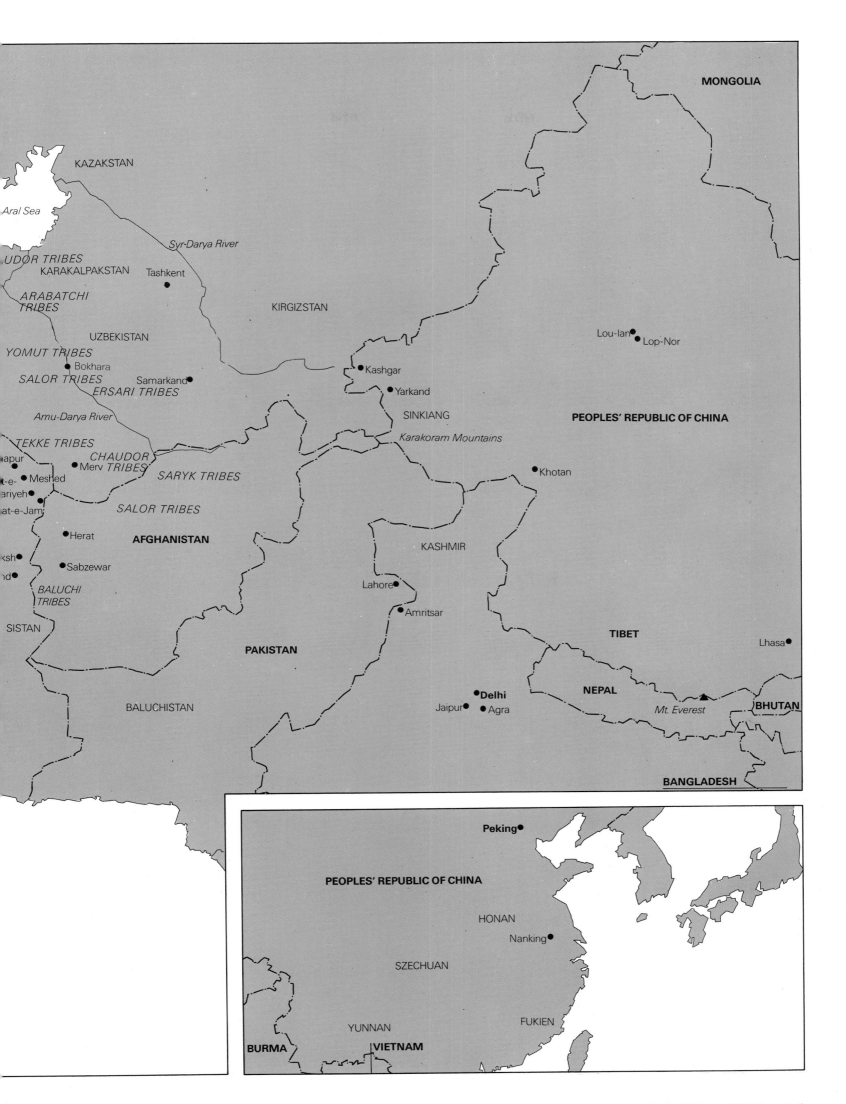

KAZAKSTAN

Aral Sea

Syr-Darya River

UDOR TRIBES

KARAKALPAKSTAN

Tashkent

ARABATCHI TRIBES

KIRGIZSTAN

UZBEKISTAN

YOMUT TRIBES

Bokhara

Samarkand

SALOR TRIBES

ERSARI TRIBES

Lou-lan Lop-Nor

Kashgar

Yarkand

SINKIANG

PEOPLES' REPUBLIC OF CHINA

Amu-Darya River

Karakoram Mountains

TEKKE TRIBES

apur

CHAUDOR TRIBES

Merv

SARYK TRIBES

Khotan

t-e- Meshed

ariyeh

SALOR TRIBES

at-e-Jam

Herat

AFGHANISTAN

KASHMIR

ksh

Sabzewar

nd

BALUCHI TRIBES

Lahore

SISTAN

Amritsar

TIBET

Lhasa

PAKISTAN

Delhi

NEPAL

Jaipur Agra

Mt. Everest

BHUTAN

BALUCHISTAN

BANGLADESH

Peking

PEOPLES' REPUBLIC OF CHINA

HONAN

Nanking

SZECHUAN

FUKIEN

YUNNAN

BURMA VIETNAM

MONGOLIA

The City of Baghdad Flooded *from a
a Persian manuscript of 1468. From
A.D. 750 Baghdad was the capital city
of the Abbasid Caliphate. British
Library, London.*

Historical Introduction

ANY STUDY OF ORIENTAL CARPETS must, inevitably, take into consideration the history and culture of a vast area stretching from the Black Sea eastward to China. This area includes those states which now form part of the Soviet Union, Mongolia, Tibet, China itself, Turkey, Mesopotamia, Persia, Afghanistan, the area of Pakistan once called Baluchistan, and India. In North Africa, we must also consider Egypt and Morocco. Apart from China and Tibet, the carpets of which form in any case a very distinct group, the cultures of all the other areas we have mentioned are linked by ethnographic ties and, most importantly, by a common religion: Islam.

The development of the art of the carpet in Islamic countries may be seen, at its most basic, as an interaction between religious and ethnic structures dating from long before the advent of Islam. This art has been shaped by economic, social and political movements caused by the development of religious beliefs and by military conquests. Thus, it is possible to define the culture of the Muslim world in terms of the movement of two major ethnic groups, the Mongols and the Arabs, and their spread through the empires of Islam.

The Caliphates

The Prophet Muhammed died in the year A.D. 632, having ten years previously moved his capital from Mecca to Medina. It is from this move that the Islamic calendar takes its starting point, the year of the Hejira. In the year of the Prophet's death, his followers sought to elect a spiritual representative, whose powers were to be both political and spiritual; they founded the Caliphate, the career of which, for some centuries, paralleled that of the Christian Papacy, although not, of course, contemporaneously. From their capital of Medina, the so-called Four Great Caliphs, Abu Bakr, Umar, Uthman and Ali, whose reigns cover the period A.D. 632–61, extended the beliefs of Islam to Syria, Mesopotamia, Persia and Egypt. In the

Left: The Triumph of Shapur I *from Naqsh-e-Rustam, Sassanian dynasty, Persia. Above: bronze water ewer. Anthropomorphic features such as the animal handles are typical of Sassanian metalwork. Victoria and Albert Museum, London.*

The Investiture of Ardeshir I.
Stone relief from Naqsh-e-Rustam, Sassanian dynasty, Persia.

following one hundred years, the Umayyad Caliphate moved its capital to Damascus and continued the conversion of the infidel with the spread of Islam to other areas of North Africa and to Turkestan and Spain.

The disintegration of the real political power of the Caliphs took place during the Abbasid Caliphate, with its capital of Baghdad (A.D. 750–1258). During this time, Islam divided itself into several factions and sects, much as the Christian church was to do at the same time and later. An anti-Caliphate of Umayyads was set up at Cordoba in Spain in A.D. 756. In North Africa, a Berber dynasty of the Shi'ite sect (the Shi'ites did not recognize the authority of the first Caliphs) was established in A.D. 909, and had spread through Egypt by A.D. 969, becoming known as the Fatamid Caliphate (the Fatamids ruled also in Sicily until the Norman invasion of 1071). Thus, by the beginning of the 11th century A.D., the diffusion of culture and learning had begun to depend less on the spread of religion and had become subject to the struggles for temporal power.

In A.D. 641, the Sassanian dynasty of Persia, which had lasted for 400 years, was overthrown by the Arabs and the country conquered for Islam. The Umayyad Caliphate established itself, and its direct rule lasted until about A.D. 750. Thereafter, the country was ruled by various dynasties, all of whom acknowledged the nominal superiority of the Caliphate. In chronological sequence, these were the Saffarid (A.D. 861–74), the Samanid (A.D. 874–928), the Ziyarid (A.D. 928–32), the Buwayhid (A.D. 932–77) and the Ghaznavid (A.D. 977–1037). In 1037, however, the country was conquered by the Seljuk Turks. These were Turkoman followers of Seljuk-ibn-Dakak who came from the Kirghiz Steppes in West Turkestan.

Top: stone relief of a kneeling captive from Bishapur, Sassanian dynasty, Persia. Left and above: unglazed pottery jar and bronze incense burner, both Persian, 12th–13th centuries. The pottery vessel, in particular, displays a Kufic base, scrolls, flower heads, animal heads and birds, motifs found in Persian weaving. Victoria and Albert Museum, London.

The Seljuk Turks

Although it was shortlived, the Seljuks formed the first great political Islamic empire, incorporating Persia, Mesopotamia, Asia Minor and Syria. In 1055, the Seljuk leader Tughril Beg was proclaimed Sultan by the Abbasid Caliph of Baghdad, but following the death of Sultan Sinjar in 1150, the empire was split first by his heirs and then by the military officers into a number of independent dynasties. Several of these states lasted until the 14th century, and in Egypt, the Mamluk dynasty, which lasted from 1252 to 1517, was founded by descendants of Seljuk Turkish soldiers.

The Mongol Invasions

In 1220, Persia was attacked by the Mongol armies of Ghengis Khan and the Il-Khanid dynasty was founded in the year 1256 by Ghengis Khan's grandson Hulagu. Two years later, Hulagu captured and partly destroyed Baghdad; subsequently, he rebuilt it and made it his capital and winter residence, Tabriz in Persia being his summer residence. During this period, the great flowering of Persian art began.

The Emperor Ghengis Khan from a Persian manuscript of 1397. Note the distinct Mongol cast of the features of the Emperor and the members of his court, and the naturalistically rendered plants in the background. British Library, London.

In the latter half of the 14th century, overall authority disintegrated, until Timur (Tamerlaine) began his conquests in 1380. Timur was himself a Mongol and a descendant of Ghengis Khan. He and his successors united Persia with Turkestan, and had their capitals at Tabriz and Samarkand. Timur himself ruled until 1405, being followed by his son Shah Rukh (d. 1447); under him, regional power devolved to several of his sons, one of whom, Baisunker Mirza, founded a great library at Herat, and another, Ibrahim Sultan, a seat of learning at Shiraz.

In the last years of Shah Rukh's reign, Persia was again invaded from Turkestan, and one tribe, the Kara-Kuyunli, under their leader Jehan Shah, captured Tabriz and built there the magnificent Blue Mosque. The Kara-Kuyunli, or 'Black Sheep' Turkomans, so-called from their heraldic emblem, were succeeded in 1469 by the Ak-Kuyunli, or 'White Sheep' Turkomans, who were led by Uzun Hassan (d. 1478), and who continued to use Tabriz as their capital. Uzun and his successors ruled until 1502 until they themselves were overthrown by a Persian dynastic group, the Safavids, descendants of Sheikh Safi-ad-Din of Ardabil. Under the Safavid dynasty, which lasted until the Afghan invasion of 1722, Persia experienced perhaps the greatest period of its history.

Left: brass bowl inlaid with silver and gold depicting mounted huntsmen with hounds. The dense, foliate ground is typical of later Persian medallion and hunting carpets. Persian, 14th century. Victoria and Albert Museum, London. Below: two scenes illustrating the life of Timur from Persian manuscripts of the 15th and 16th centuries. The scene showing Timur seated in his tent was executed in 1552 and shows an allover floral carpet which would not, of course, have been made during the ruler's lifetime. British Library and Victoria and Albert Museum, London.

Above: Bahram Gur Hunting, *a miniature in the Turkoman style of north-west Persia, c. 1490. The animal combat group in the foreground is often found in later hunting carpets; note the distinctly Chinese cloud in the top left corner. Victoria and Albert Museum, London. Above right: this was a period of continuous tribal warfare, as shown in the miniature of a skirmish between camel-mounted soldiers from a Persian manuscript of 1493. British Library, London. Right: dome of the tomb of the poet Hafiz at Shiraz, southern Persia. A typically complex geometric ornamental structure, similar to the overlaid medallions found on many Oriental carpets.*

Mesopotamia

The historical progression in the rest of the Islamic world is equally complex, but an attempt must be made to set out the chronology, so that references to particular dynasties made later in the sections on Oriental weaving may be understood.

West of Iran, there were two principal areas, Mesopotamia and Asia Minor. Mesopotamia stretched approximately 400 miles from Diyarbakir in the north (now a small town in south-east Turkey) to Baghdad in the south (now the capital city of Iraq). The area was split into three geographical divisions – Diyarbakir, Jazira (now Al Jazirah) and Iraq, each area remaining fairly autonomous. The Abbasid Caliphate ruled from approximately A.D. 750 to 945, and the city of Baghdad became an important religious and cultural centre, especially under the famous Harun-al-Rashid (A.D. 786–809).

During the second half of the 10th century and the first half of the 11th, several Emirates were established of Arab, Persian and Kurdish origin which caused the decline of the political power of the Caliphate. The Seljuk invasion of 1055 included Mesopotamia, and their domination in this area lasted some thirty years longer than it did in Persia, although by the mid-13th century Seljuk rule had fragmented into localized dynasties.

Mesopotamia became united with the Mongol Il-Khanid dynasty of Persia in 1256, but in 1336 it became allied with Azerbaijan, then the most northerly province of Persia but one which, until the advent of the Safavids, was under the autonomous rule of Turkoman princes. This was, in fact, a very confused period, with cities and areas constantly changing hands; thus, Baghdad was captured by Timur in 1393 and held for some time. In 1502, the area was united with Safavid Persia, and so remained until 1638, when it was conquered by the Turkish Ottoman Sultan Murad IV. Thus it continued until the map of the Middle East was redrawn at Versailles after the First World War.

Turkey and the Ottomans

Turkey itself consisted of an area then known as Anatolia. Until the fall of Byzantium, the area was a Christian empire. From 1077 to 1300, however, it formed part of the territories of the Seljuks of Rum ('Rum' being a corruption of Rome, the country having formed part of the Holy Roman Empire); their capital was Konya, some 400 miles south-east of Constantinople. In the second half of the 13th century, Turkey was partly in thrall to the Persian Mongols, but about 1300 the whole area came under the domination of the Ottoman Turks, originally the rulers of one of several small Emirates into which the Seljuk authority had, according to its usual pattern, divided itself.

The Ottomans became the longest-lived and arguably the greatest of all the Middle Eastern political dynasties of Islam, lasting until 1924. During their period of greatest power, from about 1450 to 1650, their lands stretched across eastern Europe, including Greece and Hungary, literally to the gates of Vienna, and took in Mesopotamia, Kurdistan, Syria and Egypt; they held sway also in the pirate states of Algiers and Tunis, which were founded with Ottoman help in the first half of the 16th century.

Egypt was captured from the Byzantines by Amir Ibn al-As in A.D. 641. For the next two centuries the country was under the rule of the Umayyad and Abbasid Caliphs, with the governmental seat at Fostat. From A.D. 868 to 905, an Emirate of Tulunids, a Turkoman dynasty, ruled under licence from the Caliphs, although it was almost autonomous. They were succeeded by another autonomous dynasty of Turkish descent, the Ikhshids.

The Berber Fatamids captured the country in A.D. 969 and ruled until 1171; they were responsible for the building of Cairo, which they made their capital. A return to the authority of the Caliphs came in 1171 with the establishment of the Ayyubid Sultanate. The Ayyubids were of Kurdish origin, and took Egypt through the military genius of their leader Salah al-Din, known in the West as Saladin. In 1250, the country was taken over by the Mamluks, a military caste of Turkish descent, and remained the Mamluk Sultanate until conquered by the Ottoman Turks in 1517. It remained a Turkish colony until the Napoleonic Wars.

India

Although the greatest Islamic art in India is associated with the Moghul Emperors, Islam had first been brought to the sub-continent by Arab invaders at the beginning of the 8th century, these having first fought their way through Afghanistan. By A.D. 900, the city of Kabul in Afghanistan was ruled by the Samanid dynasty, and from A.D. 962 to 1166, the city of Ghazna (now Ghazni), about ninety miles south of Kabul, gave its name to a dynasty, the Ghaznavids, who recognized the authority of the Abbasid Caliphate. The greatest Ghaznavid Sultan, Mahmud (998–1030), ruled an area which stretched from inside the eastern border of Persia through to the Punjab in India.

For the following 300 years, there was a fragmentation of authority. The Ghorid dynasty took control of Ghazna in 1161 and extended its rule under Sultan Muhammed throughout much of the Ghaznavid Sultanate, capturing Lahore in 1186. The Ghorids maintained control until about 1206, when the Sultanate of Delhi was founded, which attempted to control the same general area; however, several small, localized, dynasties were founded, while Afghanistan united with West Turkestan, which was, during this period, under the rule of the Seljuk Turks.

In 1526, however, Babur, the Mongol king of Afghanistan and a fifth generation descendant of Timur, overthrew the Delhi Sultanate and united the area which, on a modern map, would include Afghanistan, Pakistan, and North India, into the Moghul Empire (Moghul, of course, being a corruption of Mongol); this lasted until Disraeli declared Queen Victoria Empress of India.

Its great rulers, apart from Babur himself, who died in 1530, included his son Humayan (1330–56), who spent the last fifteen years of his reign as a fugitive at the Persian court, Akbar (1556–1605), Jehangir (1605–27), Jehan (1628–59) and Aurangzeb (1659–1707). During this 188-year period, the Moghul emperors were responsible for fostering the development of a culture which many would argue is the finest flowering of Islamic art.

China, Mongolia and Tibet

In discussing the carpets of China, we have to consider not only those pieces made in China itself, but in those countries linked by political, ethnic and cultural ties. Thus, it is meaningless to consider Chinese weaving outside the context of what is known of the carpets from Mongolia, Tibet and the area called East Turkestan. This area now includes Kirgizstan and Tadzhikstan in the southern U.S.S.R. and stretches from the towns of Tashkent and Samarkand in the west as far as Kansu in central China, taking in the area of Sinkiang.

In 1206, about the same time as the Mongol armies began pushing westwards, they conquered China and founded the Yüan dynasty (1206–1368), with the great Emperor Kublai Khan establishing his capital at Peking and renaming it Khanbaliq – 'City of Khans'. By the time the Mongols were defeated by the Chinese Buddhist monk Chu-Yüan-Chang in 1367, the cultural style of the Mongols had mingled inextricably with that of China. Chu-Yüan-Chang ascended the throne and took the title of Hung Wu; he was the founder of the Ming dynasty which lasted until 1644.

In the last years of their dynasty, the Ming Emperors grew ineffectual and the power of their central authority disintegrated. Following the suicide of the last Ming Emperor, Ch'ung Chêng, in 1643, the Chinese army asked the Manchurians for help in restoring order. The Manchurians gave it and took China for themselves. The first Manchu Emperor of the Ch'ing dynasty, Shun Chih, ascended the throne in 1644, and the rulers of China remained members of the Manchu line until the establishment of a republic in 1912.

The Turkoman Tribes

Our brief chronology of the major carpet weaving areas made frequent reference to the Turkomans or Turks. These peoples supposedly originated in Turkestan, the ill-defined area which stretches from the eastern shores of the Caspian Sea, through what are now the Soviet States of Turkmenistan, Uzbekistan, Kazakstan, Tadzhikstan and Kirgizstan to Sinkiang. As stated above, East Turkestan stretches from the eastern borders of the Soviet states through Sinkiang to Kansu; West Turkestan is defined as being the area now covered by the Soviet state of Turkmenistan, though taking in some parts of the western area of Uzbekistan, including the city of Bokhara.

Within the last century, the growing political dominance of Russia, which both under Imperial rule and latterly under the Soviets, has sought to impose a settled authoritarian regime on essentially nomadic, autocratic peoples, has meant a move of Turkoman tribes into Persia, Afghanistan and as far east as Pakistan. From the evidence of weaving alone, however, it is probable that, since the end of the Second World War, the ethnic and cultural balance of the Turkoman peoples has been all but destroyed.

Miniature from the second volume of a manuscript of the Akbar Nameh *of about 1590. The painting, composed by Miskina and executed by Tulsi the Younger, depicts the building of the Red Fort at Agra, completed in 1566, and Akbar's first major architectural commission. Victoria and Albert Museum, London.*

It is now generally accepted that of the several ethnic groups which made their homes in what are now the southern Soviet states, the Turkomans, like the Uzbeks, Kazaks and Kirgiz, are of Mongolian origin, emanating both from Mongolia itself and from Chinese Sinkiang, which the Mongols occupied before moving westward. The Turkoman peoples themselves have no recorded history, and what we know of their early history is due to the Arab historians of the 10th and 11th centuries, who attempted to codify the peoples of Islam.

At the time of the earliest recordings of the Turkoman peoples, they were located to the east of the borders of what is now the Soviet state of Uzbekistan, around Tashkent. They were referred to also as the Oghuz, and the Arabs were in no doubt that the peoples living to the west were of the same origin as the people they called the Toghuz-Oghuz, who were then still settled in Mongolia and Sinkiang.

The Arabs themselves, in their conquests, had divided the area east of the Caspian Sea into two provinces: Khorassan, south of the Oxus River (now called the Amu-Darya) which is now roughly equivalent to the present Soviet state of Turkmenistan, and Transoxania, north of the Oxus to the Jazartes River (now called the Syr-Darya), which is the area now occupied by the Soviet state of Uzbekistan.

Naturally, both provinces, being so distant from the seats of power in Damascus and Baghdad, exercised virtual autonomy and the governors spent much of their time fighting each other until the beginning of the 10th century when Ismael, governor of Samarkand, capital of Transoxania (Merv was the capital of Khorassan), conquered the whole area and made the city of Bokhara capital of both provinces. Ismael founded a dynasty, the Samanids, whose rule was independent of the Caliphs.

At this point in history, the Turkomans were still semi-nomadic herders of sheep. Indeed their nomadism long seems to have prevented them from developing into a coherent national group while they remained in central Asia. Although of Mongol origin, the Turkomans did not necessarily come to conquer, any more than the Mongol armies of Ghengis Khan intended to exert a cultural influence upon the countries they overran. Nevertheless, both branches of a common stock had a profound effect upon the political life and the art of all the countries with which they had contact.

At the end of the 10th century, the Arab ruler of Bokhara faced a revolution, and sought the aid of a Muslim Turkoman leader, Seljuk. The Seljuk Turkomans thereafter retained the patronage of the Samanid dynasty, and for the first time a Turkoman tribe moved across the Jazartes river into the region of Khorassan near the city of Bokhara itself. Other Oghuz Turkomans followed in the next hundred years or so. Such tribes – the Salors, Chaudors, Ersaris, Saryks, Yomuts, Tekkes and Arabatchis – we shall discuss later when dealing with Turkoman carpets.

As we have seen above, the Seljuks were powerful enough by the middle of the 11th century to found their own dynasty in Persia, Mesopotamia, Asia Minor and Syria and later, by descent, in Egypt. During the Mongol invasions of the 13th century, the Turkoman tribes of West Turkestan were divided in their loyalties, some fighting for the invaders and some against them.

The Importance of the Mongols

From this summary, it can be seen that the Mongols as an ethnic group were of prime importance in the development of political structures and art in central Asia. During the course of this study, it will become clear that much of an apparently indigenous style in fact emanates from the Far East. The Mongols conquered China and moved west; they had previously, in a nomadic capacity, wandered west so that, by the end of the 13th century, almost all the lands from the Black Sea to the East China Sea were ruled by peoples of Mongol descent.

I was once told by a leading figure in the London carpet trade that when he was young, he and his father, who had himself been a dealer since the end of the 19th century, used to discuss the history of carpets. His father said that when he himself was learning the trade as a boy and asked where such and such a design originated, the answer was always 'From the East'. 'It seemed,' said my informant, 'that wherever you asked the question – in Salonika or Istanbul, in Tabriz or Kabul, the answer was always the same – "From the East".' In looking at the history and ethnography of the vast area of land with which we are dealing, such an answer, instinctive though it may be, is almost unquestionably true.

Opposite: Persian miniature depicting a Turkoman captive. Late 15th century. Victoria and Albert Museum, London.

Early Weaving

SO FAR, IT IS NOT KNOWN at what time and what place pile-knotted carpets were first produced. At least one modern authority suggests that such pieces were of nomadic origin. Certainly, the rearing of sheep, the prime source of carpet wool, is a traditional nomad occupation, and the necessity of thick coverings for people having to endure extreme cold would have soon caused the development of the art of weaving to supersede the use of rough animal skins to provide such covering.

There are, of course, several references, both in ancient scriptures and in classical authors, to the art of weaving but no evidence that such references apply to pile carpets. Indeed, on the evidence of fragments found in ancient Egyptian tombs, some dating from the second millennium B.C., we know that various forms of flat-weaving were well-developed, but it is probable that pile carpets were unknown. However, we are still at an early stage in the development of carpet studies. Apart from advances in techniques and the gathering of scientific data, the modern student is the inheritor of several decades of intense research and of some remarkable discoveries. It must be added, however, that although theoretical structures have become more elaborate and some of the more obvious mistakes of early scholars have been corrected, very little in the way of concrete factual evidence has been added to that at the disposal of Martin, Kendrick, Tattersall, Bode, Kühnel and other early twentieth-century scholars.

The Pazyryk Rug

However, there is one major twentieth-century discovery of great dramatic impact, which was made by Rudenko, a Russian archaeologist, in 1947. This was the finding of a pile knotted rug in a Scythian burial mound dating from the 5th century B.C.; this rug is tied with the Ghiordes knot (200 to the square inch).

Other fragments found by Rudenko at the same site were tied with the Senneh knot. The Pazyryk itself conforms to the general schematic arrangement of later Oriental carpets, with a central field surrounded by major and minor borders. The central field has a madder red ground upon which are rows of squares containing schematized floral motifs. The squares are themselves contained within a border of octagons resembling the guls of later Turkoman weaving. The first major border contains a procession of elks; there is then a minor border of floral motifs which follow the designs within the field squares, but in reverse colouring. The second major border is filled with a procession of horses on a madder field, some being ridden and others being walked by grooms. Each horse, it is interesting to note, has a richly embroidered saddle-cloth, the design of which appears to resemble closely that of the Pazyryk rug itself. There is then an outer border of octagons, the designs of which are identical to those running round the outer edge of the field.

Discussing the Pazyryk rug, Dimand remarks that it shows a mixture of Assyrian, Achaemenian and Scythian motifs. He prefers to regard it as of Persian origin, giving as his principal reason its similarity in design to alabaster slabs found at the palaces of Sennacherib (705–681 B.C.) and Assurbanipal (668–26 B.C.). Instinctively this seems wrong. The Altai Mountains are located nearly 2,000 miles north-east of the present border of Persia, in the region above Sinkiang and Mongolia, which was populated then, as it is now, by peoples of Mongol descent. The Scythians were themselves migrants from the region of Mongolia and, in common with early Mongol artists, frequently used animal imagery. Although the origin of the Pazyryk rug will never be known with absolute certainty, it is reasonable to conclude that it was woven approximately in the region in which it was found, and by Scythians of Mongol descent who had moved from their original lands during a general migration of Mongol peoples westward. Since we know or, on strong presumptive evidence, can assume, that the art of the pile carpet began in the East Turkestan-Mongolia region, an area largely populated by nomadic sheep-herders, it is perverse to suggest, as Ulrich Schürmann has done, that the Pazyryk was woven in Azerbaijan or indeed any part of Persia; this would mean that it was then taken thousands of miles *eastward* by the same people who had, for decades, if not centuries, been moving *westward*. Throughout the history of Oriental carpet weaving, we shall return again and again to the theme that the patterns and techniques of carpet weaving originated somewhere in the East, among the Mongol peoples, and eventually moved west.

Early Fragments

Some carpet fragments were found in the 1920s by Sir Aurel Stein of the British Museum, during the excavations at Lou-lan, one of the towns in East Turkestan on the trade route west. Again, the majority of these were tied with the Ghiordes knot, although there were some tied with the Spanish knot. Although it is arguable that these fragments are remains of trade goods *from* the west, this again seems unnecessarily contentious, when their manufacture in the area in which they were discovered is easily acceptable. They date from the 2nd to 3rd centuries A.D. and add weight to the argument that the knotting of pile carpets was a well-developed and frequently encountered art form in East Turkestan-Mongolia long before it migrated west.

There is evidence, of course, that pile carpets were produced in Persia during the Sassanian dynasty (A.D. 224–641) and in other areas of the Middle East during the same period. Fragments of pile carpets, unearthed in the city of Dura-Europas can, on the evidence of dated monuments, be ascribed to the first half of the 3rd century A.D.; these fragments are tied with both the Senneh and Ghiordes knots. The Chinese Sui Annals (A.D. 590–617) mention woollen carpets being produced in Persia, and in A.D. 638, when the Sassanian King Chosroes II was defeated by the Byzantine Emperor Heraklius, a huge carpet called the Spring Carpet of Chosroes, was found at his palace at Ctesiphon. This piece, said to have been brocaded with gold and silver thread, was studded with jewels and pearls; both

The Pazyryk rug. Excavated in barrow 5, the burial mound of a Scythian prince, by S. R. Rudenko in 1947 in the Altai Mountains of Siberia, and datable to the 5th century B.C. There are over 200 Ghiordes knots per square inch. A fragment of another pile carpet excavated in the same region has a knot count of about 450 to the square inch. 6 ft. 8 in. × 6 ft. 3½ in. (200 × 189 cm.). Hermitage Museum, Leningrad.

Detail from the monumental felt appliqué wall hanging from barrows at Pazyryk, depicting in repeat rows a mounted prince before a seated goddess. The hanging, which now exists only in fragmentary form, still measures 21 ft. 8 in. × 15 ft. (650 × 450 cm.). Hermitage Museum, Leningrad.

its size and technique lead one to the conclusion that it was not a pile carpet, but some type of flat-weave. It has been calculated that it would have weighed over two tons and could not have been woven in one piece. Fragments of true knotted carpets, tied with the Spanish knot, have been excavated in Egypt, and have been dated to the 5th century A.D. They are attributed to the Christian Coptic sect.

Early Persian Weaving

Following the fall of the Sassanian dynasty and the establishment of the Caliphate, the evidence for weaving in Persia becomes clearer, if only because Arab historians and geographers took their task of examining and codifying the peoples of Islam seriously; thus we have a wealth of written material. We know that carpet weaving was carried on at Fars, Majanderan and Gilan to the south-west and, according to Muhddasi writing in the 10th century, in the Kainat. Although Arab historians do not describe the type of weaving, it is safe to assume that pile carpets were made and were almost certainly the products of tribal nomads, who could have moved down from the north of the country in search of fresh pastures. It is worth making the point that the imagery of many early tribal pieces, and of those from the 19th century – Turkoman, Baluchi, Yuruk and Kashgai – is so similar that it is difficult to believe that they are not fragmented folk memories of a common heritage of symbols. And as I have suggested before, this common heritage is probably Far Eastern and, more specifically, Mongolian in origin.

Following the conquest of Persia by the Seljuk Turks in about 1037, many areas of the country became settled by peoples of Turkish descent who brought their own language and culture; they colonized the areas of Azerbaijan and Hamadan, where they remain to this day. However, A. Cecil Edwards is incorrect when he says that the Seljuk women who were the weavers introduced the Turkish knot into these provinces. As we have seen, the Ghiordes knot was woven in Persia by the 3rd century B.C. (and if one follows the opinion of those who believe that the Pazyryk is of Persian origin, by the 6th century B.C.) just as the Senneh or Persian knot was used in East Turkestan by the beginning of the first millenium of the Christian calendar.

No Persian Seljuk complete rugs or fragments are known, but several from Asia Minor exist, which would certainly not have differed from those woven in Persia under Turkish influence. There are three main groups of discoveries – the three intact carpets and five fragments found in the Alaeddin Mosque in Konya, the Seljuk capital, in 1905, a further group discovered in the Eshrefoglu Mosque in Beyshehir in 1929 (Dimand says 1930) and a third group consisting of seven fragments found in the ruins of Fostat in Egypt. The Alaeddin Mosque was built in 1220 and the Eshrefoglu in 1296 (1298 according to Erdmann). Since it is probable that both of these august institutions would have acquired new carpets, the known Konya fragments cover the whole of the 13th century.

The Seljuks were, of course, of Turkoman stock. All the Seljuk fragments are of stylized, geometric, floral patterns, some of which lived on into the 15th and 16th centuries with the Holbein and Lotto patterns. There are also fragments with rows of red octagons which are obviously part of the common heritage of nineteenth-century Turkoman weavings. There is also a clear affinity between the fragments and early Mongolian and Chinese weaving. One of the Beyshehir rugs is woven with a light blue ground upon which are dark blue lozenges containing stars, the centres of the stars being vermilion. The edges of the lozenges are decorated with a series of hook motifs in a reciprocal pattern. This design was derived from the Chinese meander pattern and can also be seen in Mongol rugs from East Turkestan which may be late twelfth- or early thirteenth-century. Two of the pieces, including a complete carpet (16½ feet long) from Beyshehir, have dark blue grounds upon which are woven geometrically stylized floral scrolls in light blue. The scrolls have attached hooks and lotus palmettes. Such designs were derived from Chinese silks, which had reached Turkey and Persia by the 13th century. The border of the complete carpet has angular interlacings bearing stylized trefoils in black on a mauve ground. Trefoils were also a popular design in Chinese textiles from the time of the Han dynasty (206 B.C.–A.D. 220). They are also to be found in the appliqué felt saddle-cloths of twelfth- and thirteenth-century Mongol horsemen.

Thus, in the earliest existing examples of Islamic weaving, a clear stylistic connection can be established with the Far East, aside from the fact that they were woven by people of Far Eastern descent. Looking forward, we can also see a clear connection with Turkoman tribal weavings of the 19th century: the octagons, hooked diamonds which can be connected with Yomut *dyrnak* guls and, in one Alaeddin fragment, geometrical rosettes reminiscent of Yomut *kepse* guls as well as motifs which appear in Turkish and Caucasian weavings for many centuries after. Even at this seminal period, therefore, it is possible to appreciate the existence of a well-established vocabulary of motifs, the result of centuries of development from what was probably a single source. That heritage, although in a deplorably debased form, is still alive today.

More documentary evidence, but no actual examples, of weaving exist from the period of the Mongol Il-Khanid dynasty from 1220 to 1380. For roughly three centuries, from 1155 to 1424, the Bakhtiari region of Persia west of Isfahan was ruled by the Atabegs of the Fasluyeh dynasty, and one visitor to their capital, the town of Idhej, was Ibn Batuta, who mentioned that a green rug was spread in honour before him. We know that the Emperor Ghengis Khan covered the floors of his administrative buildings near Tabriz with rugs made in Fars and that he sent similar pieces as gifts to the Mausoleum of Sayfaddin Khalid ibn Khalid in Damascus. More important, however, is the survival of a number of illuminated miniatures depicting rugs and carpets in use. When Marco Polo visited the Mongol Persian empire in the 13th century, he noted the abundance of beautiful silks, tapestries and rugs. The first Il-Khanid emperor, Hulagu, established his summer residence at Tabriz, and under his successors, the city was made into a great cultural centre. In the suburbs of the city, Rashid ad-Din, the chief minister of Ghazan built the Rab-i-Rashidi, a great college of science and art. He is known to have commissioned many manuscripts, one of which survives. Not surprisingly, the illustrative style of this work, the *Jami-al-Tavarikh* (Universal History), which is dated A.H. 707 and 714 (A.D. 1307 and 1314), shows strong Chinese influence in its overall conception.

But for the study of early Persian weaving, as for the study of early Persian illumination, the most important manuscript is the famous Demotte *Shah Nameh*, datable to the mid-14th century. This book, named after the New York dealer who, on failing to sell it complete, divided it up early this century, is ascribed by Dimand to Tabriz, although the majority of today's scholars favour the Il-Khanid capital and winter residence of Baghdad. Three of its miniatures depict rugs, two of which have an allover field pattern of interlaced ovals, unlike anything seen in later Persian weaving, but similar to patterns found in Caucasian weaving of fairly recent date. The third rug has stylized animals in double octagons, similar to known Turkish weaving of the 14th century, and may well be of Turkish origin. Another manuscript of slightly later date, the *Divan* (Book of Poems), also has a famous miniature which depicts two rugs, one with an allover pattern of stars and octagons on a pale yellow ground and the other with an allover pattern of polychrome squares.

At this time, the rugs of Persia, as far as we can tell from available evidence, were of a stylized, geometric design. Yet the Mongol conquerors brought with them a liking for the Chinese style of art, with its naturalistic rendering of animals, flowers and birds, together with various well-established symbolic motifs. Under the Il-Khanid rulers, but more especially under the succeeding Timurid dynasty, the influence of Chinese art was to have a profound effect upon the development of the Persian style.

The invasions of Timur began in 1380, and in 1405, the year of his death, he became ruler of Persia. The 15th century saw the beginning of the classic period of Persian art, and from the last two decades, we have the first surviving examples of Persian rugs which show the change from rectilinearity to floral asymmetry. This change came about not only because of the infusion into Persian art of Chinese motifs, but also because, during this period, rug weaving ceased to be solely a nomadic folk art and began to be practised by skilled weavers working in royal manufactories. The new style of the Timurid period, which made its first appearance in book illustrations and bindings, is characterized by the use of scrolling leaves and blossoms – peonies, pomegranate palmettes, fungus – interlaced with geometric motifs and arabesques. In some designs, real and imagined beasts appear, such as wild cats, dragons, phoenixes and other birds and deer.

Again, manuscript illuminations provide the only visual evidence we have of early Timurid weaving. The Timurid Emperors Shah Rukh (1404–43) and Baisunker Mirza extended the great seats of learning and culture at Baghdad and Tabriz by founding similar academies at Samarkand in East Turkestan, Bokhara and Shiraz, the last named built by Shah Rukh's son Ibrahim Sultan. The Timurid capital was Herat in the most easterly

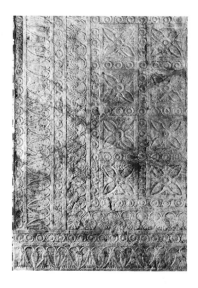

Stone pavement slab simulating a carpet from the north palace of King Assurbanipal at Nineveh, c. 640 B.C. The similarity of this design and others found on different slabs from the same location and that of the Pazyryk rug has led scholars to suggest a Persian or Mesopotamian provenance for the latter. 10 ft. × 8 ft. 1 in. (304.6 × 246 cm.). British Museum, London.

Persian province of Khorassan (the town is now in Afghanistan). In all of these new academies and in the old ones, the style of painting did not change much during the early years of the 15th century. The Chinese influence was strong and there was an important trade with China. Ming porcelain appears in Timurid miniatures and at least one leading Persian artist, Ghiyath ad-Din, visited the Far East. It would seem as if, for the fifteenth-century Persian painters, China was as important an influence as Italy was to be for European artists of the 18th and 19th centuries.

As with painting, the style of rug weaving, to judge from early Timurid miniatures in which pieces are depicted, did not change much initially. It would seem that the major centre of weaving was Herat, for it is in Herati miniatures that rugs are most often depicted. They remain close to Turkish geometric prototypes and a number of scholars have suggested that they may not even be of Persian workmanship, but are Turkish imports.

Rugs with allover geometric patterns appear frequently in miniatures at this time.

The Bier of Iskandar, *miniature from the Demotte* Shah Nameh, *Tabriz or Baghdad, 14th century. The carpet depicted has an allover field pattern of interlaced ovals and a Kufic border. Freer Gallery of Art, Washington.*

Dimand illustrates several examples, including one from a *Shah Nameh* of 1429–30 in the Gulistan Palace, Teheran; this shows a rug with a repeat pattern of octagons, alternately red and green, formed by knotted bands, and filled with leafy devices. Several examples similar to this appear in early Italian paintings, which may have been either embroideries or pile carpets. There are two pieces very close to Dimand's example in the *Polyptych: Madonna and Child Enthroned with Six Angels* by Taddeo Gaddi in the church of San Giovanni Fuorcivitas in Pistoia; this altarpiece, it should be noted, is dated 1353.

Another miniature illustrated by Dimand, from Sadi's *Gulistan*, shows Sadi and his teacher seated on a rug with a pattern consisting of cross motifs and stars, connected by knotted interlacings. This manuscript is dated 1426–7. However, in the British Museum, there is an Italian manuscript address from the people of the town of Prato to Robert of Anjou, King of Naples, datable to about 1335–40. The king is shown seated upon a throne which is covered with a carpet or embroidery of similar pattern to that in the Gulistan miniature, the red and blue crosses of the weaving forming reciprocal eight-pointed stars on a pale green ground.

Such patterns, appearing as they do in several Italian paintings of the 14th and early 15th centuries, were not, of course, confined to carpets. Many of them, in the form of altar cloths and draperies, were made of silk and other stuffs. This is not surprising as the European weaving industry was confined almost solely to plain fabrics in wool and linen, until silk weaving became well established in several Italian towns at the end of the 14th century, notably in Venice, Genoa, Lucca and Florence. Therefore, until around 1400, great quantities of silk embroideries, woven with a repeat pattern on a draw loom, were sent from China and the Middle East to Europe, as well as from Byzantium and Moorish Spain. The funerary garments of Can Grande della Scala, Lord of Verona, who died in 1329, were almost all of silk from central Asia, and in the tomb of the Duke Rudolf of Austria, who died in 1365, was found a silk woven with the name of the Persian ruler Abu Said.

Donald King, in an essay on the medieval textile trade between Europe and the East, has also suggested that Islamic silks of an earlier date which reached Europe had an unquestionable influence on Romanesque artists and architects. As is pointed out later in connection with Pintoricchio's frescoes in Siena, the floors of many churches and castles in medieval paintings and miniatures are inlaid with tiles in geometric patterns probably derived from Oriental textiles. And for textiles, one of the most popular motifs seems to have been a repeat of an endless knot in a square; an Italian miniature in a manuscript in the British Museum, depicting a Genoese banking scene of the early 15th century, includes a tile floor almost identical in design to one of the rugs depicted in the Demotte *Shah Nameh*.

By the 1480s, cartouche designs, and rugs with flowers, animals and birds, had appeared. We have as evidence for this several miniatures, including one by Bihzad in a manuscript of Sadi's *Bustan* (Fruits of the Garden), which is dated 1487, and, most importantly, in a miniature attributed to the same artist in a *Zafar Nameh* (Book of Timur's Victories) in which, for the first time, there is depicted a medallion carpet. Again, however, there is some evidence from Italian painting that allover patterns of floral arabesques may have first appeared considerably earlier than Oriental manuscript illuminations would have us believe. In two works by the Florentine Master of the Straus Madonna, *Madonna and Child with Four Saints* (private collection) and *Polyptych: Madonna and Child Enthroned with Eight Saints and Two Angels* (San Donato, Citille), there appear on the floor beneath the Virgin's feet either embroideries or rugs with floral arabesques. The Master of the Straus Madonna was active between about 1380 and 1420.

It should not be forgotten, however, that during the Timurid period, the north-west Persian province of Azerbaijan was under Turkoman rule, firstly of the Kara-Kuyunli and then, after 1469, of the Ak-Kuyunli. Their capital was Tabriz, and European visitors to the court of Uzun Hassan, among them the Venetian Ambassador Giuseppe Barbaro in 1471, testify to the existence of carpets on the floors of royal buildings. From the evidence of the Blue Mosque, built by the Black Sheep Turkomans in Tabriz, floral decoration was well-known in this kingdom and several authorities have suggested that some of the rugs now ascribed to the early Safavid period might well have been woven in Tabriz in the late 15th century. Certainly it was in Tabriz that the Safavid Shahs established their first political and cultural capital.

Safavid Weaving

IN 1499, THE SAFAVIDS began their conquest of Persia. Shah Ismael I was crowned in 1502 and ruled until 1524. He was followed by Shah Tahmasp (1524–76), Shah Ismael II (1576–87), Shah Abbas I (1587–1629), Shah Safi (1629–42) and Shah Abbas II (1642–74). This period, lasting 175 years, was the golden age of Persian art, and carpet weaving was perhaps the greatest of these arts.

The Safavid rulers, notably Tahmasp and Abbas I, the latter a skilled weaver himself, established several royal factories or *karkhanes* for the manufacture of all types of woven materials, the major ones being at Kashan, Kerman, Isfahan (Shah Abbas' capital), Joshaqan and Tabriz. Others were at Yezd, Shiraz and, to the east, Herat and Sabzawar, the former now well inside the border of Afghanistan and the latter not to be confused with the Afghan town of the same name.

The rugs of Safavid Persia have been divided into several categories, based primarily upon motifs, but also, in some instances, named for historical or technical reasons. The principal categories are medallion, vase, garden, hunting and figure, compartment, large and small silk Kashans, and Polonaise. There are several other groupings of specific types, some of which, like the Portuguese, fall outside any of the above categories (although they may sometimes be classified with medallion carpets), and others, like the Sanguszko group, the tree and shrub carpets and the floral Herat carpets (some of which are called Isfahans), which may be related to the major groups, as indeed some of the major groups are related to each other. There are also prayer rugs, which do not, however, form as important a part of Persian weaving as they do of Turkish.

The setting up of the royal factories meant that a significant quantity of pieces was produced under Imperial patronage. They were designed by some of the leading artists of the day, and carpet weaving at its highest level ceased to be the product of a nomadic or village way of life in Persia but became a highly sophisticated art form. The change in the circumstances of carpet weaving may be seen in the emphasis during the 16th century on carpets of curvilinear, rather than rectilinear, design – a change in emphasis which bespeaks a new social origin for carpets as well as a new artistic approach.

A further change was the growing number of new designs. This was the result not only of designers giving free reign to their artistic imaginations and moving away from the dictates of tradition and tribal custom, but also of the pressure on the weavers to produce new designs for carpets, which the Imperial Government used increasingly for the furnishing of palaces

Medallion carpet with hunting scenes. Signed 'Gyath u-Din Jamai' (or 'Ghiyath al-Din Jami' or 'Ghyias ed Din Sami') and dated 929 of the Hejira (A.D. 1522–3) or 949 (A.D. 1542–3). The sixteenth-century dating of this carpet has recently been called into question. 19 ft. × 12 ft. 2 in. (570 × 365 cm.). Poldi Pezzoli Museum, Milan.

87

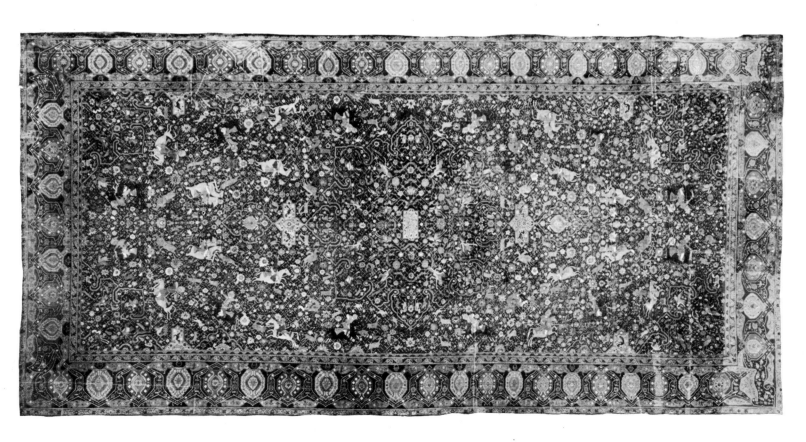

and governmental buildings and for diplomatic gifts and barter. By the middle of the 16th century, carpets were also being woven on commission for the European nobility.

Medallion Carpets

One of the earliest of the new designs was the medallion carpet. There are in fact three Persian carpets bearing dates before 1600: the two medallion carpets, probably from the Shrine at Ardabil, now in the Victoria and Albert Museum, and the Los Angeles County Museum of Art (the latter the gift of J. Paul Getty), and the hunting carpet in the Poldi Pezzoli Museum, Milan (the authenticity of which has recently come under close scrutiny). The Italian piece has a date which is difficult to read; it is either 929 of the Hejira (1522/3) or 949 (1542/3); most scholars rule out the first date. The full inscription reads:

'By the diligence of Gyath u-din Jamai was completed
This renowned work that appeals to us by its beauty. In the year 949.'

The inscription on the Ardabil carpets was first translated by Edward Stebbings in his monograph on the Victoria and Albert Museum carpet, published in 1892:

'I have no refuge in the world other than thy threshold.
There is no protection for my head other than this door.
The work of the slave of the Holy Place.
Maqsud of Kashan, in the year 946.'

However, a more recent translation by Rexford Stead of the Los Angeles County Museum of Art reads somewhat differently:

'Except for thy haven, there is no refuge for me in this world;
Other than here, there is no place for my head.
The work of a servant of the Court, Maqsud of Kashan, 946.'

According to Stead, the Persian word *dargah*, rendered by Stebbings as 'Holy Place', can also mean 'court' (although whether in the sense of 'courtyard' is not made clear, since there are several translations which render *dargah* as 'threshold'). Similarly, *bandah-i*, translated by Stebbings as 'slave', should more properly be rendered as the less pejorative 'servant'. The first two lines of the inscription are taken from a *ghazal* or ode by the leading fourteenth-century poet Hafiz.

The Ardabil carpets were brought to London by Ziegler's, a Manchester firm who were the earliest European dealers and manufacturers of carpets active in Persia, in the late 1880s. Robinson's, the carpet dealers, effected the sale of one piece to the Victoria and Albert Museum in 1893 for the then enormous sum of £2,000 (not £2,500 in 1892 as stated in Erdmann's *Seven Hundred Years of Oriental Carpets*). They did not disclose the fact that there were two identical pieces and that the Victoria and Albert carpet had been rendered 'complete' by using large areas of its pair. The remaining portion of the second carpet, consisting of most of the central field area, is now in California, although there are several small fragments in various collections both public and private.

The Victoria and Albert Museum carpet measures 37 feet by 17 feet 6 inches. It has a silk warp and weft and a wool pile; it is woven with 297–324 knots to the square inch (not 350 as is usually stated). The Los Angeles carpet provides an added mystery by being more finely woven – with 380–420 knots per square inch. Since it has been estimated that each carpet took a minimum of three and a half years to weave, and it is unlikely that both were woven simultaneously, the finer knotting of the Los Angeles piece has been taken as an indication of a slightly earlier date. This would mean that the London carpet was completed some years after 946, but the date of the first was woven into what was intended to be a matched pair.

The London carpet has a field, two inner guards, a border and an outer guard. The centre of the field is a circular medallion, around which are arranged sixteen ogee palmettes; from the central palmettes on the long axis hang mosque lamps on four chains. The central arrangement of circular medallion and palmettes appears quartered in the four corners of the field. The field colour is a deep midnight blue; the colour of the large central medallion is yellow, and woven upon it are arabesques ending in broad leaves in green-blue and red. The field is covered in an allover pattern of stems and flower heads of extraordinary complexity, and

*The Ardabil Shrine carpet. Signed
'Maksud of Kashan' and dated
A. H. 946 (A.D. 1539–40). The
pair, lacking its borders, is in the Los
Angeles County Museum, the gift of
J. Paul Getty. 36 ft. 6 in. × 17 ft. 6 in.
(1051.56 × 553.40 cm.). Victoria
and Albert Museum, London.*

this is continued on the field of the wide central border. In this border are alternate rectangular cartouches in red and circular medallions in yellow. The first of the inner border guards has green and yellow flowers on a red ground, the second has a predominantly red and blue scroll and cloud-band pattern on a yellow ground. The outer guard has a pattern of arabesques alternating with flower heads in bright green on a red ground. At one end of the carpet, the last piece to be woven, is the inscription in a rectangular yellow cartouche. The overall effect is of the utmost sumptuousness.

As to the place where the Ardabil carpets were produced, it is a puzzle to tease scholars. The traditional theory is that they were woven on the orders of Shah Tahmasp for the Shrine of Safi at Ardabil, and that Maksud (Maqsud) was probably the overseer of the factory where the pieces were made. Recent scholarship, however, has not necessarily accepted that these are self-evident truths, and with some justification. The problem as to whether Maksud was master weaver or donor neatly divides students, and will probably never be satisfactorily solved. There is also some evidence to suggest that the carpets were not woven for the Ardabil Mosque.

There is no absolute reason, as Rexford Stead has explained in his short monograph, *The Ardabil Carpets*, why the Ardabil carpets should be regarded as 'holy', and there was no room in the shrine complex at Ardabil large enough for the carpets to be hung or placed without being obstructed in some way.

There is also in existence an apparently complete list of carpets and other possessions of the Ardabil shrine attested by the Mutavalli of the shrine in 1759; it gives the size of all the carpets, none of which are as large as even the fragmented Ardabil, and there is no mention of any carpet with an inscription.

Rexford Stead also relates the visit of a Major R. Jackson to the Victoria and Albert Museum in 1966. In 1919, when in Persia, the Major had become friendly with W. L. Flynn, an employee of the house of Ziegler. According to Flynn, his company had purchased the Ardabil in Tabriz, having heard that it came from the Mosque of Imam Riza in Meshed. This shrine, the holiest in Persia, is one of the great places of pilgrimage in the Muslim world, and the announcement of such a provenance would unquestionably have proved diplomatically embarrassing. However, Shah Tahmasp, like Shah Abbas, was a great benefactor to this mosque, which certainly has rooms large enough to accommodate both Ardabils. Ziegler's were offered the second, more damaged carpet subsequently and used it for restoration to the London piece.

Unfortunately, there is also contrary evidence. In 1845, an English traveller, Richard Holmes, published *Sketches on the Shore of the Caspian*, in which he wrote of his visit to the Ardabil Mosque in 1843: 'On the floor (of the long lofty ante-chamber to the principal tombs) were the faded remains of what was once a very splendid carpet, the manufacture of which very much surpassed that of the present day. At one extremity was woven the date of its make, some three hundred years ago.'

Stead suggests that this 'long, lofty' room was 'probably the main body of the prayer hall, known as the *ghandil khaneh* or lamp room because of its hanging gold and silver lamps. But the clear floor space of this hall measures only 29 feet 2½ inches by 19 feet ½ inch, making it impossible to lay out a single Ardabil, no less a pair!' However, in fairness to Holmes, he only saw one carpet, not two, and we know that after the work done on the pieces by Ziegler's, neither is the same today as it would have been in 1843 (and we are only dealing with a discrepancy of about six feet between the length of the room and the present length of the Victoria and Albert Museum carpet). There may well have been a room in the sixteenth-century mosque to accommodate both pieces.

As for Major Jackson's story, Kurt Erdmann in *Seven Hundred Years of Oriental Carpets* has an alternative, although equally unsubstantiated tale, relating to repairs to the vault of the prayer hall, to pay for which the mosque authorities may have sold carpets.

We note, of course, that the building which underwent repairs was the very same in which Holmes apparently saw one of the carpets some forty years previously, so that its present size and disposition cannot be taken as indications of its original suitability for housing one or both of the carpets. On the present evidence (assuming that Erdmann is correct), the traditional attribution to Ardabil is not seriously undermined. Certainly it is incontrovertible that the prayer hall was restored, thus rendering Stead's strictures about its present size irrelevant.

There are strongly held views also regarding the location of the factory which made the Ardabils; Erdmann seems to favour Tabriz or Kazvin. Dimand, however, comes down very heavily in favour of Tabriz in his catalogue, *Oriental Rugs in the Metropolitan Museum of Art*. Among earlier scholars, Kendrick and Tattersall suggested Ardabil itself as the place of weaving, Bode and Kühnel stated categorically that it must be Tabriz, as did Pope and Sarre and Trenkwald. Arberry and Edwards favoured Kashan. The compilers of the catalogue for the *Arts of Islam* exhibition held in London in 1976 are less specific. They suggest the Poldi Pezzoli carpet may have been woven in Tabriz or Kazvin, while the Ardabil carpets are assigned to 'Central Persia', presumably Kashan. Rexford Stead accepts the Tabriz attribution, but the latest display notice at the Victoria and Albert Museum indicates a preference for Kashan. Certainly Dimand's attribution to Tabriz seems a little too dogmatic. There is no evidence that Tabriz weavers were any more capable of producing highly complex work such as the Ardabil carpets than the weavers of Kashan, Kerman or Herat. If Maksud *was* the supervisor, why bring him from Kashan if the weavers of Tabriz were so skilled?

Most significantly, however, there is one major historical barrier to Tabriz; A. Cecil Edwards has pointed out that Tabriz was captured by the Turks in 1533, six years before the Ardabil was completed. He therefore concludes that Tahmasp would have been unlikely to have left his factory behind in the town under Turkish occupation.

In fact, the Turks first captured Tabriz in 1514, and it was a battleground for nearly half a century. Edwards suggests that the Ardabils may have been woven at Kazvin if Tahmasp moved his factory there, but he, like most other scholars, finds this an unlikely hypothesis, since there is not a great tradition of weaving in that town.

Erdmann's point that the master weaver only added his birthplace when weaving elsewhere is also not proven (as we shall see when discussing Pope's attribution of a group of tree carpets to Joshaqan), and it is just as likely that it would have been added as an extra means of identification on what was obviously an extremely important commission. An attribution of the Ardabil carpets to Kashan itself seems a logical hypothesis, even if impossible to prove.

The Ardabil carpets are the most famous of a large group of medallion carpets, the origins of which are not settled, nor are ever likely to be. Dimand assigns a considerable number to Tabriz and others to Kashan. However, one of the carpets assigned by him to Tabriz, the medallion and animal carpet in the Instituto de Valencia de Don Juan, Madrid, has been assigned over the last few years by several authorities to Kashan, Isfahan, Yezd or Kazvin respectively! Again, this piece is now considered part of a group of a dozen or so carpets, called collectively the Sanguszko group, after a particularly fine example in the collection of Prince Roman Sanguszko, Paris. We shall consider these pieces in some detail later.

Medallion carpet with animal combat groups and dragons. A member of the Sangusko group of carpets. Probably Kashan or Kerman, late 16th or early 17th century. 14 ft. 1 in. × 7 ft. 2 in. (430 × 215 cm.). Instituto de Valencia de Don Juan, Madrid.

Among the earliest of the medallion carpets attributed to Tabriz is one in the Metropolitan Museum with a light blue medallion on a terracotta field, and with an arabesque border. In common with most of the carpets woven in northern and central Persia during the Safavid Dynasty, it is woven with the Senneh knot and has a cotton warp and weft (although some will have either silk warp and weft, or a cotton warp and silk weft). It is ascribed by Dimand to the late 15th century, and this early date is principally suggested by the absence of Chinese-inspired cloud-bands in the design, motifs which became more popular during the 16th century.

In a number of medallion carpets thought to have been made in the early years of the 16th century during the reigns of Shahs Ismael and Tahmasp, the field design consists either of an allover arrangement of arabesques or may incorporate animals and figures.

Several authorities have pointed out that in the first two decades of the 16th century many of the leading artists were brought from Herat and other cultural centres to the capital at Tabriz, including Mirak, Mirza Ali, Sultan Muhammed and Mir Sayyid Ali. Bihzad moved to Tabriz in 1510, and was appointed head of the library and royal painting studio in 1522. It is probable, therefore, that the growing sophistication apparent in the designs of carpets made during the first decades of the Safavid Empire was due to the presence of the artists, who made designs and cartoons for the weavers. Nevertheless, we have to remember that Tabriz was under Turkish rule from 1533 to about 1555, so that the existence there in that period of a flourishing Safavid court art seems, to say the least, politically unlikely.

However, one of the finest medallion carpets, the Anhalt, now in the Metropolitan Museum was, by tradition, captured as booty by the Duke of Anhalt after the Turkish retreat from the Siege of Vienna in 1683. The presence of this piece in Turkish hands suggests the possibility that it was woven in Tabriz during the period of Turkish occupation. In other words, the Turks allowed Tahmasp's workshops to continue production, keeping some of what was made for themselves. On the subject of this prize, Erdmann has written, 'It is worth noting that all the pieces associated with the victory of 1683 are of Persian origin. This is probably no mere accident, for although Turkey had its own carpet production, Sultans and high dignitaries seem to have had a taste for Persian rugs and preferred them to local products.'

It should be said that Erdmann tends to dismiss the claims of many of the carpets captured in this way because of their age, saying, 'In the Orient, carpets have never been regarded as rarities and we can hardly assume that an Ottoman Wazir at the Siege of Vienna would take about with him carpets 150 years old.' However, there is good reason to suppose that the Metropolitan carpet was so acquired by its Western owner, and if so, the Wazirs obviously did carry early pieces around with them.

Even if we accept Erdmann's dating of the 17th century for the Anhalt carpet (which is difficult), it would still have not been new at the time of the Siege of Vienna. Even the carpet which did definitely come from the Siege, a Shah Abbas silk Polonaise now in a private collection, which has a seventeenth-century ink inscription on its back detailing its provenance, must have been woven at least fifty years before it found its way west.

In order to accept a Tabriz origin for the Ardabil carpets, however, we would have to accept the hypothesis that the commission for their weaving was placed before the Turkish occupation of the city in 1533, that the Turks allowed work to continue on them for nearly a decade and then allowed what were obviously masterpieces of the art of carpet making to go to their destination in Persia, possibly out of respect for the sanctity of the mosque. All this seems most unlikely.

Medallion carpets ascribed to the first twenty years of the Safavid dynasty – that is, to the reign of Shah Ismael – include: a medallion and corner carpet in the Metropolitan Museum, New York (the 'corner' referring to the quartered cartouches in the corners of the field), with medallion and escutcheon panels on either side of the long axis in dark blue on a red field; another carpet in the Metropolitan Museum with the same general design and colour scheme, and other examples in the Victoria and Albert Museum, the Joseph V. McMullan Collection and the Gulbenkian Foundation, Lisbon. Another was in the Staatliche Museum, Berlin, but was almost completely destroyed during the Second World War.

Dimand, in accepting its earlier dating, also assigned the medallion hunting rug in the Poldi Pezzoli Museum to this group. He compares the drawing of the figures to Herati miniature by Sheikh Zad in the Khamsa of Nizami in the Metropolitan Museum. However,

this piece is not so straightforward as might appear. Bode and Kühnel remarked on its 'astonishingly austere and commonplace drawing and the utterly inadequate treatment of its corners'. Other authorities have noted the clumsy effect of the cross-hatching, created by the floral stems on the ground. The way the corners repeat not only a section of the central medallion but also a section of the bar-and-palmette appendage is again unusual, being a device found often in Ushak designs, but not in Persian pieces.

Erdmann has suggested that the criticism of the coarseness of the drawing stems partly from comparisons with the Vienna silk hunting carpet, which is far more closely woven and in a finer material. Nevertheless, the oddity of the Poldi Pezzoli piece is causing a younger generation of students to question the validity of its inscription. Not known before 1925, this piece may well be much later in date than has hitherto been supposed.

There is also a small group of carpets of similar design which were probably made during the second quarter of the 16th century, in an Ismael/Tahmasp transitional period. The best known of this small group is the so-called 'Coronation' rug, now in the Los Angeles County Museum, the gift of J. Paul Getty.

This has a large central medallion with escutcheon panels at either end on a white ground. The starred corner panels contain figures of houris, and the central medallion contains forty flying crane and two pairs of reclining gazelles. The field has woven upon it floral arabesques and animals, some in combat. When shown in the 1976 *Arts of Islam* exhibition in London, it was described thus: 'This carpet depicts the Persian conception of Paradise. To the Safavid designer Paradise was set in a fertile garden with flowering trees, birds and animals – some of which were familiar from life on earth such as the cranes in the centre, while others, like the phoenixes and dragons, were borrowed from Chinese mythology.'

In the form of the medallion and accompanying panels, as well as in some of the decorative motifs, the Los Angeles carpet clearly resembles the Poldi Pezzoli dated carpet. Other pieces more closely related to the Coronation carpet (usually called the Getty crane carpet) are known. The Mantes Cathedral carpet, now in the Louvre, has a star-shaped central medallion with a dragon and phoenix combat. One carpet, on a white ground, is cut in half and divided between Cracow and the Musée des Arts Décoratifs, Paris; there is a fragment of another in the Philadelphia Museum of Art. Two others, with blue grounds, are the Prince of Schwarzenberg carpet and the fragmentary Steiglitz carpet in Leningrad. A second crane carpet was seriously damaged in Berlin in the Second World War.

Another group which has been linked stylistically with the foregoing has a repeat pattern of cartouches and lobed medallions. An example in the Metropolitan Museum has eight

lobed medallions containing the dragon and phoenix combat, the cartouches and medallions being in red, blue, green or brown on a white field. There are other examples in the Musée des Tissus, Lyons, the Düsseldorf Art Museum (fragment), and a pair split between the Kunsthistorisches Museum, Vienna, and a New York private collection.

Again, the attribution to Tabriz is by no means certain; in the catalogue of an important exhibition (Sheffield and Birmingham, England, 1976) entitled *Carpets of Central Persia*, Dr. May Beattie notes that the Steiglitz carpet appears to have the weave and colour of many vase-technique carpets, and that there was therefore no reason why a design of this type should not have been made in several different centres.

It would seem, therefore, as if there is no factual, very little circumstantial, but much hypothetical evidence to suggest that some of the early Safavid carpets were woven at

Above left: the Berlin crane carpet, almost completely destroyed in the Second World War. Above centre: the Chelsea carpet (detail). Central Persia, mid-16th century. 17 ft. 9 in. × 10 ft. 4 in. (541 × 315 cm.). Victoria and Albert Museum, London. Above right: medallion carpet woven for the 'Darius of the World'. Central Persia, mid-16th century. 16 ft. 7 in. × 7 ft. 10 in. (505.5 × 239 cm.). Poldi Pezzoli Museum, Milan.

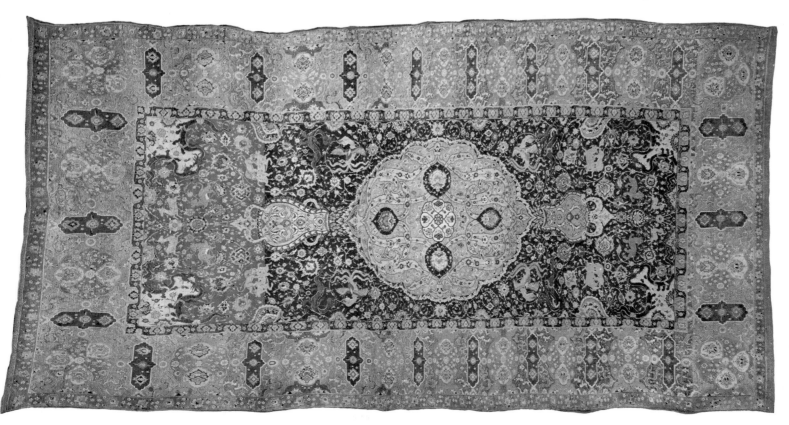

Right: fragment of a medallion carpet with animals, 16th century. 10 ft. 5 in. × 10 ft. (317 × 305 cm.). Museo Civico Bardini, Florence. Below left: medallion and compartment carpet, central Persia, 16th century. 24 ft. 7 in. × 12 ft. 4 in. (737 × 370 cm.). Österreichisches Museum für angewandte Kunst, Vienna. Below right: fragment of a medallion carpet woven on a yellow ground with arabesque scrolls and birds. Probably Kashan, 16th century. 12 ft. 4 in. × 7 ft. 10 in. (370 × 240 cm.). Musée des Gobelins, Paris.

Tabriz, others at Kashan, others – such as the Paris/Cracow fragments – in the province of Khorassan, possibly at Herat, and still others at Kerman.

The major wool rugs assigned to the period of Shah Tahmasp are the Ardabil Mosque carpets; the Anhalt medallion rug, with its gold-yellow field, red cartouches and escutcheons and small peacocks woven in mosaic-like patterns; a medallion rug in the Poldi Pezzoli Museum with flowering trees and animals, woven with a central blue medallion, two Chinese vases on the long axis, flowering trees, foliage and animals on a red ground and an inscription saying that it was woven for the 'Darius of the World'; the magnificent Chelsea carpet in the Victoria and Albert Museum, with a multiple blue medallion on a red field and with animals among flowering and fruiting trees and foliage; a medallion rug partly brocaded with metal thread, with a design which includes peacocks and a Chinese bowl, in the Metropolitan Museum, New York; and the Poldi Pezzoli dated carpet, if we accept the second of its two possible datings in the 16th century.

To the same reign are assigned the small and large silk carpets of Kashan. Four large pieces have survived, all of which are assumed to have been woven in the 1530s. The most famous is the rose-ground hunting carpet in the Österreichisches Museum für angewandte Kunst, Vienna; the others are in the Museum of Fine Arts, Boston, (ex-Rothschild Collection), in the possession of the Royal House of Sweden, Stockholm, and the last in the possession of the Polish Government.

Large Kashan Silk Carpets

The Vienna hunting carpet, once in the Hapsburg royal collection, is of the medallion and corner type, with a green eight-lobed central cartouche; it measures 22 feet 4 inches by 10 feet 6 inches, has a knot count of about 785 to the square inch and has silver and silver-gilt brocading. The field is woven with myriad small groups of huntsmen, some mounted and some on foot, the horses grey, black, chestnut or white; they are charging after, hacking to pieces with swords, spearing or shooting with bows and arrows various forms of game, including leopards, lions, wolves, deer, gazelle, hares, etc. Between the two guards, there is an extraordinary, wide border representing Paradise, with the winged blessed being waited upon by houris, as promised in the Koran, amidst floral arabesques and flying birds. The ground colour of this border is a rich deep crimson, perhaps an indication of what the original field colour must have been like, before it faded to its present unsatisfactory salmon pink.

The design of the Vienna carpet is of the utmost beauty, with brilliant draughtsmanship. As early as 1908, F. R. Martin, in his pioneering book *A History of Oriental Carpets before 1800*, suggested that the design should be connected with Shah Tahmasp's court painter Sultan Muhammed (died *c.* 1555) and this has been accepted by most authorities since.

The same authorship may be true of the Boston carpet, once in the Rothschild Collection and acquired by the Museum of Fine Arts in 1966. Again, a central medallion shows the dragon and phoenix combat, and the field is dominated by hunters. The general concept of the border design is also the same, with seated figures with various offerings amidst trees and flying birds. The fact that these figures, unlike those in the Vienna carpet, are wingless, suggests that this represents an earthly scene (or 'princely garden party' as Dimand put it). The outer guard of the Boston carpet has what appears to be geese among floral scrolls. Like the Vienna carpet, it has silver and silver-gilt brocading and is woven with the Senneh knot, with a count of between 728 and 812 to the square inch. It is smaller than the Austrian piece, measuring approximately 16 feet by 7 feet 6 inches.

The third example, the Branicki carpet, is not, strictly speaking, a hunting carpet. It has no huntsmen, but animals either singly or in combat. Supposedly captured after the Siege of Vienna, it was apparently destroyed during the bombing of Warsaw in the Second World War. It has a pale green field and large quatrefoil centre medallion, palmette escutcheons and corner pieces. It measured 25 feet 4 inches by 11 feet 8 inches. In design, it was close to some of the Sanguszko pieces, especially to that of Prince Sanguszko himself, a carpet which had also been in Poland for many generations.

The fourth example, the hunting carpet in the Royal Palace of Stockholm, is probably of a slightly later date, around the end of the 16th century. Woven on a red field, the drawing is less refined, although the figures, in Erdmann's words, 'show great power of movement'. It measures 18 feet 6 inches by 9 feet 6 inches.

The Imperial silk hunting carpet. The finest surviving example of silk weaving from sixteenth-century Kashan, possibly after a design by Sultan Muhammed, Shah Tahmasp's court painter. 22 ft. 4 in. × 10 ft. 6 in. (681 × 320 cm.). Österreichisches Museum für angewandte Kunst, Vienna.

Small Kashan Silk Carpets

More numerous – about fourteen examples are known – are the small silk carpets of Kashan, which many scholars, including Erdmann, have studied in detail as a group and whose findings are now generally accepted. There are two basic groups – those with a central medallion and those without medallions and with an allover pattern of pictorially arranged animals. There are ten medallion pieces and four animal ones. They are to be found in the following locations:

Metropolitan Museum, New York	3 medallion and 1 animal
Art Institute, Detroit	1 animal
Gulbenkian Foundation, Lisbon	1 medallion
Bavarian National Museum, Munich	1 medallion

Above: the Branicki carpet (detail). Woven in silk with medallion and animals on a pale green ground. Kashan, second half of the 16th century. 25 ft. 4 in. × 11 ft. 8 in. (760 × 350 cm.). Property of the Polish Government, presumed destroyed in the Second World War.

Small silk animal carpet, Kashan, late 16th century. Three other animal carpets from this group are known. 7 ft. 10 in. × 5 ft. 10½ in. (235 × 175 cm.). The Metropolitan Museum of Art, New York, Bequest of Benjamin Altman, 1913.

Top: small silk medallion carpet. Kashan, 16th century. Rose-coloured ground. Carpe s of the same design are in the Metropolitan Museum, New York, and in Coimbra, Portugal. 8 ft. 10¼ in. × 5 ft. 2½ in. (266.5 × 156.5 cm.). Bayerisches Nationalmuseum, Munich. Above: small silk medallion carpet. Kashan, 16th century. Executed from the same cartoon as the Altman carpet. 7 ft. 10 in. × 5 ft. 10½ in. (235 × 175 cm.). Detroit Institute of Arts, Edsel Ford Gift, 1925. Right: small silk medallion carpet. Kashan, 16th century. Rose-coloured ground. Carpets of a similar design are in the Metropolitan Museum, New York, and the Gulbenkian Foundation, Lisbon. 8 ft. 4 in. × 4 ft. 11 in. (250 × 150 cm.). Musée des Gobelins, Paris.

Musée des Gobelins, Paris	1 medallion
Louvre, Paris	1 animal (the Peytel)
Textile Museum, Washington	1 medallion
Rijksmuseum, Amsterdam	1 medallion
Museum für angewandte Kunst, Vienna	1 medallion
Coimbra Museum, Portugal	1 medallion
Ex-Aynard Collection, Paris	1 animal (auctioned 1913, present whereabouts unknown).

Of the medallion rugs, Erdmann has defined three types with sub-categories. The first group, simple medallion without appendages, can be divided into two groups, the first with quatrefoil medallion and the second with a diamond overlaid with a quatrefoil to form an octafoil. The first sub-category includes the Musée des Gobelins, Gulbenkian and one of the Metropolitan rugs; the second, one of the Metropolitan pieces and the rug in the Rijksmuseum, Amsterdam. The second type, medallion with appendages, also has two sub-headings: with band framing medallion (rugs in the Metropolitan, Munich and Coimbra) and with cartouches grouped around the central medallion, which is the most elaborate of the medallion forms and includes the rugs in Washington and Vienna. The third group consists of the animal carpets.

Erdmann suggests further that within this group of fourteen carpets, there are six identifiable cartoons; in other words, it would seem as if the workshop in Kashan was supplied with designs, probably by a leading artist, which were then interpreted in such a way as to produce carpets which, although not identical, clearly had a common source.

The Gulbenkian carpet appears to have been done from a cartoon of which there is no other known version. One of the Metropolitan rugs and the Musée des Gobelins rugs are twins, as are the Amsterdam rug and another of the Metropolitan pieces, and the Washington and Vienna pieces; the fifth medallion cartoon is represented by the third Metropolitan piece and those in Coimbra and Munich.

The animal rugs without medallion form the sixth cartoon. The Detroit and Metropolitan pieces are indeed very similar. Both have six rows of polychrome animals, consisting of leopards, lions and other wild cats attacking game, and single animals; the bottom row of each piece has identical groups, with a bird perched on a tree in the bottom left hand corner. They are roughly the same size, 7 feet 10 inches by 5 feet 10 inches, and both are woven on red grounds. The Peytel Kashan, however, is woven on a dark blue ground, with a red main border, and is approximately half the size of the other two, with only three rows of animals. However, several of the same animal groups appear, so that it was obviously woven from the same cartoon or, as may be the case with animal carpets and rugs in general, from a pattern book of motifs.

Vase carpets

Perhaps the most complex of the many problems surrounding sixteenth-century Persian weaving is the definition of the term 'vase carpet', and from which particular region such pieces originate. In simple terms, vase carpets may be defined in two ways: as a reference to a design found upon a field or a generalized description of a particular structural technique common to many carpets of widely differing designs.

Within the wide grouping of 'vase carpet' Dr. May Beattie has defined several individual groups by design in her exhibition catalogue of *Carpets of Central Persia*: garden carpets, centralized designs, multiple medallion designs, directional designs, sickle-leaf designs, arabesque designs, and lattice designs; the last-named is further sub-divided into three-plane lattice, three-plane large-leaf lattice, two-plane lattice and single-plane lattice. Although complex, these are the best definitions yet offered.

Unlike medallion carpets, the pieces stylistically defined as vase carpets have a design which is one-directional only: if viewed from the wrong end, the design is upside down. The vases themselves are often well-hidden within the highly complex floral pattern of the field. In the best-known types, a fine example of which is in the Baltimore Museum of Art, the field is divided from side to side by rows of floral lozenges, the individual fields of which are in different colours and each one of which contains a Chinese vase.

Such carpets are defined by Dr. May Beattie as 'two-plane lattice'. In contrast to the Baltimore rug, which is the most easily recognizable type, another form of the two-plane lattice is represented by carpets in the Victoria and Albert Museum and Colonial Williamsburg, both of which have floral medallions in rows divided by large and small polychrome flower heads.

The Baltimore carpet once formed the pair to an example in the Berlin Museum destroyed by fire in the Second World War. Their dates are still a matter of controversy. Some modern scholars, including Charles Grant Ellis and May Beattie, incline to the belief that the stiffness of the drawing makes it unlikely that they are from before the mid-17th century, but Erdmann and Dimand stick to dates in the late 16th century.

*Vase carpet of the
lattice type.
Central Persia,
possibly Kerman,
early 17th
century. 12 ft. 9 in.
× 7 ft. 8 in.
(389 × 234 cm.).*

The other major group of vase carpets is the 'three-plane lattice'. This has a field design of great complexity which Doctor Dimand has described lucidly in his important Metropolitan Museum catalogue:

'At first glance it may seem that the large palmettes are placed arbitrarily over the field. However, analysis of the design reveals a definite pattern based on three systems of wavy scrolls forming a lozenge diaper. The large palmettes are surrounded by floral sprays, smaller palmettes and leaves. Usually two or three motifs are superimposed, some containing floral sprays, others the characteristic lyre-shaped lilies. The ground colour is usually red or blue; occasionally it is white.'

The Schwarzenberg medallion carpet. Central Persia, mid-16th century. Woven on a blue ground with animals and cypress trees. 19 ft. × 12 ft. 4 in. (570 × 365 cm.). H.S.H. Prince Charles of Schwarzenberg.

Various fine examples of this type are known. There is a complete example in the Metropolitan Museum and fragments from two others in the same institution. Another important piece, once in Berlin, was destroyed almost totally during the Second World War; this has been described by Erdmann as 'one of the earliest and most important on account of the precision of its drawing and the richness of its colour'. Its pair was in the collection of the late Lady Baillie. There are also published fragments in the Baltimore Museum, the Iraq Museum, Baghdad and the Glasgow Art Gallery (Burrell Collection). There is a particularly beautiful large fragment in the Fogg Art Museum, the gift of Joseph V. McMullan, and two in the Victoria and Albert Museum, one of which once belonged to William Morris.

Dr. May Beattie has also published a fragment of what she terms 'three-plane large-leaf lattice' designs, in which large palmettes are grouped in fours within large serrated leaves, which form lattice patterns (superficially such pieces resemble the two-plane lattice carpets). Although there are several fragments of such carpets scattered throughout the world's museums, no complete examples are known; however, the largest fragment, in the Istanbul Museum, is 15 feet 9 inches by 9 feet 4 inches, thus showing the full length and only slight cutting on the sides. The examples which contain four palmettes within each lozenge have monochrome fields, but there are several fragments known with the lozenge containing six flower heads, and these have multicoloured fields similar to the two-plane lattice carpets of the Baltimore type.

Also within the three-plane lattice group are carpets with vases arranged in rows with stylized flower bouquets emanating from them. A fine pair on green grounds is split between the Museum für angewandte Kunst, Vienna, and the Rijksmuseum, Amsterdam.

Thus far, we have described pieces which, on stylistic grounds, may be defined as vase carpets. There are, however, other groups of technically related pieces. As we have seen, the vase carpets so far discussed have all conformed to Dr. May Beattie's 'lattice design' categories. Leaving aside for the present the tangled question of how the Sanguszko carpets relate to this group, three well-defined types are the directional designs, the sickle-leaf design and the arabesque designs.

The carpets with directional designs may have rows of either animals, animals and equestrian hunters, or flowering plants, shrubs and trees. An extremely beautiful example of the middle category is in the Musée des Arts Décoratifs, Paris, and inevitably invites comparisons with the small Kashan silk animal rugs. So, too, do the designs of single animals and game being pursued by wildcats, among cypress trees, other flowering trees and flower heads. Such designs, found on fragments in the Museum für Kunsthandwerk, Frankfurt-am-Main, and the Bernheimer Collection, Munich, not only remind one of the Kashan silk rugs, but also of such pieces as the Schwarzenberg medallion carpet and the Getty crane carpet.

Another carpet with animals amid cypress trees was in the Berlin Museum, but virtually destroyed in the Second World War. This is described as a 'directional' carpet of the Sanguszko type. The directional designs with rows of flowering plants are known from several fragmentary examples and a fine, complete example in the Metropolitan Museum, New York, woven on a red ground and ascribed by Dimand to early seventeenth-century Isfahan. As many authorities have pointed out, such designs were popular with Moghul weavers, and we illustrate an Indian piece which was obviously inspired by Persian carpets of this type.

The finest and most famous of the sickle-leaf designs is unquestionably the splendid throne rug in the Corcoran Gallery of Art, Washington. The basic pattern consists of six pairs of long, elegant, sickle-shaped leaves arranged in three rows along the long axis, each pair forming a 'shell' within which is a palmette. There are four large palmettes down the long axis, from each of which emanate arabesques which connect to the other palmettes between the sickle pairs and on the edge of the field; there are also two cypress trees woven

301

Above: the Sanguszko medallion and animal carpet. Central Persia, late 16th or early 17th century. 20 ft. 1¼ in. × 10 ft. 9 in. (604 × 322 cm.). Prince Roman Sanguszko, Paris. Above right: arabesque carpet woven in the vase technique. The wide arabesques are in blue on a red ground. Possibly Kerman, early 17th century. 11 ft. 10 in. × 7 ft. 6½ in. (355 × 225 cm.). Ex-Eric Tabbagh Collection, Paris; it is now in the Kunst und Gewerbe Museum, Hamburg.

in the centre of the field. The rug probably represents a bird's eye view of a wooded landscape seen, as it were, through vines and foliage. It derives its name from the suggestion put forward by Arthur Upham Pope that its size (8 feet 8½ inches by 6 feet 5 inches) indicates that it could have been used on the dais of a throne. The leaves and flowers, woven in a polychrome palette, in which yellow, green and blue predominate, are on a rich red field with a deep blue floral border.

No other sickle-leaf carpet compares in quality to the Corcoran throne rug. Erdmann, in *Seven Hundred Years of Oriental Carpets*, illustrates two – one in a Swedish private collection – in which the design, while adhering to the same principle, is stiffer and more angular, and with shorter, fatter leaves which destroy the overwhelmingly elegant effect of the Corcoran rug. One of these he tentatively attributes to southern Persia and the other to Herat. To this sickle-leaf group can be assigned a carpet with multiple medallions in the Robert Lehmann bequest to the Metropolitan Museum, and a fine rug in the Gulbenkian Foundation, Lisbon.

The designs of arabesque rugs are of several different types, some of which continued to be made well into the 18th century. The finest have a red field with a system of powerful wide blue bands and trefoils, with a further and secondary system of palmettes, blossoms and cloud-bands.

A fine pair was once split between the Berlin Staatliche Museum and the Corcoran Gallery, Washington, but the former was yet another casualty of the last war; another example, once belonging to Eric Tabbagh, is now in the Kunst und Gewerbe Museum,

Hamburg. Dimand shows that there are several depictions of similar carpets in sixteenth-century miniatures, including examples by Mir Sayyid Ali.

Later carpets, with lateral systems of wide arabesques and dense floral patterns, are attributed to the 17th and 18th centuries and were probably made in Kurdistan. One example in the Metropolitan Museum is dated 1794 and is inscribed with the fact that it was made to the order of His Excellency Ali-Riza Khan in Garus, a district of Kurdistan. There is obviously a stylistic connection between these pieces, some of the late Kurdistan tree and garden carpets, and the floral and dragon carpets of the Caucasus.

A different form of arabesque is found in the beautiful medallion and corner rug in the Burrell Collection, Glasgow; in this piece, the arabesques are organized round a central pink medallion on a yellow field. The arabesques move in a highly structured way on the field, forming themselves into four quatrefoils and cartouches at either end of the field on the long axis of the carpet.

Related to the vase carpets, although no actual vase appears in the design, is the unique Havermeyer carpet in the Metropolitan Museum; the floral decoration of the field is woven on a background of overlapping, cross-shaped cartouches in a polychrome palette. The effect of the 'patchwork' design can be linked with the Baltimore two-plane lattice carpet with its polychrome diamonds interlocking but not overlapping. As Maurice Dimand has noticed, the design structure of the Havermeyer carpet is connected with a pair of contemporaneous silk Polonaise carpets given to the Metropolitan by John D. Rockefeller Jr.

Although the floral aspect of the Havermeyer carpet, as well as its technical structure, is the one which links it most closely with the vase carpets, the idea of the multiple medallion or cartouche design, either overlapping or independently placed, connects it to other carpets; and these are the ones of the so-called Sanguszko group. With a discussion of these carpets, we come across one of the most interesting, and yet complex, questions the study of Oriental carpets can offer.

The Sanguszko group was first isolated and described by Kurt Erdmann in 1932, following the great exhibition of Persian art in London. In Dr. May Beattie's words, it is named after 'a handsome medallion-and-corner carpet in the possession of Prince Sanguszko . . . First shown in Leningrad in 1904 and said to have been taken at the Battle of Chocim in 1621'. Although there is no firm classification for the group, about fifteen carpets and fragments are generally included within it; they are as follows:

Thyssen-Bornemisza Collection, Lugano	medallion and animal design (the Behague carpet)	
Textile Museum, Washington	medallion and animal design (fragments)	
Duke of Buccleuch	multiple medallion and animal design	61
Museum für Islamische Kunst, Berlin	medallion, animal and corner design (the Cassirer carpet)	
Victoria and Albert Museum, London	medallion, corner and animal design	
Musée des Tissus, Lyons	multiple medallion and animal design	
Staatliche Museum, Berlin	directional design with animals (almost completely destroyed in the Second World War)	
Ex-Baron Havatny, Budapest	medallion and animal carpet (fragment)	
Prince Roman Sanguszko, Paris	medallion and animal design	60
National Gallery, Washington	medallion and animal design (the Widener carpet)	
Instituto de Don Juan, Madrid	medallion, corner and animal design	48
Philadelphia Museum of Art	medallion and animal design (the Williams carpet).	

There are, in addition, the Benguiat, Kelekian and Yerkes/Trevor carpets. As can be seen from this list, the principal attributes of most of the Sanguszko carpets are medallions and animals, the latter within flowers and foliage representative of landscapes.

As to where and when the different carpets of the vase-technique were woven, the innocent seeker after scholarly enlightenment might well wish, after studying the available literature, that he had never embarked upon the task. There are four main contenders – Kerman, Isfahan, Kashan and Joshaqan. But one should not forget, of course, the possibility of Tabriz, Kazvin, Yezd or even Herat (for if Joshaqan has been taken seriously, then Herat can hardly be considered eccentric).

The earliest vase carpets were probably woven in the second half of the 16th century during the first years of Shah Abbas's reign. Certainly, the two fragments of a three-plane lattice carpet, one in Berlin (Inv. 1-8-72) and the other in the Textile Museum, Washington (Inv. R. 33.6.5), are freer and more active in design than the other pieces we have mentioned previously, certainly more so than the destroyed Berlin pieces, the first of which, as we noted earlier, was described by Erdmann as 'one of the earliest and most important', and dated by him to the first half of the 16th century, a dating which could possibly be as much as a century too early.

Charles Grant Ellis, in his 1968 essay on vase rugs in the *Textile Museum Journal*, considered the stiffening of the small flowers in the borders in square blocks – the so-called 'frozen' border – an indication of late work. He dated the Baltimore two-plane lattice to the second half of the 17th century (and thus by extension its destroyed pair in Berlin); on the

Two single-plane lattice vase carpets of the type traditionally associated with Joshaqan. Late 18th or early 19th century. Left: 15 ft. 8 in. × 8 ft. 4 in. (477.5 × 254 cm.). Ex-Kevorkian Collection. Below: 15 ft. 10 in. × 6 ft. 6 in. (483 × 198 cm.).

basis of the 'frozen' border, we could also date Erdmann's 'first half of the 16th century' carpet to the second half of the 17th century, as well as its ex-Lady Baillie pair, and similarly the Istanbul three-plane large-leaf carpet and the Colonial Williamsburg two-plane lattice carpet. And if we assign the last-named to the late 17th century, so also we must the Victoria and Albert Museum's two-plane lattice, with which the Williamsburg carpet has much in common. (Personally, I believe the Victoria and Albert piece to be even later, probably eighteenth- or nineteenth-century Kurdistan, albeit that the latter carpets are usually woven on blue fields.)

There is certainly some evidence that the Victoria and Albert and Williamsburg pieces are late, for in the Sarajevo Museum there is a fragment of a multiple medallion carpet with which the other two were first grouped by Martin in 1908, which is dated 1067 of the Hejira (1656). It would seem as if the dating of any of the one- or two-plane lattice designs, and the majority of the three-plane lattice pieces, to before the beginning of the 17th century is difficult to justify.

The same general dating – the first half of the 17th century or later, depending on the quality of execution – can be assigned to most of the other vase-technique types. The Havermeyer floral compartment or multiple medallion rug in the Metropolitan Museum is assigned by Dimand to the first half of the 17th century and, although he links it with both the Victoria and Albert Museum and Colonial Williamsburg pieces, there is good reason to suppose, looking at its style and quality, that it is earlier than those two. There is also its strong resemblance to known Polonaise carpets to enforce a reasonably early dating in the 17th century.

The arabesque carpets are, again, assigned by most authorities to the 17th century. However, the suggestion that the Hamburg and Corcoran (ex-Senator Clarke) carpets are late sixteenth-century or early seventeenth-century seems justifiable. As Dimand remarks: 'The use of arabesque bands is also to be seen in faience mosaic decoration of the late 16th and early 17th centuries in Ardabil and Isfahan, notably those of Mashid-i-Jami and the Lutfullah Mosque, both in Isfahan.' The sickle-leaf and directional designs are also considered to be early seventeenth-century.

As to the place of origin, Kerman in south Persia has been the favourite choice of scholars for fifty years or more. Like many other Persian cities, it is mentioned in the literature of the Shah Abbas period as a place where fine rugs were woven; references occur not only in Persian manuscripts but also in Indian, such as the *Akbar Nameh*. Floral rugs of the sickle-leaf variety were imported into India, and had considerable influence on Moghul weavers; and, as many writers have pointed out, eighteenth- and nineteenth-century carpets known to have been woven in Kerman do bear a strong resemblance to earlier pieces attributed to the town. There does seem good reason, therefore, to conclude that the attribution to Kerman is the most likely.

Erdmann argues that the lattice layout must have come to Kerman from the Caucasus. This, however, presupposes that tribal weavers of Caucasian origin settled in and around Kerman almost exclusively. This, of course, is not so. The province of Kurdistan lies be-

Two shaped silk carpets woven with directional designs of flowering shrubs and cypress trees, from a set of thirteen woven for the Mausoleum of Shah Abbas II at Kum. Below: signed Nimat Allah (or Ni'matullah) of Joshaqan and dated 1671. 6 ft. 3 in. × 2 ft. 10 in. (188 × 85 cm.). Below right: late seventeenth-century Joshaqan. 30 ft. 9 in. × 13 ft. 7½ in. (823 × 408 cm.). Iran Bastan Museum, Teheran, on loan from the Mausoleum of Shah Abbas II at Kum.

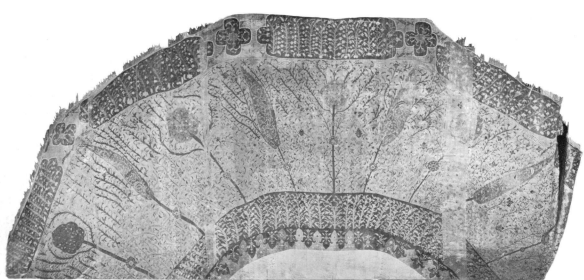

tween the present eastern border of Turkey and north-west Iran, quite some distance from Kerman. Caucasian and Turkish nomads roamed this area at will and moved the whole way down the western part of Persia, settling around Hamadan, Bijar, Senneh, Malayer, Saruk and as far south and east as Shiraz and Kerman.

It is hardly possible to dispute Erdmann's observations about rugs of the last hundred years or so woven in the Kerman area – one thinks not only of adaptations of the lattice and garden designs woven in the town itself under commercial conditions, but the stylization of some of the Afshar floral and tree motifs which are woven into their rugs by Afshar tribesmen, who are descended from Turkish tribes originally from Azerbaijan.

However, the same observations could be made about the modern production of the Herez-Tabriz area in the north-east, and the production in the region of Meshed and the Fars tribal rugs in the south. And, as Dimand has pointed out, weavers from the Caucasus were also to be found in Isfahan in the 17th century, which leads him to believe that many of the vase carpets were woven there.

As we have said before, the multiple medallion carpets of the vase-technique group can also be linked stylistically with some of the Polonaise silk carpets which very probably *were* woven in Isfahan.

However, to confuse the matter further, Arthur Upham Pope in his *Survey of Persian Art* has pointed out that there are silk carpets of the 17th century in the Mausoleum of Shah Abbas II at Kum, which have either a vase in the decoration or a repeat pattern of cypress trees. One of these is inscribed, 'The work of the Master Nimat Allah of Joshaqan in the year 1082 (1671).' Because of this, and because there are also other carpets of the 18th and 19th centuries bearing resemblance to the vase carpets which Pope also attributed to Joshaqan, he suggested that not only did many of the silk Polonaise carpets originate in Joshaqan, but many of the vase rugs also.

This idea, which has been treated seriously by scholars, even if not accepted by most, gives a clear indication of the contradictions which abound in the world of carpet scholarship. For, if we remember, one of Erdmann's main arguments against the title 'Maksud of Kashan' pointing to a Kashani origin for the Ardabil carpets was that weavers only put their place of origin if weaving elsewhere!

If we believe Pope, we have a strong argument for believing that the Ardabils were woven at Kashan (although Pope himself blithely attributes them to Tabriz). If, however, we accept Erdmann's argument, then we must assume that Pope's attribution of carpets to Joshaqan is unjustified, at least on the evidence of a place name woven into a carpet. I incline to the same view with these pieces as I do with the Ardabil carpets – that the weaver was proud of his work and wished, by giving his place of origin, to bring honour to his home as well as to himself, but this attribution is irrelevant to vase carpets.

By now, the reader will be aware of the difficulty, if not the impossibility, of assigning exclusive provenance to not only the vase carpets, but the majority of Safavid carpet production. A skillful advocate can, as many have done in the past, put forward a number of widely differing places as the source of a particular type of carpet. But to attribute vase carpets of the lattice design in particular to a specific town is to do so on the basis of circumstantial evidence, a large part of which is highly subjective.

There seems no reason to suppose, to repeat Dr. May Beattie's remarks about the Steiglitz Carpet, that carpets so handsomely designed, and made over a period of a century or more, were not woven in several different locations, especially if we remember that artists and designers were moved from one city to another.

In all probability, vase carpets were woven in Tabriz, Kashan, Isfahan, Yezd, Kerman and Herat. There is certainly no evidence to say that they were not, and no conclusive body of evidence to pin-point one place to the exclusion of the others. It is to be regretted that so many scholars play such pointless guessing games, which tend to confuse rather than enlighten the layman.

Even the simple single-plane lattice carpets, which resemble the Baltimore two-plane lattice carpet, and are usually considered to have been woven in the 18th century, have not found unanimous support for their place of origin. Many scholars have thought Joshaqan a likely provenance, especially as carpets are still produced there in this style. However, single-plane lattice designs are also produced today in Tabriz and elsewhere in Persia, so that what appears to be a continuing Joshaqani tradition cannot really be described as such; in fact,

63

the 19th and 20th centuries saw the introduction of designs based upon carpets of the Safavid period by European merchants into towns and villages where they may not have been woven before.

The copying of actual carpets and the adaptation of sixteenth- and seventeenth-century designs was current in Persia in the late 19th century. Erdmann and Ellis were both of the opinion that the single-plane lattice designs originated from Kerman (although Erdmann dated them to the second half of the 17th century).

The Sanguszko Carpets

The problem of the place of origin of the Sanguszko carpets is just as difficult to resolve. In considering the carpets we have listed earlier, we have to remember that there are several carpets not usually categorized as Sanguszko pieces which are, nevertheless, closely linked to them stylistically. The Poldi Pezzoli dated carpet, the Getty crane carpet, the Schwarzenberg, Steiglitz and Paris-Cracow carpets, the Chelsea carpet, the Poldi Pezzoli 'Darius of the World' carpet, the Anhalt carpet and the Branicki carpet have all been mentioned.

Medallion carpet with arabesque foliage and birds on a beige ground. Possibly Herat, mid-16th century. 7 ft. 7 in. × 5 ft. 1 in. (227 × 152 cm.). Gulistan Museum, Teheran.

We should remember that in the cases of the Paris/Cracow and Getty carpets, two pieces which one would have thought so closely linked that there would be no discussion about a common place of origin, some modern scholarship is of the opinion that the former was woven in Khorassan and the latter in Tabriz – in other words, at opposite sides of the country. If such is the case, what possible hope is there of giving accurate provenances to the rest?

Erdmann is of the view that the carpets of the Sanguszko group containing animals and figures are from Kashan. He was led to this conclusion by a close stylistic comparison between them and certain silk pieces, the provenance of which he felt was certainly Kashan. Pope, on the other hand, thought that they were certainly from Kerman and there is one piece of historical evidence to bear this out.

Engelbert Kaempfer, a visitor to Isfahan in 1684, remarked that the woollen carpets with animal designs he saw in the reception hall were woven in Kerman. Since we know that Shah Abbas I also established workshops at Kashan, Isfahan and Yezd and continued the ateliers at Tabriz and Herat, there is every reason to suppose that medallion and animal carpets in wool were woven at all of these places and that the Sanguszko carpets could have been woven at any of them. To repeat once more, master weavers and master painters were moved from place to place, presumably taking their techniques and designs with them.

Floral carpets

To the city of Herat, once in the Persian province of Khorassan, but now inside the border of Afghanistan, is assigned a group of carpets with floral designs. Herat was the centre of Timurid court art and possibly the oldest weaving centre in Persia. The earliest geometric Persian rugs are presumed to have been woven there (although they may well have not been woven in Persia at all but imported from Turkey) and during the 16th and 17th centuries a specific style of dense floral patterning is attributed to the looms of Herat.

The majority of such pieces do not contain animals or birds, although a few such pieces are known. A particularly fine pair, called the Emperor's carpets, a supposed gift from Peter the Great to Leopold I of Austria, is now split between the Metropolitan Museum and the Österreichisches Museum für angewandte Kunst, Vienna. Woven with deep red grounds, these carpets have series of animals, either singly or in combat, arranged in rows vertically and horizontally. In the intervening field areas, there is a dense interacting floral arrangement of flower heads and scrolls.

Naturally, the forms of the carpets invite comparisons with other animal carpets, both in silk and wool. The silk Kashans come to mind, as do a pair of red-ground animal carpets split between the Metropolitan and the Mrs. John D. Rockefeller Collection, which came from the shrine of Sheikh Safi in the mosque at Ardabil. This pair was assigned by both Erdmann and Dimand to sixteenth-century Tabriz.

Certainly the arrangement of the Ardabil animal carpets is more formal and less flowing than the Emperor carpets, but the attribution of one pair to Tabriz and the other to Herat is based on little evidence, visual or otherwise. The Herati borders of both pairs are similar and an attribution to Kashan rather than to Tabriz seems to make better sense.

Again, if one can make attributions to specific towns based upon visual evidence, I find

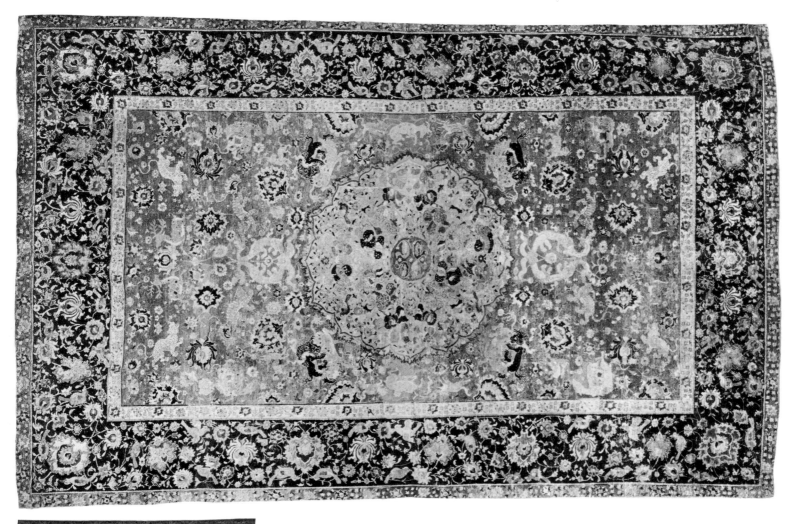

Above and below (detail): one of a pair of animal rugs attributed to late sixteenth-century Herat. 8 ft. 4 in. × 5 ft. 10 in. (250 × 182.5 cm.). Metropolitan Museum of Art, New York. Left: floral Herat carpet, late 16th or early 17th century. 16 ft. 2 in. × 7 ft. 1 in. (493 × 216 cm.). Ex-collection of Grace, Countess of Dudley.

Right : one of a pair of wool and silver brocade carpets with a silk foundation, from the Ardabil Shrine, the other in the Rockefeller Collection, New York. Probably late sixteenth-century Kashan. 11 ft. 7½ in. × 5 ft. 11 in. (327.5 × 175 cm.). Metropolitan Museum of Art, New York. Far right : Herat carpet of the so-called 'Isfahan' type, late 17th or early 18th century. 6 ft. 3 in. × 4 ft. 2 in. (190.5 × 127 cm.). Ex-Kevorkian Collection.

Right : Herat wool carpet with silver brocading. Late 16th century. 9 ft. 9 in. × 5 ft. 2½ in. (293 × 156 cm.), reduced in length by three horizontal cuts. Formerly in the Figdor and Cassirer Collections. Far right : floral carpet, wool with silver brocading, Herat, early 17th century. 18 ft. 5 in. × 12 ft. 5 in. (552 × 348 cm.). Shrine Collection, Meshed.

67 it difficult to believe that the Emperor's carpets and the small pair of medallion and animal rugs, also in the Metropolitan Museum and attributed to sixteenth-century Herat by Dimand, were woven in the same place at the same time. The same statement holds true for the Ardabil animal carpets and the Ardabil medallion carpets; the difference in quality must surely be self-evident.

66 The attribution of the floral rugs to Herat is safer; the majority of the rugs have no figures, but a small number do have birds. These bird pieces are considered the earliest examples, dating from the late 16th to the early 17th century, of a tradition which lasted well into the 18th century, although with a steady worsening of quality. A fragmentary example, woven with pheasants and with metal brocading, is in the Victoria and Albert Museum, London; a fine and complete example on a blue ground, containing birds of Paradise and other birds, is in the Metropolitan Museum.

70 Of the purely floral rugs, Dimand has noted that the Isfahan type was imported into Europe in great quantities. These carpets are indeed depicted in many seventeenth-century paintings, including works by Velazquez, Rubens, Van Dyck, Vermeer, Terborch, de Hooch, Bol and Metsu.

The leaf patterns are characterized by a widespread use of serrated leaves in pairs and flower heads, the so-called Herati or 'fish' pattern. The angularity of the leaves, solidly drawn, contrasts with the flowing structural arabesques of the main design.

It should be noted that the name 'Isfahan' for floral Herat carpets of various sizes was given to the group by European merchants since that city was the market place for such pieces. Confusion between place of origin and place of marketing becomes ubiquitous in the late 19th and 20th centuries. The influence of early Herati designs was widespread, great numbers of pieces being imported into Europe and India. Floral carpets from all over Persia show the influence of Herati weaving; it is especially noticeable in the sickle-leaf pieces discussed above, and also in copies made in Isfahan and the districts of Azerbaijan and Kurdistan. There are even pieces made in the Caucasus which can be linked stylistically with Herati weaving, demonstrating the wide currency of the patterns.

The dominant theme in Persian Safavid weaving is the garden, as Donald King wrote in the catalogue of the *Arts of Islam* exhibition held in London in 1976: 'The idea of a garden in perpetual springtime – the flowers, the trees, the sound of water and of birds – has remained especially pleasing to the peoples of Islam, many of whom dwell in relatively arid climates, and it is constantly evoked in their carpets and textiles.'

All Safavid carpets contain floral elements arranged in formal patterns, so it is arguable that they are all, to a certain extent, intended to create an impression of living things. In the animal and hunting carpets, there is also the depiction of life in a fertile land, with trees, water and abundant game.

Other carpets we have noticed – the Schwarzenberg medallion, the Getty crane carpet, the Corcoran throne rug – are all idealized, schematic renderings of bountiful landscapes. The borders of the great silk hunting carpets in Vienna and Boston depict people at ease in gardens, the one heavenly, the other earthly. Similar scenes occur in the famous silk kelim in the Residenz Museum, Munich.

Evidence that these carpets represented gardens comes also from the verses found in the borders of many of them, sometimes culled from the work of leading poets, but often composed by unknown writers for a particular carpet. The Baker animal and medallion carpet in the Metropolitan Museum, New York (the authenticity of which we shall discuss later), has a verse in the cartouche which reads in the later translation by Dimand from Sarre and Trenkwald:

Floral Herat rug of the Isfahan type, late 17th or early 18th century. 5 ft. 8 in. × 4 ft. 5 in. (173 × 135 cm.).

'*When the first down appeared around thy face,*
From the streaming of our tears is the carpet of spring
the charter of our good and evil fortune is a down,

which grows on the rosy cheek of a youthful lover.
A down, fragrant as musk, has come up around thy cheek
O Cypress, when thou was bending towards the rose garden,
Hidden in thy breath were cypress and poplar green.
Al Khizr in the spring, in quest of the water of life
Has again appeared at this season, enveloped in green,
As though the earth, through the bitterness of parting, has sucked up the water.
From it springs up grass in every verdant meadow.
Sufi, burn the blue robe, now that there is a temptation
From wine and flute to turn aside to the green river.'

Inscriptions such as this appear on some forty carpets, mostly with the same sentiments and often with the same imagery. Tulips and narcissi are mentioned frequently (the Baker carpet has such a verse in its medallion which is very similar to the small medallion carpet in the Musée des Arts Décoratifs, Paris) and the analogy between the flowers of spring and a young man's first beard – the rising sap – is used frequently as a symbol of procreation.

Such carpets, therefore, not only served the functional purpose of adding warmth and comfort to their owners' lives but also, through their designs, were a constant reminder of pleasant days in spring and summer. They served a further purpose of bringing to mind the pleasures of Paradise which would await those who kept the faith on earth. Some authorities have taken the theological content of such carpets further by suggesting that the medallion may be taken as the dome of heaven and the hunting and animal combat scenes as allegories of the battle between good and evil. The verses certainly suggest that the pictorial elements of the carpets may be read on two levels.

Floral Herat carpet (detail), probably late 16th century. 25 ft. 10 in. × 10 ft. 3 in. (787 × 312 cm.). Ex-Kevorkian Collection.

These are all, as we have said, idealized poetic renderings. There are, however, carpets which attempt to depict gardens in a more cartographical way. These are the *Chahar bag* or 'four gardens' carpets which reflect the layout of the classic Persian garden in which the land is divided into four sections by canals. The carpets depict such gardens from a hypothetical bird's eye view.

There are two principal groups of *Chahar bag* carpets, the one of squarish form with a fairly dense foliate background, and the other consisting of pieces, usually of great length, in which the garden has been subjected to a more stylized, geometric rendering, although the layout is described with greater topographical accuracy than the first group. Of the first group, the only known examples are in the Museum für angewandte Kunst, Vienna (the Figdor garden carpet). Were it not for the division of the field into areas by means of 'water channels', this piece would bear little resemblance to the second group of carpets, which includes the major garden carpets.

The Figdor piece is on a red ground, the field being divided into six sections, each one of which contains a small central medallion, four with floral centres and two with tree and animal centres. There are a further three medallions split by the central canal on the long axis. The wide canals around the field and through the centre contain fish, as do six small pools in the field. There are also two pools containing single ducks and six with duck entwined with fish. The quadrilateral field compartments contain, apart from the medallions, flowering trees, shrubs and, in the bottom two compartments only, birds. This piece is usually dated to the 17th century and assigned to south Persia; most carpet scholars believe that it can be classified as Kerman with reasonable confidence.

The Wagner garden carpet (Burrell Collection, Glasgow) is later in date and in technique is part of the vase group; again on technical grounds, it has even been assigned to the Sanguszko group. The dark blue field is divided into four compartments by an H-shaped canal system with a central pool. Thus, the two outer sections of the garden run the length of the field on the long axis, with the central section divided into two by the cross bar of the H. The water channels are woven in pale blue and have naturalistically rendered ducks and fishes. The central pool, woven in white, also has fishes and ducks, four of the latter on the water and one in flight. The two outer longitudinal panels are mirror images, with trees

Above: Rudaba Lets Down her Tresses for Zal to Climb, *miniature from a Moghul* Shah Nameh *of c. 1580. Note the similarity in the layout of this* Chahar bag *garden to the prayer rug below right. Below left: the Figdor garden carpet. The closest variant is the prayer rug below right. Central Persia. 6 ft. 3 in × 5 ft. 1 in. (187 × 151 cm.). Österreichisches Museum für angewandte Kunst, Vienna. Below right: garden prayer rug, signed by Muhammed Amin. 4 ft. 8 in. × 3 ft. 9 in. (140 × 113 cm.). Meshed Shrine Collection.*

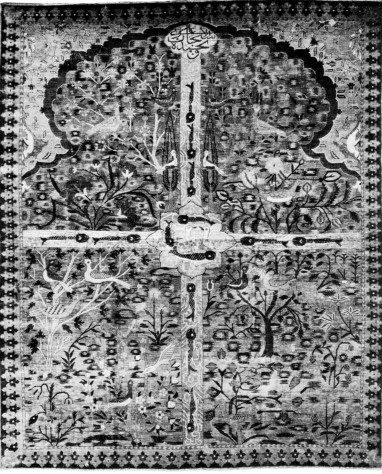

Details from the Jaipur garden carpet. From the labels on the back of the carpet, it must have entered the Moghul Imperial Collection before 1632; it is the finest existing example of the Chahar bag type, predating other known examples by at least a century. Possibly south Persian. The complete carpet measures 28 ft. × 12 ft. 4 in. (840 × 370 cm.). Jaipur Museum, India.

Previous page: Rustam and Mihrafruz Converse in a Garden Pavilion. *Painting on cotton from the* Hamza Nameh, *executed in the Imperial studio between 1567 and 1582. Victoria and Albert Museum, London.*

growing horizontally outward at the bottom, and vertically at the top; there is a variety of game birds and animals, while each panel contains, a little incongruously, a vase of flowers. The bottom centre panel has two rows of trees growing horizontally inward toward each other, each being a mirror of the other; animals and birds include deer, hare, birds of paradise and cranes. The top centre pattern displays the same mirror diptych pattern but the trees and shrubbery grow vertically. The yellow border is woven with an Herati pattern.

Writing in 1908, Martin regarded this piece as 'a vivid illustration of the Spring Carpet of Chosroes', but Dr. May Beattie has suggested that it represents 'an enclosed plantation rather than a conventional garden with flower beds, and the network of water lines also differs from the usual parallel and diverging arrangement used to indicate moving water.'

Of its origins and date, the Wagner carpet has, as we said, been linked with the Sanguszko group of animal carpets, but recent scholarship tends to follow the view, originally put forward by Martin, that it is from Kerman. Some support for this attribution is afforded by a prayer rug of related design in the collection of the mosque at Meshed which is signed Muhammed Amin of Kerman and dated 1651; Erdmann, however, regards the date on this piece as being too early and it may indeed be a century or so out, if not a nineteenth-century copy. The angular drawing of the Wagner carpet suggests a late date, and the guesses of modern scholars range from the late 17th century to Erdmann's early 18th century. Dr. Beattie suggests that the absence of transverse symmetry and the rather square shape of the carpet may mean that only part of a cartoon, possibly intended for a much longer carpet, was used in this instance.

More prevalent is the second, and major, group of garden carpets. The earliest and most important of these is an early seventeenth-century example in the Jaipur Museum which was discovered in a sealed room in the Maharajah of Jaipur's palace at Amber in 1937. Later examples, all of which are ascribed to the 18th century, include the following: the

The colour scheme, technique and character of this garden carpet indicate that it is actually Kurdish. 22 ft. × 8 ft. (670 × 244 cm.). Fogg Art Museum, Cambridge, Mass. McMullan Collection.

McLaren carpets in England; the two which were dispersed from the Kevorkian collection at Sotheby's in 1970 (the one now in the Islamische Museum, Berlin, the other still on the market at the time of writing); three destroyed in Berlin in the Second World War; three in the Metropolitan Museum, New York, including a large fragment similar in style to the McLaren carpets. Other examples are in the Fogg Art Museum, Harvard (gift of Joseph V. McMullan) and the Victoria and Albert Museum, London; another large fragment of a McLaren-type carpet, possibly from the same example as the fragment in the Metropolitan, was sold at Sotheby's in London on 14 April 1976, and several other large and small fragments scattered throughout the major museums of the world.

All these late pieces are ascribed to Kurdistan, but the Jaipur carpet, possibly once part of a sizable group which inspired the Kurdistan pieces, is attributed to Isfahan by Dimand. Erdmann, however, with a blithe disregard for the quality of his evidence, suggests that 'because of its structure, colouring and design, especially that of its border, this must be assigned to the group of Persian vase carpets probably from Kerman.' (Erdmann also makes the cheerful *non sequitur* that proof of an attribution to Kerman is furnished by Abu Fadl (*sic*), historian of the Emperor Akbar, when he says that 'carpets were imported from Kerman, Joshaqan and other Persian places'! As for the movement of the design from south Persia in the 17th century to Kurdistan in the 18th and 19th centuries, Martin has suggested that Nadir Shah moved weavers to Kurdistan in the mid-18th century to the area around Hamadan.

The naturalistically rendered flora and fauna in the Jaipur carpet are reduced to a geometric formula in the latest Kurdistan pieces, a reduction which is not in itself unattractive, but which is somewhat sterile compared with the richness of the earlier piece. As we have said, the largest examples of this group can attain a length of over thirty feet (the complete McLaren carpet), but there are some whole examples which are only about a third of this length and thereby lose the powerful visual effect of the large examples.

The complete McLaren carpet (there is a fragmentary example of the same type also in this collection), and associated fragments are brighter, yet more subtle and have a more lively floral patterning than the Kevorkian type of late garden carpet. It may be that the former should be assigned to the first half of the 18th century, or even to the late 17th century, and the others, especially the simplified small rugs, to the second half of the 18th century, or later.

The Kevorkian type, however, does not represent the final stage in the development of this motif. Kendrick and Tattersall, in *Hand-woven Carpets*, illustrated a piece once in the Orendi Collection in which the design is reduced to an overall pattern of squares containing single, highly stylized flowers. The 'pool' is a large central square containing stylized flower heads radiating from a cross-pattern stem. The 'water channel' surrounding the pool contains motifs strongly resembling those found in bird Ushaks.

In another example in Berlin, all semblance of the earlier schematic rendering of gardens has disappeared with the whole field covered with a lattice of squares containing single plants. Such pieces may be dated to around 1800–50.

Tree and Shrub Carpets
Related to both the medallion and animal carpets are the so-called tree or shrub carpets which were woven from the 16th century onwards. One group of these can be related structurally to the vase carpets and the other, late seventeenth- or early eighteenth-century examples from Kurdistan, resemble visually not only the vase-technique arabesque carpets from the same area but also, and by extension, the Kuba dragon rugs from the Caucasus.

Of the first group, the earliest and most famous is the Williams tree carpet in Philadelphia, which, like many of the early pieces, is woven on a red ground and is assigned by Dimand to Tabriz. The flowering branches of the cypresses, flowering trees and shrubs form a dense floral patterning. The marked angularity of the drawing style, which Dimand takes as an indication of an early date, is also, of course, one of the most obvious characteristics of the later tree and garden carpets from Kurdistan, with which the present piece is obviously connected. Another, less usual, form of tree carpet, is found in a rug in the Metropolitan Museum, New York. This is an adaptation of the medallion design, the medallion itself being in the form of a pool with fishes, around which are arranged, in an engaging pattern, flower heads and trees in a non-directional design.

The directional-row format of the Williams tree carpet became simplified in the 17th century with the directional tree carpets, some of which we have discussed previously in the section on vase-technique carpets. There are two fine examples in the Metropolitan Museum (one with trees arranged around a star medallion), one previously in the Goldschmidt Collection, New York, and several other complete carpets and fragments in museums and private collections throughout the world.

78 In some of these, the rows are contained within a lily-like trellice pattern; the finest example is probably the ex-Lady Dudley carpet sold at Sotheby's in April 1976, while another smaller piece is in the Musée des Arts Décoratifs, Paris. The Sotheby catalogue dates the Lady Dudley Carpet to the 16th century, whereas a dating to the 17th century is probable, and makes the odd remark, 'This carpet . . . was almost certainly woven in Joshaqan.' Modern scholarship does not even admit Joshaqan as the origin of the stiff, single-plane lattice, vase-technique carpets, the best known example of which is in the Victoria and Albert Museum, preferring Kerman. It must be said, however, that in nineteenth- and twentieth-century carpet production, the single-plane lattice design is associated primarily, although not exclusively, with Joshaqan, and there is no reason to doubt this.

Two tree carpets of the shield type, north-west Persian, late 18th century. Left: complete carpet with an exceptionally beautiful white ground and floral border. 20 ft. 8 in. × 8 ft. 8 in. (634 × 234 cm.). Private collection, England. Right: reduced in length, and with the usual palmette and leaf border. 16 ft. 4 in. × 9 ft. 1 in. (490 × 277 cm.). McIlhenny Collection, Philadelphia Museum.

Carpet with a directional design of trees, shrubs and animals. Attributed by Dimand to Kerman, although the borders are reminiscent of carpets attributed to Tabriz. Late 17th or early 18th century. 26 ft. 8 in. × 10 ft. 9 in. (813 × 328 cm.). Ex-Kevorkian Collection.

Directional shrub carpet with lattice. Probably the finest existing carpet of its type. Possibly Kerman, 17th century. 11 ft. 6 in. × 9 ft. 5 in. (351 × 287 cm.). Ex-collection of Grace, Countess of Dudley.

80

138

As we noted earlier, directional tree and shrub designs were very popular among Moghul weavers. The Persian examples may also be connected with eighteenth-century Kurdistan carpets with rows of very angular trees. There is a parallel between these directional designs and the unusual Amsterdam/Vienna three-plane lattice pair mentioned previously. There are also eighteenth-century Kurdistan carpets with hunting scenes and animal groups.

A famous complete example was shown in the 1932 London exhibition of Islamic art at Burlington House, belonging then to an Istanbul dealer, while two fragments from a single carpet, one in the Museum für Kunsthandwerk, Frankfurt, and the other in the Bernheimer Collection, Munich, were shown in the *Carpets of Central Persia* exhibition in Sheffield and Birmingham, England, in 1976. Another complete example is in the Metropolitan Museum.

The fragmented carpet has less angular and stylized drawing than the Istanbul piece and is obviously earlier in date. However, Dr. May Beattie has remarked of it, 'From the structure . . . I would not have expected the carpet to have been woven in Tabriz or even in Northwest Persia.' In an essay published in 1968, she suggested an attribution to Kerman, while Otto Bernheimer, in the catalogue of his collection published in 1959, suggested Isfahan-south Persia. An attribution to south Persia is justified on both stylistic and structural

So-called Indo-Persian animal carpet. Possibly attributable to eighteenth-century Herat. 27 ft. 6 in. × 9 ft. 3 in. (838 × 282 cm.).

grounds, for they are obviously slightly coarsened versions of such directional animal carpets as the Musée des Arts Décoratifs piece and, of course, the small silk Kashan animal rugs.

However, it should be noted that in her discussion of garden carpets, Dr. May Beattie does remind us of Martin's theories concerning Nadir Shah transferring Herat and Kerman weavers to the area of Hamadan. If this was so, it would justify a north-west Persian provenance for the Frankfurt/Munich fragments and related carpets – a justification which would extend to the structure of such pieces.

On balance, it seems reasonable to ascribe all these carpets, whether from the 16th, 17th or 18th centuries, to north-west Persia; the style of drawing certainly seems consistent throughout this long period. And the style of the Williams tree carpet, if it is sixteenth-century Tabriz work, makes the attribution of such pieces as the Ardabil carpets to the same town and period even less convincing.

The second group of carpets have what we might call the 'tree-shield' design and are ascribed to late seventeenth- to early eighteenth-century Kurdistan. The field, usually dark blue, has horizontal rows of medallions, either two or three complete ones and two halves to each row. From alternate medallions in alternate rows grow four trees in opposite directions, north-west, north-east, south-west and south-east, which form shield-like compartments around the other medallions and half medallions in the same rows. The longer, pendant-shaped medallions in the non-tree-growing rows are surrounded by the flowering branches of the trees and themselves contain flower heads or shrubs. The medallion colours are usually light tan and green-blue for the large, and red and white for the small.

One of the finest examples, with an unusual white ground floral border, was sold at Christie's in November 1976, and is now in a private English collection; other examples are in the Metropolitan Museum (McMullan Collection) and the Philadelphia Museum (McIlhenny Collection).

Polonaise Carpets

One of the best-documented groups of Safavid weaving consists of the Shah Abbas silk carpets, which have become widely known under the generic, but inaccurate heading of 'Polonaise'. Numerous accounts by seventeenth- and early eighteenth-century travellers, missionaries and diplomats speak of the silk weaving of Isfahan and Kashan. There are several carpets in European collections today which can be traced back to diplomatic gifts in the 17th century.

The misnomer 'Polonaise' occurred as a result of the Paris International Exhibition of 1878, in which was shown a silk carpet from a Polish collection, the Czartoryski, bearing

Below: animal and tree carpet, attributed to north-west Persia, but considered by some to be Caucasian. A late eighteenth-century stylized version of the Safavid animal carpets. 14 ft. 9 in. × 8 ft. 8 in. (442.5 × 260 cm.). Ex-collection S. Haim, Istanbul. Below right: Paolo Veronese: The Marriage Feast at Cana *(detail), 1562–3. Hanging from the balcony high to the left of the painting is a representation of a pile-knotted carpet of medallion and corner design, which is close to certain Kashan silk pieces. Representations of sixteenth-century Persian carpets are rare in Italian painting. The Louvre, Paris.*

77

what was then wrongly assumed to be their coat-of-arms. It was also assumed that the piece was of Polish workmanship and even when its proper place of origin was established, the label 'Polonaise' stuck. The Czartoryski carpet is now in the Metropolitan Museum.

In the spring of 1601, the King of Poland, Sigismund Vasa III, instructed an Armenian merchant to visit Kashan and purchase silk carpets and tapestries. Such things had, of course been known in Europe before this time and there is at least one fine silk piece of Polish provenance, the Branicki carpet, which pre-dates the Shah Abbas pieces. Sigismund's merchant was successful in his undertaking, and on 12 December 1602 presented a bill to the Polish Treasury which included the cost of eight carpets.

There exists evidence, then, of carpets being in Poland by the end of 1602, thus pre-dating the first Venice gift of 1603, to which Dimand refers as 'the first known appearance in Europe of these rugs'. According to Erdmann, the eight carpets listed by Sigismund's merchant are the ones now in the Residenz Museum, Munich. Certainly, a pair of tapestry-woven, silk carpets in the Residenz, once the property of the Wittelsbach family, bear the arms of Sigismund III; they passed into German possession on the marriage of the Polish Princess Anna Katherina Konstanza to the Elector Palatine Philip Wilhelm in 1642. With the other six pieces, this pair formed part of her dowry.

The second documented group, mentioned above, consists of eight carpets brought in successive embassies to Venice in 1603, 1622 and 1638. The first brought one, the second

Two Shah Abbas silk and metal thread Polonaise carpets. Above: an example dating from the early 17th century. 13 ft. 4 in. × 6 ft. 5 in. (406 × 195.5 cm.). Above right: the design divides the field into two halves. 6 ft. 9 in. × 4 ft. 9 in. (206 × 145 cm.). Ex-Kevorkian Collection.

four and the third three. Five of these are still preserved in the Treasury of St. Mark, including the 1603 piece, of a medallion and corner design, which was presented to the Doge, Marino Grimani, by an embassy of Shah Abbas led by Fethi Bey. The ambassador explained to the Doge that the Shah wished the carpet to become part of the Treasury.

The other four are from the second embassy. From the third, sent by Shah Safi, none is known definitely to have survived; Erdmann has suggested that two pieces in the Museo Correr, of unknown provenance, but with some stylistic resemblance to the later Venice pieces, may be part of this gift. There are also another five examples in the Ca d'Oro, Venice, although these are considered minor.

There is another important small group in the Rosenberg Castle, Copenhagen; these were given by an embassy of Safi to the Duke Frederick of Holstein-Gottorp in 1639, a magnificent gift which also included brocades and velvets. Another superb Polonaise was given to the Queen Sofie Amalie of Denmark in 1662 by the Dutch East India Company and this is also in the Rosenberg Castle.

Of a pair of carpets once in the possession of the Prince Doria, one is now in the Metropolitan Museum (the gift of John D. Rockefeller Jr.) and the other was sold by Colnaghi's of London in 1976. The Metropolitan also possesses a silk kelim once belonging to the Royal House of Saxony, as did a pair now split between the Textile Museum, Washington, and

Detail of the silk and gold thread Polonaise carpet given by the Dutch East India Company to Queen Sofie Amalie of Denmark in 1662 (not 1666, as stated by Dimand). This carpet would have been new when the presentation was made. In spite of its superb condition, its sickly colours and uncoordinated design (continued overleaf)

84

clearly demonstrate the decadence of late Polonaise carpets. Rosenberg Castle, Copenhagen. Top right: silk and silver thread Polonaise, one of the carpets presented to the Doge of Venice in 1622. 8 ft. 7 in. × 6 ft. 1 in. (259 × 182 cm.). Basilica of St. Mark, Venice. Above: one of a pair of silk and gold thread Doria Polonaise carpets, the other being the gift of John D. Rockefeller Jr. to the Metropolitan Museum, New York. This piece is notable for its brilliant colouring and magnificent condition. 13 ft. 8 in. × 6 ft. (410 × 180 cm.). P. & D. Colnaghi & Co. Ltd., London.

the Islamisches Museum, Berlin. To judge from the high cost of such pieces illustrated in the account presented to Sigismund, only the nobility would have been able to afford them.

It is obvious that not only were such carpets highly regarded in Europe, but also in Persia itself and further east. Several writers have described examples they saw in Persia. The Carmelite missionaries Father Paul Simon and Father Peter visited Kashan in 1607–8 and left accounts of the carpets they saw, as did Sir Anthony Sherley. The latter's *Brief and True Report* of his Persian journey published in London in 1600 mentions 'Persian carpets of a wonderful fineness.' Sir Thomas Herbert visited the country in 1627–9, and wrote of the Palace of Isfahan:

'*Within, the rooms . . . are enlightened with trellices; the rooms are embossed above, and painted red-white, blue and gold; the side painted with sports and landscape; the ground, or floor, spread with carpets of silk and gold, without other furniture.*'

The French merchant, J. B. Tavernier, visited Persia in 1664, and wrote:

'*The floor was spread with gold and silk carpets, made specifically for the palace, and there was a large scaffold covered with a magnificent carpet . . . After I had laid out my goods upon a fair table covered with a gold and silver carpet . . . the King entered, attended by only three eunuchs for his guard, and two old men, whose office it was to pull off his shoes when he goes into any room spread with gold and silk carpets, and put them on again when he leaves.*'

Sir John Chardin visited the country in 1666 and 1672, writing subsequently of his travels; he commented in particular on the weavers of Isfahan. John Fryer, who visited the same city in 1676, described the carpet bazaar which sold pieces 'woollen and silk, intermixed with gold and silver very costly, which are the peculiar manufacture of this country.' Another visitor, the Polish Jesuit missionary, Krusinskij, lived in Persia from 1702 to 1729, during and just after the last years of the Safavid dynasty. He wrote of the manufacture of silk textiles and carpets of Isfahan, which were made under strict supervision for use in the royal palace, although there was also a brisk export trade with Europe and India.

There is preserved in the Shrine of Imam Ali at al-Najaf, about six miles west of Kufa in Iraq, a group of four complete and three fragmentary brocaded carpets in wool and silk. One of the woollen pieces has an inscription to the effect that it was presented by 'the dog of this shrine', that is, Shah Abbas, who is known to have referred to himself as 'the dog of Ali'. Evidence that the carpets were highly regarded in India comes from Krusinskij, while one of a group of three known multiple medallion and animal silk kelims is in Japan, where it has been since the 16th century; it was used as a campaigning cloak by the Samurai Toyotomi Hideyoshi, who died in 1598.

Some 300 or more pile or tapestry-woven Shah Abbas silk carpets have survived. In an article entitled *Persian Silk Carpets* (*The Connoisseur*, July 1975), Maurice Dimand described their motifs in some detail.

Kelims

The tapestry-woven pieces, or kelims, form a distinct group. Their brightness of colour and the frequent use of animals and birds in the decorative scheme – things rarely, if ever, found in pile carpets – suggest that they may have been woven in Kashan; if we assume that the sixteenth-century silk pile carpets discussed previously were woven in Kashan, the kelims certainly fit logically into the hypothetical construction of a body of work woven in that town over a period of a hundred years or so.

The fields of the silk kelims are usually of the same basic design – central diamond or ovoid-lobed medallion with bar-and-palmette appendages at either end of the long axis and quartered cartouches in the corners of the field. This pattern can be seen in the best-known pieces: the Doisteau kelim (the Louvre, Paris), the Bliss kelim (Metropolitan), the Berlin Pardisah kelim and its companion piece, lacking the inscriptions, in the Textile Museum, Washington, and the Wittelsbach Paradise kelim (Residenz Museum, Munich) which has the field only, the borders lacking.

The kelim with the coat-of-arms of Sigismund Vasa III in the Residenz Museum also adheres to this format, but the central medallion is square. Two examples in the Metropolitan Museum, New York, ex-Saxony and ex-Bliss, are floral in character and the second piece has no corner cartouche, with the central medallion being contained within a large

palmette star. Another, probably later, example in the Karlsrühe Landsmuseum conforms to the general medallion, appendages and corner format, although the floral scrolling is far less free in many respects. It bears an uncanny resemblance to nineteenth-century *suzanis*, the majority of which are supposed to have been woven in Uzbekistan in the Caucasus.

The multiple medallion kelims are the rarest. Only three examples are known: the Figdor, the Toyotomi Hideyoshi in Japan, and the example published by Gertrude Robinson in the *Burlington Magazine* in 1938, which subsequently disappeared and then reappeared after nearly forty years. It was sold at Sotheby's on 18 November 1976 as the property of Baron Giorgio Franchetti; it fetched the enormous price of £63,800 ($111,630) and is now in a Swiss private collection. The relationship between these pieces and the silk and wool medallion and hunting carpets we have discussed previously. The frequent use of Chinese motifs, the integration of animals and birds into a well-structured floral background, make the drawing of parallels between the large and small silk carpets of Kashan and the Sanguszko group virtually inevitable.

On the evidence of imports into Europe, most examples of the kelims, as well as the pile carpets, are datable to the first half of the 17th century; but since there is evidence that at least one piece, the Hideyoshi kelim, was in Japan well before the beginning of the 17th century, an earlier dating for some of the best pieces seems certain.

86

Two flat-weave silk and metal thread Polonaise carpets. Above left: 6 ft. × 3 ft. 6 in. (200 × 118 cm.). Above: 10 ft. × 4 ft. 6½ in. (300 × 136 cm.). Ardabil Shrine Collection.

It should be noted, however, that many of the pile carpets are very coarsely woven in view of the material and are often on a cotton web; the brocading of silver and silver-gilt threads is also comparatively crudely done, not passing about every second warp as in most of the sixteenth-century pieces, but passing over several warp threads. Despite their attraction and glamour, many of the pile Shah Abbas carpets which, apart from Kashan and Isfahan, were probably woven in other cities as well, must be taken as decadent examples of a great tradition.

The Portuguese Carpets

An odd group of carpets are the so-called 'Portuguese' pieces. These have a huge central medallion taking up most of the field, but either with concentric, faceted rims or with very bold floral outlines. In the four corners of the field appear ships, a man in the sea and fishes. There are about eight of these pieces known, which are located as follows: Museum für angewandte Kunst, Vienna; Berlin (completely destroyed in the Second World War); Lord Sackville, Knole, England; Metropolitan Museum, New York; Winterthur Museum, Delaware; Gulbenkian Foundation, Lisbon; Musée des Tissus, Lyons; Rijksmuseum, Amsterdam. There is also a fragment illustrated by McMullan in *Islamic Carpets*.

The origin of these pieces is mysterious. The Vienna carpet was displayed at the *Arts of Islam* exhibition in London in 1976, and the catalogue noted: 'The carpet could have been made in Southern Persia, or in Gujarat, or, as the oldest theory suggested, in Goa.'

Sixteenth-century Persian medallion carpet. Possibly north-west Persia. This piece is reduced in length by approximately 9 ft. (300 cm.). It now measures 26 ft. 3 in. × 12 ft. (800 × 365 cm.).

Wool and metal thread prayer rug. Many examples of this type are known, including one in the Metropolitan Museum. Although a few writers persist in calling them sixteenth- or seventeenth-century Persian, the majority of scholars are now of the opinion that the rugs are the products of the nineteenth-century Imperial Ottoman factories. 5 ft. 5 in. × 3 ft. 7 in. (162 × 107 cm.). Ex-Paravicini Collection, Cairo. Below: Turkish carpet in silk and metal thread, possibly woven from the same cartoon as the Salting carpet, but slightly later in date, c. 1870. 6 ft. 7 in. × 4 ft. 5 in. (201 × 135 cm.).

The model for the scene may be a lost miniature or even a European print. Persian weavers worked in India under Moghul patronage, so similar decorative features are to be found in the carpets of both Persia and India at this time.'

The attribution to Goa is now generally rejected, although some scholars think that Gujarat is a workable hypothesis. South Persia, however, is the generally accepted attribution, with a date in the 17th century. It is interesting to note that there are Caucasian carpets usually attributed to the region of Kula woven in the late 17th and 18th centuries with a layout similar to the Portuguese carpets and some nineteenth-century Moroccan pieces, with their multiple-edged stepped lozenges, might also be compared. The Viennese carpet, with its strange colours, certainly aroused lively suspicions when it appeared in London in 1976 at the *Arts of Islam* exhibition; there is no trace of any of these pieces existing before the Berlin carpet was acquired in 1887.

Dating Problems

In the Poldi Pezzoli dated carpet and the Portuguese carpets, we encounter even more difficulties. There are other groups of carpets traditionally described as sixteenth- to seventeenth-century Persian which must again be considered dubious. One group consists of long or short wool carpets with medallion and animal (or bird) designs; they usually have woven inscriptions and brocading. The best-known examples are as follows: the Salting carpet, Victoria and Albert Museum, London; the four Rothschild carpets (sold at auction in Paris in 1966); the Marquand carpet, Philadelphia Museum of Art; the Baker carpet, Metropolitan Museum, New York; and a carpet in the Gulistan Museum, Teheran.

A second group consists of prayer rugs with floral mihrab (prayer arches) and extensive inscriptions from the Koran in the field and borders. The best-known example in the West is in the Metropolitan Museum, New York, the pair to which, along with about thirty-six others, may be found in the Top Kapi Museum, Istanbul.

The Salting carpet in the Victoria and Albert Museum may be taken as the focal point of the first group. Its attribution to sixteenth-century Persia has been suspected since the beginning of the present century and it is now generally assumed to be nineteenth-century Turkish work, probably from the royal looms in either Istanbul or Hereke. Like the other carpets associated with it, it is extremely finely woven – about 880 Persian knots to the square inch. The Baker carpet in the Metropolitan Museum has about 550 Persian knots to the square inch, while that same institution's two prayer rugs, also assigned to the 16th century by Dimand, have 552 and 342 Persian knots to the square inch respectively. Like most of the other carpets associated with it, the Salting carpet has a silk warp and weft and has woven stanzas of poetry in the border.

The attribution to Turkey makes logical sense. The Top Kapi Museum, as we have said, has a large holding of the prayer rugs, and the Koum Kapou carpets to be discussed later are of superb workmanship, and in the Persian style, thus giving us certain evidence of weaving of this kind in Turkey during the 19th century. Erdmann assigns both groups to the early 19th century. This means that either these pieces were made at the end of the 19th century – perfectly possible – or at the beginning of the 19th century or earlier in Istanbul or Hereke, which is more probable.

Some as yet unqualified evidence for the latter conclusion is afforded by one of the Rothschild carpets, of typical animal and medallion design which, having been sold at auction in Paris in 1966 and again in 1968, appeared at Sotheby's in London in April 1976. Although catalogued as sixteenth-century Persian, an attribution to nineteenth-century Turkey was made by the auctioneer from the rostrum. Not surprisingly under such circumstances, the carpet failed to sell. Subsequent scientific tests undertaken on Sotheby's behalf on the brocaded areas suggested a date earlier than 1850.

One of the main problems with both groupings is the source of inspiration. As far as can be judged, none of the sixteenth-century Persian rugs known to us today are accepted as genuine. Thus, the Turkish designers of these pieces would have had to have created the designs using elements of sixteenth-century Persian floral ornament. The origins of the medallion and animal pieces is clearer; both the silk Kashan carpets and the Herat medallion and animal carpets were used.

Two carpets, in the Musée des Arts Décoratifs, Paris, and the Thyssen Collection, Lugano (ex-von Pannewitz Collection) are hesitantly accepted as being genuine sixteenth-century Persian; if this is so – although there seems no reason why these should be accepted and the others not – then they form the closest parallels. It has to be admitted, however, that too little is known at present about the nineteenth-century Turkish court looms to make definitive statements, and future students of Oriental weaving may have very different views on the carpets we have mentioned above. It must be added that were it not for its coarser weaving – less than 250 knots to the square inch – one might be tempted to assign the Poldi Pezzoli dated carpet to this group, though in many respects this piece is too crude to be placed convincingly with any group.

Early Ottoman Weaving

WE HAVE DISCUSSED THE SELJUK CARPETS and fragments found in the two mosques and at Fostat. These are assumed to have been woven at Konya, which was the main centre, or at either Sivas or Kayseri, both towns renowned for weaving, and which were visited by Marco Polo in the 13th century. Around 1300, Othman, founder of the Ottoman dynasty and one of several petty rulers who had presided over the decline of Seljuk power, unified the country and made Bursa (often spelled Brusa) the capital in 1326, the year of his death. Forty years later, the principal city of the Ottomans was the ancient Byzantine city of Adrianople, now referred to as Erdine.

The earliest carpets of the Ottoman period date from around 1400, and one of these is arguably among the most famous of all existing carpets; it is certainly the one which has been known the longest to scholars. This is the dragon and phoenix carpet discovered by Wilhelm von Bode, director of the Berlin Museum (where it is today), in a central Italian church in 1886. Subsequently, another rug of the same period, the Marby rug, was discovered in a Swedish church in Marby (Jämtland), and is now exhibited in the Historiske Museum, Stockholm.

Neither piece represents the earliest development of its particular design. Both are already highly stylized. The Berlin carpet, woven on a brilliant yellow ground, which bespeaks Chinese influence, is divided into two squares, each of which shows an identical combat scene between two animals. One of these is easily recognized as a dragon, but the other, presumably a bird with three tail feathers, and other geometrically rendered ornithological features, has been identified as a phoenix, thus tending to point to this being a schematized west-Asian rendering of a far older Chinese image. It can be dated with a certain degree of accuracy by the existence of a carpet with similar motifs depicted in a fresco by Domenico di Bartolo in the hospital of Santa Maria della Scala in Siena, which is known to have been executed between 1440 and 1444, and by carpets in other early fourteenth-century Italian paintings.

As with the purely abstract motifs of the Seljuk pieces discussed earlier, the evidence for the depiction of animals and birds in Turkish weaving goes back before the beginning of the 15th century. A small fragment, depicting a single bird within an octagon, was discovered at Fostat, and is assumed to be fourteenth-century; like the dragon and phoenix rug and the Marby rug, it is tied with the Ghiordes knot.

Domenico di Bartolo: Marriage Ceremony, c. *1440–4. Fresco in the hospital of Santa Maria della Scala, Siena. The carpet, with its octagons containing stylized dragon and phoenix motifs, differs from many animal carpets found in paintings in that it has an elaborate border system.*

The Berlin dragon and phoenix carpet. Although generally considered complete (except for the right-hand border), this may well be a fragment of a much larger carpet. It was discovered by Wilhelm von Bode in a central Italian church in 1886 and is usually dated to early fifteenth-century Anatolia. Its date has recently been questioned by Hübel and others. 5 ft. 9 in. × 3 ft. (172 × 90 cm.). Islamische Museum, Berlin.

Below: Niccolo di Buonaccorso (active 1372, died 1388): Betrothal of the Virgin, *National Gallery, London. Right: Fra Angelico:* Madonna and Child with Saints, *altarpiece, 1438–40. Museo di San Marco, Florence. Note the animal carpet showing pairs of quadrupeds. Below right: Jaime Hughet:* Madonna and Child Enthroned *(detail), c. 1455–6. Museo de Arte de Cataluña, Barcelona. The carpets in the Niccolo and Fra Angelico paintings differ from that in the Spanish painting, a fragment of which type is preserved in the Mervlana Museum, Konya.*

Early Ottoman Carpets in European Painting

In the period between approximately 1350 and 1450, four principal types of animal carpets are found depicted in European paintings: heraldic birds (possibly eagles), as in the Fostat fragment, groups of animals or animals in combat, as in the Berlin dragon and phoenix rug, pairs of facing birds on either side of a tree, as in the Marby rug (Erdmann suggests that the above mentioned Fostat fragment may also be of this type) and single standing beasts within octagons, of which no actual examples survive.

Animal combat carpets, of the Berlin type, appear in works by Domenico di Bartolo (fresco in the hospital of Santa Maria della Scala in Siena, *c.* 1440–4), Pisanello (*The Annunciation* in San Fermo, Verona) and, most clearly, in a work by the late fifteenth-century

Domenico Ghirlandaio:
Madonna Enthroned, *mid-15th century. The painting shows a geometric rug with Kufic borders close to large pattern Holbeins. Uffizi Gallery, Florence.*

Veronese master Domenico Morone (once in the Este Collection, Vienna). Single birds and single-standing beasts appear in paintings by Italian masters such as Niccolo di Buonaccorso (*Betrothal of the Virgin*, National Gallery, London) and Ambrogio Lorenzetti (*Madonna Enthroned*, formerly Baer Collection, Berlin), both of which are datable to the 1340s. An example also appears in a work by the Sienese master Giovanni di Paolo, datable to the early 15th century, in the Galleria Doria, Rome (*The Marriage of the Virgin*). Pairs of birds are shown in paintings by, among others, Lippo Memmi, datable to about 1350, in Sano di Pietro's *Betrothal of the Virgin* (Pinacoteca Vaticana, Rome) and in Mantegna's *Martyrdom of St. Christopher* in the Eremitani Chapel, Padua, datable to about 1451–3. Pairs of quadrupeds appear in *The Madonna of the Snow* by Sassetta, the Sienese master (Uffizi, Florence). The incidence of such depictions grows in the 15th century but, according to Erdmann, ceases around 1500.

They are also found in northern European works, and in Spanish art. A dragon and phoenix rug appears in Hans Memlinc's *Bathsheba in the Bath*, and in the Spaniard Jaime Hughet's *Madonna and Child Enthroned*, probably executed in the 1450s, there is a rug with free-standing birds, probably cockerels. Despite Erdmann's comment about no piece appearing in a European painting after 1500, it should be noted that an admittedly debased version is depicted in an early seventeenth-century English portrait of Lady Dorothy Cary and further evidence of the continued production of animal carpets of this type is afforded by Dimand, who suggests that a cockerel carpet similar to the one which appears in Hughet's painting, now in the Mervlana Museum, Konya, is not in fact fifteenth-century, as catalogued by its owners, but a seventeenth-century copy of a fifteenth-century prototype.

However, the Fostat fragment creates something of a problem. A. G. Hübel, in *The Book of Carpets*, considered the Berlin and Stockholm rugs not to be fifteenth-century, but early eighteenth-century copies of textiles not necessarily Turkish in origin (several authorities have considered the possibility that these carpets may be Caucasian). The Fostat

fragment is more finely woven than the other two more complete pieces. John Mills, in a well-argued passage in his pamphlet *Carpets in Pictures* draws attention to a number of significant facts regarding the animal and bird rugs depicted in early paintings. Firstly, they are large, and secondly they are depicted on the floor in a utilitarian fashion, in contrast with the habit of using later Turkish pieces as throne, dais or table rugs or as hangings; this suggests that the earlier pieces were not so highly regarded by their owners. Thirdly, in many of the early carpets, there are clearly discernible transverse woven lines suggesting a very coarse and specific type of knotting, and fourthly, they do not usually have borders. Mills is of the opinion that these pieces may be 'the tail-ends of a Byzantine tradition of floor-carpet making' and may be loop-knotted. Certainly the Fostat fragment suggests that true pile-knotted carpets of similar design were also produced, but its quality, superior to the Berlin and Stockholm pieces, lends weight to Hübel's theory that the latter two may be some 300 years later in date than almost all writers have supposed. It should also be noted that what seem to be large standing birds are depicted on small rugs used for hanging from balconies in *The Tournament*, a panel inset into a mid-fifteenth-century *cassone* in the National Gallery, London. This same picture also contains rugs with purely geometric designs of repeat-pattern diamond lozenges and, according to Mills, this is the only known early painting in which both bird and geometric rugs appear together.

There is evidence of the continuing popularity of the geometric designs first seen in the Seljuk pieces in a number of European paintings of the 14th and 15th centuries.

Holbein Carpets

During the second half of the 15th century, during which time the depiction of geometrically designed pieces, as opposed to animal rugs, becomes more frequent, there began to appear with some regularity a group of pieces with variations on octagon motifs. These are the earliest examples of a particular family, known somewhat inaccurately as Holbein carpets. They make their earliest appearances nearly a hundred years before Holbein the Younger was painting and, although this specific type is credited to the 15th century, it must of course be connected with earlier geometrically designed pieces of the Seljuk period, and should be seen as part of a developing tradition. It should be noted at this stage that within the general term Holbein, there are two distinct groups, known as 'small pattern Holbeins' and 'large pattern Holbeins'. The former are thought by some to have appeared at an earlier stage than the latter.

The large pattern design is most frequently depicted and is characterized in its earliest form by two or three large octagons within squares in bold primary colours; these octagons are filled with geometric ornament, possibly a stylized floral design, while the borders and details have interlaced ornament of a highly complex nature. Several fifteenth-century paintings from both Italy and Flanders contain such pieces. Mid-fifteenth-century Italian works include: Piero della Francesca's *Sigismundo Malatesta as Donor* in the church of San Francesco, Rimini, and his *Madonna and Child* in the Brera, Milan; Fra Carnevale's miniature in the *Codex Urbinensis* depicting Frederigo da Montefeltro and the scholar Landino; Mantegna's polyptych of *Virgin and Child Enthroned with Saints and Angels* in the church of San Zeno, Verona, datable to 1456–9, *Ludovico Gonzaga and his Family* in the Camera, Mantua, datable to about 1474, and *San Bernadino* in the Brera, Milan, now thought to be by a follower of Mantegna. (This may be an animal rug, as Erdmann suggests, although there is too little of it showing beneath the Virgin's feet to be absolutely certain.) There is also an example in Jacopo Bassano's *Annunciation* of *c.* 1445 which is to be found in San Alessandro, Brescia.

96 Most famous, however, are pictures by the Venetian masters Vittore Carpaccio and Carlo Crivelli. In Carpaccio's *St. Ursula and the Prince Taking Leave of their Parents* in the Scuola di Sant'Orsola, Venice, dated 1495, there are depicted no less than six examples, all variations on the large octagon theme, draped over balustrades and balconies in the foreground and middle distance, and another fifteen or so of various designs hanging out of windows in the background. Other Holbein carpets appear in the artist's *Theseus Receiving the Embassy of Hippolyta, Queen of the Amazons* (Musée Jacquemart-André, Paris), executed in about 1500, and two more in *St. Tryphon Exorcising the Daughter of the Emperor Gordianus* in the Scuola di San Giorgio degli Schiavoni, Venice, executed in about 1508. The best-

97 known Crivelli is the *Annunciation* in the National Gallery, London.

Opposite, top left: Jan van Eyck; Triptych (centre panel), 1430–31. Gemäldegalerie, Dresden. Opposite, top right: Jan van Eyck and Petrus Christus: Madonna of Jan Vos, 1441–3. Frick Collection. New York. Opposite, bottom: Jan van Eyck: Madonna of Canon George van der Paele, 1436. Musée Groeninge, Bruges.

Fra Carnevale: Frederigo da Montefeltro and the Scholar Landino. Frontispiece from the Codex Urbinensis, mid-15th century. Biblioteca Apostolica, the Vatican.

Above and right (detail):
Vittore Carpaccio: St. Ursula
and the Prince Taking Leave of
their Parents, *1495. From the*
cycle of the Scuola di Sant'
Orsola, Accademia, Venice.

Opposite: Carlo Crivelli:
Annunciation with St. Emidius,
altarpiece, second half of 15th
century. National Gallery,
London.

Another design is illustrated in *Madonna and Child* by Raffaelino del Garbo, once in the Staatliche Museum, Berlin, and destroyed during the Second World War. Datable to about 1500, this picture showed a rug with squarish octagons alternating with rows of ovoid octagons; it also had a wide and very handsome Kufic border.

One of the best depictions of an early Holbein, however, may be found in Pintoricchio's cycle of frescoes devoted to the life of Pope Pius II, Eneo Silvio Piccolomini, in the Piccolomini Library in the Siena Duomo. Executed in the first years of the 16th century, the scene depicting the then cardinal as Ambassador to the Scottish Court has a tri-octagon rug with squares within the octagons, and a wide green border containing a key design. Although the artist has probably simplified the detail, the rug serves as a focal point of the picture, and its pattern is followed in the depiction of the marble floor.

Northern European representations include Hans Memlinc's *Donne of Kidwelly Altarpiece* in the National Gallery, London, the *Madonna and Child with Angels* in the Kunsthistorisches Museum, Vienna, and his *Madonna* in the Washington National Gallery,

OPVS CARO
LI CRIVELLI
VENETI

·1486·

LIBERTAS · · · · ECCLESIASTICA

*This page and opposite page,
left to right: Hans Memlinc:*
Triptych *(centre panel), c. 1480;
School of Roger van der Weyden:*
Madonna and Child Before an
Altar, *late 15th century;
Domenico Panetti;* Madonna
Enthroned with Four Saints,
1503; Vicenzo Foppa: Madonna
and Child Enthroned with
Saints, c. 1480.

*This page and opposite page, left
to right: Hans Memlinc:* Donne
of Kidwelly Altarpiece, *second
half of the 15th century, National
Gallery, London; Domenico
Ghirlandaio:* Virgin and Child
with Saints, c. 1485, Galleria
Antica e Moderna, Florence.

which depicts a large double-octagon rug; other examples appear in the Master of St. Giles' *Mass of St. Giles* in the National Gallery, London, and in Gerard David's *Triptych* in the Louvre, Paris. Several others appear in paintings by Flemish masters active in the last thirty years of the 15th century.

Erdmann suggests that about fifty intact or fragmentary examples of this type survive. There is an early fragment in the Berlin Museum, while the most important intact surviving example is the piece in the McIlhenny Collection, which has three squares containing double octagons, a red field, and elaborate geometrical borders and guards. This piece is dated to the second half of the 15th century, roughly contemporary with a fine double-octagon rug in the Istanbul Museum. Both these pieces, as well as those depicted by Pintoricchio and other artists, have close stylistic links with nineteenth-century weaving; the early Holbeins resemble closely rugs associated latterly with Bergama and indeed may themselves have been woven in that town. There is also a strong similarity to certain nineteenth-century Caucasian types, the Istanbul carpet being especially close to Karatchoph-Kazaks. And, naturally, the use of strong octagonal motifs, with the frequent employment of rich reds as ground colours, form links with nineteenth-century Turkoman weavings. Even in the Berlin dragon and phoenix carpet, with its highly stylized ornament and hooked octagons, we see an incontrovertible link with the geometric stylization of Tekke, Salor and Yomut weaving. Once again, a common Turkic-Mongolian heritage reveals its presence in another area of carpet and rug making.

Lotto Carpets

Related to the Holbein carpets are those pieces bearing what is called the Lotto pattern, another useless misnomer. As we noted, the octagonal designs associated with the Holbein rugs evolved out of the animal rugs which can be dated back with some certainty to the 13th century; the abstract designs began to appear in European art in the first half of the 15th century, by which time, they were presumably well established in their country of origin. The Lotto pattern, although related to these earlier 'solid' geometric designs, makes its first appearance in Europe at the beginning of the 16th century (specifically in a portrait group by Sebastiano del Piombo, dated 1516, in the National Gallery, Washington). It takes the form of a skeletal pattern of alternating rows of octagons and crosses made up of stylized foliage; these are almost always woven in yellow, with blue details, on a red ground. Although a few pieces of large size are known, the majority of carpets exhibiting this pattern are fairly small.

Its origin as a design format has given rise to much scholarly debate; Erdmann thought that the carpets were made in the same district of Western Anatolia as the small pattern Holbeins. He also advances the theory that the pattern of these carpets did not evolve, but was deliberately designed, like that of the Holbein carpet.

From European paintings, then, we have evidence of the small and large pattern Holbeins, the former with rows of lozenges and octagons, and the latter with two or three large octagons, being produced from about the early to mid-15th century, and the arabesque or Lotto designs from the beginning of the 16th century. Of course, in several paintings, most notably the Carpaccio *St. Ursula*, small and large pattern Holbeins appear side by side; and in other paintings by the same artist, there are variants of the large Holbein pattern: for instance, a central square surrounded by four smaller squares, as in the carpet represented in the *Embassy of Hyppolyta*. In the *Birth of the Virgin* in the Scuola degli Albanesi, Bergamo, there is represented a carpet with a large star medallion surrounded by smaller eight-pointed, square-centred stars and with very unusual arabesque corner panels; a similar piece (although the field is unclear) appears in the *Virgin and Child Enthroned with Saints* of 1518 in the church of San Francesco, Pirano.

Similarly, the Italian painter Lorenzo Lotto did not confine himself to representations of carpets bearing the particular arabesque design which has been named after him. In fact, a look through the artist's complete *oeuvre* demonstrates the full extent of the misnomer. The 250 or so authentic works by the artist include the following paintings which depict Oriental carpets:

1. *Virgin and Child with Four Saints* (San Cristina al Tivarone, Treviso), 1507. Field with small free-standing cypress trees and floral motifs – one border forming itself into an octagon

and containing a floral star. This is a frequently encountered feature of Turkish carpets from the 16th century. Dimand illustrates two prayer rugs once in the Ballard Collection and now in the Metropolitan Museum; another two in the McMullan Collection are illustrated in his *Islamic Carpets*, plate nos. 100 and 101; they are described by their owner as a mixture between a highly stylized garden theme and double-arched prayer rugs. No. 100 in particular has cypress motifs similar to the piece illustrated in the Lotto painting.

2. *Portrait of Pompeo Colonna* (Galleria Colonna, Rome), 1509. Stylized Kufic border and part of floral border – no field visible.

3. *The Protonotary Giovanni Giuliani* (National Gallery, London), 1519–20. Detail of a field with scattered motifs including eight-pointed stars.

4. *Virgin and Child Enthroned* (San Spirito, Bergamo), 1521. Similar border and border arch to no. 1.

5. *The Marriage of St. Catherine with Niccolo Bonghi as Donor* (Accademia Carrara, Bergamo), 1523. Large pattern Holbein.

6. *Husband and Wife* (formerly Gatchina, near Leningrad), *c.* 1524. The carpet is similar to nos. 1 and 4 but with a wider and more elaborate main border, similar to that found in some small pattern Holbeins.

7. *Portrait of Antonio Correr* (formerly to be seen on the London art market), 1525. Large pattern Holbein.

8. *Portrait of Laura Pisani* (now thought to be by Dosso Dossi – ex-Cornbury Park Collection), 1525. Small pattern Holbein.

9. *Portrait of a Gentleman* (Cleveland Museum of Art, Ohio), 15(3)5? Small pattern Holbein.

10. *St. Anthony Giving Alms* (SS. Giovanni e Paolo, Venice), 1542. Three carpets: one Lotto pattern and two scattered cypress and palmette (as in no. 3), assumed to be Turkish or Egyptian compartment rugs.

11. *Family Portrait* (National Gallery, London), 1547. One Lotto pattern carpet.

We can see that, although Lotto frequently painted various geometric rugs in his pictures, only on two occasions, at the end of his career, do Lotto patterns appear. Their incidence in seventeenth-century paintings by northern European artists seems to have been much greater. Lotto, of course, was a Venetian, and it is noticeable that the greatest quantity of rugs of many varieties appear in Venetian paintings in the 16th century, hardly surprising as that country was the major European importer. From the evidence of European paintings in general, we can see a progression from the highly stylized carpets of the 13th, 14th and early 15th centuries through the various geometric patterns of the 15th and 16th centuries, of which the Lottos, arabesque or open medallion carpets, are perhaps the final culmination.

Most scholars are agreed that the Turkish carpets of which we have knowledge in the West represent but a fraction of the many designs which were produced; without a more exact knowledge, it seems a fairly pointless exercise to try to decide their provenance. The best supported suggestion is that the large pattern Holbeins originate from Bergama, and the small pattern and open medallion carpets from Ushak. Of the Bergama hypothesis, it can be said that, in a country where the traditions of weaving remained more constant than in most other known carpet-producing centres, the rugs of nineteenth-century Bergama provenance bear a close resemblance to the fifteenth- and sixteenth-century examples. There is, however, no firm evidence.

Lotto carpets continued to be made throughout the 16th, 17th and 18th centuries, although the design became heavier, more angular and more coarse; the elegant Kufic borders of the early pieces, matching the beautifully constructed arabesque repeat of the field, also disappeared, to be replaced by wholly inappropriate floral or cloud-band borders. In some of the later pieces, these borders are much too wide, destroying the well-designed ratio of field to border found in sixteenth-century examples. A carpet from the McMullan Collection, now in the Metropolitan Museum, exhibits many of the worst features of these late pieces;

the cross pattern has become thicker and more solid, the vertical beams being either red or blue and the horizontal beams yellow or red. The width of the main border and two thin guard stripes equal roughly half the width of the field. This piece, which is dated to the mid-18th century, has one unusual feature, however: it is one of very few examples woven with a blue ground.

Above: two arabesque or Lotto pattern rugs, showing the coarsening of the design in later pieces. Left: early to mid-17th century. 5 ft. 7 in. × 4 ft. 3 in. (170 × 129.5 cm.). Right: late 17th century. 5 ft. 3 in. × 4 ft. (160 × 122 cm.).

Ushak Carpets

The city of Ushak in western Turkey is associated with several important types of sixteenth- and seventeenth-century carpets. Like Istanbul, which, as Constantinople, had been finally conquered by Mehmet II in 1453 (he ruled from 1451 to 1481, and began the building of the Top Kapi Saray) and Bursa, which became the Ottoman capital in 1326, Ushak was one of the centres of Ottoman court weaving.

The development of new carpet styles is associated with two major historical events. The Sultan Bayazid II (1481–1512) was a strict Sunni Muslim, and objected to the Shi'ite faith of his Safavid neighbours. Relations with Persia deteriorated and under Bayazid's successor, Selim I (1512–20), war broke out. Ismail was defeated and the city of Tabriz captured for the first time in 1514; at the same time the Ottomans began their conquest of North Africa, overthrowing the Mamluk Sultanate in 1517. Under perhaps the greatest of the Ottoman Sultans, Suleyman the Magnificent (1520–66), the empire reached its apogee. The conquest of such vast territories naturally had its effect upon the culture of the conquerors as well as on the conquered.

Both Cairo, the seat of Mamluk power, and Tabriz, the Safavid capital, had brilliant and thriving carpet-weaving factories; it would seem as if the contact with the Persian manufactories changed the Turkish style, while the Turks may have utilized the skills of the Mamluk workshops to produce carpets to the specifications sent to them from Turkey itself.

To Ushak are ascribed five principal designs: the double-ended mihrab prayer rugs (and some single-ended ones), the star pattern rugs, the medallion pattern carpets, the misnamed bird pattern and the balls and lines pattern (sometimes called the 'Arms of

Ushak prayer rug. Probably the finest surviving example of its type. Early 16th century. 5 ft. 11 in. × 3 ft. 11 in. (180 × 120 cm.). Islamische Museum, Berlin.

Tamerlaine'), the last two invariably woven on white grounds. It is generally assumed that the various names found in European inventories of the 16th century: Damascene, Smyrna, Turkey, etc. relate to the various designs produced in Ushak, some of which are woven with European coats-of-arms, or to the products of Egyptian workshops. There is ample evidence to prove their importation into Europe, usually via Venice, in vast numbers; the famous order for sixty such pieces by Cardinal Wolsey for Hampton Court in 1520 is the most often quoted. His order was placed through the Signory of Venice.

The variations played by Turkish weavers on the theme of the prayer rug are perhaps Turkey's greatest contribution to weaving. The earliest examples which have survived are dated to the 16th and 17th centuries, but the tradition must be considerably older. There is, for instance, a representation of such a piece in a Persian Timurid miniature of 1436. The motifs of the prayer rug are universal in the Islamic world. The primary one is an arch shape in the centre of the field called the mihrab or pulpit, a reminder of the pulpit in the court-yard of the Prophet's house at Mecca from which he preached to his followers. In addition, there may be found representations of lamps, as well as water ewers and combs, both sym-bolic of the cleansing of the body which to the Muslim is an essential adjunct of prayer; stanzas of the Koran may be found woven in the field and borders, but there is never any representation of living creatures, in accordance with Sunni edicts (although not specifically forbidden in the Koran).

The earliest Turkish prayer rugs, of which there is a famous example in the Islamische Museum, Berlin, are assigned to sixteenth-century Ushak; the Berlin piece measures 5 feet 11 inches by 3 feet 11 inches; the mihrab is dark blue edged with light blue at the base, and the surrounding field area is brilliant red. In the spandrels on either side of the trefoil arch are stylized arabesques in light blue resembling heraldic beasts. The floral ornament in the arched base of the mihrab, with its 'head' (which has 'eyes' and a 'mouth'), eight 'legs' and 'antennae', resembles some grotesque, spider-like insect hanging from the surrounding arabesques. This is one of the strangest motifs to be found in any Oriental carpet. The arch of the mihrab ends in a trefoil, the centre flange of which is of an arrowhead shape. In the area of the field above the mihrab are arabesques of related type to the Lotto arabesques; the bottom part of the field eats into the base of the mihrab with a large diamond formation containing stylized floral motifs. Related examples are known, two of which were once in the Ballard Collection and have, by tradition, been attributed to the weaving town of Konya. That the general format continued in popularity is evidenced by an example with a double-ended mihrab attributed to eighteenth-century Konya, which appeared in the London salerooms of Lefèvre in 1977. This had an aubergine mihrab with a central octagon contain-ing flower heads; from the octagon radiated yellow poles, the two on the long axis having palmette and escutcheon motifs and those on the short axis palmettes. The blue spandrels at either end contained arabesques related to the Lotto type. However, in the Lefèvre catalogue, this piece is not described as a prayer rug, and with reason; in the mihrab are stylized flower heads, small star shapes and four small quadrupeds. It would appear that this piece, too, is a strange mixture of a highly stylized garden carpet and a prayer rug, borrowing motifs from both, yet being neither.

In the 17th century, the Ushak prayer rugs usually contain a double-ended mihrab; this frequently contains a star medallion, and free-standing, scattered floral motifs. The spandrels invariably contain the arabesque interlacing of the Lotto type, an interlacing which, the more one looks at it, seems to resemble a stylized mixture of floral motifs and Kufic script; the borders usually have cloud-band motifs. In addition to this principal type, there are also multiple mihrab rugs called saphs. Examples are rare in collections in the West, although a fragmentary one, dated to the late 17th or early 18th century, is in the Textile Museum, Washington. A complete example, with two rows of six mihrabs, each one of which contains a hanging lamp at the top and schematic renderings of two feet at the base, is illustrated by Erdmann in his *Oriental Carpets*. It is attributed to seventeenth-century Ushak and its present whereabouts is unknown. In *Seven Hundred Years of Oriental Carpets*, the same author illustrates another example, with five and a half plain mihrabs, which is given the same date and provenance; it is a fragment, probably representing less than half of the complete saph, and is now in the Berlin Museum. Other fragments are in the Turk ve 107 Islam Museum in Istanbul, and Erdmann suggests that the earliest of these probably dates back to the 15th century. Saphs continued to be made in the 19th century.

The medallion and star Ushaks are the most famous seventeenth-century products of this town. The former can attain considerable lengths, examples being known which measure up to thirty feet. The star Ushaks are usually of smaller size; they begin to appear in European paintings about the middle of the 16th century and continued to be made, in a debased form, into the 19th century. The earliest depiction of the field of a star Ushak occurs in a painting by Paris Bordone, *The Doge's Ring* (Accademia, Venice) of 1530. The medallion pattern appears slightly later; a rug in a *Portrait of Henry VIII and his Family*, executed in about 1570 for Queen Elizabeth, depicts a carpet which some authorities describe as a star Ushak (for instance, the compilers of the catalogue for the *Arts of Islam* exhibition held in London in 1976) and others as a medallion Ushak (for instance, Louise W. Mackie in *The Splendour of Turkish Weaving*).

The field of the star Ushak has rows of eight-pointed stars alternating with smaller, stepped-diamond lozenges; both are usually outlined in yellow, have blue fields, and contain floral arabesques in yellow, with red details. They are woven on a red field, which contains a broken lattice of flowers and leaves, giving a scattered effect; the whole pattern is an endless repeat, with edges of new rows of diamond-star or star-diamond appearing at one or both ends. The field sizes of these pieces vary, thus giving different numbers of motifs.

In the most normal size, around 14 feet by 7 feet, there is the following layout: $\frac{1}{6}$ star; $\frac{2}{3}$ star – diamond – $\frac{2}{3}$ star; diamond – star – diamond; $\frac{2}{3}$ star – diamond – $\frac{2}{3}$ star; diamond – star – diamond; $\frac{1}{4}$ star – $\frac{1}{2}$ diamond – $\frac{1}{4}$ star. Examples with this layout are in the Metropolitan Museum and on the London art market (Christie's, London, 13 January 1975, and the same carpet again at Lefèvre on 14 February 1977). Slightly smaller versions, for instance that at Hardwicke Hall, have $\frac{1}{4} - \frac{1}{2} - \frac{1}{4}$ rows at top and bottom, with $\frac{1}{2}$ diamond – star – $\frac{1}{2}$ diamond; $\frac{1}{2}$ star – diamond – $\frac{1}{2}$ star; $\frac{1}{2}$ diamond – star – $\frac{1}{2}$ diamond rows intervening (the order of rows may be reversed and the amount appearing at top and bottom may differ; for example, $\frac{1}{6}$ to $\frac{2}{3}$ as in the example in the Kunstgewerbemuseum, Cologne). Another size, for instance the piece in the Bernheimer Collection, Munich, has a $\frac{1}{6}$ row, then $\frac{1}{6}$ diamond – star – $\frac{1}{6}$ diamond; $\frac{1}{3}$ star – diamond – $\frac{1}{3}$ star; $\frac{1}{6}$ diamond – star – $\frac{1}{6}$ diamond; and then a $\frac{1}{3}$ row.

In two examples illustrated by Dimand in his catalogue of the Metropolitan Museum Collection, there are differing fields; in one, measuring 9 feet 1 inch by 5 feet 7 inches, there are three large stars down the long axis, touching the edges of medallions on the long borders; another has large diamond – star – diamond – $\frac{1}{4}$ star on the long axis, the diamonds being linked on either side with star points on the edges of the field. Both these are ascribed to the 17th century.

Erdmann illustrates other variants; two pieces, one in the Berlin Museum almost completely destroyed in the last war and the other in the Kunst und Gewerbe Museum, Hamburg, have patterns of two squared lozenges in geometric lattices alternating, on the long axis, with a large eight-pointed star flanked by two smaller and more floral, eight-pointed stars; the Hamburg piece, assigned to the 17th century, is considered by Erdmann to be slightly later than the Berlin carpet. Yet another unique variant is an extant Berlin piece which has a system as follows: $\frac{1}{2}$ star; up-winged palmette; $\frac{1}{4}$ star – diamond – $\frac{1}{4}$ star; down-winged palmette; star; up-winged palmette; $\frac{1}{4}$ star – diamond – $\frac{1}{4}$ star.

Finally, we should mention the carpets in the collection of the Duke of Buccleuch. One has alternate rows of star – diamond – star – diamond – star and star point – diamond – star – diamond – star – diamond – star point; this piece, however, bears the Montagu arms and the date 1584. A second example bears the date 1585 and a third, although contemporary, is undated. These are now thought by the majority of scholars to be of English workmanship (although Bode and Kühnel, for instance, were adamant that this was not the case, saying that they were woven on commission in Ushak). Kendrick and Tattersall maintained that the initials 'E.B.' and 'A.N.' found in the borders are those of English weavers, and pointed out that the warp is of hemp, never found in Turkish weaves. Stylistically, the Buccleuch carpets exhibit more motifs in the field than are found on any Turkish Ushak star carpet: motifs which, as Dimand points out, are unusually elongated. He suggests as a provenance the town of Norwich, well known for its woven carpets in the later Middle Ages.

For the medallion Ushaks, there are two basic colour schemes: one with red medallions on a blue field, and the other reversed. The medallions are of ovoid form (sometimes called ogival), one of the favourite motifs in the court manufactories at Istanbul. Again, the field is subjected to many variations on the basic theme. In some cases, the medallion arrangement

*Star Ushak carpet. First
half of the 17th century.
13 ft. 3 in. × 7 ft. 2 in.
(430 × 218 cm.).*

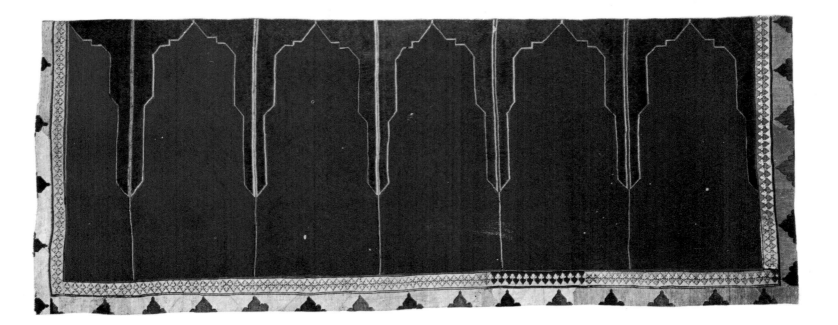

seems to have been derived from typical Safavid medallion carpets, with central medallion and corner pieces. Unique to the Turkish variety of medallion carpet, however, is the habit, in very long carpets, of having the central medallion begin a repeat at either end. Thus, even in this pattern, the closest to the Persian developments the Turkish designers came, they could not disband the concept of the endless pattern.

The best-known medallion Ushaks include the Stroganoff carpet, which has a large central medallion with small palmette attachments at either end on the long axis; small portions of the medallion (including palmette attachment) appear at either end of the field on the long axis; on each side of the field, above and below the central medallion, appear halves of large and ornate star medallions. The oval medallion is red, and contains floral patterns in blue, green, yellow, etc.; the star medallions are pale blue and the field dark blue with yellow floral arabesques. The same colour scheme applies to a superb medallion carpet which appeared in the London salerooms of Lefèvre in February 1977; this had a scheme of two pale blue, half-star medallions-and-palmette at either end, large, oval, red medallions and palmettes down the centre of the piece, each of which was flanked by approximately one-eighth sections of similar medallions curtailed by the borders of the field; between the two complete oval medallions were two star-and-palmette medallions shown approximately four-fifths complete. The guard stripe was dark blue with yellow floral motifs matching the field, and the main border was the same red as the oval medallions and with the same floral colour scheme of yellow, light and dark blue, and green.

The same layout as the Stroganoff carpet is found in an example recently acquired by the Kunst und Gewerbe Museum, Hamburg, whilst a unique fragment in Berlin has a light blue star medallion and dark blue field, but with an oval medallion in pale yellow edged with red, an effect which Erdmann describes as 'striking but not aesthetically satisfying . . . presumably an experimental piece.' Another famous blue-ground piece, in the Museum für angewandte Kunst, Vienna, has serrate-edged, red medallions which have been flattened into hexagonal forms. In Berlin, there is a late red-ground piece, with a single central ovoid medallion and detached escutcheons on the long axis; the central medallion contains a smaller quatrefoil lobed medallion. There are corner pieces to the field, apparently one-eighth sections of huge stars; all idea of a repeat pattern has disappeared from this unusual carpet. It bears the arms of the Wiesotowski family and, with its pair, preserved in Poland, is assigned by Erdmann to about 1700. The lateness of the dating is justified if a comparison with the large example in the Metropolitan Museum is made. This, too, is on a red ground and the central medallion contains an identical quatrefoil; however, the field contains part ovals at either end and stars above and below the central medallion – in other words, it adheres to the endless repeat pattern of the earlier blue-ground medallion carpets.

As we have indicated, there is a third class of Ushak which has the characteristics of both the star and medallion patterns. An example in the Metropolitan Museum has two hexagonal medallions on the long axis, with sections of lobed cartouches down each side of the field. The field is dark blue, the hexagons and lobed portions red. The field and interiors of the figures are decorated with floral arabesques. This piece is assigned to the mid-17th century. Another variation, represented by a destroyed piece once in Berlin, another once in a Berlin private collection, another in the Staatliche Museum, Berlin, and a fourth (of about twelve known) in Detroit, has a pattern of large red eight-pointed stars on a blue ground with yellow arabesques; the normal pattern is 1 star; 2 half stars; 1 star, etc. Although the shape of the medallions connect these pieces with the star Ushaks, the overall effect, predominantly due to the colour scheme, is closer to the medallion carpets.

Another type, represented by examples in Berlin, St. Louis, Lisbon (private collection), the Victoria and Albert Museum and the Metropolitan Museum, has large quatrefoil medallions taking up the whole width of the field, alternating with single diamonds in the centre of the field on the long axis; the complete example in the Metropolitan Museum measures 9 feet 5 inches by 4 feet and contains only one medallion and two half diamonds. Another, in the same institution, a fragment from the McMullan Collection, has the more usual multiple medallion layout, the medallions in blue and red, and the diamonds in blue, on a red field. All these examples are assigned to the 17th century. It is interesting to note that another McMullan gift to the Metropolitan is a nineteenth-century Turkish village rug which has the same format as the smaller of the two seventeenth-century pieces, thus exemplifying the strong traditionalist elements in Turkish weaving we have mentioned previously in this chapter.

One does not have to look far for the origins of the medallion Ushak design. Until its appearance, Turkish weaving, as far as we know from examples to have reached the West, was geometric and rectilinear. In the years following the capture of Tabriz in 1514, however, a change occurred not only in Turkish weaving, but in many other branches of the arts. It is probable that during the Turks' sporadic forty-year occupation of Tabriz, in which there was a flourishing weaving manufactory and scriptorium, vast quantities of early Safavid art were taken to Turkey as booty, to influence both the taste of the patrons and, by extension, those they patronised.

There are several examples in Persian manuscript art of the early 16th century of ornamental pages very similar in design to medallion Ushaks. The colour scheme of the Koran (opposite) is gold medallions with red details, and the field channels dark blue with yellow and red cloud-bands and floral details. It is interesting to speculate that the fragment of Ushak medallion carpet in Berlin, which has yellow medallions, represents an initial attempt to reproduce in yellow-dyed wool the rich gold leaf of manuscript illumination; this proving unsuccessful, red medallions were substituted. However, in a Moghul miniature depicting *A Celebration in the Women's Quarters of the Palace*, from a late sixteenth- or early seventeenth-century *Akbar Nameh* (Kevorkian sale, 1971) there appear four carpets, the largest one of which, from the scale of those upon it, measures about ten feet in length; this closely follows the design of the Koran pages and Ushak medallion carpets. It has gold (yellow) medallions with red arabesques, and blue field channels with yellow, white and red floral arabesques.

It is worth noting that the design of an endlessly repeating medallion is indigenous to Persian manuscript art, and was thus transferred to carpet design by the Turks; the Persians themselves preferred the enclosed medallion for weavings as they did for book-bindings. However, it should be said that the corner pieces in many Persian medallion carpets are quartered sections of the central medallion – for example, the Ardabils – which, of course, suggests the possibility of an infinite repeat.

The rugs with the balls and stripes pattern intrigue scholars, and the origin of the design has been the subject of much speculation. The original derivation, which was thought once to be the Buddhist *tchintamani* emblem, is believed by many scholars to be a schematic rendering of the skin of the leopard or other spotted cat. It is known that ancient Iranian and Turkoman rulers looked upon the leopard skin as having particular talismanic powers and the wearing of one was considered an important ritual. The same was true of tiger skins and it may be that the pattern that has emerged is a combination of the chief markings of both these animal skins. Although most of the pieces that have survived are of medium carpet size (excluding silks and velvets), there is a prayer rug in the Art Institute of Chicago with the balls and lines pattern in the mihrab and the balls alone in the spandrels.

The second principal white-ground pattern is known as the bird Ushak. This began to make its appearance in European paintings in the second half of the 16th century. Dimand

110

Small bird Ushak with a white ground. Late 17th or early 18th century. 5 ft. 10 in. × 4 ft. 8 in. (178 × 142 cm.).

Double page from a Koran, Persian, dating from the early 16th century. An interesting comparison may be made with the layout of medallion Ushak carpets.

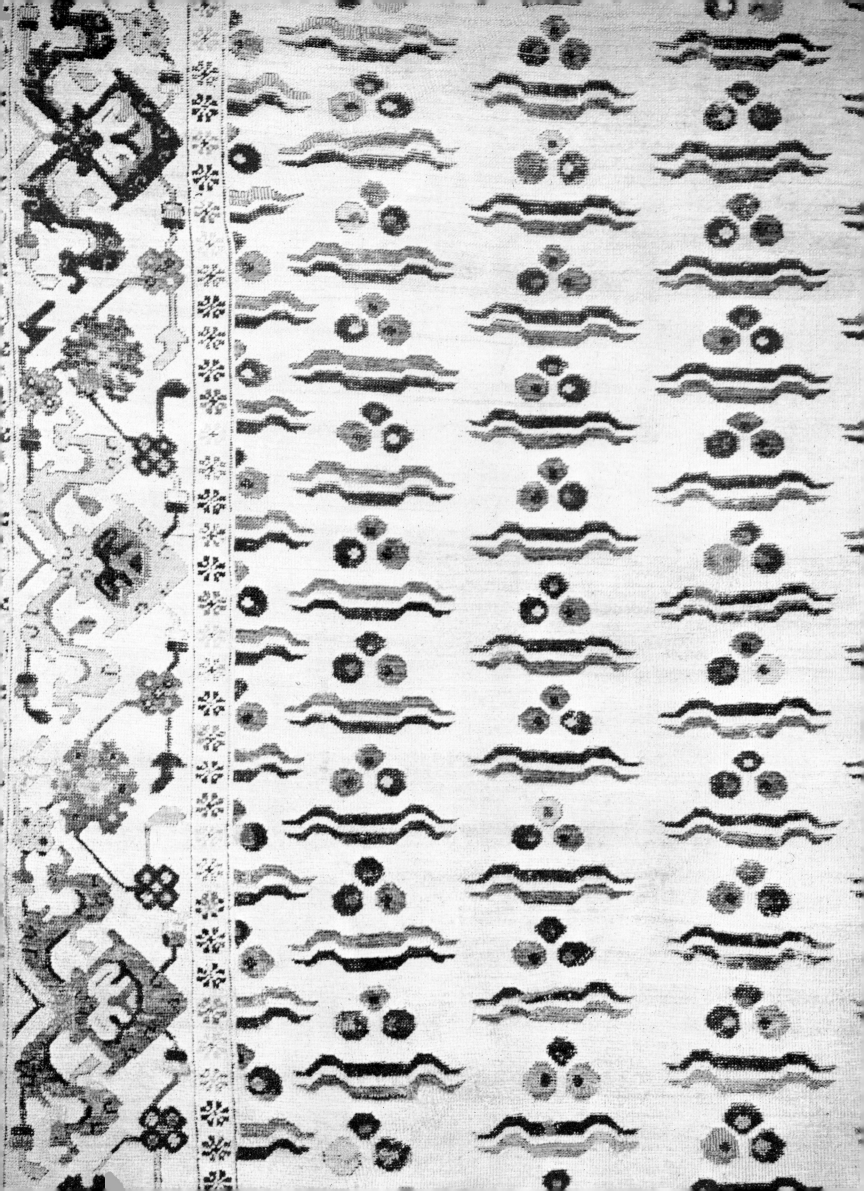

illustrates a *Portrait of a Man* by the German Hans Mielich, datable to about 1557, and now in the Kress Collection; Erdmann, in *Seven Hundred Years of Oriental Carpets*, illustrates a *Portrait of a Man in Armour*, attributed to the school of the French artist François Clouet, *c.* 1560–70, now in the Lazaro Collection, Madrid. Bode and Kühnel illustrate a picture by Varotari, once on the Berlin art market, and another example appears in a painting by the same artist now in the Hermitage, Leningrad, which is dated 1625. A fourth example appears in the ceiling frescoes by Pietro Candido for the Royal Palace in Munich, executed in 1625–6. Bode and Kühnel point out also that there is an actual example bearing the arms of an Archbishop of Lemberg (1614–30) and another, dated 1646, in the church at Schaessburg, Transylvania. The 'birds' are in fact rhomboidal shaped leaves, the sides of which resemble wings and the ends a beak and a tail. The normal layout is for the leaves to be horizontal and vertical in alternate rows, thus forming a square diaper in which are two schemes of geometric floral rosettes, one large and one small. In some rugs (for instance, an example in the Textile Museum, Washington) there are also arrowhead-shaped leaves, so that the lateral rows read upright-arrow-upright-horizontal etc.; the rows of leaves like arrowheads face alternately left and right. The field pattern is in a polychrome palette, featuring yellow, red and blue.

One other variant of the repeat motif on a white ground consists of longitudinal rows of highly stylized geometric floral motifs between columns composed of cypress motifs and rosettes. Examples are in the Museum of Applied Arts, Budapest, formerly in a private collection in Chemnitz (illustrated by Erdmann in *Oriental Carpets*, plate no. 150), and in the Protestant Church at Richisal, Transylvania (illustrated by E. Schmutzler in *Altorientalische Teppiche in Siebenburgen*, Leipzig, 1933, plate no. 36). There are two rows of motifs in these carpets; the design is supposed to be an even more schematic rendering of the bird motif, but the cataloguers of the *Arts of Islam* exhibition of 1976, in which the Budapest example was shown, suggested that 'the elongated blossoms with asymmetrical angular stems seem rather to be direct descendants of the flowers in the ground pattern of star Ushak carpets'. This group is dated to the late 17th or early 18th century.

Small Ushak medallion carpet. First half of the 17th century. 9 ft. 9 in. × 6 ft. 6 in. (297 × 198 cm.).

Opposite: detail of a balls and stripes Ushak carpet with a white ground. Late 16th century. 10 ft. 6 in. × 5 ft. 8½ in. (315 × 171 cm.). Formerly in the collection of Wilhelm von Bode, now the Dumbarton Oaks Collection.

Mamluk and Ottoman Weaving in Egypt

FROM THE CAPTURE OF EGYPT in 1517 to the Napoleonic campaigns of the late 18th century, the life and culture of Egypt were controlled by her Ottoman overlords. Thus we must examine now the early weaving of the Mamluks and the changes wrought by the Turks in succeeding years.

The scholarly discussion surrounding Egyptian carpets is very confused. There are, however, three main problems. When were the Mamluk geometric carpets woven? Where were the Cairene court carpets produced? Is there any distinction to be made between places of manufacture for the Cairene court carpets woven on wool and those which, woven on silk, also used undyed cotton in the white areas of the design? There is also a fourth problem concerning the question of origin of certain classes of compartment rugs.

Scholarship on the first point is divided between the traditional view that the Mamluk carpets were woven during the late 15th and early 16th centuries and the view put by Dimand that they were woven during the first years of Ottoman domination, from about 1520, through into the late 17th century (he suggests, in other words, that the term 'Mamluk' is historically unjustified). These are the carpets which some scholars, notably Kühnel, who was one of the first to attempt a classification of Egyptian weaving, associate with the Damascene carpets mentioned in Italian inventories, as a result of which they were thought for some years to have originated in Damascus.

Bode and Kühnel give what is perhaps the best description of Mamluk design when they describe it as 'a kaleidoscope translated into textile form'. The usual format is a central medallion, frequently consisting of an octagon, a square and a diamond superimposed, thus giving the impression of an octagon within an eight-pointed star. The rest of the field is divided into smaller units containing stars, octagons and stylized floral motifs; these units are arranged around the large central motif like planets round a sun. The borders, which do not contrast with the field but echo its designs, usually have a system of alternating oblong cartouches and rosettes. Such rugs can attain lengths of up to thirty feet.

In some of the smaller examples the field consists of one large, ornate medallion and surrounding system; in the largest, there can be as many as five medallions and systems on the long axis, or a layout of two small systems, one large and then two more small ones. The colour scheme is confined to a palette of rich cherry red, green and blue, with touches of yellow and white; this, combined with a glossy wool, gives the shimmering surface which led Kühnel to suggest that they should be identified with the Damascene rugs of old inventories. He assigned them to the last quarter of the 15th century.

Dimand, as we said, is of the opinion that all Mamluk carpets are sixteenth- and seventeenth-century, and should, therefore, be classed with other varieties of Ottoman weaving; he points out that the borders of the rugs have alternate cartouche and medallion designs, which do not appear in Persian rugs before the 16th century. He also remarks that examples are found in frescoes by Moretto in the Salvadego Palace, Brescia, and that since these are datable to the second quarter of the 16th century, it is probable that Mamluk rugs were not woven before the beginning of that century.

The attribution of these kaleidoscope carpets to the Cairo factories of the late 15th and early 16th centuries was first put forward by Frederick Sarre and followed by Ernst Kühnel and Kurt Erdmann. By stylistic analysis, they assigned such pieces to Egypt rather than Damascus (in which city, as far as is known, carpets have never been produced). Kühnel also cites the travels of Giuseppe Barbaro in 1474, in the description of which the manufacture of carpets in Cairo is mentioned (Barbaro is also the first to mention Bursa in Turkey as a carpet weaving city). Kühnel, like Dimand, also mentions the Moretto frescoes, but interprets their significance in a different manner. The frescoes, which contain depictions of at least six Mamluk rugs, were executed around 1530, and it must be assumed that the rugs that appear were several years older than the painting.

There is other evidence (although it has to be admitted that Kühnel's ideas about the date of the Moretto Mamluks hardly constitutes evidence) for an earlier dating than that admitted by Dimand. Charles Grant Ellis published two carpets in his 1967 essay, *Mysteries of the Misplaced Mamluks*; these have decorative motifs apparently based upon a blazon appropriate to the use of some thirty Amirs at the court of Qatbay (1468–96). We should also consider the highly complex geometric floral motifs of Mamluk manuscript illumination

Opposite: Mamluk medallion carpet. Late 15th century. 6 ft. 1 in. × 5 ft. (185.5 × 152.5 cm.). Victoria and Albert Museum, London.

of the 13th and 14th centuries, based upon overlapping structures of octagons, diamonds and polygons. This was a style heavily influenced by Persian Seljuk illuminators of the 13th century; one of the finest thirteenth-century Persian manuscripts, a seven-volume Koran in the Bibliothèque Nationale, Paris, has a title page with a field containing six roundels which themselves contain radiating floral motifs.

From a later date, 1313, there is also the great thirty-volume Koran in Cairo illuminated by Abd Allah ibn Muhammed ibn Mahmud al-Hamadani for al-Malik an-Nasr Muhammed. The recipient is identified as either the Persian Il-Khanid Sultan Uljaytu, who took the name al-Malik an-Nasr ('Victorious King') on his conversion to Islam in about 1312, or the Mamluk Sultan of Egypt of the same name who was ruling contemporaneously. In view of the Shi'ite prayers in the manuscript (the Mamluks were Sunnis), the Persian patronage is preferred, although within ten years of its completion, it had found its way to the Mamluk court. In 1326 it was given by deed of gift (waqf) by Abu Sa'id Sayf ad-Din Baktimur as-Saqi to his funerary foundation. This manuscript, evidence of close contact between the Mamluk and Il-Khanid styles, also has splendid geometrical designs and it should be added that the border design of rosette and elongated cartouche is known from a number of fourteenth-century Mamluk manuscripts.

It should also be remembered that the Mamluks were descendants of Turkish Seljuk soldiers; thus the designs of early Mamluk carpets spring from the same source as early Turkish and Persian art, and have the same geometric structure. However, the Egyptian pieces incorporate aspects of design developed independently in Turkey and Persia and amalgamate them in a unique way with aspects of Egyptian traditional design; the synthesis is demonstrated to a point by the Turkish geometrical layout and the use of the Persian knot. From the evidence of manuscript art, we should perhaps lean more towards Kühnel's dating.

Ottoman Court Carpets

Dimand's dating of Mamluk carpets is necessitated by his theories concerning the so-called Ottoman court carpets, two groups of stylistically similar but structurally different weavings which have been attributed by the majority of scholars, either solely or in part, to Cairo, but which Dimand attributes *in toto* to Ottoman looms either in Bursa or Istanbul.

This is a difficult problem, for lying between the pure Mamluk designs, the attribution of which to Egypt is not in doubt, and the Ottoman court carpets of the floral type, there is another group of related carpets of a mixed geometric-floral design, which have been called variously 'checkerboard' rugs (Bode and Kühnel), 'Rhodian' and 'compartment rugs in the Egyptian manner'. This hybrid group is now generally assigned to Anatolia, although its relationship to Mamluk carpets is certainly as strong as it is to traditional Turkish weaving, in particular to the two classes of Holbein carpets, and it has the added distinction of being woven with the Persian knot.

Now, the difficulties are these. If we accept that both these carpets and those of the floral type were woven not in Egypt, as earlier scholars supposed, but exclusively in Anatolia, we have to accept also that in Egypt, carpets of Mamluk design were the only ones made, and that production of these tailed off in the late 17th century as Cairo sank to the status of a provincial backwater of the Ottoman Empire.

The alternatives are twofold: that some of the compartment carpets were woven in Egypt in the 16th and 17th centuries, utilizing traditional Mamluk designs, but tempered with the new awareness of traditional Anatolian weaving brought with them by the Ottomans; or, as Kühnel and Erdmann supposed, that the floral designs were woven in Cairo to the specifications of Anatolian designers. Erdmann, it should be said, is not confident of this hypothesis. In suggesting that the origins of the design were probably the manufactories of Bursa, he finds it difficult to explain why the Ottomans should have sent to Cairo to have examples woven, which must 'have differed markedly from these originals in technique, material and colouring', when they could have enlarged the Bursa workshops and had them woven there.

Bode and Kühnel point out that the floral carpets were unquestionably woven under court patronage. They suggested that the general colour range of such pieces adhered to the basic Mamluk palette; the central medallion found in many of the pieces was, they supposed, carried through from Mamluk designs, rather than an adoption of Persian motifs garnered by the Turks during their successful campaign against Tabriz; they remarked

Opposite, above left (detail) and right: the Simonetti carpet. Probably the finest extant example of Mamluk weaving, and a brilliant example of the geometric formalism associated with Egyptian rugs. 15th century. 29 ft. 5 in. × 7 ft. 10 in. (897 × 239 cm.). Metropolitan Museum of Art, New York, Fletcher Fund.

Opposite, below left: Mamluk medallion rug. A number of examples with a single geometric system have survived. Late 15th or early 16th century. 6 ft. 10 in. × 4 ft. 8 in. (208 × 142 cm.).

Early seventeenth-century Ottoman court floral rug attributed to Cairo or Istanbul. 6 ft. 2 in. × 4 ft. 5 in. (188 × 135 cm.). Ex-Kevorkian Collection.

that in the earliest examples (or what they considered to be the earliest examples), the borders were not designed so as to contrast with the field, as in Turkish and Persian weaving, but so as to echo it, as in Mamluk weaving. These carpets are also woven with the Persian knot.

These, however, are comparatively minor points. No one can doubt the major stylistic differences between Mamluk geometric designs and the curvilinear floral motifs of the court carpets. The adherents to the theory that such pieces were woven in Cairo have a simple, but effective, explanation. They argue that the Turks, wishing to emulate the curvilinear designs in carpets they had seen and captured in Tabriz, decided that Cairo, which, in Erdmann's words, had 'the most important carpet manufactories in the west', with its long-established tradition of the Senneh knot, in itself more suitable for the finer knotting required by curvilinear designs, would be the most suitable place of manufacture. Therefore, Turkish designers, probably working in court workshops in Bursa and Istanbul, supplied designs to the Cairo weavers for them to execute. This would explain the sudden and radical change in Egyptian carpet design in the 16th century.

There is evidence from the diaries of the French traveller Thevenot, who visited Cairo in 1663, that rug weaving was still practised there at that date. There are also the several European inventories of the 16th and 17th centuries with references to carpets described variously as 'Querin', 'Cagiarin', 'Cairin' and 'Alkheirisch', all references to Cairo. Finally, there is the fact that in 1585, the Sultan Murad III ordered eleven Cairo weavers, plus a quantity of fine wool, to Istanbul. On the evidence of this well-documented historical event, Kühnel has suggested that the floral carpets could be divided into two groups based on structure. Those pieces woven on a wool foundation should be attributed to Cairo and those woven on a silk foundation and using an undyed cotton pile instead of wool in the white areas of the field should be attributed to a Bursa or Istanbul workshop staffed by the Cairo weavers; therefore, such pieces must be later than 1585.

Dimand was not convinced by this pretty hypothesis. He maintained, from stylistic and technical evidence, that Kühnel's Bursa or Istanbul group had to be earlier than 1585. Dimand further remarked that Bursa was a well-known weaving centre long before the arrival there of the Cairene weavers, and that a city register of 1525 listed no less than fifteen rug makers. The Turks would have been aware of Persian designs after their forays into Tabriz and would have noticed that the Senneh knot was more suited to the fine weaving demanded by curvilinear designs. There was no reason why they could not have established a suitable workshop in Turkey itself, using Turkish or even Persian weavers.

Using much cross-referencing from the designs found in Turkish ceramic art, especially mosque tiles, and fabrics, Dimand suggests that the floral motifs found in the Ottoman court carpets did not mark a radical break with tradition, but were logical extensions of motifs already in use at the end of the 15th century in the repertoire of designs of the Turkish carpet weaver. He thought that the earliest pieces, with a central medallion and dense floral patterning on a dark red field, could be dated to the first half of the 16th century; he placed a carpet in the Metropolitan Museum in this group, even though it is woven with silk warp and weft. To the mid-16th century, he assigned a carpet on an all-wool foundation, woven with multiple roundels containing arabesques, large palmettes, serrated leaves and flower sprays, again on a rich red background, and with a complementary floral arabesque and palmette border.

Floral rugs, often with no central medallion, but with large, heavy, serrated leaves are attributed to the late 16th and 17th centuries, lateness of date being determined by coarseness

Below left: an unusual Ottoman Cairene court carpet with a marked abrash. Late 16th or early 17th century. 8 ft. 2 in. × 7 ft. 7 in. (249 × 231 cm.). Below right: a rounded octagonal carpet of Ottoman Cairene design, probably made in Istanbul. Mid-16th century. A round carpet of Mamluk design is in the Barbieri Collection, Genoa. 8 ft. 7 in. × 7 ft. 4 in. (262 × 223.5 cm.). W. A. Clark Collection, Corcoran Gallery of Art, Washington.

The Ottoman court carpet at its most refined and elegant; the vivid but soft green is typical of the carpets in this group. Early 17th century. Probably Istanbul or Bursa. 8 ft. 3 in. × 6 ft. 7 in. (251.5 × 200.5 cm.).

of design and weave. Some examples, produced in the 18th century, have a Persian knot count as low as 90 to the square inch.

Related to these pieces are the prayer rugs, in which the mihrab is either plain, columned or filled with similar large-leaf foliage. The more floral of these pieces, such as the justly famous example in the Walters Art Gallery, Baltimore, have mihrabs so slightly delineated and such an abundance of floral motifs that one would be forgiven for thinking that they were not prayer rugs. An example in the Metropolitan Museum, catalogued as late 17th century, has a central roundel and palmette arrangement in the mihrab, and dense floral patterning; it can be compared to a piece in the same institution with medallions and corners, and another, also in the Metropolitan, the gift of Joseph V. McMullan.

There is also a distinct group of floral medallion and corner carpets, in which the medallions, corners and borders are filled with the usual floral motifs, but in which the rest of the field has a repeat pattern, such as the balls and stripes. Needless to say, the very rare column prayer rugs of this group, in which the mihrab is depicted with supporting columns in an architectural fashion, are held to be the precursors of the village prayer rugs – especially those from the Ghiordes and Ladik areas – which were made in the late 18th century.

Opposite: Ottoman court prayer rug, dated 1610 in a chronogram, which is the only known example of a date appearing in an Ottoman carpet. Probably Istanbul or Bursa. 5 ft. 11 in. × 3 ft. 11 in. (180 × 119 cm.). Islamische Museum, Berlin.

Ottoman court floral carpet. Probably made in Istanbul or Bursa. 6 ft. 5 in. × 4 ft. 6 in. (195.5 × 137 cm.).

The Rhodian Carpets

We come now to the other group of carpets which, on stylistic grounds, have, at some time, been attributed to Egypt. These are the compartment rugs, which are in fact a form of medallion rug. They have been associated with those pieces described in old inventories as 'tappeti rodioti' (Rhodian carpets). Bode and Kühnel suggest, a little fancifully, that the cross depicted in the centres of the repetitive star motif should be taken as the emblem of the Order of St. John, which was resident on the island of Rhodes until 1526 and that these carpets, while not of course made on the island, were produced for the knights (this is one of the dafter theories that carpet scholarship has thrown up). The two German scholars, however, were not unaware of the Anatolian characteristics of these carpets and were undecided as to their country of origin.

Structurally, these pieces are odd; they are tied with a Senneh knot, but the warp is spun and plied in the opposite direction to warps found in Mamluk carpets. They have also a foundation of goat's hair. In terms of design, the relationship to Mamluk carpets is clearly seen in the field, which contains either rows of octagons within diamonds, or a system of large and small octagons. The colour of the former group, which in general seems coarser and more archaic, is closer to that of Mamluk carpets than that of the latter group, which is richer and more closely related to the Holbein carpets. However, in many respects (the scattered cypresses and tiny floral motifs, as well as the radiating, kaleidoscopic feel of the design) they are very close also to the Mamluk pieces. In all probability, they are later in date than the first group.

The second, scattered design group is fairly homogeneous. The ground colour is red and there is a layout of a central octagon and four small octagons in the arrangement 2–1–2. Within each octagon there is an arabesque and a central star. The main border is pseudo-Kufic. This general layout can be seen in rugs in the Philadelphia Museum of Art and in the collection of Charles Grant Ellis; they can also be seen in many sixteenth-century Italian paintings, notably Lorenzo Lotto's *Portrait of the Protonotary Giovanni Giuliani* in the National Gallery, London, datable to about 1519–20, and the same artist's *Altarpiece of St. Anthony* in Venice, dated 1542 (a painting which also contains a Lotto pattern carpet). The attribution of these pieces to Egypt is highly unlikely. The use of the Senneh knot, as Dimand said, could have been learned from Persian weavers in Tabriz after its capture in 1514; the colours and the Kufic borders are alien to Egyptian weaving. It would seem as if this is a style close to established Turkish themes, but showing an undoubted awareness of Mamluk design. It should be added that the presence of such a piece in an Italian painting of 1519–20 is fairly strong evidence of a non-Egyptian origin, for in all probability the carpet shown by Lotto was woven before the Turks captured Cairo in 1517.

However, the first 'rows of octagons' group of compartment rugs differs considerably from the second. As we said earlier, the colours are much closer to Mamluk origins; none are woven with Kufic borders, and several have the rosette and cartouche borders of Mamluk rugs. There are several examples known, including ones in the Textile Museum, Washington, the Metropolitan Museum, New York, the Museum of Islamic Art, Cairo, the City Art Museum, St. Louis, the Bardini Museum, Florence, and a particularly fine example once in the Davanzati Palace, Florence, and in the Staatliche Museum, Berlin. Joseph V. McMullan, who once owned the piece now in New York, believed it to be of Egyptian origin. Most authorities suggest a date for these pieces around the late 16th and early 17th century, and later rather than earlier. It is probable that these pieces are of Egyptian origin (they retain too many characteristics of the great Mamluk pieces) and yet are obviously far below them in quality. They are a logical, if somewhat sad, epitaph to the earlier brilliance of Egyptian weaving.

Rugs and Carpets of Moghul India

THE MOGHUL DYNASTY of India was, as its name implies, ruled by emperors proud of their Mongol descent. Babur, the first Moghul Shah (1526–30), was a fifth generation descendant of Tamerlaine, and was thus related to Ghengis Khan. Formerly ruler of Afghanistan, he overthrew the Hindu Delhi Sultanate. Ten years after his death, his son and successor, Humayan, was forced into exile by an Afghan revolt and spent nine years at the Persian court of Shah Tahmasp.

On his return to India in 1549, Humayan brought with him a deep love of Persian art; two of the leading Persian court painters, Mir Sayyid Ali and Abdus Samad accompanied him, and founded the Moghul school of painting, a style which, like the carpets of the Moghul Imperial factories, blends the elegant sophistication of the Persian style with a rich exoticism which is characteristically Indian. Mir Sayyid Ali, called Nazir al-Mulk (Wonder of the Realm), illustrated a huge twelve-volume *Dastan i-Amir Hamza* (Romance of Amir Hamza) with paintings on cotton, one of the masterpieces of Islamic art and one which was to provide Moghul painters with a yardstick for years to come.

It was under Humayan's son Akbar the Great (1556–1606) that the Moghul Empire consolidated its power. Like the late Timurid and early Safavid Shahs, he established work-

The Emperor Babur entertaining Badi-Uzzalman Mirza in a tent beside the Murghab river in 1506. *The superb double medallion carpet is of a type not known to have survived. From a manuscript of the* Babur Nameh *of c. 1590. Victoria and Albert Museum, London.*

The Emperor
Akbar's entry into
Surat in 1573.
*Miniature executed
by the Persian artist
Farrukh Beg who
arrived at Akbar's
court in 1584. Note
the ornate woven
animal trappings.
From a manuscript
of the* Akbar
Nameh, *c. 1596.
Victoria and Albert
Museum, London.*

The Emperor
Akbar returning by
boat to Agra. *From
a manuscript of the*
Akbar Nameh, c.
*1596. Victoria and
Albert Museum,
London.*

shops for the production of paintings, manuscripts, goldsmithing, arms and carpets. Between 1569 and 1584, he built the city palace of Fatehpur-Sikri, having the walls covered with murals. In 1584, he established his capital at Agra.

Early Moghul Weaving

It is from the reign of Akbar that we have the first documentary evidence of carpet production. His chief minister Abu'l-Fazl (1551–1602) wrote the official history of his master's reign, the *A'in-i Akbari*, which was translated by H. Blochmann in 1873. In this, we read that the Emperor

'. . . *has caused carpets to be made of wonderful varieties and charming textures; he has appointed experienced workmen, who have produced many masterpieces. The carpets of Iran and Turan are no more thought of, although merchants still import carpets from Góskhán, Khúzistán, Kermán and Sabzwár. All kinds of carpet-weavers have settled here, and drive a flourishing trade. These are found in every town, but especially in Agrah, Fathpúr and Láhór.*'

This passage not only establishes the location of the leading weaving centres of India, but also tells us the places of origin of Persian carpets as 'Goskhan' (Joshaqan), Khuzistan (in west Persia), Kerman and Sabzewar (the small town in Khorassan we mentioned in our section on Safavid textiles). A surprising omission from this list is Herat, from which city large quantities of carpets are known to have been sent to India; the floral style of these can be seen repeated in many Indian weavings. 'Turan', referred to in the above quoted passage, is Turkestan. The proud boast that Persian and Turkestan carpets 'are no more thought of' should not, of course, be taken literally, since Persian carpets at least continued to be imported into India in great quantities during the 17th century; the Amber garden carpet, for instance, came to India in the early 17th century. Indeed, it is unlikely that any of the surviving Indian carpets predate the reign of Jehangir (1605–27).

Persian Influence

The Amber garden carpet comes to mind when discussing a group of extraordinary fragments from at least two carpets of Moghul origin, which are assumed to be among the earliest extant examples of Indian weaving, dating from around the first decade of the 17th century. The designs are free and asymmetric, one of the principal features of many Indian carpets. One group of fragments has figures of animals, some real and some imaginary, either singly or in pairs, attacking and devouring each other. The best known fragment, once in the McMullan Collection, is now in the Metropolitan Museum; this has double-bodied, six-headed birds; other pieces from the same carpet may be found in St. Louis, Boston; Detroit, Washington, the Louvre and in the Burrell Collection, Glasgow (the ex-Loewenfeld fragment). The second carpet has animal heads dotted around the field, which is covered by a wide spiralling arabesque; the animals represented are elephants, deer, lions, wolves, geese, etc. Fragments of this carpet may be found in Lyons, Paris, Boston and Hanover. According to Erdmann, other fragments (in Glasgow, Stockholm, and a private French collection) may be from a third 'fantastic animal' carpet.

Although more grotesque than the Amber garden carpet now in Jaipur, certain elements of the Moghul fragments – the polychromy and angularity of drawing – are very close. It may be that the Amber carpet (which was probably one of several imported examples) influenced the Moghul designers in the production of their bizarre carpets. This would mean that the existing fragments should perhaps be given a slightly later date than has been supposed hitherto.

Moghul Animal Carpets

Although the majority of surviving Moghul carpets are of a formal floral design, there is a small group of exceptional animal carpets extant, all of which are dated to the early 17th century. The three most famous are the Widener carpet in the National Gallery, Washington, the Peacock rug in the Österreichisches Museum für angewandte Kunst, Vienna, and the Boston hunting carpet. There are several features in these pieces which bespeak their Indian origin: flowers and animals, such as elephants, never found in Persian weaving, and more importantly, a pictorial realism and asymmetry which are unique to Indian weaving at this date and which betray the presence of Hindu designers and weavers.

Prince Salim, afterwards the Emperor Jehangir. *Painting by Bichitr*, c. 1630. Note the realistic floral borders of this miniature. Victoria and Albert Museum, London.

Fragment from a grotesque animal carpet. Scattered fragments from at least two, and possibly three, such carpets are known. 2 ft. 6¼ in. × 1 ft. 9½ in. (77 × 55 cm.). Metropolitan Museum of Art, New York, Gift of Joseph V. McMullan.

Top: bird and tree carpet known as the Peacock rug. Possibly designed by Mansur, court painter to the Emperor Jehangir. Early 17th century. 7 ft. 10 in. × 5 ft. 2½ in. (235 × 156 cm.). Österreichisches Museum für angewandte Kunst, Vienna. Above: an almost complete Indian silk tree carpet, mid-17th century. 12 ft. × 4 ft. 6 in. (360 × 135 cm.). Musée des Tissus, Lyons. Right: Indian hunting carpet of the early 17th century. Typical asymmetrical design. 8 ft. × 4 ft. 11 in. (244 × 150 cm.). Museum of Fine Arts, Boston, Gift of Mrs. F. L. Ames in memory of Frederick L. Ames.

The Boston carpet is probably the finest of the three we have mentioned. At the top it depicts scenes within the interiors of pavilions; further down the field, there is a leopard attacking a spotted bull (a group reminiscent of those found on Persian animal carpets) and single beasts; in the centre is the depiction of a hunter on foot, followed by an ox cart being driven by a bearer, on the back of which is chained what is usually described as a leopard, but which is actually an extremely faithful rendering of a cheetah, known to have been a favoured hunting animal among Indian princes; another bearer follows the cart. The

practise of keeping hunting cats chained on the back of carts for transport to the field is referred to by a French traveller, François Bernier, who visited India between 1658 and 1668. Three-quarters of the way down the field appear a tiger and a winged elephant, the latter straight out of Hindu mythology, while at the bottom is depicted a wildcat of indeterminate species chasing two deer. The field is dotted with trees and flowering shrubs simulating a landscape, to which the animal figures bring a sense of movement.

Like the Boston carpet, both the Vienna and Washington pieces are planned with a complete lack of symmetry, and delineate plants, animals and birds with the greatest realism and in rich profusion. The Vienna piece has several varieties of birds (peacocks, cranes, chickens, turtledoves, hoopoes, partridge, etc.) among foliage. It is thought possible that it may have been designed by Shah Jehangir's court painter Mansur, and is generally considered to be of slightly earlier date than the other animal carpets of 1605–10.

The Widener carpet in Washington, datable to around 1625, contains many of the elements found in Persian carpets, although the Chinese elements are considerably less marked. The design is, again, far more free-ranging, and the figures – both human and animal – are designed on such a scale as to make them dominate the field, rather than be absorbed into a general decorative scheme, as in Persian carpets. Among the fantastic wealth of animal life depicted in this carpet may be seen a rhinoceros, deer, hyenas, a dragon, what appears to be a crocodile, fighting bulls and rabbits; the centre is dominated by a figure mounted on an elephant. The border has a rosette and cartouche design.

Another important member of this group is the large animal and tree rug in the Metropolitan Museum, just over thirty feet in length, and ascribed to the early seventeenth-century looms at Lahore. This has a field covered with large flowering shrubs and palm trees, the latter motif peculiar to Indian carpets at this date. Running through this 'jungle' are a variety of wild cats, game, birds etc., some in combat groups. The border is an unusual one of interlocking stars and star-cartouches. Although the effect of the field is rich and varied, it is perhaps a little too overcrowded, and the drawing style stiffer than is usually found. Related to this piece is the exceptionally rare silk tree carpet in the Musée des Tissus, Lyons, which although incomplete, measures twelve feet in length. This is even stiffer in design than the Metropolitan Museum carpet, the design being a mirror image on either side of the long axis. There are few animals, but several varieties of birds with wings outstretched.

From the above descriptions, it will be seen that the Moghul weavers in general remained more faithful to a sense of pictorial space, derived from miniature painting. Occasionally, however, animal carpets were designed in a more geometric fashion. The Lyons silk carpet is one example; a more unusual piece is in the Metropolitan Museum, apparently the only one of its type to have survived. This has a field with two panels of interlaced bands forming swastikas; in the seven geometric spaces left by the bands are large birds. The rug has wide arabesque borders, with large palmettes. The overall impression left by the geometric formations is closer to certain Turkish rugs than to Persian, although the naturalism of the birds is totally alien to Anatolian weaving.

Moghul Floral Carpets

Different in style, but of the same period, is a group of floral carpets, the patterns of which seem to derive from contemporary Herat pieces. Of these a number were woven in India on commission for European clients. The most famous is the Girdlers' Carpet still in the possession of the Girdlers' Company in London, one of the medieval trade guilds. The most unusual feature about this piece is its design; twenty-four feet in length, the design is vertical on the long axis; in other words, the piece resembles a European tapestry strip, or table carpet. The field contains five shields. At either end are heraldic devices – shields azure, eagles displayed argent, in chief three fleur-de-lys or per shield. Flanking the large central coat-of-arms are shields woven with the initials 'R.B.' and a merchant's seal. The initials stand for Robert Bell, Master of the Girdlers' Company in 1634, and a director of the East India Company. The central arms are those of the Girdlers' Company, with its motto 'Give Thanks to God'. The red field is woven with large flower heads on foliate stems, and these are reciprocated on the blue border.

This carpet must be considered as one of the masterpieces of the reign of Shah Jehan (1628–59), celebrated as the builder of the Taj Mahal, although in many respects its design is closer to a European conception of a carpet. A related piece, which can be linked with animal carpets, is the fragmentary Fremlin carpet, named after the arms of the Fremlin family of Kent which appear woven into the border and field; the red field is woven with winged beasts and combat groups. Other palmette or Herati carpets of Moghul origin which can be connected with European commissions are in the collection of the Duke of Buccleuch, having been imported by his ancestor the Earl of Montagu.

We have mentioned before Jehangir's court painter Mansur. He was commissioned by his master to produce albums of flower paintings, over a hundred of which survive. It is

assumed that the Emperor's great love of flowers gave rise to a special feature of Moghul art in the 17th century, the depiction of large flowers and shrubs, rendered in glowing colours and faithful detail. The largest surviving group, the so-called 'Lahore carpets' are preserved in the Jaipur Museum. They were made originally for Rajah Jai Singh I (1622–68) for his palace at Amber, built in 1630.

There are, essentially, four groups of Moghul floral rugs. One has a lattice pattern, with either palmettes and blossoms or single flowering shrubs contained within a white trellice framework; the trellice itself is constructed of either long slender leaves, arabesque scrolls or acanthus leaves. An example of the first type, with foliate scrolls, large flower heads and a lattice of long lanceolate leaves, is in the Metropolitan Museum, New York, and is dated by Dimand to the first half of the 17th century.

More common is the second type, with single flowering shrubs contained within an abstract lattice, the flowers in white, pink and yellow, with green stems and leaves, on a red ground. Examples include the ex-Kevorkian carpet, sold at Sotheby's in 1970 (one of eight Moghul carpets in this extraordinary collection), a similar, but finer example obtained by the Hamburg Museum in 1961, a large fragment in the Victoria and Albert Museum with a continuous serrated lattice of ogee form, another fragment in Düsseldorf which is thought to be from the same carpet, and yet another fragment in the Metropolitan Museum, the arabesque lattice of which contains large, single flower heads surrounded by smaller scattered leaves and flowers; a similar fragment is in the Victoria and Albert Museum. The third variety, with acanthus trellice, is the rarest; a very fragmentary example is in the Metropolitan Museum, New York.

The second floral group is the one particularly associated with the Lahore carpets; the design consists of directional rows of whole flowering plants on a red ground. Probably the finest surviving example, and the earliest, is the ex-Kevorkian piece purchased by the Metropolitan Museum at Sotheby's in 1970 for what now appears to have been the minimal

Late seventeenth- or early eighteenth-century Moghul flowers-in-a-lattice carpet, a design derived from Persian prototypes. 11 ft. 10 in. × 6 ft. 8 in. (361 × 203 cm.) Ex-Kevorkian Collection.

Watercolour of the Girdlers' carpet by Ada Hunter, 1899. This accurate depiction is shown here, since it is not possible to photograph the actual carpet in colour. The original measures 24 ft. × 8 ft. (732 × 244 cm.); it is dated 1634 and is the property of the Girdlers' Company, London. Victoria and Albert Museum, London.

Above left: Moghul carpet with directional design of single shrubs. Lahore, period of Shah Jehan, first half of the 17th century. 14 ft. × 6 ft. 7 in. (427 × 200.5 cm.). Formerly in the Kevorkian Collection, now Metropolitan Museum of Art, New York. Above: detail of an exceptionally large Moghul floral and medallion carpet based on a Persian vase carpet. Period of Shah Jehan. 52 ft. 4 in. × 10 ft. 8 in. (1595 × 325 cm.). Ex-Kevorkian Collection, now private collection, London.

 sum of £14,000 ($24,500). The rows of carnations, tulips, iris, chrysanthemums and primroses are executed realistically in a polychrome palette. The borders are based on the Herati pattern. Another example, also once in the Kevorkian Collection, has rows of plants which are designed to be viewed vertically on the long axis. This piece is part of a particular group; two quadrilateral pieces are known (this example, fifteen feet in length, and another of twenty-four feet were once in the collection of Lionel Harris). Three other carpets from the same group are seven-sided pieces obviously made to fit around a central structure, possibly a throne or fountain. According to Kendrick and Tattersall, they were woven specially for a room in the Amber Palace; the flowers depicted include roses, irises, lilies, violets, bell flowers, peonies, carnations and tulips. There is also an apparently unique rug in the Frick Collection, New York, which has rows of trees at the base of which grow flowers. This had been sent as a gift to the Ardabil shrine by Shah Jehan.

In discussing the Girdlers' Carpet and related pieces, we have pointed out their connection with the palmette or Herati carpets. Other Indian carpets, based on either floral Herat carpets or Persian vase carpets of the two- or three-plane lattice types, are frequently encountered. A fine Herat-type piece, once in the Altman Collection, is now in the Metropolitan Museum; the design is stiffer than the Persian prototypes, although the delineation of the flowers is more realistic. The borders, however, are the features which in particular betray the Moghul origin; they are woven with the rows of single flowering plants found in the directional carpets discussed above.

Another example in the Metropolitan Museum has what Dimand describes as 'racemes of wisteria-like blossoms' alternating with lanceolate leaves. Also showing a strong Persian influence was the piece woven with predominantly yellow flowers, with vivid touches of red, blue, green and white, in the first Kevorkian sale at Sotheby's in 1969; again, this had borders of whole flowering shrubs, contained within eight-pointed stars. A more unusual example, in the Museum of Islamic Art, Istanbul, has a repeat white arabesque in the field intertwined with flowers. The borders are reminiscent of the 'wisteria and lanceolate' leaf design found in the field of the Metropolitan Museum carpet mentioned above. Other carpets of similar type are in the Berlin Museum and the Cleveland Museum.

Possibly the most extraordinary of all surviving Indian floral carpets is the ex-Kevorkian piece sold in 1970 and now in an English private collection. This measures fifty-two and a half feet in length and was almost certainly an Imperial commission. Along its entire enormous length are ogee and square medallions surrounded by radiating systems of flower heads and stems, each system differing from the next one. Maurice Dimand has pointed out that, in style, it seems to be a mixture between Persian vase and garden carpets. It is probable that the Persian originals on which it is based are themselves early seventeenth-century, so a dating to the period of Jehangir seems less likely than one to the period of Shah Jehan or thereabouts.

However, the former hypothesis is not impossible and indeed there is evidence to suggest that it may actually have been woven during the time of Jehangir, who was a contemporary of Shah Abbas of Persia. At least one carpet, now known from fragments, is thought to have been commissioned by Abbas from the looms at Lahore. It was intact in 1887 and was in the Chihil Sultan Kiosk in Isfahan. The fragments now extant, including ones in the Victoria and Albert Museum, the University Museum, Cleveland, and the ex-Haim piece illustrated by Erdmann in *Seven Hundred Years of Oriental Carpets*, show that the design of this piece was also derived from Persian vase carpets. Since it is known from the description of Sir James Morier, writing in 1812, that there were several carpets in the Chihil Sultan, the ex-Kevorkian piece may well be from the same group.

Although most scholars have quite correctly pointed out the specifically Indian characteristics of the floral carpets, it would be wrong to underestimate their close relationship with Persian weaving; however, the Indian designers and weavers do not seem to have had a delayed reaction, a feature of one country influencing the designs of another. The Indian carpets of Persian inspiration seem to have been virtually contemporaneous with the

One of a group of shaped Moghul carpets possibly made for the Amber Palace or, according to Dimand, the Taj Mahal. Period of Shah Jehan, first half of the 17th century. 14 ft. 8 in. × 8 ft. 8 in. (447 × 264 cm.). Ex-Kevorkian Collection.

originals. The directional rows of flowering shrubs, while characteristically Indian, are not, as we have seen, specifically so.

In our section on Safavid weaving, we mentioned such pieces as the Ballard red-ground tree rug in the Metropolitan Museum (a misleading description; it is more accurately a flowering shrub rug), dated to early seventeenth-century Isfahan; the McMullan shrub rug with central star-shaped medallion and corners, also in the Metropolitan; the directional vase carpets, such as the Washington fragment; and the shrub carpets which have single plants contained within a lattice. All these are very close indeed to Moghul designs, yet none can be much earlier than the first quarter of the 17th century. There may, therefore, have

Detail of a band of cut velvet, with a design of naturalistically rendered flowers, typical of Moghul work. 17th century. 9 ft. 11 in. × 5 ft. 3 in. (298 × 158 cm.). Victoria and Albert Museum, London.

Akbar II holding a durbar in the Diwan-i Khass of the Red Fort at Agra. *Note the similarity of the design of the throne surround to that of the rug with three arches illustrated here.* C. *1820. India Office Library, London.*

been a greater measure of mutual interdependence between Persian and Indian designers, rather than the one-way traffic which has been supposed hitherto.

The fourth group of Indian floral weavings are the prayer rugs. Of these, one particular type is outstanding and exceptionally rare. In such pieces, the mihrab contains one large flowering plant. One of the finest is now in the Metropolitan Museum, the gift of Joseph V. McMullan. This has an over life-size chrysanthemum, with five brilliant white blooms and green stem and leaves; the field is the usual rich crimson associated with Indian weavings and at the base of the stem is hilly ground. On either side of the stem grow small tulip plants.

The arch of the mihrab is formed by a white arabesque of the type found in some of the lattice-pattern floral carpets, and the spandrels are filled with large flower heads amid scrolling foliage; these are echoed in the more formal arrangement of the borders.

Despite its small size (4 feet 11½ inches by 12¾ inches) this is a piece of great splendour. It also has another characteristic of small Indian weavings: an exceptionally fine knotted pile. Though piled in wool, it has a count of 728 Senneh knots to the square inch. Approximately two other complete examples of the type are recorded: a piece with an identical arrangement, but with a dark-bloomed chrysanthemum, is illustrated by Bode and Kühnel and was in the Paravicini Collection, Cairo. This is the carpet which McMullan mentions as being in the Engel-Gros Collection; it was sold in the Paravicini sale in Paris in 1963, and is now in the Pincket Collection, Grimberg. The other is in the Thyssen Collection (ex-Aynard); this piece may be a fragment of a multiple mihrab saph. A later and less densely woven saph is in an English private collection. The fragment of yet another, a genuine seventeenth-century Moghul silk piece is in the Metropolitan Museum. It has a most unusual colour scheme with a white-grey field; its most incredible feature, however, is its knot count of 2,552 to the square inch. Its total amount of knots complete would have been around four million. The Kashan silk rugs, by comparison, have a knot count of around 500 to 650 per square inch. It should be noted that this extreme fineness of knotting does not apply only to silk rugs. The Metropolitan acanthus-leaf trellice fragment has a wool pile with 1,258 knots per square inch, and the Hamburg trellice carpet has over 1,000 knots per square inch, densities far higher than any found in Persian weavings.

Another complete carpet of this design in silk was sold in the Benguiat sale of 23 April 1932, lot 14. This had been published by Martin in 1908 as Moghul *c.* 1640. In her discussion of the Thyssen rug, May Beattie mentions the Benguiat piece, remarking that it is now considered to be later in date. However, when it appeared at Christie's on 5 May 1977, lot 32, it became obvious that it was in fact an early twentieth-century Hereke or Istanbul piece, probably copied from the Engel-Gros/Paravicini rug.

216

Opposite page, top: detail of a large Moghul carpet with directional rows of flowering plants. Mid-18th century. 27 ft. 5 in. × 10 ft. (832 × 305 cm.). Ex-Kevorkian Collection.

Opposite page, bottom left: Portrait of the Emperor Aurangzeb. *Early 18th century. Victoria and Albert Museum, London. Opposite page, bottom right:* Portrait of the Emperor Bahadur Shah Zafar, *1838. Victoria and Albert Museum. London.*

Caucasian Weaving

Opposite: Daghestan prayer rug, dated 1826. 5 ft. × 3 ft. 6 in. (152.5 × 106.5 cm.).

CAUCASIAN CARPETS come from an area of approximately 160,000 square miles; the region is situated in the land between the Black Sea and the Caspian Sea. Although many of the carpets of the so-called 'north-west Persian-Caucasian' group were probably woven inside the present borders of Iran in the region between the towns of Tabriz in the south and Erivan (now called Yerevan) in the north, the majority were woven in, and north of, the regions called Armenia, Karabagh, Kazak, Moghan and Shirvan on old maps, regions now incorporated into the modern Soviet states of Armenia and Azerbaijan. We note, of course, that before the border between Russia and Persia was settled in about 1869, the area called Azerbaijan stretched well south into Persia, its capital being Tabriz. Many of the names of regions and towns given to various types of Caucasian weavings are no longer found on maps of the U.S.S.R.; they are the result of traditional scholarship. For the purposes of any discussion of Caucasian weaving, however, they must be retained.

The carpets of the Caucasus mirror the ethnography of their creators. Until the Russian conquests of the late 18th and 19th centuries, the area had been for over 800 years an ethnic, cultural and religious melting-pot and a ceaseless battleground. Arabs, Tartars, Turks, Mongols, Persians, Russians and so on were constantly seeking to make the region theirs, either for political or religious reasons. Even in the 19th century, Shamil, leader of the

Late eighteenth-century hunting carpet. Possibly southern Caucasus, but probably Kurdistan. 12 ft. 8¾ in. × 6 ft. 2¼ in. (386.5 × 188.5 cm.). Metropolitan Museum of Art, New York. Gift of Joseph V. McMullan.

Cherkess tribe, declared a Muslim Holy War on the Russian conquerors. One of the leading cultural groups, the Armenians, remained Christian, despite terrible persecution, culminating in the mass-murder and deportation of millions by the Turks during the First World War. Both the cultural mix and the barbarism are displayed in Caucasian carpet design, and in the use of a brilliant hot palette in many of the types.

Dragon Rugs

The earliest Caucasian weavings are the dragon rugs. The date of the pieces, of which between fifty and a hundred examples survive, is a matter of controversy, as are the circumstances of their production. One theory suggests that, since the designs are based on Persian vase rugs of the Shah Abbas period and later, the earliest examples cannot date from much before the end of the 16th century, and continued to be made into the 19th. The other view is that they must be dated considerably earlier than this, with an origin in the 15th century or even earlier. This is the dating put forward by many of the leading German scholars, including Kühnel, Erdmann and Ulrich Schürmann. It is suggested that certain fifteenth-century Italian and Flemish paintings (Jan van Eyck's triptych in the Dresden Gemäldegalerie, which we have mentioned in connection with early Ottoman geometric 95 designs, the *Virgin and Child* attributed by Berenson to 'Amico di Sandro', and Piero Pollaiuolo's *Annunciation* in the Dresden Gemäldegalerie) show rugs with a lozenge diaper typical of early Caucasian weaving.

By inference, Schürmann suggests in *Caucasian Rugs* that the animal combat rugs, such as the Berlin dragon and phoenix carpet, may also be of Caucasian rather than Anatolian origin. Although this is not the generally accepted view, many authorities have pointed out the similarities between carpets such as the Berlin piece and later Caucasian weavings, and it has to be said that the stylization of animal forms is a more prevalent characteristic of Caucasian weaving than it is of Turkish. It should be noted in this context that the Seljuk Turks invaded and conquered Armenia, Georgia, and the surrounding areas in the 11th century and remained thereafter one of the principal cultural influences in the area. Although the effect of Persian weaving may be seen in Caucasian rugs from the 16th century onwards, the technical structure of all Caucasian pile carpets is Turkish; that is, they are woven with the Ghiordes knot. It might also be added that there is no actual evidence, apart from the finding of fragments dating from Seljuk times in Turkish mosques, that they were woven in Turkey rather than in a Turkish milieu in the Caucasus. On stylistic evidence, the latter is certainly a hypothesis which cannot be dismissed.

The evidence of the paintings cited above is, however, equivocal. Only the haziest notion of the field pattern can be gathered from the Pollaiuolo; the field pattern of the van Eyck carpet does have a lozenge diaper, as does the carpet in the *Lucca Madonna* in Frankfurt and the one in the *Madonna of Jan Vos* in the Frick Collection; the effect, however, is totally 95 uncharacteristic of the dragon rugs with which they have been associated. I do not believe it to be feasible to take the carpets displayed in any of these paintings as evidence of Caucasian weaving in Europe in the 15th century. The earliest dated pieces are a fragment in the Textile Museum, Washington, woven with the name of the client for whom it was produced, Husayn 142 Beg, and the date, which can be read as either Muharram 1001 or 1101 (October 1592 or 1689), with most scholars preferring the later date and calling it a Kurdish copy of a dragon carpet; the second example, which is a floral rather than a dragon rug, is inscribed, 'I, Gothar, full of sin and feeble in soul, have made this with my own hands. May he who reads this pray for my soul'. There follows the Armenian date of 1129, corresponding to A.D. 1679, although Erdmann pointed out that the date appears to have been tampered with and should read 1779. However, he admitted that he had not examined the carpet, which had disappeared. Ettinghausen, in 1936, suggested that the date, which is rendered in chronogramatic form, should read 1149 (A.D. 1699–1700). This latter dating was confirmed (and there is no sign of it having been tampered with) when the carpet, still in superb condition, reappeared at an auction in London on 20 May 1977.

Again, the circumstances under which the early pieces were woven have given rise to some controversy. Dimand states categorically that the rugs of the Caucasus were made by peasants and nomads. There was, in other words, no urbanization and patronage as found in Turkish, Persian and Indian weaving. This, however, was not the view of Erdmann in *Oriental Carpets*; he pointed out that many of the dragon carpets attain lengths of up to twenty feet (and more) and have a brilliant and diverse colour range. This suggested that such pieces could not have been woven on nomadic looms, but were made in city workshops, and that, in addition, they were produced from cartoons. Although it is impossible to make a categoric statement one way or the other, Erdmann's hypothesis is not generally accepted by other carpet scholars.

As controversial are the questions of where and by whom the dragon rugs were woven. One of the most prevalent theories of old carpet literature was that they were the exclusive product of Armenians; recent scholarship favours a more north-easterly provenance, suggesting that they emanate from the northern part of Azerbaijan and the southern part of Daghestan, specifically from in and around the town of Kuba. This latter hypothesis is based upon structural characteristics, such as fineness of wool and the tightness of knotting. However, there is evidence that such carpets, and the related floral types, were woven by Armenians, and it seems likely that they were woven not in one specific area, but throughout the Caucasus.

The dragon rugs can be divided into four chronological groups. The earliest examples, probably dating from the late 16th and early 17th centuries, are based on a lozenge diaper of serrate leaves, a formation found in Persian vase carpets. The finest, and probably the earliest, is the so-called 'Graf' rug, which by tradition came from a mosque in Damascus in the late 19th century (an unlikely provenance considering its clearly discernible animal motifs), and in 1905 passed to the Berlin Museum. Originally measuring 22 feet 7 inches in length, its partial destruction in the Second World War was described by Erdmann as the greatest loss suffered by the Berlin collection. It was remarkable not only for its richness of colour, but also for the denseness of its design: a transverse lattice of five lozenges, as opposed to the usual three. The designs within each diamond vary from row to row, some having large, single palmettes, some appearing to be highly stylized trees; while others have pairs of facing animals, single animals or combat groups. In the spaces between the diamond rows are elongated, spotted dragon forms (which resemble a mixture between a sea horse and a giraffe) and combat groups between black and white animals. Several other animal forms can be seen, such as Chinese dragons and unicorns, and the carpet has a surrounding border of palmettes and arabesques.

No other dragon rug has the same complicated design structure. Although Erdmann's dating of this piece to around 1500 is probably too early, the carpet has a splendour unknown in any other example and if any dragon rug can be dated to the first half of the 16th century, this is it. Other early examples can be found in the Victoria and Albert Museum and in the Metropolitan. The Victoria and Albert piece comes closest to emulating the richness of the Graf rug; the Metropolitan example is a far more formal affair, although all three have virtually identical borders and have the serrate leaves of the lozenges alternately red and yellow at the top and bottom of each diamond. The Metropolitan carpet has three clearly demarcated lozenges per row, each of which is filled with a large, stylized palmette; the spaces between the rows have dragons rampant, either facing or back to back in alternate rows, and between each dragon is a large palmette. Although this dragon motif cannot be said to have degenerated, its stiffness and regularity mark out the carpet as being slightly later than the Berlin and London pieces, probably early seventeenth-century.

The second group, dating from the mid- to late 17th century, includes carpets in the Metropolitan Museum, two in the Textile Museum, Washington, two in Philadelphia, two in the Victoria and Albert Museum, two in Berlin and several in various private collections. In these carpets, the lozenge diaper, clearly discernible in the earlier pieces, begins to disintegrate and the elongated dragon forms become more schematic. There is also less wealth of detail, and a cruder colouring.

The third group, from the late 17th and early 18th centuries, shows an even greater degeneration of the original form. Examples are in Washington, Detroit and Berlin. Dimand also assigns the McMullan rug to this group, but this may be too late a dating. It retains many of the elements of the first group (including the border). It may well be part of the second group; the animal forms are still clearly recognizable although the diaper has that elongation typical of later pieces. McMullan himself, in an article in *The Connoisseur*, remarked that the border of his piece was 'identical' with that of the Persian Figdor garden carpet; this is certainly not true, although there is some similarity.

The Washington piece in this third group is the dated example referred to earlier.

Late eighteenth-century Kuba carpet with the avshan *design. Kufic borders. 12 ft. 9 in. × 5 ft. 1 in. (389 × 155 cm.).*

Kurdish copy of a Caucasian dragon rug. Signed 'Hasan Beg' and dated 'Muharram A.H. 1011' (October, A.D. 1689), 14 ft. 6 in. × 6 ft. (453 × 180 cm.). Textile Museum, Washington.

The Nigde carpet (detail). Traditionally attributed to Kuba, but possibly Shirvan or Shusha. Early 17th century. 24 ft. 8 in. × 10 ft. (752 × 305 cm.). The Metropolitan Museum of Art, New York, Gift of Joseph V. McMullan.

It shows the same formalism as the early Metropolitan carpet described above, and has particularly realistic deer as well as schematic dragons; the lattice, however, is no longer composed of realistically rendered serrated leaves, but of leaves stylized to the point of geometrical abstraction. There is also a certain static quality in the design. This odd mixture confused earlier writers; Kühnel for instance, remarked that the date of 1689 was unacceptable. However, this piece has now been recognized as a Kurdish copy of a dragon rug, an attribution which reconciles the contradictory nature of the design.

The rugs of the fourth group, dating from about 1750 to 1850, are naturally the most prevalent. With these pieces, the original format has become so geometric as to be almost unrecognizable. There are also some fine examples in the Soumak flat-weave technique. It is worth saying that, while we talk of the design of the dragon rugs as having degenerated, there is a distinct continuity of style, and many of the late examples are of fine quality. What we may also be dealing with is not so much a degeneration as a development from realism to abstraction, a perfectly acceptable progression in most art forms.

In the context of the dragon rugs, we should also mention the existence of a few animal carpets closely based on Persian prototypes, but with a schematization of motifs. We have mentioned in our section on Safavid carpets the often illustrated piece once on the Istanbul art market. This, like the tree carpets, is usually described as 'north-west Persian-Caucasian' and, although far more geometric in detail than the animal carpets from central Persia, it still retains enough realism to make an attribution to Kurdistan or southern Azerbaijan the most likely. The same remarks apply to the beautiful piece woven on a red ground given by Joseph V. McMullan to the Metropolitan Museum. This has trees, scattered flowers, deer and other game, eight horses, seven of which have riders, and two huntsmen on foot. The riders are suggested by the most schematic forms (indeed, they resemble birds more than humans), although the horses, despite their carousel colouring – white, dark blue, light blue, yellow or green, with multi-coloured spots – are more realistically rendered. The piece also has a wide palmette-and-escutcheon border atypical of Caucasian weaving.

80

138

Floral Rugs

Concurrent with the production of dragon rugs were the floral rugs, which are assigned by all early authorities to Kuba. However, Schürmann points out that although there is technical evidence to prove a northern Caucasian provenance for many of these pieces, there is also evidence to prove that many were woven by Armenians, probably in the southern Caucasus. The latter are often very long and, compared to the examples from Kuba, the colouring is dull; the weave is also much more coarse. There does, then, still remain some doubt as to the exact provenance of this category of rug.

There are three principal varieties of floral or blossom carpet with either a Caucasian or north west Persia-Caucasian provenance. The first consists of large pieces adapting many of the designs found in Persian vase carpets, and rugs from Herat. The second contains the tree rugs and the third has rows of individual palmettes. Of the first group, probably the greatest example is the Nigde carpet, the gift of Joseph V. McMullan to the Metropolitan Museum. Nearly twenty-five feet in length, this carpet may lay just claim to being the most splendid intact example of Caucasian weaving. It is datable to the early 17th century, and like the dragon carpets, is based on a transverse diamond lattice. The system reads $\frac{1}{2}-\frac{1}{2}-\frac{1}{2}$; $1-1$; $\frac{1}{2}-1-\frac{1}{2}$; $1-1$; $\frac{1}{2}-1-\frac{1}{2}$; $\frac{1}{2}-\frac{1}{2}$, thus giving the impression of an endless repeat. In the $1-1$ rows, the large lozenges are woven with dark blue-black grounds and contain cruciform motifs, which themselves contain four large palmettes springing from a cartwheel motif. On the other rows, the lozenges are either blue-yellow-blue or white-red-white. They contain large palmettes growing from an angular stem-system, and two large cloud-bands. On the bars of each lozenge, there are large palmettes. The character of the design, although typical of what we would expect from Caucasian weaving, retains very strong Chinese elements, and the stem system in the floral (as opposed to the cruciform) lozenges is reminiscent of the designs found in Khotan carpets from East Turkestan. Another fragmentary carpet of the same date is in the Berlin Museum, although this latter piece is woven on a blue ground.

143

Right: floral carpet (detail) of the shield group. Kuba or Shirvan, late 18th or early 19th century. 9 ft. × 5 ft. 3 in. (274 × 160 cm.). Far right: floral rug. Kuba or Shirvan, twentieth-century copy. 9 ft. 2 in. × 5 ft. 10 in. (279 × 178 cm.).

*Above left: floral carpet,
traditionally attributed to Kuba,
but possibly Shirvan or Shusha.
Mid-18th century. 6 ft. 2 in. ×
5 ft. 1 in. (188 × 155 cm.).
Above: floral rug, Kuba or
Shirvan, possibly 18th or 19th
century. 10 ft. 7 in. × 5 ft. 5 in.
(322 × 165 cm.). Metropolitan
Museum of Art, New York,
Theodore M. Davis Collection,
Bequest of Theodore M. Davis,
1915.*

As with the dragon carpets, the floral lattice design continued to be used for the next two centuries, although the system became more schematic and simplified. The large palmettes, cloud-bands and cruciform motifs were retained, but in formalized rows across the field. The nineteenth century rugs, as the examples in the Metropolitan attributed to Shirvan (Dimand catalogue nos. 168 and 169), retain the large palmettes, but the lozenge system has become skeletal. The design of no. 168, with its pseudo-Kufic border design derived from Anatolian weaving, is close to contemporaneous Kurdish weaving (although there are technical differences in the weave).

The tree carpets are problematic, in that they were probably woven in Kurdistan, as were the late garden carpets we have discussed in our Safavid section. Although many scholars catalogue the former group with Caucasian weaving and the latter with Persian, the tree carpets are usually woven with the Persian knot and the garden carpets with the Ghiordes or Turkish knot! Since these pieces were woven in an area which always was, and still is, part of Persia, we prefer to call them Persian, although recognizing, in the angularity and stylization of design, a close link with Caucasian weaving. However, one atypical piece is the carpet illustrated by Ulrich Schürmann in *Caucasian Rugs* (plate no. 2) which contains elements of both the tree and garden carpets and with a geometric flower and branch system reminiscent of the Nigde carpet. It also has a border of lyre-shaped floral motifs characteristic of Caucasian weaving and was probably made in Azerbaijan.

The third group consists of carpets with rows of individual flower forms which are often rendered with a considerable degree of abstraction. Such pieces are again associated with Kuba and the surrounding areas. The earliest examples probably date from the mid-18th century, and production continued throughout the 19th and into the 20th century. The floral forms in the earliest examples are often rendered as rows of flower heads of tulip-like form, but so geometric as to resemble shields; each 'shield' is flanked by two banners, which are, in fact, schematic wedge-like renderings of serrate leaves on stems. Another design,

Floral carpet traditionally attributed to Kuba, but possibly Shirvan or Shusha. 17th or 18th century. 9 ft. 11 in. × 7 ft. 10 in. (302 × 239 cm.).

of which there is a particularly fine example in the Metropolitan Museum, has rows of elongated formalized renderings of the Herati pattern, with two huge lanceolate leaves enclosing a ragged half-palmette.

Other designs consist of allover patterns of candelabra-like sprays of small flowers, which in later examples from the 19th century become so geometric as to resemble heraldic devices. The earliest pieces are obviously derived from Persian carpets of the late 17th century. From eighteenth-century Armenia came rugs with three poles on the long axis, broken at regular intervals with even more geometric renderings of the shield and banner motif described above; these are usually woven in a palette of red, blue and yellow on a white ground. Such allover designs continued to be among the most popular of all Caucasian decorative schemes. To some of the early Kuba examples, one of the most magnificent examples of which is the piece given by Joseph V. McMullan to the Metropolitan, can be traced the so-called 'eagle' motifs of the Chelaberd rugs made in the 19th and 20th centuries. The McMullan rug also has a border of cypress trees, motifs which are found in the field of an interesting Caucasian fragment in the Turk ve Islam museum; this latter piece, probably based on a Persian vase carpet, also has stylized renderings of people sitting in small pavilions. Before moving on to further discussion of nineteenth- and early twentieth-century Caucasian weaving, we should take note of the large, stepped medallion rugs which have been mentioned in connection with the problematical Persian 'Portuguese' carpets. There are examples of these rare Caucasian weavings in the Washington Textile Museum and in the Metropolitan Museum. Dimand describes the Metropolitan piece as a floral lozenge rug, and dates it to the 17th century. The centre of the field has a stepped star shape, from which radiate six stepped bands, thus giving the impression of a huge diamond, the sides of which are cut by the border. Within each band are blossoms on stems and small stylized birds. The central lozenge is woven with a cream ground, and the bands are salmon-pink, green, crimson, purple and yellow. The four corners of the field, woven with a cream ground, have trees, flowers and animals, including antelope and spotted deer.

Weaving in the 19th and 20th Centuries

Caucasian weaving of the last 180 years is a complicated affair. There is, as we have indicated earlier, an extraordinary multiplicity of cultural and ethnographical influences in the area. Other influences on weaving have been political, religious, and the considerable differences in climate and available pasture which occur between the high mountainous areas and the lowland. In recent years, the large numbers of Caucasian pieces on the market, and the fine quality of rugs made well into the 20th century, has caused much study of weaving in this area and there is now a well-organized body of scholarship. We can do no more than touch on some of the more obvious styles, and refer the reader interested in a more detailed discussion of the subject to specialist monographs such as Ulrich Schürmann's *Caucasian Rugs*.

In general, the designs and colours of Caucasian rugs are not in themselves sufficient to determine the place of origin with absolute certainty. There are, of course, some particularly well-documented designs which have been traced to source, but they represent only a small part of the exceptionally wide range of designs found in Caucasian weavings. The one important factor in determining the regions from which specific carpets originate is the type of wool used, and the length of pile. Heavy wool rugs are good insulators and the sheep reared in the mountainous districts grow a heavier, shaggier and longer fleece than those reared in the lowland areas. The rugs woven in the mountain villages have a richer, longer and heavier pile, and their colours tend to be hotter. Thus the areas which produce long-piled rugs are Kazak, Gendje, Lesghi, and several varieties of Karabagh; medium piles are found on Talish, Lenkoran and Daghestan weavings, and a fine low pile on Shirvan, Kuba and Baku rugs.

As to the proliferation of designs, there are some 350 different tribes in the area, speaking approximately 150 different dialects. The south-west, in the Armenia-Kazak area, is peopled by Christian Armenians; in the south-east are Tartars of Mongol descent, and Persians; to the north, the principal tribes are the Shirvans, Daghestans, Chechens and Lesghis, and to the north-west are Cherkesses (Circassians), the last-named a fair-skinned people who are the denominating factor in the 'Caucasian' description of European peoples. There are, of course, cultural and ethnic overlaps in all these areas. To give some indication of the difficulty in ascribing particular designs to specific locations, the Russian scholar S. Zerimov, in his study *Azerbaijan Carpets*, gave the names of 123 villages in the southern and mid-Caucasus which produced carpets of distinctive design. For the whole of the Caucasus, we would probably have to multiply this figure by a factor of at least four. Many of the schematic animal motifs found in Caucasian weavings can be traced back centuries, and are probably of Scythian origin.

For convenience, it is possible to divide the Caucasus into ten weaving areas: Kazak, Karabagh, Gendje, Talish, Moghan, Shirvan, Baku, Kuba, Daghestan and Derbend. It should be noted, however, that the generic name Kazak is often applied to a wide variety of Caucasian rugs which have not necessarily been woven in the Kazak district.

Kazak Weavings

Kazak consists of the western area of the Caucasus stretching from Erivan in the south to Tiflis in the north, and is not to be confused with the state of Kazakstan. Within the Armenia-Kazak area are several small towns and districts associated with certain well-known designs. The most important are (reading from south to north) Karatchoph, Karaklis, Idjevan, Lori-Pambak, Lambalo, Fachralo, Schulaver and Bordjalou. As we have indicated, the population is principally Armenian, although there is a high incidence of nomadic Kurdish tribesmen. It is from this region that many of the seventeenth-century floral carpets

Below: Kazak rug of the type attributed to Lori-Pambak. Late 19th century. 8 ft. 8 in. × 6 ft. (264 × 183 cm.). Bottom: Kazak rug of the type attributed to Bordjalou. Late 18th or early 19th century. 7 ft. × 4 ft. 1 in. (213.5 × 124.5 cm.).

11

Two Kazak prayer rugs. Right:
5 ft. 5 in. × 4 ft. 7 in. (165 ×
139.5 cm.). Below: 4 ft. 11 in. ×
3 ft. 7 in. (150 × 109 cm.).

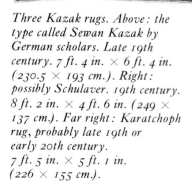

Three Kazak rugs. Above: the
type called Sewan Kazak by
German scholars. Late 19th
century. 7 ft. 4 in. × 6 ft. 4 in.
(230.5 × 193 cm.). Right:
possibly Schulaver. 19th century.
8 ft. 2 in. × 4 ft. 6 in. (249 ×
137 cm.). Far right: Karatchoph
rug, probably late 19th or
early 20th century.
7 ft. 5 in. × 5 ft. 1 in.
(226 × 155 cm.).

Chinese bronze mirror. Note the similarity of the central medallion to that on the Lori-Pambak rug. 1st century A.D. Victoria and Albert Museum, London.

with ascending designs originate, their strong Persian characteristic no doubt brought north by the Kurds.

The predominant motifs of the Kazak weavers appear to be highly stylized renderings of floral motifs, many of which would not be recognizable as such were it not for our knowledge of earlier Caucasian weavings. In a number of eighteenth- and early nineteenth-century pieces not assignable to any particular district, there is an ascending pole-like structure, which is obviously a schematic rendering of the degenerated lozenge system of the dragon rugs. These rugs, like many Caucasian weavings, are characterized by large blocks of plain colour – red, blues, greens and yellows predominating. Within the pole medallions there may often be found scorpion motifs realistically rendered on earlier pieces, but totally unrecognizable on later ones. In fact, it is probable that these are not representations of scorpions but, like the 'birds' of Ushak carpets, merely stylized renderings of floral motifs.

The designs of the Bordjalou district may be recognized fairly easily. The field pattern 147 generally consists of various single motifs woven on a red ground. These are obviously stylized renderings of scattered floral patterns. The shapes vary from rug to rug, some having serrated diamonds, others multi-coloured octagons, and others hexagons. Some examples have large hooked motifs in the borders with three or more large hooked diamonds on the long axis in the field, surrounded by scattered floral motifs; these are exceptionally colourful pieces. This layout is fairly often found on Caucasian weavings. Other Bordjalous have a row of quadrangles on the long axis, surrounded by geometrical motifs of a floral nature.

The Fachralos, Lori-Pambaks, some Karatchophs and many of the rugs described 147 simply as Kazaks have designs which have become almost synonymous with Caucasian weaving. These consist frequently of one or two large medallions – hooked or starred octagons – with small geometric motifs, or flower heads, at either end of the field. Within the central medallions are smaller motifs, either octagons or stylized cruciforms, the latter similar to those found on early Chinese bronzes. There is usually a strong echoing of colour from one area of a

Top: Armenian Kazak rug dated in Western Arabic numerals A.D. 1890. 7 ft. 4 in. × 4 ft. 3 in. (213 × 129 cm.). Above: Karabagh rug from Chondzoresk of the type once called 'cloud-band Kazak'. Early 19th century. 8 ft. 5 in. × 5 ft. 5 in. (257 × 165 cm.).

Karabagh rug from Chelaberd, of the type called 'eagle Kazak'. Mid-19th century. 7 ft. × 4 ft. 10 in. (208 × 147.5 cm.).

rug to another. A variation is to have one huge cruciform medallion running the entire length and width of the field, with stylized tree and floral motifs in the four remaining corners of the field.

Karabagh Weavings

To the east of the Armenian-Kazak region is Karabagh. The principal weaving towns and areas are Chelaberd, Chondzoresk, Shusha, Channik and Goradiz; there are also embroidered pieces, woven by nomadic Kurdish tribesmen, called Kasim-Ushags. The most famous Karabagh pieces are the Chelaberds; these have a huge cruciform medallion in white with a large blue or green centre cross. There is some resemblance between these medallions and the

Russian double-headed eagle, with the result that in the carpet trade they have become known as 'Adler' or 'eagle Kazaks'. Of course, they are not from Kazak and the medallions, as can be seen from earlier Caucasian weavings, such as the large McMullan rug mentioned above, are almost certainly stylizations of floral motifs. On the earliest examples, there are usually only one or two medallions in the field down the long axis, with a huge hooked bar at either end. The total medallion-and-bar form, therefore, may be a gargantuan stylization of the Herati pattern found, albeit in stylized but clearly recognizable form, on seventeenth- and eighteenth-century Caucasian pieces. There are also examples with no bars, and simplified medallions of St. Andrew's cross form but without the centre cross; there may be three or four such medallions down the centre of the field, and Schürmann has suggested that they are probably eighteenth-century forerunners of the later pieces of more complicated design. On the very late examples, woven from around 1800 until comparatively recent times, the colours are duller and there may be three or four medallions down the centre of the field separated by straight horizontal bars.

Other rugs from the Karabagh district exhibit a wide range of design. From Chondzoresk come rugs with three conjoined octagons down the centre of the field containing motifs made up from flat, worm-like cloud-bands characteristic of many types of Caucasian weaving. Not surprisingly, this type used to be known in the trade as 'cloud-band Kazaks', a nomenclature which, unlike 'eagle Kazaks', has largely disappeared from modern carpet literature. Carpets with conjoined serrate-edged bands forming a lozenge diaper were also produced in this area; examples woven with pale, pastel borders are attributed to Channik. Unusual designs of a repeat pattern of red, red-brown, pink and cream *botehs* (the large curving leaf or palm pattern associated with Persian weaving) on a black ground were woven at Goradiz, and in

Above left: prayer rug, probably Chan Karabagh, but possibly Marasali. Early 19th century. 6 ft. 2 in. × 3 ft. 4 in. (188 × 110 cm.). Above: Karabagh rug; late 19th or early 20th century. 6 ft. 10 in. × 4 ft. 9 in. (208 × 145 cm.). Below: detail of a Karabagh corridor carpet in the European taste. Dated A.H. 1294 (A.D. 1877). 15 ft. 9 in. × 5 ft. 4 in. (480 × 162.5 cm.).

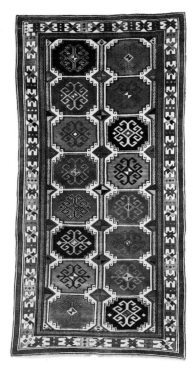

Moghan rug. The characteristic layout of two rows of hooked octagons should be compared with the motifs found on carpets in early Flemish paintings. Early 19th century. 8 ft. 6 in. × 4 ft. 1 in. (259 × 124 cm.).

Karabagh carpet made for the Western market. 19th century. 18 ft. 9 in. × 7 ft. 1 in. (570 × 216 cm.).

the Shusha district there were woven rugs with a rich red field with a pole medallion running the whole length of the field and surrounded by geometric motifs representing vases of flowers and *botehs*. The unusual aspect of the last-named design is that all the field motifs are not woven 'solid', but in a way which resembles filigree; indeed, these rather unattractive pieces bear a resemblance to the more commercial types of Indian filigree work.

From Shusha, as from other areas of the Caucasus, come rugs with floral medallions containing bouquets of roses. The first rugs with this type of decoration, alien to the Oriental tradition, were produced around 1800 and continued to be made throughout the 19th century. They were the direct result of contact with officers of the Russian army, and the diplomats who followed in their wake; the Russians wished to utilize the weaving skills of the areas which they conquered for the production of rugs in the European – specifically French – style to fit in with the French furniture and decorations of their homes. Although there is nothing slavishly imitative about these Caucasian rugs, the weavers were obviously not comfortable with the strictly representational designs of French carpets, and the result is a strange mixture of authentic Caucasian motifs with French floral patterning. Many such pieces, however, are surprisingly attractive.

Adjoining Karabagh to the south is a region called the Karadagh; the rugs woven here are similar to Karabaghs, but the region's closer proximity to Persia gives the weavings a softer, more Persian, quality. The fields usually have a design based upon Persian bar-and-escutcheon medallions and corners, with small stylized human, animal and bird figures in the field, as well as typically Caucasian stylized floral motifs.

Gendje Weavings

To the north of Karabagh is the Gendje region. The rugs produced here have a wide range of designs emanating from the surrounding districts of Kazak, Karabagh and Shirvan. The town of Genje itself was called Elizabethpol by the Russians. The rugs are largely woven by Armenians and therefore structurally resemble those made in the Armenia-Kazak area; the finest pieces have a silky, thick wool with a long pile, although the quality of pieces varies greatly. Some rugs have six or eight squares in the field containing X-form medallions, the squares being surrounded by stars. Rugs with large hooked diamonds and octagons, surrounded by small stars on an open field, can also be found. One of the favourite designs, common to many other regions of the Caucasus, was a field decorated in its entirety with diagonal bars of different colours; these bars usually contain floral forms and can be of varying widths. On pieces with wide bars, *botehs* will often be found. Many such pieces are very long in relation to the width and were obviously intended for use as runners or corridor carpets. There are also rugs with one huge medallion – formalized renderings of the medallion-and-bar motif of Persian carpets – woven with large blocks of bright colour on a red ground, and surrounded by stylized *botehs* and geometric forms.

Moghan Rugs

The rugs of the Moghan Steppes are rare. In general, they conform to a basic pattern. The colours, compared to many of the rugs we have discussed, are subdued, although the design as a whole has a subtle polychromy. The most usual design is a double row of hooked octagons down the field. These octagons are filled with either stars, hooked cruciform medallions or the stylized design found often on Caucasian weavings and referred to in older literature as the 'tarantula', which, again, is probably fanciful.

Talish Weavings

East of Moghan, on the coast of the Caspian Sea, is Talish. Carpets from this area are particularly well woven with a fine soft wool of medium pile. The sizes of Talish carpets are always between about 3 and 5 feet by about 7½ to 10 feet in length. One of the most famous Talish designs has a long narrow field of monochrome blue or blue-green without any decoration, except for a serrated edge of a contrasting colour. It is surrounded by four guard and border stripes, the wide border having a series of round floral motifs. The borders in total are about one and a half times the width of the field. A very fine example of this type, sold at auction by Lefèvre in London in 1976 had a field piled in several shades of blue and blue-green; in the centre was a small cream quadrangle containing an inscription and the date 1851. Other Talish rugs have the same general layout, but the field is filled with star motifs within an octagonal lattice, or with myriad small polychrome stars resembling flower heads. Rarer are the designs of three hooked diamonds on the long axis, the edges of which are echoed by a wide parallel zig-zag on either side, in the channels of which are parallel rows of small petaloid motifs.

In the Talish area is the coastal town of Lenkoran which produces carpets differing in design from the main Talish types. One has an enormous series of *boteh* medallions and scorpion-like bars in the field. A superb example illustrated by Schürmann and dating from the 18th century, is woven in a rich subtle palette of red, aubergine, green, blue, brown, yellow, cream and purple on a dark blue-black field with a reciprocal trefoil border in red-brown and white. Another design, again on a blue-black field, has a series of large and small octagons and cruciform medallions down the length of the field. The large octagons are flanked by S-shaped motifs which, it is reasonable to suppose, were derived from earlier dragon carpets.

Shirvan Weavings

The rugs of the Shirvan area, between Karabagh and Daghestan on the shores of the Caspian, are among the finest woven in the Caucasus, with the area being one of the most prolific producers of weavings. There are a number of small towns and villages with which particular designs can be associated – Chajli, Marasali, Bidjov and Akstafa, as well as the generic name Shirvan. Almost all the designs we have encountered previously can be found on Shirvan weavings. We have mentioned the ascending designs of rows of floral palmettes of shield-like form, which were woven in eighteenth-century Shirvan. Other examples have more realistic flowers contained within an overall lattice possibly derived from Persian vase carpets; in some of the early examples, from the 18th and beginning of the 19th centuries, parts of the flowers are woven in silk.

There are also early eighteenth-century pieces, the designs of which seem to mark an intermediate stage between dragon rugs and the pieces from Chelaberd – the eagle Kazaks. Schürmann has suggested that this transmogrification of design may have been a conscious attempt on the part of the weavers to avoid changing the three-dimensional animals and flowers of earlier carpets into a two-dimensional rug pattern.

Moghan rug. 19th century. 6 ft. 11 in. × 4 ft. (211 × 122 cm.).

Below, left to right: Shirvan rug from Chajli; late 18th or early 19th century. 7 ft. 7 in. × 4 ft. 3 in. (231 × 129.5 cm.). Shirvan rug, possibly from Marasali; late 19th century; 6 ft. 1 in. × 5 ft. 5 in. (185.5 × 104 cm.). Talish rug of typical design; mid-19th century; 7 ft. 6 in. × 3 ft. 1 in. (228 × 94 cm.).

Right: Shirvan rug of the type called Akstafa. Late 19th century. 8 ft. 2 in. × 3 ft. 11 in. (249 × 119 cm.). Far right: one of a pair of Shirvan long rugs. Late 19th century. 13 ft. × 3 ft. (396 × 91.5 cm.).

Kuba rug from the village of Chichi. The slanting band and rosette border is a characteristic feature. Early 19th century. 4 ft. 6 in. × 3 ft. 2 in. (137 × 96.5 cm.).

There are eighteenth-century carpets from north Shirvan with large cruciform medallions on the long axis, separated by smaller motifs reminiscent of those found on the Chelaberds; there are also single flower heads on angular yellow stems, small free-standing palmettes and cloud-bands. Woven on a red ground, many of the decorative elements are of Persian inspiration. However, the overall impression is that such pieces may well have derived their design from star Ushaks. The cross medallions suggest that they were probably woven by Armenians.

Many varieties of large geometric medallion rugs were woven in Shirvan, in common with other Caucasian districts. One particular type is woven with a palette consisting of various shades of two colours, yellow and blue being the most prevalent combination. There are also pieces woven with geometric rows of cloud-bands and octagons, particularly associated, as we shall see, with Perepedil.

To the Chajli are attributed carpets with a design of three large octagons on the long axis containing stylized tree motifs; the surrounding field is filled with scattered flowers and hooked diamonds, the motifs associated with certain classes of Turkoman weaving. The fields of these pieces are either red, blue or, very rarely, white. Small floral rugs were woven in Bidjov, the brilliant polychromy of the field contrasting with the austere dark blue-black ground. The carpets and runners of Akstafa again have a brilliant polychromy, and are distinguished by the invariable use of highly stylized birds and animals, combined with large geometric medallions and scattered flowerheads. They are close to Persian tribal weavings.

Baku Weavings

Roughly midway up the Caspian coast is the Aspheron peninsular on which is located the town of Baku; here, and in the surrounding towns – Surahani, Chila and Saliani – are woven distinctive Caucasian rugs. Compared to many other types of Caucasian weaving, the Baku rugs have a fairly subdued palette, without loss of the subtle polychromy which is one of the chief virtues of weaving from the Caucasus. Like some Shirvan pieces, the characteristic palette of Baku weavings is duochromatic: yellow and blue. Chila rugs have a wider use of colour; one type, called in the trade the 'Boteh-Chila' has, as its name implies, a field woven with polychrome *botehs* and serrate-edged octagons (although in some examples there are simply rows of large *botehs* in the field). On some examples, small birds and animals are found in the borders. The so-called 'Arshan-Chila' is similar to designs found on some early Turkish carpets, and we will discuss this motif in our following section on Kuba rugs. Surahanis have large pole medallions surrounded by, and enclosing, scattered floral motifs; the borders are frequently pseudo-Kufic. Saliani is close to Talish and the rugs are similar in shape and overall effect; the Saliani pieces, however, are less formal and have a greater use of scattered floral decoration.

Kuba Weavings

In the area between Shirvan and Daghestan in the eastern Caucasus is Kuba which, with its surrounding villages, is the most prolific and justly celebrated source of Caucasian weaving. The principal villages are Konagend, Perepedil, Sejshour, Zejwa, Chichi, Dara-Chichi and Karagashli. The variety and richness of design and colour is extraordinary and no generalized statement can be made about Kuba weaving.

As we have noted, many of the dragon rugs and floral designs possibly emanated from the Kuba region which would thus have probably the longest weaving history in the Caucasus. Many of the floral pieces relate to Persian vase rugs; the dragon carpets have been attributed by some scholars to a Persian inspiration, while others have suggested a closer link with early Seljuk weaving. It is noticeable that amongst eighteenth- and nineteenth-century carpets from north Shirvan and Kuba, there are many examples with a mixed floral-medallion field and pseudo-Kufic borders, which seem to derive at least in part from small pattern Holbein rugs. Erdmann, in *Oriental Carpets*, illustrates a fine example (plate no. 11) which he attributes to Kuba, *c.* 1800. Kendrick and Tattersall illustrate another (plate no. 119) which has the same field, but a geometric palmette border. An identical piece (it may indeed be the same) is illustrated in Schürmann's *Caucasian Rugs* (no. 96) and another with the same Kufic borders but a field design of scattered star-like floral motifs is in the Metropolitan Museum, attributed by Dimand to early nineteenth-century Shirvan. Schürmann also illustrates another piece (no. 95) which has a more floral, Persian design in the field, but again has Kufic

Top: pictorial rug attributed to Shirvan, but possibly Kurdish, c. 1880. 5 ft. 7 in. × 3 ft. 9 in. (170 × 140 cm.). Above: Baku rug of the type known in the trade as 'Boteh-Chila' (or 'Hilah'). 19th century. 12 ft. 5 in. × 5 ft. 3 in. (377 × 160 cm.).

Below, top, left to right : Kuba rug from Perepedil ; dated three times at the top in the Christian calendar, 1901 ; 6 ft. 10 in. × 5 ft. 5 in. (208 × 165 cm.). Kuba rug from the village of Chichi ; 10 ft. 8 in. × 5 ft. 4 in. (325 × 162.5 cm.). Star Kuba floral runner dated A.H. 1301 (A.D. 1884) ; 14 ft. 2 in. × 4 ft. (432 × 122 cm.). Below, bottom, left to right : Kuba rug from Perepedil ; dated in both the Christian and Islamic calendars, A.H. 1324 and A.D. 1906 ; 6 ft. 6 in. × 4 ft. 1 in. (198 × 124 cm.). Kuba rug possibly from Konagend ; second half of the 19th century ; 5 ft. 11 in. × 4 ft. (130 × 122 cm.). Karabagh floral rug from Chila ; 19th century ; 8 ft. 4 in. × 3 ft. 8 in. (254 × 112 cm.).

borders; what we would describe as a Caucasian version of small pattern Holbeins is known as the *arshan* design and is found in both Karabagh and Chila weavings.

The majority of Kuba rugs of the 19th century display crowded floral motifs, either free standing, combined with large geometric motifs, or retained within an allover lattice. Konagend pieces tend towards a greater geometricity of motif, whilst the pieces from Perepedil, which are often woven in a sombre palette of yellow, brown and blue on a black ground, display a large handle-bar motif in rows which may be derived from cloud-bands, but which is referred to by Caucasian scholars as the ram's horn (*wurma*) design; this is alternated with other bar medallions and serrated diamonds, and the intervening field has rows of stylized flowers, humans and animals. This is among the most distinctive of all Caucasian designs. Perepedil also produced small rugs woven with a stylized version of the Herati pattern in the field. The rugs of Chichi and Dara-Chichi, two small villages situated to the south-west of Kuba, usually have a dark blue ground filled with small stepped polygons interlocking so as to form a large irregular shape. The border has flower heads alternating with diagonal bands. The characteristic Karagashli design is one of slanting irregular rhomboids in red, usually on a blue field. The rugs of Sejshour are found in a variety of floral and geometric designs, frequently having large St. Andrew's cross medallions. There are also Russian-influenced carpets woven with rows of roses.

It should be noted that in earlier rug books the trade name 'Cabistan' was applied to many varieties of east Caucasian rugs, before proper identification became available. This word, which applies to no known tribe or village, has now largely disappeared.

Kuba rug of Lesghi design, with the typical stars associated with Lesghistan tribal weaving. Mid-19th century. 5 ft. 8 in. × 4 ft. 7 in. (173 × 140 cm.).

Rugs of Daghestan and Lesghistan

The two most north-easterly Caucasian provinces are Daghestan and Lesghistan, the former inhabited by the Chechis and the latter by the Lesghis. However, the Lesghis themselves are found in Daghestan and there is little difference between the rugs of both areas. Some particularly fine pieces were woven here in the late 17th and early 18th centuries. The beautiful dragon rugs in the Soumak technique are attributed to Daghestan, as are some magnificent pieces with rows of shield medallions containing heraldic-like devices which are, in fact, stylized flowers. These latter pieces are usually woven in predominant yellows and blues on a red ground. To the particular Daghestan village of Mahatschkala are attributed rugs with long pole medallions interlocking with seven to eight small octagons per pole, which themselves contain the usual stylized floral motifs. An interesting example illustrated by Schürmann has a wide border containing motifs resembling those found on bird Ushaks and on certain Turkoman *juvals*, especially those of the Yomut.

Daghestan also produced long corridor rugs, which can contain a variety of floral motifs including interlocking rows of multi-coloured stepped octagons. To the Lesghis are attributed rugs with three or four large geometric motifs down the centre of the field; in one example, three star-like medallions in white alternate with blue rectangles, the rectangles containing repeats of the star medallion in green. Within each of the resulting five star medallions there is a small octagon, each one of which is woven with a different geometrical motif in the centre; the surrounding field contains tiny scattered floral and geometric motifs and one small stylized quadruped.

Kuba prayer rug close in design to Daghestan pieces. 19th century, 5 ft. × 3 ft. 4 in. (152.5 × 101.5 cm.).

Derbend Weavings

On the Daghestan coast is the town of Derbend, which produces carpets in a variety of styles culled from the other regions of the Caucasus and generally of a medium to poor quality One particularly nasty carpet illustrated in *Caucasian Rugs* is assigned by Schürmann to Derbend; woven with realistic (by Caucasian standards) pink, white and blue roses with green leaves on a pale rust-red ground, it is attributed to around 1800 or even earlier.

Prayer Rugs

139 The Caucasus produced prayer rugs in great numbers, and there do not seem to have been any qualms about weaving into them figures of humans and animals. Indeed, the field and border patterns remain close to those of secular rugs and are distinguished only by the typically Caucasian six-sided geometrical mihrab arch and spandrels woven at the top of the field. Many of the pieces with field patterns of overall rows of *botehs*, flowers or flowers within a lattice have the mihrab arch woven rather incongruously on top.

Weaving of the Turkoman and Baluchi Tribes

Turkoman Weaving

Turkoman weavings were produced predominantly in the three Soviet states of Turkmenistan, Karakalpakstan and Uzbekistan. The primary influences on the life and culture of these warlike regions have been Mongolian and Turkish and many of the motifs found in Turkoman weavings can be traced to these sources.

The origins of existing Turkoman weaving are a matter of some controversy. The traditional view was that the Turkomans, being essentially nomadic peoples, used their carpets as functional objects in their everyday life and did not regard them in any special way. Thus the weavings had a comparatively short life. This view was enforced by the fact that, although weaving has been known in this region for many centuries, only pieces of a comparatively recent date seem to have survived. More recent scholarship, however, has not accepted this hypothesis in its entirety. It seems clear that the Turkomans did regard their weavings with respect and looked after them. It has also been established that they wove pieces not only for use in their tents (*kibitkas*) but also for urban dwellings. Near large cities, such as Merv, Pendeh and Khiva, semi-nomadic tribes would weave rugs for barter. Such pieces are often considerably larger than those intended for tribal use.

However, no known Turkoman carpets can be dated as early as surviving Turkish, Persian, Caucasian and Indian pieces. The only real point of controversy is whether certain existing pieces, obviously of considerable age, should be dated to the 18th or early 19th centuries. In this, scholarship seems neatly divided, although the more likely view is that no Turkoman carpets can be dated before 1800 with any degree of certainty and this view does not seem likely to be seriously challenged in the near future.

As we have noted several times in our foregoing sections, many early carpets bear a stylistic resemblance to nineteenth-century Turkoman weavings. Even the Pazyryk rug, with its layout of formal geometric and floral motifs, can be taken as an ancestor of this group. Among the Seljuk fragments are many pieces which bear the characteristic octagonal motifs of Turkoman weavings. The Swedish scholar Carl Johann Lamm, in an essay published in 1973, reconstructed from fragments of Seljuk pieces excavated in Fostat, the field patterns of whole carpets which, although dating from the 13th and 14th centuries, could

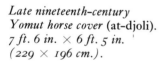

Late nineteenth-century
Yomut horse cover (at-djoli).
7 ft. 6 in. × 6 ft. 5 in.
(229 × 196 cm.).

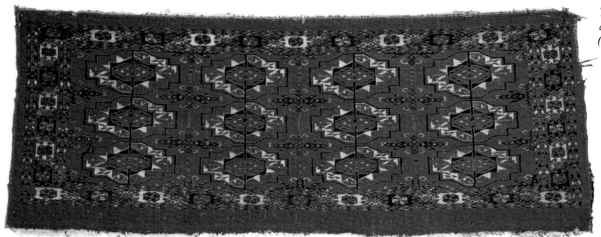

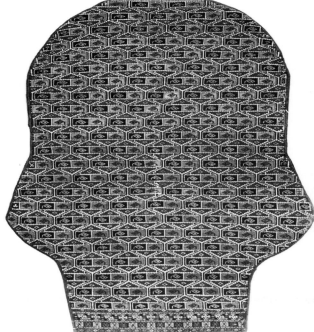

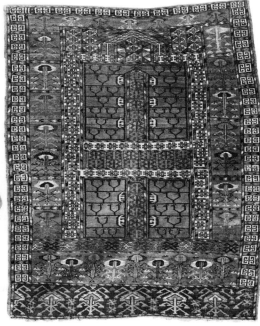

have been woven by the Saryks or Yomuts in the last century. Similarly, stylistic features of later Ottoman, Safavid and Caucasian weavings are found in Turkoman pieces.

Although scholarship in the last few years has devoted much time to chronology, stylistic development, technical structure, tribal inter-relationships and the resultant movements of particular design features, it is still possible to make two general and basic statements. Turkoman weavings have a predominant colour scheme of red, red-brown and red-blue; and, secondly, the principal decorative motif is the 'gul' (variously spelled 'ghul', 'ghol' or 'gol'). This is an octagon, or variant on that geometric form, with differing motifs contained within it.

The Turkoman Gul

There are two theories about the gul; it is the Persian word for flower, and one theory is that it is merely a highly formalized floral motif. The second hypothesis may not necessarily be a contradiction of this but an amplification; it was first put forward by the Russian scholar W. G. Moshkova (who was also responsible for the first systematic classification of the various types of Turkoman weavings and their uses.) She suggested that the gul was not so much a flower as a tribal symbol – a heraldic device. Each tribe had its own distinctive gul, which appeared or disappeared according to the tribe's fortune. Since many tribes were established as autonomous entities in central Asia by the 15th century, Moshkova's theory presupposes that such tribes had also established their right to a specific rendering of the gul by this time, which remained their exclusive use until they were absorbed or conquered or simply died out. Of course, no Turkoman weavings of such an early date survive, nor did the Turkoman tribes have a written history. However, since distinctive forms of guls are still used as one of the most accurate ways of making tribal attributions, when taken in conjunction with highly sophisticated structural analysis, Madame Moshkova's theories cannot be dismissed as being too conjectural. These two generalizations apart, there are four principal aspects of Turkoman weaving.

Structure in Turkoman Weaving

The structural analysis to which we have referred above, is a highly complex science, which has been developed in latter years by such scholars as May Beattie, Siawosch Azadi, Charles Grant Ellis, Ulrich Schürmann and Jon Thompson. It is a skill which requires a deep knowledge of comparative weaving methods, since the establishment of different tribes or areas by reference to structure, as opposed to design, which is an easy but unreliable and frequently contradictory guide, necessitates the scholar working with a large group of pieces of a similar decorative scheme. This is particularly true of Turkoman carpets, and structural analysis is now an important branch of carpet scholarship, and many of the attributions of Turkoman weaving which we will be using have resulted from it.

Turkoman Tribes

The second aspect is the understanding of the various tribes which make up the Turkoman peoples, since modern literature refers to the weavings of this area not by any generic term, as was the case in the past, but by specific tribal names. The most often encountered are the Tekke, the Yomut, the Salor, the Saryk, the Chaudor (or Chodor), the Ersari and their sub-tribes of the Beshir, Kizil-Ayak and Arabatchi, and the Karakalpak. Weavings produced by Turkoman tribes in Afghanistan were known as Afghans in the carpet trade, but the classi-fication of distinctive styles and their attribution to various tribes and sub-tribes has also been attempted recently by George O'Bannon and others. Carpets were, and in some cases still are, also referred to by the names of the places in which they were woven or marketed; thus we find descriptions like Merv, Pendeh, Khiva and Bokhara. Such names were often used by the carpet trade to distinguish particular designs before tribal classification became as reliable as it is today. The worst abuse was the term 'Bokhara', which was applied to any carpet which looked like a Tekke. This abuse lingers on in the modern carpet industry with the term 'Pakistani Bokhara'! 'Pendeh' is still used by scholars to describe fine old Turkoman weavings which cannot necessarily be ascribed to any particular tribe.

Woven Utensils and Decorations

The third aspect is the classification of the different types of Turkoman weaving in terms of their function. As important as carpets are the different types of objects woven for everyday use by nomadic peoples; on these objects – bags, tent hangings of many kinds, animal trappings, etc. – was lavished the same degree of care as on the carpets, and in the analysis of Turkoman styles, they are certainly as significant.

For use in the tent itself were the following objects:

The main carpet (khali) Most carpets intended for use in the tent do not exceed ten feet in length. However, Chaudor and Ersari-Beshir pieces are frequently longer, as are pieces woven in the more settled encampments near large towns, intended for com-mercial sale in the urban centres.

Odshak bashi This a U-shaped rug for use in the tent as a stove surround, two often being used together to form a circle. Rarely found.

Dip khali Small rugs used on the floor at the tent opening.

Engsi Rugs made for the entrance to the tent in place of doors. They have a characteristic cross-shaped motif, which has led them to being called *hatchli engsi* or simply *hatchli*. It was once thought that they were used as prayer rugs.

Kapunuk A three-sided weaving for use as a tent entrance surround.

Yolami, bou or yup Narrow woven bands flat-woven in white, with the designs in pile. They encircled the interior of the tent, covering up the join between the lower sections and the roof poles. A band can attain lengths of up to sixty-five feet.

Namazlyk and aytalyk The former is a prayer rug and the latter a funeral rug used to take the deceased to the grave but not buried with him. The *namazlyks* are often mihrab-shaped – that is, they have three straight sides and an arched top side.

Salatchyk These resemble small *namazlyks*, but were used as cot rugs for small children.

The second group of Turkoman weavings consists of many types of bags:

159 *Juval or chuval* The largest of the bags which, when not in use as containers, were used as decorative hangings in the tent. They have either pile or flat-woven fronts and either flat-woven backs, or ones consisting of canvas decorated with a thin strip of polychrome embroidery.

Mafrash (or kap) A narrow bag usually measuring 2–3 feet in width by about one foot in depth. A small type, the *aina kap*, is a mirror-bag.

Torba A bag about the same width as the *juval* but half the depth; in other words, a slightly larger version of the *mafrash*.

Tutash or tudadj or ghazan tutash Small pentagonal weavings about eight inches across, and made in pairs joined at the top by a thin woven band. Used as pan-holders.

Dis or duz torba Small hexagonal bag used for storing salt.

Boktsche A very rare type of bag consisting of four triangular flaps sown down at the base to a flat-woven square.

Darak bash or dokme darak A small pentagonal pouch used as a comb cover.

Chemche torba Long narrow bag twice as deep as wide, used for storing articles such as spoons.

Tufek bash Long thin bags used as gun covers.

Khordjin Joined pairs of small bags used for slinging over the saddle of a horse or camel. Ubiquitous in the Middle East and woven in a variety of techniques.

The third group of weavings are those made for the ornamentation of camels and horses during ceremonial occasions such as weddings. They are as follows:

158 *At-djoli (or tainaktshe or konaktsha)* Large polygonal horse blankets, pile or flat-woven.

Tsherlik (or eyerlik) Small saddle covers with three straight sides and an arched top which has a slit in the centre to accommodate the pommel. Another variety is hemispherical.

Khalyk An ornamental weaving looking much like a small *kapunuk*, but with an added arrowhead section in the centre of the lower edge. According to Moshkova, they were used for decorating the breasts of camels during wedding processions, and seem only to have been woven by the Tekke. Azadi interviewed an old Tekke tribesman in Meshed who said that they had been used 'a long time ago' to decorate the exterior of the door of the litter (*kadjaveh*) in which the bride was carried. These weavings are now becoming extremely rare.

Below left: Yomut asmalyk *or camel flank hanging. Mid- to late 19th century. 3 ft. 9 in. × 2 ft. 5 in. (114 × 74 cm.). Below: a late nineteenth-century or early twentieth-century Pende* juval *face, adopting the Salor turreted gul. 5 ft. 9 in. × 3 ft. 4 in. (175 × 102 cm.).*

Djah dizluk Small pentagonal weavings made in pairs to decorate the front knees of camels.

Uk bash (or ukudshi) Conical bags made to fit over the ends of the bundles of tent rods which were bound to the flanks of a camel during the wedding procession. They have mistakenly been called camel hats or covers for water vessels. Usually woven in pairs, only Yomut examples are known.

Asmalyk (or asmalik) Large pentagonal weavings to decorate the flanks of camels. Owing to a mis-translation, these are sometimes mistakenly called *osmalduks*.

At-torba Bag similar to the *chemche torba* used as a feed bag for horses.

At-chechi Long knotted girth for horses.

Many of the small pieces, especially *mafrashes*, *torbas*, *asmalyks* and the smaller bags, as well as a few of the larger pieces like *kapunuks*, have long tasselled fringes. On many bags, these can be dark blue and two or three times as long as the bag's depth. The majority of bags have lost their canvas or flat-woven backs, which were removed to lessen the weight of bales sent to Europe in vast numbers at the turn of the century and during the 1920s and 1930s. We should emphasize once again that these small pieces are frequently of superb quality and often display designs unknown in larger pieces.

Turkoman Design

The fourth important aspect of Turkoman weaving is the design. As we have said, the characteristic, though not invariable, motif is the octagon, called the gul. The guls are woven in parallel rows on the large carpets and on many of the *juvals* and larger bags. The smaller pieces just as often do not have guls, but some other geometric motif. The recognition of the gul type is one of the most crucial, and superficially one of the easiest ways, of recognizing specific tribal origin. We say superficially, because there is some truth to Moshkova's thesis concerning the waxing and waning of tribal guls according to the fortunes of the tribe, in which context she speaks of 'living' and 'dead' guls. Although her emphasis might be thought incorrect, one of the most complex aspects of Turkoman design is that, as tribes were absorbed and sub-tribes evolved, the guls of one group were adopted by another.

Thus the form of a gul may be taken as evidence of a particular tribal origin but not as proof that it was actually woven by that tribe on the piece at which we are looking. To give

Tekke juval *face adopting the Salor turreted gul. Mid- to late 19th century. Approximately 4 ft. × 2 ft. 6 in. (122 × 76 cm.). Victoria and Albert Museum, London.*

one quick example, the famous turreted gul of the Salor, which we discuss below, appears on weavings by the Tekke and other tribes after the Salor submitted to wars and forced migration and virtually died out as an autonomous unit. The appearance of their gul on many Tekke pieces in the second half of the 19th century and later is evidence of what we already know, that the Tekke were primarily responsible for the decimation of the Salor. It must also be remembered that many tribes had more than one distinctive gul of their own.

Salor Weavings

Of the tribes we have listed, it is assumed that the Salor are the oldest. Originally the most powerful of the Turkomans, centuries of war and decimation scattered them to the north near Bokhara and to the south into Afghanistan. As with the other tribes, we have no real concept of what Salor weaving in the 15th, 16th and 17th centuries looked like. They may have displayed the same degree of continuity as is found in Turkish village and nomad weaving, or the designs may have become steadily more schematic over the years, as is true of Caucasian weaving. However, the turreted gul of the Salor is considered among the most archaic of all Turkoman designs.

The Salor turreted gul is at once the most celebrated of Turkoman designs and the most difficult because of its use by other tribes. It exemplifies the problems inherent in Turkoman weaving design analysis, as do the motifs of the Salor in general. The Salor turreted gul has an outer edge of between twenty-four and twenty-seven star points from which spring hooked stems (a form known in European Gothic art). The inner field of the gul, often woven in rose-coloured silk, has a further twelve to sixteen hooked star points. In the centre is a hooked cruciform design called, according to Azadi, *aina-kotshak* (*aina* = mirror, *kotshak* = ram). In the field between the major guls are minor guls, crosses made up of thirteen small squares with a central *aina-kotshak* motif. What we have described is one of the characteristic field patterns of very old Salor *juvals*. At the base, there is a skirt of about four to six inches decorated with between twelve and twenty double diagonal rows of three-stemmed flower sprays, the stem of each double row alternately blue and red. The basic field and border colour is a tan red. The details are in pink (the centres of the major and minor guls), two or three different shades of red, two shades of blue, brown and yellow.

Tekke carpet. Second half of the 19th century. 12 ft. × 5 ft. 9 in. (364 × 175 cm.), including flat-woven ends.

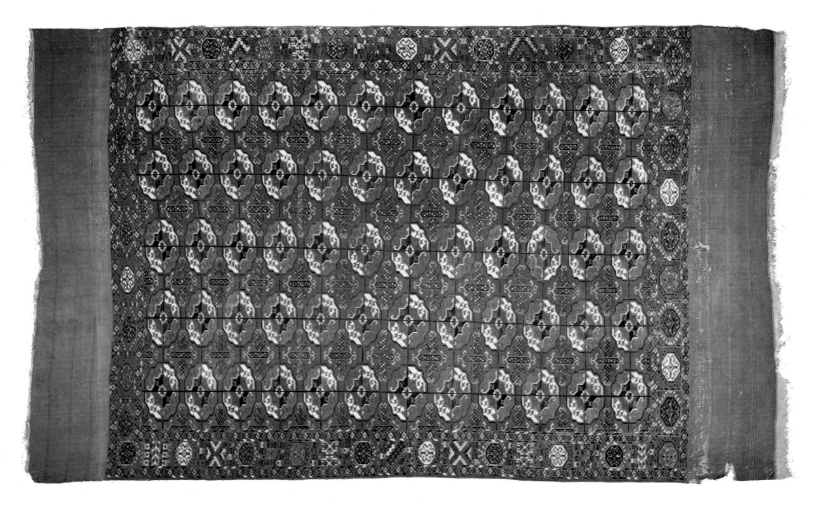

There is another major Salor gul, which is a large, roundish, stepped octagon. Within it are eight tulip-like motifs facing inwards, four star-shaped floral ornaments, two at either end of the gul, and a central knot-sided octagonal motif. Running along the top and bottom edges of the field facing inwards are six to eight wide arrowhead motifs connected by bars; each arrowhead stem contains the same tulip motif found in the principal gul. The minor guls are small diamonds with turrets. The overall colour of these *juvals* can vary considerably from a dark plum red to a light tan; the same is true of the turreted pieces mentioned above.

Although all genuine Salor weavings are rare (as opposed to later pieces woven by other tribes using Salor motifs), the *juvals* probably outnumber the rugs. Two of the latter, both in private collections, are illustrated by Ulrich Schürmann in *Central Asian Rugs* (nos. 8 and 9). The first is an extraordinary piece woven with three rows of eight turreted guls on a white ground, this last feature being extremely unusual. Between these rows are rows of minor guls of flattened octagonal shape connected by poles with diamond extrusions. The second piece has a rich orange-red field. The major and minor guls are almost identical to those of the white ground piece, although the minor cruciform or stepped octagon guls have hooks at the ends of the four arms. The major stylistic differences in the second piece are the lack of the connecting diamond poles between the minor guls, and the borders. The white ground piece has borders consisting of three strips, the inner and outer containing floral motifs and the centre one made up of small hooked motifs resembling the 'tarantula' design (although it is probably, in this case, a version of the *aina-kotshak*) on the long sides, changing to rectangles containing the same motif on the short sides. The red ground piece has a series of narrow guards containing small floral and geometric motifs with a skirt at either end and with minor diamond guls, the edges of which have a comb-like pattern.

Saryk Weavings

The early weavings of the Saryk, who lived east of the Murghab river close to the borders of Afghanistan, are closely linked with those of the Salor. There are at least three forms of the Saryk gul, which are flatter and more angular than those of the Salor. The principal gul is a stepped octagon with twenty-four sides. This is found on the majority of Saryk weavings; minor guls, if they appear, are frequently of the same geometrical form, although the inner decoration may be different. Jon Thompson, in his edition of the famous monograph on Turkoman weavings by Andrei Andreyevich Bogolyubov, *Carpets of Central Asia*, the original of which was published posthumously in St. Petersburg between 1908 and 1909, has described what he considers to be the chief characteristics of Saryk weaving (although all of them need not necessarily be present in one piece). The Salors used a particular dark blue, which is almost black; the field colour is a brownish red, varying from brown-red to brown-purple; a very dark green is used. The areas of white are piled in cotton, and there is a frequent use of silk which becomes more lavish in later pieces. The Turkish knot tends to be used more frequently.

Tekke Weavings

The Tekke were the largest and most powerful of the Turkoman tribes, and their weavings, along with those of the Yomut, are the most common. The Tekke were to be found principally north of the town of Ashkhabad in southern Turkmenistan just beyond the Persian border, and further east around Merv. Their principal gul was a roundish stepped octagon of soft outline containing stylized twigs and leaves. It is quartered by four blue lines which join the guls on the long and short axes. The minor Tekke gul is a cruciform motif with hooked ends. The interior of the major gul has two sections, the outer quartered cream and red, and the inner quartered red and black, or red and blue or red and green, the last named combination a characteristic of older pieces. The borders are elaborately woven with a variety of geometric and semi-floral motifs and at either end of the field there are often wide skirts woven with more recognizable floral motifs. Tekke carpets also have wide red kelim ends, which are, however, frequently missing.

159
162
163
165

Yomut Weavings

The Yomuts were found principally to the north-west of Turkmenistan. They were prolific weavers and many examples of all types have survived. The rarest are those woven by the so-called Ogurjalis on the eastern shore of the Caspian Sea, supposedly the oldest branch of the Yomut tribe. The most famous Ogurjali gul is oval-shaped with the top and bottom planes serrated and with two-tined fork motifs at either end. The best known example is in the Metropolitan Museum, the gift of Joseph V. McMullan. It has three rows of Ogurjali guls, the outer rows containing eight guls each, and the centre seven complete guls and two halves at top and bottom. The field colour is a rich plum-red; the guls themselves have an outer border containing italic-shaped petaloids, then another regular octagon, which contains a square, which in turn contains a geometric motif of a floral nature. The guls are made up of the following colours – crimson-red, russet-red, green, blue, white and yellow. The yellow is used sparingly and confined to the petaloids; the inner square is always russet-red; the outer gul border is either blue, crimson-red, or green. When it is crimson, the inner octagon may be either green or blue, when blue either red or white and when green it is crimson. The main borders have the serrated zig-zag pattern in two shades of red, green and blue with ship-like floral motifs in the troughs on a white ground.

This border pattern, with the trough motifs more obviously floral, is found in Anatolian weavings, for instance the carpet illustrated by Erdmann in *Oriental Carpets* (plate no. 153) dated to around 1800. The inner and outer guard stripes have a reciprocal red, blue and white floral motif. On the long sides of the field, between the guls, are rows of four star-shaped flower heads arranged in a cruciform pattern.

This piece, the finest of its kind, is variously dated between 1750 and 1825. Other, and presumably later, examples do not have the same richness of colour and simplicity of pattern. A beautiful piece sold at auction by Lefèvre in London on 25 March 1977, had a more russet-red field and the rows of guls were alternately $\frac{1}{2}-1-1-1-\frac{1}{2}$; $1-1-1$ across the short axis, and forming a diagonal pattern of ten or nine and two halves on the long axis. They were thus smaller than those of the McMullan carpet. They did not have the same colour range, being either light blue with an interior red octagon or red with an interior dark blue octagon. The main borders on the long sides were the same as on the McMullan carpet, with slight variations at either end. The Lefèvre piece had woven skirts, which were decorated with the Yomut tree-of-life pattern.

Another example, in the Textile Museum, Washington, has roughly the same lateral layout of guls, but on the long axis, they read seven halves and a quarter; one half and seven complete; seven complete and one half; one half and seven complete; seven complete and one half; one half and seven complete; seven halves and one quarter. The colours of the guls are alternately red outer border and black interior octagon and green centre square; or green outer border, red interior octagon and black centre square. The skirts at either end have two forms of Yomut minor cruciform guls and the main borders are woven with the Yomut birds-on-a-pole motif.

A fourth example, in a private Hamburg collection, is darker than the preceding three pieces, the guls being alternately crimson with a black interior octagon and vice versa. The border is a more schematic rendering of the zig-zag and trough pattern and there are no skirts. A fifth example is illustrated by Kendrick and Tattersall in *Hand-woven carpets* (plate no. 183). It should be noted that in discussing the Hamburg piece, Siawosch Azadi, whose *Turkoman Carpets* is considered to be one of the most authoritative books on the subject, remarks that the gul cannot be associated with any particular tribe, and many belong to a tribe which, having merged with another, has lost its identity. He makes no reference to the commonly held Ogurjali Yomut theory. A sixth example, with a squarer gul, is in a private Milanese collection and is illustrated by Schürmann.

This particular gul is not the only one associated with the Ogurjalis. The other is a spread-eagle gul, which is similar to the Caucasian eagle Kazak medallion. It is combined either with various large and small guls and other geometric motifs, as in the incredibly complex carpet illustrated by Schürmann (*Central Asian Carpets*, plate no. 23), or more commonly, combined with a Yomut *dyrnak* gul, the latter a large hooked diamond found as a major gul on many Yomut carpets. However, it is interesting that a carpet with a *dyrnak* gul, which would normally simply be described as Yomut, is described as 'antique Ogurjali carpet' by Bogolyubov. The skirt is woven with a design of cruciform motifs which is rarely found in Ogurjali weaving.

The fourth major Yomut gul is the *kepse*; this is a flattened diamond with four high turrets on either side; the colours can be a combination of green, blue, crimson, brown-red, yellow and cream. The skirts usually have a tree-of-life or stylized flower pattern. As with

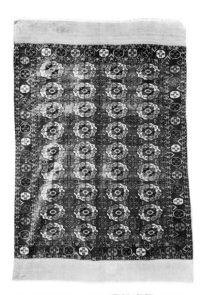

Top: Tekke carpet; the large guls indicate a slightly earlier date than the carpet illustrated on p. 163. Mid-19th century. 8 ft. 8 in. × 6 ft. 4 in. (264 × 193 cm.). Above: Ersari carpet with tauk naska *guls. Second half of the 19th century. 8 ft. 2 in. × 6 ft. 7 in. (249 × 201 cm.).*

Yomut carpet with kepse *guls. Second half of the 19th century. 9 ft. 6 in. × 5 ft. (290 × 152.5 cm.).*

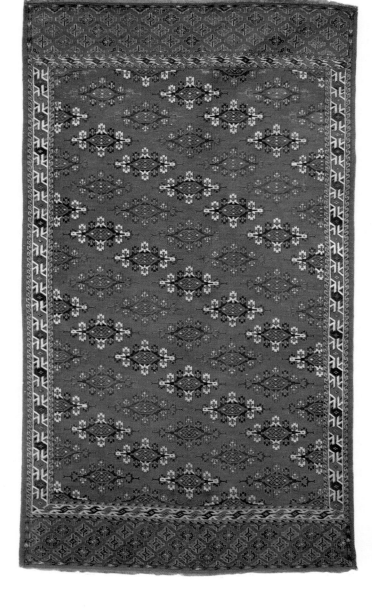

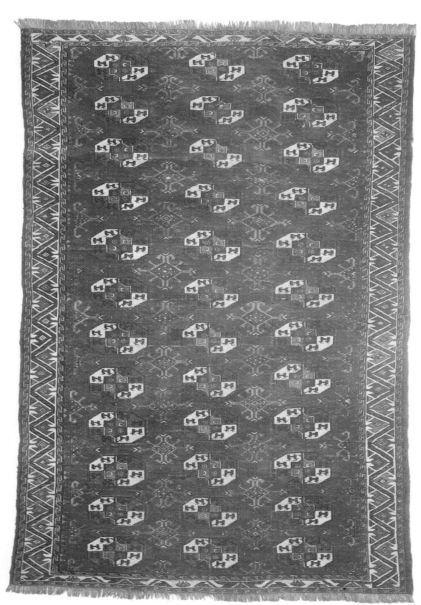

Above: Yomut carpet with kepse guls. Second half of the 19th century. 9 ft. 6 in. × 5 ft. (290 × 152.5 cm.). Above right: Yomut carpet with tauk naska guls. Mid-19th century. 8 ft. 5 in. × 5 ft. 6 in. (256 × 167.5 cm.).

other Yomut carpets, the field colour can range from a light red, through purple-red to a rich purple-brown. Another Yomut gul, which is also associated with the Arabatchi, Ersari, Kizil-Ayak and Chaudor, is the so-called *tauk naska* gul, a regular octagon with a central decahedron and two animal forms in each quarter (the word *tauk* means 'chicken' and these figures presumably once resembled birds). Another gul found on Yomut pieces as well as those of other tribes, is a flattened octagon. One carpet with the *tauk naska* major gul and the typical Yomut minor gul, is in the Vereinigte Werkstatten Collection, Munich, and is attributed by Schürmann to the Yomut of the Ogurjalis. Many Yomut weavings are characterized by particularly vivid blues and greens.

Chaudor Weavings
The Chaudors were located in the northern part of Turkmenistan on the Amu-Darya river, and their weavings are among the rarest of the Turkoman pieces. Although they produced examples similar in style to the Yomut and Saryk, their characteristic gul is a large roundish octagon with either stepped or zig-zag sides within a thin zig-zag lattice; there is a wider use of cream-yellow than in most other Turkoman weavings.

Weavings of the Ersari Tribes
There are three principal tribal units of the Ersari important in the context of weaving: the Ersari proper, the Ersari-Beshir (usually simply called the Beshir) and the Kizil-Ayak, named after a small village once just inside the Turkmenistan border with Afghanistan. The Ersari proper lived in southern Turkmenistan and over the border with Afghanistan; the Beshir, a sub-group of the Ersari, were found in the Khanat of Bokhara.

165

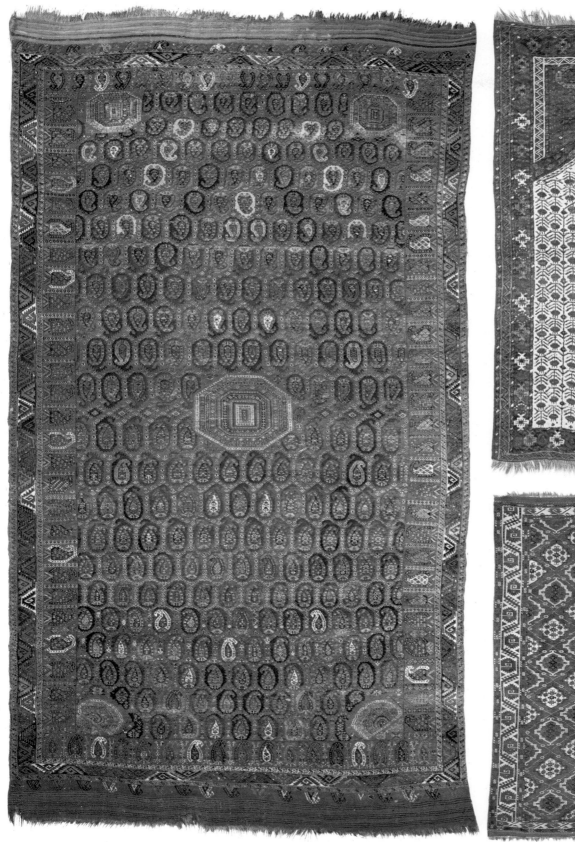

The Beshir had a distinct weaving style, less geometric and more floral than the other
168 Turkoman tribes. They used bright colours and large motifs, as well as designs such as allover field patterns of cloud-bands and octagons, stylized tulips and other flowers. They also
wove some characteristic prayer rugs with a four-sided mihrab surmounted by a knop; the
broad mihrab structure or the field around it, being woven with a white field on which are
floral motifs (pomegranates being among the most popular).

Pure Ersari weaving is often closer to the general concept of Turkoman design, but they
also produced unique patterns; on both carpets and bags, one finds a row of large conjoined
diamonds on the central axis, surrounded by parallel bold zig-zags. Similar designs were
produced by the Karakalpak, who lived far to the north on the southern shores of the Aral

*Above left: large Beshir carpet
with* botehs. *Probably first half
of the 19th century. 16 ft. ×
8 ft. (488 × 244 cm.). Top
right: Beshir prayer rug. Mid-
to late 19th century. 5 ft. × 3 ft.
(150 × 90 cm.). Above:
Chaudor carpet. Second half of
the 19th century. 9 ft. 2 in. ×
7 ft. 7 in. (275 × 228 cm.).*

Above, left to right: three Beshir carpets. Conjoined diamond design; second half of the 19th century; 7 ft. 10 in. × 4 ft. 7 in. (239 × 140 cm.). Diamond lattice design; early 19th century; 7 ft. 7 in. × 4 ft. 7 in. (231 × 140 cm.). Herati design with octagons; mid- to late 19th century; 11 ft. 2 in. × 5 ft. 6 in. (339 × 168 cm.).

Sea, and on nomadic weavings from Turkey, the Caucasus and Persia. There are also rugs with quartered star-shaped guls.

In Afghanistan, early in the 19th century, the Ersari wove large carpets with russet-red fields decorated with the very large Ersari gul called the *gulli-gul*, the interior of which is quartered and contains branches with three schematic fruit (although some are found with the *tauk naska* motifs). Jon Thompson, in his discussion of an Afghan Ersari with the *gulli-gul* illustrated in Bogolyubov, remarks that such pieces were probably first woven near Bokhara, where the Ersari were settled, and only in Afghanistan from the second half of the 19th century. Schürmann, however, dates an Afghan piece with the Ersari version of the *tauk naska* gul to *c.* 1800. The *gulli-gul* appears on a carpet illustrated by Azardi (plate no. 8), attributed to the early 19th century. This has a brilliant red field uncharacteristic of the Afghan pieces and was probably woven in Turkmenistan; it also has a number of different minor guls including the *dyrnak*.

The Kizil-Ayak are generally, though not unanimously, considered a sub-tribe of the Ersari. Certainly one of the principal Kizil-Ayak guls has the roundish but angular form associated with the Ersari, and a similar use of colour. An example is illustrated in the English edition of Bogolyubov's book.

Arabatchi Weavings

Azadi also illustrates a Kizil-Ayak carpet woven with three rows of two *tauk naska* guls of flattened octagonal form, with a cruciform minor gul. The style is similar to that of the Yomut, as is the Arabatchi carpet, also illustrated by Azadi, which has tree-of-life skirts, the zig-zag and trough border design and the combination of dark purple-brown field and brilliant blue ornamental details found in Yomut pieces. Another Arabatchi rug with similar main guls but differing minor guls was sold by Lefèvre in London in March 1977. It also differed from the Azadi piece in that the borders were decorated with small geometric motifs and there was no skirt. The field was a reddish brown colour which is a characteristic colour of Arabatchi weaving.

Dr. Thompson also notes that the Arabatchi continued to weave until the late 19th century, since examples are known with synthetic dyes. However, according to Thompson, 'the oldest and certainly the most beautiful example of the weaving of the tribe' is a small rug made from the two pile fields of a pair of saddle-bags in the Metropolitan Museum, New York. This piece has the typical Tekke rounded soft-edge gul, although the interior details are different (Dimand, not at his best on Turkoman weavings, catalogues it as Tekke). The Metropolitan Museum also has a carpet (catalogue no. 192) which is similar to the Kizil-Ayak and Arabatchi pieces with octagonal *tauk naska* guls, and this is catalogued as Ersari which, indirectly, it is.

Smaller Turkoman Weavings

So far, we have concentrated our descriptions on the largest Turkoman weavings, the central carpets. The small pieces, if anything, exhibit a wider variety of design. In many cases, of course, they follow the typical gul patterns of the full carpets, but they may also exhibit designs which, on the carpets, are only found in the borders or skirts. Thus there are Yomut *asmalyks* with tree-of-life or birds-on-pole field patterns, in addition to the usual Yomut *asmalyk* field of serrated diamond octagons within a lattice, a design not found on the fields of carpets. Other pieces may have different techniques, such as the Yomut *juvals* and tent bands, partly woven flat and partly pile-knotted. We are unable here to explore fully all the designs found on Turkoman small pieces, and recommend the reader to such specialist monographs and catalogues as we have mentioned in the course of this chapter.

Before moving to a brief discussion of Turkoman weavings in Afghanistan and else-where, we should mention the enigmatic 'S-group', the definition of which has been one of Jon Thompson's principal contributions to Turkoman scholarship. The pieces so classified do not exhibit any particular design – although one of the characteristic features on many of them is a thin guard stripe exhibiting a pattern of alternate X's and diamonds. It includes such designs as the Salor turreted gul, found principally on *juvals*, the more rounded Salor gul, the stepped diamond gul pieces which seem closer to the Saryks, and a piece with a

Although described by previous writers as Yomut or Kizil-Ayak, technical analysis has proved that the rare and beautiful prayer rugs of the type illustrated here should be ascribed to the Arabatchi. Second half of the 19th century. 4 ft. 8 in. (142 cm.) square.

Opposite: Afghan Ersari
pardah of hatchli design.
Touches of silk in the border.
c. 1900. Approximately 7 ft. 6 in.
× 5 ft. 7 in. (231 × 170 cm.).

magnificent deep red field and the roundish *gulli-gul* in the McMullan Collection which Schürmann and others have catalogued as a particularly fine early Saryk Afghan, although it seems to have characteristics of the Tekke, Ersari and Yomuts and a colour scheme unlike any Afghan. Another piece tentatively included by Thompson in his 'S-group', is the *juval* illustrated in Bogolyubov, which has the X and diamond stripe and a field pattern of rectangular guls with an Ogurjali fork motif on each side, contained within an angular yellow lattice structure.

Dr. Thompson has also identified door surrounds and *engsis* which he would include in the 'S-group'. Thus their identification relies not so much upon design as on a technical analysis of the weave; the pieces all have a deeply depressed warp, a Persian knot wrapped round the right of the pair and open to the left, wefts sometimes dyed light red, a fairly long pile, a thick heavy handle, extremely fine wool, silk in the pile but no cotton and a pinkish-red corrosive dye. However, it is possible that within this group there is a sub-group, since there are pieces typical in most respects which have a Persian knot open to the right and a brownish-red field. Thompson is of the opinion that the 'S-group' represents true Salor weaving, untainted by other tribes. Later pieces exhibiting many of the Salor motifs – especially the turreted gul – were woven by the Tekke. It has to be said that the theory of the 'S-group' is still in the early stages of exegesis and as with Turkoman weaving in general, much remains to be discovered and codified.

Turkoman Weaving in Afghanistan

As the Russians established political dominance over Turkmenistan during the 19th century, finally agreeing on a border with Afghanistan in 1884, many of the major Turkoman tribes set up villages in Afghanistan; they also moved into Persia. Turkoman weavers are still active in Afghanistan, but produce pieces of a commercialized and highly bastardized design.

As we remarked above, Afghan Turkoman weaving has had a long history. From the 1880s, however, tribes mingled and differences of design became merged. New sub-groups evolved from the confusion, and often produced pieces of a size or design unknown in genuine Turkoman weavings or, more usually, a mixture of the design characteristics of individual tribal groups. The majority of the weavings produced in Afghanistan over the last hundred years or so has been by Ersaris, Tekkes and their tribal off-shoots. The Ersari carpets are named after different tribal groups, which are themselves named after the villages or regions in which they are to be found – Daulatabad, Kunduz, Charshango, Chob-Bash, Beshir, Labijar, Kizil-Ayak and Waziri, although some sub-groups obviously kept their traditional names. The Charshango, it is thought, were once a sub-group of the Salor, since

162

Below: Afghan Charshango
torba, with dark blue fringes.
Late 19th century. 4 ft. 6 in. ×
1 ft. 8 in. (137 × 51 cm.).
Below right: north Afghanistan
Turkoman prayer rug, dated
A.H. 1342 (A.D. 1925). 4 ft ×
2 ft. 10 in. (122 × 86 cm.).

Afghan Waziri Turkoman rug. Early 20th century. 5 ft. 3 in. × 3 ft. 1 in. (160 × 94 cm.).

assimilated by the Ersari, while the Chob-Bash are probably of Chaudor descent. The Kizil-Ayak rugs were originally woven by an Ersari sub-group living in a town of that name in the Pendeh oasis. A village with the same name is also located in Afghanistan.

Different names apply to the types of weaving produced by the Turkomans of Afghanistan. Thus we have names like *kalin* (a carpet larger than 6×9 feet), *kalincha* (rug less than 6×9 feet), *joi namaz* (prayer rug), *balisht* and *pushti* (bags of the same size or smaller than *torba*), *kharin* (double-pocketed saddle-bags), *toushah* (the *juval*), *pardah* (a weaving with the *engsi* design, but too large to have been used as a door hanging), and *jollar* (a piece similar to the *mafrash* and *torba*). The term *mauri* (literally 'of Merv') is used to describe carpets of varying qualities and designs in the Tekke style.

Much Turkoman weaving carried out in Afghanistan in the 19th century follows the traditional patterns and is difficult to distinguish purely visually. Several examples illustrated in the catalogue of the exhibition held in Washington in 1972, *Weavings of the Tribes in Afghanistan*, could just as well have been produced on the other side of the border. Thus there are Beshir prayer rugs of traditional design, Ersari *torbas* exhibiting the well-known zig-zag pattern, a Chaudor rug indistinguishable from pieces woven in Turkmenistan and Tekke and Yomut *juvals* of traditional design, although the guls have become smaller and more cramped. One fine design apparently peculiar to the Afghan Kizil-Ayaks is a prayer rug with a pictorial representation of the mosque at Mecca. There are also very large Afghan Ersari *juvals* with a copious use of silk and large quartered guls. Although there is no simple rule for recognizing Afghan weavings, it should be noted that they do not use much blue, and that the selvedges, invariably blue in Turkmenistan weavings, are usually brown in those from Afghanistan.

In recent years, the export trade has been responsible for the extraordinary colours in which pieces woven with traditional Turkoman designs are produced. At the beginning of this century, pieces exported to the United States were washed with chemicals to tone down the deep reds to a pale rose. They were also treated so that the red changed to gold and the results were dubbed 'golden Afghans' in the trade; naturally, they were later woven with gold-yellow dyed wool. In Persia, the Yomut tribesmen began to produce pieces with the Tekke gul (very few Yomuts settled in Afghanistan). No Turkoman weavers have been active in Pakistan, but since 1947, very inferior pieces woven with Turkoman designs have been made in factories in Lahore and Karachi, with green, grey, yellow or other field colours.

Baluchi Weaving

A book written on carpets ten years ago would not have devoted much time to Baluchi tribal weavings. In the hierarchy of carpets, if such a thing could exist, they would have been placed firmly in the position of the humblest serfs. This is not an entirely fanciful analogy since one of the principal criticisms of Baluchi weavings is that they have no independence of design, but are a hotch-potch amalgam adapted from Persians, Turks, Caucasians and Turkomans. They were also categorized as being coarsely woven; many pieces, however, have over 100 knots per square inch and a sizeable number have over 150, not particularly coarse by the standards of tribal and village weaving in general. Many rug dealers active since the 1920s will say that even fifteen years ago, fine Baluchi pieces were given away as presents to clients buying expensive Persian or Turkish pieces. They were considered to have no lasting value.

It is only in recent years that serious interest has arisen in the products of the Baluchi, stemming from a wider study of Turkoman and other tribal weavings. The collecting of Baluchi rugs still goes hand in hand with an interest in Turkoman pieces, as it did with the great specialist collectors of the past, such as Bogolyubov. Two important exhibitions – *Baluchi Rugs*, held by the International Hajji Baba Society of Washington in 1974, and *Rugs of the Wandering Baluchi* organized by two young London dealers, David Black and Clive Loveless, in 1976 – together with several mixed exhibitions of Afghan and Turkoman weaving, have done much to rectify the unjustifiable lack of attention given to Baluchi pieces; it is unlikely that anyone will be giving them away again.

The origins of the Baluchi, like those of other nomadic peoples, are difficult to establish with any degree of certainty. Of Indo-Aryan stock, it is said that they may have originated in Arabia itself, or possibly in the vicinity of modern-day Iraq. It is known from Arab geographers that they were settled in south Persia, in the vicinity of Kerman, by the 10th century, and it is probable that they were scattered north and further south by the Seljuk conquest of Kerman in 1037, and then again by the Mongol invasions of the early 13th century. In the 19th century, many of the Baluchi still settled in the southern part of Persia and Afghanistan in the region of Sistan were sent in forced migrations ordered by Nadir Shah north into Khorassan, near Meshed, in the regions of Torbat-e-Heydariyeh and Torbat-e-Jam. In the area below the Persian-Afghan border, the Baluchis set up a loose federation called Baluchistan, now part of Pakistan. Although nearly half the present Baluchi population of around two million are still to be found in Baluchistan, this area has virtually no significance for the student of weaving. Only kelims and a very small number of poor-quality knotted pieces are produced there. The town of Torbat, sixty miles south of Meshed, was and remains the principal market-place for Baluchi weavings.

The main Baluchi weaving area is a stretch of land straddling the Persian-Afghan border from a line drawn between Sabzewar, Meshed and Sarakhs in the north of Zahedan, a town just inside the Persian border some three hundred miles to the south. In the north, from whence came the most important Baluchi carpets, were the areas of Torbat-e-Heydariyeh, Torbat-e-Jam, Nishapur and Sarakhs. Here were located various Baluchi tribes, the best weavers being the Salar Khani (or Said Muhammed Khani), the Ali Akbar Khani, the Khodada'i, the Husseinza'i and the Djanbeghi. In Sarakhs itself were the Brahni and the Rahim Khani, the latter a splinter group of the Salar Khani. In this area, and further south-east in Afghanistan, there is another tribal people who, although distinct from the Baluchi, produced some weavings which are usually classified with them. These are the Tshahar Aimak ('Four Peoples'). To this ethnic group belong the tribes of the Balhuri and Timuri who both produced (the latter especially), weavings similar to the Baluchi. Other Baluchi tribes, around Herat and further south, are the Dokhtar-e-Ghazi and the Jakub-Khani. In north-east Persia are found various sub-groups of the Timuris, Kurds and Arabs, and in Afghanistan, sub-tribes of the Hazaras, Ghilzas and Timuris, all ethically different from the Baluchi, although much intermingling through marriage has taken place. Some of these groups, such as the Hazaras, are of Mongol descent.

This list is by no means exhaustive, and there still remains considerable confusion over the ethnic origins of some of the smaller groups. The Badjiz in the far north-west of Afghanistan, although they now claim to be Baluchi, were probably originally Arab (although some would claim that the Baluchi were of similar origin). There are also the Otak and Shazka'i tribes who weave kelims and are Pathans (peoples of Afghan origin), as are the Bobakza'i at Adraskand, one of the principal rug-weaving centres of the Baluchi; the Bobakza'i are, apparently, a part of the Nunza'i sub-tribe of the ancient Duranis. Other Tshahar Aimak peoples, such as the Taimani, Firuzkuhi and Djamshidi, are also to be found in Afghanistan and may be of Turkish or Persian descent. There are also, of course, tribes of Turkoman origin, such as the Karakalpak, Yomut and Ersari, whose weavings we have described above. It should be said that it is difficult to ascribe the weavings of the Baluchi and Tshahar Aimak to any particular sub-tribe or group.

The Baluchi, like the Turkomans, usually wove carpets of small size, under ten feet in length, and a variety of bags. They lived in more primitive tent-like constructions – *ghedan*, or collectively, a *toomuri* – than the Turkomans, which were described by Charles Masson in his *Narratives of Various Journeys in Balochistan, Afghanistan, the Panjab and Kalat, etc.*, published in London in 1844:

'*The dwellings . . . are formed by a number of long slender poles bent and inverted towards each other, over which are extended slips of the coarse fabric of camel hair, and dyed generally black. The direction of the length is from east to west, the better to exclude the sun's rays. The interior management is as simple as the exterior – on the one side are piled up their bags of grain and flower, and other necessities, which are concealed from view by a carpet spread over them in front, while above them are piled their stocks of carpets and felt, neatly folded. They place their cakes of bread in carpet bags, also their flower and salt.*'

Masson also left a long description of the methods used by the Baluchi to produce some of their textiles:

'*The wool of the sheep is beaten by slender sticks or rods held in either hand, and alternately descending, until it be reduced to a pulp fit for the fabric of namads or felts. It is also spun into carpets, which are coloured with madder, indigo, turmeric, etc., all of which operations are carried out within toomuns. The leaves of the apple-trees are collected at their fall in autumn, and preserved for use as a yellow dye, which is, I believe, a novel application of them. The hair of camels is often used as a base of the carpet, upon which the lines, or various patterns in worsted, are worked. It is exclusively adapted to the fabric of the coarse black coverings for tents, and for a variety of furniture for the living animal. As well as wool, it is employed in the construction of ropes and strings. Cloaks, here called shawls, are made of the same materials, and are in general use varying in fineness of texture; some of them are gaudily decorated with floss silk, or varied colours.'*

The weaving was carried out principally by women and girls, especially by girls weaving the household effects they would need in their own homes, which they produced in the period between betrothal and marriage.

Although it is difficult to distinguish between the various types of Baluchi weaving, it is accepted that the finest pieces, no surviving example of which can be dated earlier than the mid-19th century, were woven in north-east Persia, in the region of Torbat-e-Heydariyeh. They were woven with a fine lustrous wool as soft as velvet, one of the most distinguished aspects of Baluchi weaving. The colours are deep and rich dark blues and reds, with the designs decorated with black, brown and small amounts of white. The ends of these and many other Baluchi carpets have wide and distinctive kelims, frequently embellished with weft-float brocade.

Baluchi Design

There is no particular design belonging to the Baluchi, unless it be the large tree-of-life motif which they weave in a distinctive manner. Their pieces are recognized rather by the quality of wool and the combination of colours. Although sombre is an adjective frequently applied to Baluchi rugs, the finest pieces have a beauty and depth of colour which is the equal of some of the best Turkoman weavings.

It is thought that when Baluchi weavings display characteristic designs of other peoples and tribes, they were probably woven by the Baluchi tribes closest to them. Thus many of the Torbat-e-Heydariyeh pieces are woven with designs derived from Persian carpets. Border designs appear which are adapted from Herati patterns, as well as motifs found in Caucasian and Turkish carpets.

One of the most popular designs is the zig-zag and trough border which is more properly known as the Turkoman line and which, as we have seen, is associated principally with the Yomuts, but is also found, in more realistic form, in the borders of Anatolian weavings.

In terms of colour, the primary influence would seem to be Turkoman weaving, and many Baluchi pieces also have designs based closely on Turkoman rugs and bags. David Black and Clive Loveless, in the beautifully produced catalogue of their exhibition, illustrated a bag-face with two turreted Salor guls. In the carpet illustrated on the facing page, a strange totem-like motif found on the right edge of the field is also found on numerous Turkoman weavings, especially on those of the Afghan Ersari. The bag-face, quite logically, is assumed to have been woven by Baluchis in Sarakhs or Merv, who would have been in contact not necessarily with genuine Salor pieces but with Tekke adaptations, the Tekke having settled around Meshed, south of the Kopet Dagh mountains. The Baluchi sub-tribes of the Rahim Khani or Brahni are other possibilities.

Baluchi Prayer Rugs

Inside the borders of Afghanistan, a nomadic Baluchi tribe, once considered to be the Dokhtar-e-Ghazi, but now thought unidentifiable, wandered between Herat in the north down to the Sistan region in the south. The weavers of the tribe wove a distinctive type of prayer rug. This has a small mihrab contained between two decorative panels. Below the mihrab is another decorative panel, which in some pieces resembles an altar upon which the mihrab stands. At the top of the mihrab, above the spandrels, is another panel containing representations of three domed and pillared mosques. It is not known from where this particular design originated; we remember that the Kizil-Ayak Turkomans wove prayer rugs with full length representations of the Mosque at Mecca; such pieces were produced in Afghanistan, though further east than the Baluchi are thought to have been. O'Bannon, in

177

Opposite: Meshed Baluchi rug. The wool of this rug is of exceptional fineness. The design may have been adapted from Beshir weaving. Mid-19th century. 6 ft. × 4 ft. 4 in. (180 × 132 cm.).

his *The Turkoman Carpet*, also illustrates a Tekke Afghan with the same general layout as the Baluchi pieces. However, he remarks that such Tekke pieces have been woven for at least forty years. It may be, therefore, that the idea was copied from the Baluchi by the Afghan Turkomans, rather than the reverse.

A type of prayer rug which can be associated with the Dokhtar-e-Ghazi has a wide mihrab with a long, tubular, arch. The entire field of the mihrab and spandrels is filled with a tight floral lattice, an effect similar to some Caucasian prayer rugs, especially examples from Daghestan. Even this attribution is not universally accepted, however, the carpet trade preferring to call them simply Herat Baluchis.

Meshed Baluchis

It is, however, for those pieces called 'Meshed Baluchis' that the weavers are primarily renowned today. As we have said, such carpets and bags are woven predominantly in a combination of red and dark blue, the latter often of an amazing density and richness, and called *surmey*. Among the finest existing examples, although badly damaged, is a carpet shown as no. 39 in the Black-Loveless exhibition. The field, a deep indigo, is woven with a serrated lattice in diamond formation, in red with touches of white. The serrated forms are woven alternately solid and in outline. At the intersections of the lattices are Maltese crosses in red with a hollow white square at the centre of each. Within each diamond is a large central motif, similar to the tarantula, two white flowers and between three and five tiny schematic renderings of deer (and in one diamond only, an equally tiny representation of a man). The inner guard stripe is woven with a reciprocal running dog pattern in brown and white, found on many Baluchi weavings, and a wide border, unfortunately severely cut, which is decorated with two forms of gul, alternating with long fir-cone-like designs. The pile is long and silky, with a feel almost like that of Cashmere.

The Mina Khani *Design*

The *mina khani* design, from which some elements in the above rug are derived, is found on Persian weavings, although its appearance on Baluchi pieces is considerably less complicated. It is supposed to have been named after a certain Mina Khan of Tabriz, but this suggestion should perhaps not be taken too seriously. The Persian design consists of large palmettes between other large palmettes of different form, the latter having two arabesque tendrils emanating from them with small flowers at the ends; the tendrils form a continuous snake-like line up the length of the field. In the Baluchi pieces, the design is usually found in stylized geometric form with rows of square floral forms with white triangles at the corners; the spaces between the square flowers thus become octagonal and gul-like, taking the place of the large free-standing palmettes of the Persian *mina khani* design. This rendering is found on both Baluchi carpets and bag-faces. In the superb fragmented piece mentioned in the previous paragraph, the lattice effect, which is latent in the Persian version, is emphasized. In other pieces (for instance, Black-Loveless no. 30), the lattice is made from a thin red line of alternate hexagons and diamonds; the hexagons contain large floral motifs, the diamonds smaller ones. Also in the field are two rows of white five-petalled flower heads, the petals of somewhat angular and disjointed form. These white flower heads, standing out strikingly from the dark background, are frequently encountered on Baluchi weavings from north-east Persia. In some cases, the field is quite small and surrounded by a very wide and elaborate border woven with a madder-red ground.

On other early pieces, the lattice is smaller and tighter, each diamond containing a small floral motif, which on some examples, such as the one illustrated here, take on the appearance of European heraldic devices, such as the *fleur de lys*, or, more frequently, schematic forms such as the tarantula. In an often encountered type of rug, the diagonal nature of the lattice is emphasized by making alternate rows light red and dark brown-red on the diagonal axis. Also popular is a vertical hexagon motif with hooked edges, resembling a cross between the scorpion pattern and a squared-off fir cone. This can be found in the borders – for instance the fragmented piece we have mentioned above – or as an allover field pattern. Usually within each hexagon will be found a small formalized tree-of-life pattern with ten branches. In some cases, there is no other field decoration except for these large motifs, in others there will be small scattered flowers and other motifs including *botehs*; one or more hexagons may also be outlined in white. This hexagonal form is probably derived from similar designs found on late Caucasian carpets which, in turn, are derived from the palmettes found on dragon carpets. In Baluchi weaving, it is particularly associated with the Adraskand Valley.

Carpets woven in the northern regions of Persia rarely use yellow. To the Persians, this was the colour of sickness and misery (a meaning which has spread to the west – for instance, the yellow flags of ships in quarantine). Pieces woven further south, however, in the Sistan province are characterized by their use of a red-brown, buff-yellow colour range, often with a dark black-brown tree-of-life motif down the centre of the field, while those pieces from further east into Afghanistan are more coarsely woven – therefore looser and floppier to handle – and use a distinctive russet colour. This latter colour is also characteristic of Timuri weavings, which tend to follow Baluchi designs; the Timuris probably did not have a weaving history independent of the Baluchi. Their weavings are virtually duochromatic – russet on a more powdery blue than the colour found on north-Persian Baluchi pieces; there may also be small touches of white. The Timuris also wove some larger carpets than the Baluchi, although these rarely exceed about fourteen feet in length; the largest examples are usually woven in two vertical strips.

Baluchi prayer rug, probably from Sistan in south-east Persia. Early 20th century. 3 ft. 11 in. × 2 ft. 6 in. (119.5 × 76 cm.).

Baluchi Tree-of-life Rugs

One of the most easily recognizable forms of Baluchi weaving is the tree-of-life prayer rug, woven in all the principal Baluchi areas of Persia and Afghanistan. This has a relatively consistent design. There are up to twelve narrow borders and guard stripes. The mihrab is eight-sided, the top being square. In the spandrels on either side of the mihrab arch are square or rectangular panels of the same field colour as the mihrab itself. The field of the mihrab is woven with between one and four trees with branches at either right-angles or at forty-five degrees to the trunk. Each branch has bunches of leaves of serrated maple-leaf form. The most usual colour scheme is for the borders, the spandrel-square designs and the field designs to be in dark shades of brown, green, and aubergine, with small details in white. The field of the mihrab and spandrel squares are of a natural camel hair. The central tree trunk may go up into the mihrab arch, or there may be a separate geometric motif there, which is often echoed at the base of the mihrab and in the spandrel squares. In some rugs, the tree may be highly formalized, and there may be in addition a large hexagonal medallion with hooked sides, of the type we have described previously, in the centre of the mihrab. As we might expect, the prayer rugs of this type woven in Sistan and Afghanistan are lighter and brighter in colouring than those woven in north Persia; there is, for instance, a greater use of brown-red, blue and white in the border. The tree-of-life motif, it should be noted, is not confined to prayer rugs but can also be found on the fields of small secular pieces.

Other Baluchi Weavings

As with the Turkomans, the Baluchis wove many pieces for special functions. One interesting example is the *soffré* rug, which takes its name from the Turkish word *sofra*, meaning a dining table. These pieces are generally about four feet square; the borders are pile-knotted but the large field is a monochrome kelim, with a few scattered floral motifs and a zig-zag surround in weft-float tapestry brocade and Soumak brocade. As their name implies, such pieces were used as table spreads for the ground and were brought out only for special guests. The same mixed technique was used for wedding rugs (*jahizi*).

Other forms of Baluchi weaving include animal trappings, gun-cases, double-pouched saddle-bags, single bags, salt bags, long bags used for pillows, etc. (the Baluchi apparently did not make pieces of the same size as Turkoman *juvals*). Such weavings, usually in a combination of very dark colours – red, aubergine, green, brown, blue and black, with details in white, show the same richness of design as the rugs. The Baluchi rarely used silk, but occasionally very small areas – ranging from a single knot to a cluster of half a dozen or so – can be found, pale green, vivid pink or white being the most common. On many of the pieces are found rows of geometric floral motifs, on others designs derived from Turkoman, Persian and differing tribal sources such as Kurdish and Kashgai. Although commercialism, with its stereotyping of design, politics, with its destruction of the nomadic way of life, and science, with its production of chemical dyes, has had the same effect on the Baluchi as on other tribal peoples, pieces are still occasionally found of good quality and of fairly recent date. A few retain the dark and glowing colour combinations of earlier examples, although the handsome decorated kelim ends no longer appear.

Baluchi prayer rug with typical tree-of-life design in the mihrab. Late 19th century. 5 ft. × 2 ft. 10 in. (152.5 × 86 cm.).

Modern 'black' Baluchi carpet with a design of conjoined diamonds, possibly adapted from Beshir weaving. 7 ft. 7½ in. × 4 ft. 9 in. (231.5 × 144.5 cm.).

Baluchi Motifs

We should not leave our study of Baluchi weavings without saying something about the origins of their designs. As we have noted, many of them are derived from other sources, although the use of colour, characteristic of the Baluchi and the inevitable simplification of the designs which they borrowed, make it impossible to confuse their pieces with those of the Turkomans, Kashgai, Caucasians or Kurds. Certainly, the tree-of-life motif is the one design which, in this particular rendering, is peculiar to the Baluchi. As to its original usage, Noel Hobbs, in an interesting essay in the Black-Loveless catalogue, notes that the origin of the word Baluchi is the Persian *baloc*, meaning cockscomb or crest. It is possible, therefore that many of the most frequently used Baluchi motifs, like those of the Turkomans, were originally clan crests, like the *tamgas* or brand marks used for cattle and sheep, which would immediately indicate a specific tribal origin.

In the 19th century, with war, forced migration, and the break-up of specific tribal structures, such symbols of autonomy began to disappear or merge with those of other tribes into a common stock (the same, as we have seen, happened with the Turkoman guls). Only in the obvious differences between the weavings of northern Persia, southern Persia and Afghanistan do vestiges of Baluchi autonomies remain. Jon Thompson, in an essay in the same Black-Loveless catalogue, suggests that certain motifs, particularly the highly formalized animal and tree design found within the guls on some Baluchi bags, and the tree-of-life motif itself, may relate back to shamanic totems of pre-Islamic times.

Far Eastern Weaving

Early Weaving in Mongolia and East Turkestan

The area described as East Turkestan stretches from Samarkand in the west to beyond Khotan, one thousand miles to the east. The principal cities are Samarkand, Tashkent, Yarkand, Kashgar and Khotan. The first is now located in Soviet Uzbekistan, Tashkent is on the borders of Soviet Kazakistan and Kirgizstan, and the remaining three are in the huge western Chinese area of Sinkiang (sometimes called Chinese Turkestan). The part of Sinkiang in which Yarkand, Kashgar and Khotan are located is known as the Tarim basin, and was not a permanent part of the Chinese empire until the 18th century; it was, however, in the direct line of the great silk route west, and was one of the first significant areas outside China to rear silkworms.

Until its conquest by the Chinese, the area had been subjected to centuries of various political, religious and cultural influences. In the early centuries of the Christian era, it knew the Graeco-Roman style of art, as is evidenced by numerous fresco fragments and artifacts excavated there. The Tarim basin, in basic geographic terms, is at the pivot of the Eurasian land mass, the city of Khotan being almost equidistant from London and Tokyo. Thus, during the first Christian millennium, the area received strong influences from Turkey and Persia in the west, from India in the south and from the important areas of Mongolia and China in the north and east.

Archaeological work undertaken by Sir Aurel Stein and others in the first decades of the present century proved that by the 4th century A.D., the principal language of the area was of the Indo-Aryan group, and was called Tokharian, a language hitherto unknown; surprisingly, Tokharian was a member of a group of languages called Kentum, then supposed to be the property of the western peoples of the Indo-Aryan language family. The speakers of Tokharian were found to have lived as much as 1,000 miles east of Khotan, in the present province of Kansu. It was here that Stein discovered frescoes which could just as well have been painted in Italy or Alexandria.

In these early centuries of the Christian era, the huge empire of Kushan stretched from the eastern borders of Persia through to the north of what is now Pakistan, and north-west India, and included areas of the southern Soviet states and all of Afghanistan. It is here that

Interior of a silver bowl from Samarkand, showing strong Indo-Persian influence. 15th century. Victoria and Albert Museum, London.

Buddhist art from India and Graeco-Roman art from the West merged into that style known as Ghandara, which spread eastward and influenced much Chinese art. Several examples of Ghandara influence on works of art dating from between the 3rd and 9th centuries A.D. have been found in the Tarim basin, and among such artifacts are fragments of pile-knotted carpets. Until the discovery of the Pazyryk carpet, these were the oldest known examples of pile knotting.

At this early period, various religious influences made their presences felt in the Tarim basin, including Manicheeism – the heretical sect of Zoroastrianism outlawed in Persia, Nestorian Christianity, Buddhism and the Shamanism of the nomad tribes. By the end of the 4th century A.D., the region had ceased to be a part of the Kushan empire, being conquered first by the Hephtalites, or White Huns, and later, in the mid-6th century, by the Turks. In the 7th century, it was ruled briefly by the T'ang emperors, and in the 8th by the Tibetans. In the 12th and 13th centuries, it was part of the Empire of the Kankatai, a Mongolian people, and then became part of the Mongolian empire of Ghengis Khan. It became known subsequently as part of the domain of the Chagatai, named after one of the sons of Ghengis Khan. Such Mongols were originally of Shamanic belief, Islam only taking a firm hold in the 14th century.

Thus far, we have described one set of historical facts relative to the region of East Turkestan. In the western part of the Tarim basin, the influence was to remain principally Turkic. In the 11th century, the city of Kashgar gave its name to the province, Kashgaria, which became an important cultural centre of the Turks, the language of the eastern Turkish Uygurs of Kotsho being the most prevalent. It was through the Turkish influence also that Islam began to establish itself in the 10th century. The northern tribes of the Chagataid empire, the main part of which was north of the Tien Shan mountains, remained Shamanist, but when some branches moved south into the Tarim basin, they soon adopted Islam, which thus became the predominant religion of the area. During the Timurid invasions of the early 15th century, the Chagataid empire was reduced to provincial status, but during the mid part of the century, two rulers, Essen Buka II and Yunus, maintained close contact with the major cities of the eastern part of the Persian Timurid empire, Bokhara and Samarkand; Yunus, especially, became interested in Timurid culture. Kashgar itself became one of the major cities of the Timurid-Chagataid cultural axis.

In the second half of the 17th century, the Chagataid dynasty was overthrown by the Mongolian Oirats, Kashgar, Yarkand, and the city of Aksu becoming fluctuating seats of power. In 1759, the Chinese conquered Kashgaria, although a brief secession took place in the 19th century under Yakoub Beg, a Turkoman mercenary. His rule, however, lasted only from 1865 to 1878, when the Chinese once again took over the area. This second invasion was backed by the British who, fearful of Russian expansion, looked to preserve the Indian border by aiding the Chinese armies, which were virtually their puppets at that time.

As we have suggested in the opening section of our study of Oriental weaving, the fact that the earliest examples of pile-knotted carpets have been found in the environs of Central Asia close to Mongolia, is probably indicative that the art itself may have been originated there by the various tribes and dynasties of Mongol descent, who were to be predominant in central and western Asia for the next 1,500 years. We have discussed the significance and probable origin of the Pazyryk rug. Several centuries, however, separate this and the fragments excavated in the northern part of the Tarim basin at the town of Lou-lan by Sir Aurel Stein, and published by him in 1928. Most of these have uncut weft loops, and are not true pile-knotted carpets. One fragment, however, dated to the 2nd or 3rd century A.D., is a true pile-knotted fragment. This, and the weft-loop pieces, although very small, suggest that stylized floral and geometric patterns were already characteristic designs. The pile-knotted piece is woven in numerous colours, including black, dull white, red, pink, buff, yellow and bright blue, on a red-pink ground. The pile is unusually long, about half an inch or more, a characteristic of Khotan rugs of a much later date, and of certain Caucasian pieces with which some of the East Turkestan weavings of the last 100 years have much in common.

Lou-lan was a post on the main Chinese trade route east, and it has been suggested that Stein's fragments should be connected with Chinese culture rather than with the shifting ethnic mix of the Tarim basin. However, scholars, following Folke Bergman, have pointed out that both weft-loop weaving and pile-knotting are alien to what is known of Chinese culture at this time. The earliest representations of rugs in Chinese art occur during the Sung dynasty (960–1279), and it is noted that such representations always show what appear to be pile-knotted pieces in use by Mongols, rather than by the Chinese themselves (the Chinese looked down upon wool as a barbarian material). Yet according to Dimand, in a statement which is difficult to understand, 'Ethnologists agree on the traditional Mongolian lack of interest in weaving'. He goes on to say that 'cities of Central Asia and Persia were famous long before the Mongol invasions for their rugs and textiles'. This presumably refers to the Mongol conquests of the 13th and 14th centuries, but no one has ever suggested that these conquests were the prime reasons for the art of pile-knotting to have been transported from east to west.

Almost a thousand years before (as early, indeed, as the Pazyryk rug itself) Mongol people had begun to move westward, settling central Asia and Anatolia. It is possible that such peoples, practising rug weaving far from their ancestral homelands, were then responsible for it moving to the east, but such a hypothesis flies in the face of logic. That designs and motifs did move east is indisputable but that such was the case with the art itself seems highly improbable. Certainly the evidence of the Pazyryk rug, both its style and its place of discovery, and the Stein fragments, which predate any hard evidence of rug weaving in the west by several centuries, suggest strongly that rug weaving was widespread in Mongolia long before it was in the west. And it should be added that the first real evidence we have of rug weaving in China itself, comes in the years following the Mongol Yüan dynasty (1206–1368).

Evidence for taking a positive view of Mongolian weavings is to be gained from a study of the Sung paintings mentioned above. Dimand himself has pointed out the existence of a group of Sung paintings in which Mongol rugs are depicted, the most important being a thirteenth-century example in the National Palace Collection, Taiwan. This, like all the others, depicts the Lady Wen-Chi, who was captured by the Mongols, taken to their country, and forced to marry a Mongolian chief with whom she lived for the next twelve years. The Taiwan painting shows Wen-Chi and her husband seated cross-legged upon a rug approximately eight feet in length. It has a red field and a central square medallion containing a diamond lozenge. Within the diamond is a cruciform motif of Chinese inspiration. The piece has frayed ends and is almost certainly a pile-knotted rug. This, and others with allover field patterns, or fields divided into geometric sections containing schematic motifs, clearly depicted in scroll paintings in a New York private collection, demonstrate that pile-knotting was a sophisticated art form in Mongolia by at least the 12th century.

Dimand points out that the geometric designs prefigure those found in later Seljuk pieces depicted in fourteenth- and fifteenth-century Italian paintings (notably two frescoes of the 14th century at Assisi reproduced in Erdmann's *Oriental Carpets*, nos. 17 and 18). It has also been suggested by the Oriental scholar Otto Kummel, that in 1262 a carpet factory was established in Karakoram, which had been made capital of Mongolia by Ghengis Khan, in order to provide carpets for the Chinese Imperial Court in Peking. If such was the case, it is the earliest establishment of its kind of which we have evidence. By the time the factory was founded, Karakoram was no longer the Mongol capital, Kublai Khan (1260–1294) having established it at Kai-pin-fu, not far from Peking.

Weaving in East Turkestan, 17th–19th Centuries

The majority of surviving carpets from East Turkestan date from the late 18th and early 19th centuries, and on into the 20th century. However, there are a significant number of pieces which may be dated from the early 18th century, and perhaps even into the 17th. Before describing these, we should elucidate some anomalies of nomenclature which exist in the field of East Turkestan weaving.

In a book published in England in 1928, *Buried Treasures of Chinese Turkestan*, the explorer Albert von le Coq remarked on the many carpets 'with beautiful patterns, known as Samarkands'. Similarly, Chinese dealers referred to East Turkestan carpets as 'Kansus'. Both names derive from the place of marketing and not that of manufacture. Similarly in the West, rugs with the allover pomegranate and tendril-lattice pattern were known as Kashgar, although they were actually woven in Khotan and possibly Yarkand. Despite using the name Kansu generically for East Turkestan carpets, the Chinese dealers, according to H. A. Lorentz in *A View of Chinese Rugs*, considered only those pieces with the flattened disc medallions to be true Kansus; the view of those so close to the centres of production cannot be ignored, but there is no evidence to prove that such pieces were woven exclusively, if at all,

Silk carpet with pomegranate design and trefoil border. Yarkand or Khotan. Mid-19th century. 11 ft. 11 in. × 6 ft. 4 in. (363 × 193 cm.).

in Kansu. A provenance further west seems certain. Certainly none of the carpets once known in the West as Samarkands were woven in that city.

Secondly, East Turkestan carpets have been until recently among the least appreciated examples of Oriental weaving in Europe and the United States, which in part accounts for their rarity in comparison to the abundance of Persian, Turkish, Caucasian and Turkoman pieces. An example of the denigratory attitude of Western dealers may be found in a book written by the American dealer Charles W. Jacobsen, *Oriental Rugs, a Complete Guide* (a useful book, but one which must be approached with caution). Of Kashgar he writes, 'None are available . . . the rug is too unimportant and unknown to give it space . . . they were very coarse, poor rugs'. And of Samarkands, 'This name should be of no interest to one seeking floor coverings . . . The antique Samarkands, with few exceptions, had little to recommend them . . . very coarse, flimsy . . . third rate rugs.' And lest it be thought that these are the views of half a century ago, the quotations are taken from the latest edition of Mr. Jacobsen's book, published in 1972.

Even today, it has to be said that the best examples of East Turkestan weavings that come onto the market are inexpensive relative to, say, the prices of Turkoman weavings. At Christie's, London, in 1976, a beautiful, though worn, silk Khotan of the late 18th/early 19th century, woven with a red pomegranate trellice on a dark blue ground, and an exact pair of the example in the Metropolitan Museum illustrated by Dimand in colour in his catalogue, failed to sell at £4,200 ($7,350); in the Akeret sale at Sotheby's, also in 1976, a beautiful nineteenth-century wool Khotan, woven with a medallion and floral motifs on a rust-red ground, fetched a mere £1,650 ($2,900). The highest auction price to date is probably the £6,800 ($11,696) given for an early nineteenth-century wool Khotan, woven with rows of flower heads and eight-lobed medallions on a rust-red field, which was sold by Lefèvre on 8 July 1977. Considerably higher prices are now paid for good, but not outstanding, Yomut, Tekke, Saryk and Salor pieces, and would be considered low for Persian silk rugs of comparatively recent date.

Ulrich Schürmann, in his book *Central Asian Rugs*, made the bold and fascinating suggestion that the earliest examples of East Turkestan weavings (aside from the antique fragments of Stein), are those fragments of the huge carpet once housed in the Chihil Sultan Kiosk, Isfahan. We remember from our section on Moghul weaving that this carpet is supposed by most scholars to be of Indian origin, it being noted by Sir Cecil Smith in 1887 that it was brought to Isfahan 'from distant lands on two elephants'.

The field of this carpet was once a rich crimson, although most of this wool has eroded away. The field decoration consists of an angular yellow lattice intertwined with green tendrils and lanceolate leaves. These tendrils appear to grow from small vase-like motifs, and lead into round but faceted discs which Schürmann says are pomegranates, but which, woven in yellow and brown, resemble rather the interiors of sunflowers or chrysanthemums. The main border is similar in design, and the two guard stripes on either side have a continuous scrolling vine pattern with realistic flower heads. Schürmann remarks that 'the design is not at all Indian, nor can there be any question of an Indian copy of a Persian pattern'. It has to be said that this design also bears only the most superficial resemblance to the earliest East Turkestan weavings. Its similarity in style to the large Kevorkian carpet which we mentioned in connection with the Chihil Sultan piece is apparent, and the field colour is one rarely found on East Turkestan weavings, a point conceded by Schürmann himself. Despite Schürmann's argument, a Moghul provenance still seems the most likely for this noble, but now fragmentary, carpet.

The regions of Kashgar, Yarkand and Khotan have been known for the production of carpets since the T'ang dynasty. Dimand quotes the Buddhist monk Hieun Tsiang who wrote of Kashgar during that period: 'They export fine wool (hair) fabrics and weave fine wool rugs.' Hieun Tsiang makes much the same comment about Khotan, adding 'fine woven silk fabrics' to his catalogue. However, the available literature on the carpets of East Turkestan suggests that there is absolutely no certain way of differentiating between the fabrics of Kashgar and Khotan. Schürmann suggests that those of Yarkand can be separated from the other two by particular characteristics in their structure, Yarkand pieces having warp threads which lie obliquely to each other, and a blue cotton weft.

An unusual type of rug, assigned by all recent authorities to Khotan, has a dark blue field. On this is woven, in either silk or wool, with gold braiding, systems of angular tendrils

131

Far left: Khotan carpet with a dark rust-red field, with pomegranate design in blue and white and Yun-Tsai-T'uo border. 19th century. 12 ft. 7 in. × 6 ft. 4 in. (384 × 193 cm.). Left: silk Khotan rug, with an aubergine field and a single pomegranate system. 19th century. 6 ft. 11 in. × 3 ft. 9 in. (211 × 140 cm.).

and green leaves, interspersed with what appear to be bird and insect motifs, and equally schematic and hardly recognizable versions of the dragon and phoenix combat. The wide borders are in the same style as the field, although the pattern consists more of an arabesque interspersed with a few green leaves and flowers. A complete version of this type in silk is in the Victoria and Albert Museum (inexplicably described by Schürmann as a fragment) and has a running-T border; a fragment of the field of another carpet woven in wool is in the Museum für Kunsthandwerk, Frankfurt.

Schürmann illustrates a small silk yellow ground weaving, measuring 3 feet 2 inches by 4 feet, in the Victoria and Albert Museum. This he dates to seventeenth-century Kashgar. The piece is of squarish form with rounded corners. A very similar piece, in slightly finer condition, is in the Metropolitan Museum of Art. This, and another of similar design and colouring, but with a stepped lunette-shaped top edge, are dated by Dimand to the 19th century, and are chair or throne seat coverings and back coverings respectively; they are ascribed to Khotan. Dimand convincingly justifies his late dating by pointing out that the angular floral arabesque of the design and the colours suggest 'a clumsy, slightly misunderstood approximation of the Ch'ien-Lung (1736–95) style seen in the decorative arts of that period'. Although his strictures on the East Turkestan pieces are perhaps a little harsh, he illustrates a Chinese embroidered silk cushion cover dating from the reign of the Emperor Ch'ien Lung which, as we said, justifies his suggestions as to the origins of the designs of the East Turkestan pieces.

As for Dimand's attribution of such pieces to Khotan, rather than Kashgar, there seems little to substantiate it; the author obviously considers all silk pieces to have been woven in Khotan, although this is surely a dubious assertion. He points out correctly that another group of rugs traditionally associated with Khotan has a delicate allover lattice, with a trellis of stems and flower heads; these decorative elements are often pile-knotted in silk of pastel shades reminiscent of Polonaise carpets, on a field flat-woven in silver and/or gold thread. An example in the Metropolitan Museum (catalogue no. 230), and dated to the 18th century, is similar in design to a piece in wool woven in yellow on a pale blue field in the

Victoria and Albert Museum, and the silk piece woven in green, blue and orange on a pale grey ground once in the collection of French and Company and illustrated by Schürmann (plate no. 74). Schürmann dates the last two pieces to the 19th century, and they are probably later in date than the Metropolitan piece, but again he attributes them to Kashgar. We should also include the brown-pink silk piece illustrated in Schürmann (plate no. 72) with this group; it has a delicate quatrefoil lattice. An example very similar to the Metropolitan carpet, woven in silk on gold and silver brocade, with a gold field and silver border, is illustrated in the 1975 catalogue of the German dealer Peter Bausback, *Antike Meisterstücke Orientalischer Knupfkunst* (p. 356) and is attributed to late eighteenth-century Khotan.

To the first group we described, which included the seat covers, we should assign the yellow ground silk fragment, woven with an angular arabesque and realistic peony blossoms in light blue and red, in the Textile Museum, Washington, the fragment of a border in the Metropolitan Museum, and a silk rug with the same border as the Metropolitan fragment, in the National Museum, Stockholm. The motifs on these pieces are more boldly drawn, and less cramped than those on the chair coverings, making an earlier dating reasonable.

Another example, a fragment on a coral red ground in the Victoria and Albert Museum, has two of its extant adjacent mihrabs woven with the large single flower motif, one of which grows from a vase, and the other two woven with the lumpy, tight arabesques which appear on the chair covers. The mihrab fields and spandrels, from left to right, are yellow with a coral red spandrel, coral red with a dark blue spandrel, dark blue with a coral red spandrel and coral red with a green spandrel. Another silk piece, illustrated in the Bausback catalogue (p. 352) referred to above, has eight mihrabs, each woven with a large floral motif. The colour scheme is somewhat similar to the Victoria and Albert Museum fragment. Dated to eighteenth- or nineteenth-century Khotan, it measures nearly fourteen feet in length.

Probably the finest of the supposed eighteenth-century pieces, however, is the silk six-mihrab saph in the Museum für Kunst und Industrie, Vienna. The mihrab fields are all a monochrome grass green with no other decoration. The brick-red spandrels, this colour also being the colour of the border and the bars separating the mihrabs, are each woven with a bold floral or geometric motif.

Saphs continued to be woven in Khotan late into the 19th century. These are usually in a brilliant polychrome palette with eight or ten mihrabs. Each mihrab contains a large flower spray, although this has become more stylized than on the earlier pieces, and in an example illustrated in the Bausback catalogue mentioned above, the central mihrab has a geometric field. The principal border of these late saphs consists of a continuous series of squares, each woven in a contrasting colour to the next, and containing a single flower head or geometric motif. It should be noted that what we have described as the spray of flowers in the mihrabs is often called the 'tree-of-life motif'. This, of course, would relate such pieces to Baluchi prayer rugs (and possibly to the Moghul-Persian pieces, which do contain a large flower spray, although this may be symbolic). The East Turkestan examples might well have the same Shamanist source as Jon Thompson has argued for the Baluchi designs.

To both Yarkand and, principally, Khotan, are ascribed those pieces with one of the most characteristic of East Turkestan designs, the allover pomegranate pattern. This design can be found on a number of ground colours – pink-white, dark blue, light blue, yellow, brick-red 183 and a dark brown-red. Hans Bidder, in his classic work, *Carpets from East Turkestan*, points 185 out that this is one of the oldest designs found in the area of the Tarim basin, an example being seen in the carving of a wooden ceiling, datable to about A.D. 300, found at Niya, near Khotan. The majority of the carpets are woven in wool, but a few examples, such as the Metropolitan Museum example and two at Christie's, are woven entirely in silk. Again most pieces have a single system of angular tendrils and pomegranates growing from a small vase at the bottom centre of the field. There are examples, however, which have two or three adjacent systems growing from the same number of vases.

The pomegranate rugs, like some of the floral rugs and the majority of the medallion rugs, usually have one of the three predominant East Turkestan border systems. One consists of a continuous series of flower sprays, each with three blossoms. These sprays are set at angles to each other and woven in two contrasting colours – for instance, yellow stems and yellow flowers alternating with yellow stems and blue flowers. The second border, a stylized interpretation of the Chinese wave pattern, consists of a series of zig-zag lines surmounted by a form which resembles a ram's head with incurving horns. It is known as the *Yun-Tsai-T'uo* 185

Left: Khotan carpet with five-blossom system. Mid-19th century. 11 ft. × 5 ft. (332 × 152 cm.). Below: Khotan carpet with flattened oval medallions and madder-red field. Second half of the 19th century. 11 ft. 4 in. × 6 ft. 2 in. (345 × 188 cm.).

*Silk manufacture in China.
Boiling cocoons and winding silk.
Watercolour on silk.*

pattern. The third type of border is either found as the main border or as a minor guard in conjunction with designs described above and other floral or geometric borders found on East Turkestan weavings. This is the running-T border; like the swastika and Greek key patterns, also found on East Turkestan rugs, it was derived from Chinese weavings which made use of such motifs from very early times.

The question of what constitutes a gul in East Turkestan weaving seems to be a somewhat complicated one. Schürmann, in *Central Asian Carpets*, devoted a section to the drawing of Turkoman and East Turkestan guls. In the page devoted to East Turkestan, he drew the stylized peony design associated with early pieces, possibly from Kashgar, which he described as the Kashgar gul. He drew two of the flattened discs with differing floral interiors, and a single geometric cruciform motif, all three of which he described as Yarkand guls. There are then three motifs, one a stylized rendition of the Kashgar peony pattern, the second a stylized peony, but in a stepped square fretwork frame, and the third a large square, with fretwork in the corners and containing a large eight-pointed star motif (in reality a diamond superimposed upon a rectangle), which contains an octagon, which contains another octagon, which in turn contains the stylized peony motif. This last elaborate construction is taken from the two similar medallions which occur in the bifurcated field of a carpet in the Victoria and Albert Museum, dated by Schürmann to the 17th or 18th century. All three of the last described motifs are called Khotan guls.

Bidder and Lorentz do not consider the flattened disc a gul, but refer to it simply as a medallion; they refer to the peony as a gul, which sometimes appears on the same rug with the flattened disc medallion. It should be noted that some scholars, such as Adolf Hackmack, in *Chinese Carpets and Rugs*, and Wantg Te-Chun, in the catalogue of his collection, published in Hong Kong in 1966, considered the gul flower to be a chrysanthemum; Bidder, however, avers that chrysanthemums do not appear in East Turkestan weavings. We might add that the stylized peony design as it appears in East Turkestan weavings, seems obviously derived from more realistic Chinese renderings, and in its schematic form resembles the tarantula pattern found in Caucasian, Turkoman and Baluchi weavings, and even the spread-eagle motif of eagle Kazaks and some Yomut weavings.

Schürmann's description of the flattened disc as a gul makes sense if we think of the word in the context of Turkoman weavings, but it would seem as if the gul of East Turkestan weavings is *not* thought of in the same way. Turkic weavers themselves refer to it as the 'moon pattern'. This motif is not associated only, or indeed primarily, with Yarkand and is found on a rug illustrated by Schürmann himself (plate no. 94), which he ascribed to Khotan. This piece is interesting in that the field design seems based on the Persian medallion and corner form. The central flattened disc in dark blue contains seven flower heads. It appears quartered in the four corners of the field. At either end of the field on the long axis are blue vases facing the centre. From each emerge single stems, with angular parallel leaves and a single small flower at the top. These stems reach to the central medallion, thus, at first glance, giving the impression of a medallion-pole-escutcheon motif. These principal forms are surrounded, on the brick red field, with various floral motifs arranged in geometric formations. The border is a wave pattern of tendrils and flower heads.

Other East Turkestan carpets may be found apparently based on a Persian or Indian prototype. A silk and metal thread piece in a private London collection, and attributed by Schürmann to nineteenth-century Kashgar, has an allover field pattern of palmettes and flower heads surrounded by leaves. On two of the rows, the flower heads are bracketed by lanceolate leaves, a system based on the Herati pattern. H. A. Lorentz illustrates (plate no. 8) a red-ground rug over seventeen feet in length in the Bernheimer Collection. This is woven with a tight and dense pattern of arabesque tendrils and small palmettes. Although related to similar Kashgar and Khotan designs, Lorentz suggests that its unusually fine patterning and its field colour (remembering, of course, what Schürmann said about the Chihil Sultan carpet) indicate that it is of Indian inspiration.

Carpets with an allover trellice and floral pattern continued to be made throughout the 19th century, the lattice sometimes being very formalized and geometric, forming interlocking diamond and star motifs. Some of these motifs are woven on a dark aubergine ground. A specific design associated with this group has sprays of flowers with five flower heads. There are also rugs, attributed by Schürmann and others to Khotan, which have an allover geometric lattice on a monochrome orange-red ground, and others in which the flower heads are arranged in more formal rows. Some of these latter pieces are without a connecting stem system and betray, like the Caucasian rugs we discussed previously, the influence of Western taste, specifically French but probably coming via Russia. Such pieces often have unusual colour combinations of pink, grey, orange and white.

Weaving in China

We shall preface our discussion of Chinese carpets with three remarks. Firstly, China is not a country with extensive wool-rearing areas and, in any case, the Chinese looked down on wool fabrics as somewhat barbarian (as they did upon the Mongols from whom they probably imported the majority of the wool weavings they owned). Secondly, sericulture (the rearing of silk-worms and the production of silk from the cocoons) has been known in China for about 4,000 years. Until the Italian Renaissance, almost all silk materials in Europe were imported from the East, and the earliest known Chinese weavings are of silk. Thirdly, pile-knotted carpets of Chinese origin, whether of silk or wool, are all of comparatively recent date. Although some authors have ascribed a few examples to the late Ming dynasty (1368–1644), most scholars agree that no extant Chinese carpet can be dated much before the end of the 17th century, and the vast proportion are of the 18th century or later. Certainly, the Chinese looked upon the manufacture of pile-knotted carpets as a distinctly minor art form, if an art form at all.

In addition, Chinese carpets are distinct from those made in the countries and areas described so far. In general, the use of design and colour is different (although some confusion with East Turkestan weavings is inevitable) and, perhaps most importantly, the Chinese, unlike all the other peoples we have mentioned, were not Muslims, and did not have a sizeable nomad population, at least within the known history of rug weaving. Kurt Erdmann, in *Oriental Carpets*, remarked that Chinese carpets 'follow such individual paths that it is quite impossible to understand them in terms of the Oriental rug. It seems more likely that better conclusions might be reached by regarding their designs as derived from felted rather than knotted carpets'. Certainly, most writers on Oriental weaving have given Chinese pieces short shrift.

Erdmann's comments about felted pieces lead us to look at the earliest extant group of Chinese (although some have said Japanese) carpets, and indeed, one of the earliest groups of complete carpets known. In the Shosho-in Shrine Treasury at Nara in Japan is a group of thirty-one wool-felt rugs (pounded and matted fibres), decorated variously with flowers, birds, animals and people in shades of brown, red-brown and blue on white, pale blue or grey grounds. These pieces all bear the stamp of the Todara-ji Shrine in Nara, and although the connection cannot be made with absolute certainty, it seems likely that they form the bulk of the bequest of thirty-one patterned and fourteen unpatterned rugs given by the widow of the Japanese Emperor Shomu to the Todara-ji in A.D. 756 during the T'ang dynasty of China (A.D. 618–906). Many of the pieces show scattered designs: birds, shrubs growing from hillocks, clouds, pilgrims, etc; others have large flowers amongst scrolling arabesques of leaves and tendrils. There are also pieces with a large central floral medallion surrounded by other flowers. There is no field border layout. However, many of the designs appear virtually unchanged in pile rugs made over 1,000 years later.

Apart from felt, decorated floor coverings were made of a variety of different materials in China, including bulrushes, reeds and other vegetable matting. There were also pile rugs in use, as is evidenced from paintings of the T'ang and Sung dynasties, but these were almost certainly of Mongol manufacture. A factory was established in 1262 in the Mongol city of Karakoram to supply carpets to the Chinese Imperial Court. In 1279, the Mongols overthrew the Chinese Sung dynasty and established their own Yüan dynasty. Despite the fact that this lasted less than a hundred years, from 1280 to 1368, the Mongols had a radical effect upon Chinese culture. It seems probable that the conquerors brought with them their preference for wool pile-knotted fabrics: carpets, animal trappings such as saddle rugs, tent hangings, etc. Although no pieces exist from this period, the geometric style of Mongolian weaving, seen in the Sung paintings mentioned above, became part of Chinese design language. It continued to be used throughout the Ming (1368–1644) and Ch'ing (1644–1912) dynasties and in combination with the naturalism of Chinese art, forms a striking decorative scheme.

Certain symbolic or narrative elements enter into all carpets; to study the designs of weaving correctly, we have to assume that the designs have evolved from a structure which

Tsun *bronze inlaid with gold and silver in arabesque scrolls. Sung dynasty, A.D. 960–1279. Victoria and Albert Museum, London.*

Portrait of the Ming Emperor Wan Li (1573–1619). Note the five-clawed Imperial dragon on the floor embroidery. Victoria and Albert Museum, London.

could at once be 'read' by the beholder. Such readings can take many forms. The Persian Safavid carpets woven with flowers, hunting scenes and gardens can, as we have seen, be interpreted as hedonistic pictures of ease and fruitfulness, implying the goodness of God on earth; but they should also be seen as didactic in that they represent the gardens of Paradise which shall be given to the righteous. They are redolent with cosmological symbolism. So too, as Jon Thompson has suggested, may be certain designs found on Baluchi weavings, and the study of the design of Turkoman weavings revolves around the central question of the ethnic origins of the gul. As we noted, the most likely theory is that guls were once symbols identifying the particular tribe which wove them, and more than that, they were symbols of autonomy and possession, they were battle standards and heraldic emblems. Although the proof of such an interpretation has yet to be found, it is difficult to deny its probability, especially as so many of the pieces display a feel for heraldry inexplicable in any other terms.

Of all Eastern weavings, Chinese carpets are perhaps the most literal. Very few of their designs are purely decorative; plants, animals and even abstract motifs have an exact meaning. The Chinese weaver would often produce a decorative scheme to accord with the particular circumstances of the person for whom it was made.

In almost all cases, the Chinese use animals, plants and apparently abstract motifs to denote certain symbolic or literary meanings. In three particular cases, however, they use schematic versions of three characters. These are *shou*, *fu* and *shuang-hsi*, meaning long-life, luck and wedded bliss. The *shou* appears the most often in the form of a centralized schematic medallion; only the bottom half of the character is used and doubled in a mirror image head-to-head to form a circle. *Fu* is less often used, symbols such as bats being preferred, and *shuang-hsi* is not a true character, but a double *hsi* which, in this form, is symbolic of wedded bliss. It is usually found on embroideries rather than rugs; Lorentz, in *A View of Chinese Rugs*, illustrates an embroidery which has the unusual single *hsi* form, meaning happiness.

The symbolic meaning of many of the animals and other objects found in Chinese rugs relate to the phonetic punning system. Thus the bat (*fu*) is a symbol of prosperity because it is pronounced in the same way as the character meaning prosperity; butterfly (*hu*) has the same meaning because it is pronounced in a very similar fashion. Stag (*lu*) means official reward or well-being, and so on. Lorentz, in an interesting example, demonstrates that punning symbolism is not necessarily confined to single words, but can be found forming a whole sentence. Thus a rug or embroidery which shows a vase on a table accompanied by a sceptre reads, phonetically, *p'ing an ju'i*, which means, 'May you find peace and tranquility according to your wishes'. This is arrived at by the punning series:

vase = *p'ing* = peace	*ju* = according to	
table = *an* = tranquility	*i* = wish, desire	*ju'i* = sceptre

By the same token, peonies stand for riches, love and affection and so on. Other objects derive their symbolism either from religious or associative connotations. In the latter context, for instance, fish are symbolic of abundance, and carp, because they are supposed to be very long-lived, are a symbol of longevity. Peaches are also symbols of long life since they are supposed to be the food of the gods. The swastika (*wan*) is the Chinese character for 10,000. Thus the continuous swastika border, called the *wan* pattern, symbolizes 'ten-thousand-fold happiness'.

Among the many animals found on Chinese rugs, we have mentioned the bat, the butterfly, the stag and the fish. A number of other creatures are part of Chinese mythology. The phoenix (*feng huang*), King of Birds to the Chinese, and also the attribute of the Empress, is the bringer of peace and happiness; the unicorn (*ch'i lin*) is the animal whose appearance heralds the birth of sages and is thus the symbol of wisdom. The stork, the crane and the goose are all symbolic of long life; the Manchurian crane, being the companion of the Taoist immortals, is a symbol of immortality. The most ubiquitous of the mythological animals is the dragon, which has three symbolic aspects – as a powerful deity, as sovereign of the forces of nature, and as the attribute of the Emperor. Since Tao Ts'ou in 206 B.C. established the dogma of the divinity of kings, it was believed that, when in trouble, the Emperor could change himself into the shape of a dragon and thus defeat his enemies. Representations of the five-clawed dragon are traditionally supposed to have been reserved for the Emperor and his immediate family; no strict enforcement of this took place, however, until an edict of Ch'ien-Lung in 1783 put a stop to its indiscriminate use. It began to be widely used again after the overthrow of the Ch'ing dynasty in 1911.

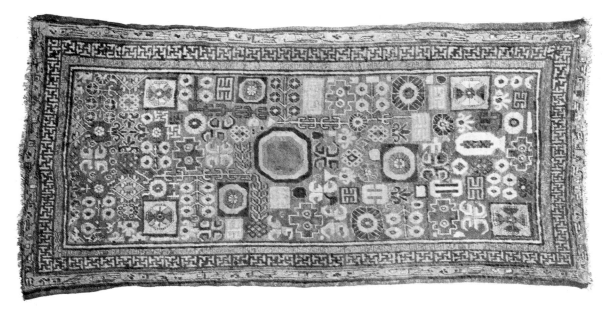

Khotan carpet. Late 19th century. Approximately 11 ft. × 5 ft. (332 × 152.5 cm.).

Flowers and fruit are also used, the lotus, chrysanthemum and peony predominating. The lotus, flower of summer, symbolizes purity; the chrysanthemum, flower of autumn, stands for longevity, and the peony, as we have indicated, for nobility, riches, love and affection. As stated before, the peach is a symbol of longevity and appears frequently with the bat as an acrostic of 'good luck and long life'. The pomegranate, with its multitude of seeds, is an apt symbol of procreation, but of male children only. The Chinese lemon, *fo shou* (literally, Buddha-fingered citron), is so-called because its rind develops into petaloid shapes which, to the Chinese, resemble the classic hand posture of the Buddha (*Fo* being his Chinese name); thus it is a symbol of great happiness. Chinese weavings also show the *Fo*-dogs who were the companions of the Buddha and who are guardians of the sacred places of Buddhism. These lion-like creatures are called *Shi T'zu*, and bear little resemblance to the modern breed of dog with the same name (which is of Tibetan origin). Horses are often shown, in some cases the eight fabulous horses of the fifth King of Chou, *Mu Wang*, who, according to the chronicle *Mu Tien Tzu Chuan*, is supposed to have used them to drive his chariot to the ends of the earth; the king reigned in the 10th century B.C.

There are also certain groups of symbols associated with particular religious beliefs and accomplishments, many of which appear in rugs. Their meanings are listed below.

1. The Eight Symbols of Taoism
These represent the Eight Spirits (*Pa Lsien*), who may be portrayed as humans or by the following symbols:
Fan – reviving the soul of the departed
Sword – supernatural power
Staff and gourd – pharmacy, healing
Castanets – soothing and comfort
Basket of flowers – supernatural power
Flute – magic
Bamboo – prophecy
Lotus-pod – supreme power

2. The Symbols of Buddhism
Wheel – the majesty of the law
Conch shell – the summons to prayer
Umbrella – dignity
Canopy – protection
Vase – enduring peace
Endless knot – destiny
Lotus flower – purity

3. The Eight Precious Things
Taken from 'One Hundred Symbols of the Book of Rites':
Pearl – purity
Coin – wealth
Books – symbolize the advantages
  of learning
Rhombus (hollow) – symbolizes victory
  and prosperity
Rhombus (solid) – painting, symbolizing
  the value of art in general
Musical stone – blessing
Rhinoceros horn – resistance
Artemisia leaf – dignity

4. The Four Symbols of Gentlemanly Accomplishments (illustration on page 193)
Flute – music
Chessboard – chess
Books – poetry
Scrolls – painting

Most of these symbols are depicted with an intertwined cloud-band motif (or, according to Dimand, a leaf). In addition, the *Ying-Yang* (male-female) symbol is often depicted, frequently accompanied by the eight trigrams – heaven, wind, earth, fire, water, mountain, thunder and clouds. The above are the major symbols. There are many more, and for a full discussion, we recommend the reader to H. A. Lorentz's book, *A View of Chinese Carpets*.

Very few extant Chinese rugs and seat covers are attributed to the 17th century. A small rug in the Textile Museum, Washington, has an allover pattern of stumpy clouds and bats. There are also ten large crane flying in the field, and one very large crane in the centre, its two curving wings forming a round medallion. Dimand, in commenting on the particular form of the clouds in this rug, notes that the wavy, scroll-like clouds of Persian carpets, derived from the Chinese, do not apparently appear on Chinese carpets. John Kimberley Mumford, in his essay on Chinese rugs published in the *Monitor* in 1916, remarked that the Chinese tended to stamp all motifs borrowed from foreign art with their own style, adapting them, as it were, to their own notions of design. Lorentz properly remarked that many of the devices borrowed from the Persians by the Chinese in the 17th and 18th centuries had, in fact, been transferred to Persia *from* China by the Mongol invasions of the 13th and 14th centuries. Both Kimberley and Lorentz also point to the appearance of Turkoman motifs in Chinese design in the latter half of the 18th century, especially through the marriage of the Emperor Ch'ien Lung to the Turkoman princess K'o Fei in 1756.

The best-known, supposedly seventeenth-century pieces include the example described above, a fragment woven with lotus and foliage on an orange ground in the Museum für Kunsthandwerk, Frankfurt, the yellow-ground runner woven with peonies and foliage in black, white and brown with a running swastika border in the Victoria and Albert Museum, London, and an orange-ground piece woven with a dragon, clouds and vases of flowers, and with a *Yun-Tsai-T'uo* border, in the Akeret Collection, Zurich.

Lorentz also attributes a group of rugs in the Metropolitan Museum to the period of the Emperor K'ang-Hsi. These include the camel-hair rug woven with 'foliage', dragons and fretwork, a carpet on a yellow ground with an allover diaper field and running swastika border, and a small yellow-ground piece woven with a blue allover fret pattern and rows of bats. In discussing the first piece, Dimand makes no note of it being woven in camel-hair, but agrees with the date, remarking that this particular 'foliage'-dragon form became very popular during the K'ang-Hsi period. The large yellow-ground piece with an allover diaper contains bats and peach sprays on alternate rows, and Dimand remarks that such rugs can be seen depicted in Ming paintings, and suggests a possibly earlier date than Lorentz. On the last piece, Dimand agrees that the style is that of the K'ang-Hsi period but is not prepared to date the rug. Dimand himself suggests that the two large rugs, in the University Museum, Philadelphia, one with a pattern of scrolling leaves and the other with an allover field pattern of linked flower sprays, may also be from the K'ang-Hsi period; however, the apparent mixture of Persian and East Turkestan influences makes a later dating more likely.

Lorentz also attributes a small blue-ground silk piece, woven with rows of what he calls 'dragons and sacrificial tables' to the 17th century or earlier, and a red-ground silk marriage carpet, woven with a rampant dragon facing a phoenix, and with a wide border containing *shuang-hsi* repeats, to the Ming dynasty. Both these are in the Metropolitan Museum. Dimand, who described the first as having a 'dragon and cloud' design, suggests that it is not from China but East Turkestan, and calls it 'somewhat crudely derived from Chinese seventeenth and eighteenth century satins . . .' He dates it to the 18th century. This piece has been reproduced many times. In the Metropolitan Museum *Bulletin* of 1909, Wilhelm Valentiner remarked that 'if ever there was a 17th century rug, this is it', and Louis Comfort Tiffany, in *Collection of Notable Oriental Rugs*, published by the Tiffany Studios in 1907, suggested that it was 'a Magistrate's rug of the sixteenth century'. Lorentz pointed out that the 'Magistrate's seal' which many authorities considered to be represented by the strange device alternating with the dragons was unknown in China and the suggestion which he adopts, coming from Valentiner, is that it represents a Buddhist altar or sacrificial table. Dimand, however, is unquestionably correct in his interpretation of the cloud, but his attribution to East Turkestan is more controversial. The design is unknown in any other weaving attributed to the Tarim Basin, and all previous scholars have been surprisingly unanimous in their attribution to China. The design, as Dimand points out, is well-known on Chinese weavings, but this particular rendering is crude and schematic compared to that found on a seventeenth-century silk banner which he illustrates as a comparison. This crudity certainly suggests a late dating, to the end of the 18th or beginning of the 19th century; like the banner, it may also have been woven for the Tibetan market. As for the marriage rug (*lung-feng*), this has a long, thick, floss-silk pile. Dimand suggests that the colours and the angularity of the drawing demonstrate that it is a nineteenth-century piece.

Throughout the 18th and 19th centuries, the Chinese style remained remarkably consistent. Carpets were frequently woven with a large round central medallion, with two smaller medallions at either end of the field; the corners had a peony trellice, and scattered on the field were peonies and foliage, butterflies, birds, bats and many of the other symbolic forms we have mentioned. In just as many examples, there were no medallions, simply an allover design of scattered motifs.

Chinese silk and metal thread carpet, with symbols of the Four Accomplishments. Late 19th or early 20th century. 7 ft. 2 in. × 4 ft. 2 in. (218 × 127 cm.).

194 To the 19th century are attributed a group of rugs of silk and metal thread (usually silvered copper). These all bear inscriptions, many of which state that they were made for use in particular imperial courts of the heavenly city. Twenty or more of these pieces are known, a group of fifteen of which was exhibited in the University of Pittsburgh in 1973 (*Imperial Carpets from Peking*). It was possible to divide them into four stylistic groups. The first had nine sinuous Imperial dragons, and a wide wave and cloud border. Although the attribution of these to the 19th century and the other carpets of the group is not now generally challenged, it should be noted that a carpet of the dragon design in the Royal Museum, Ontario, bears the inscription, according to Lorentz, *Ch'ien Lung yu Chih* – 'Made for the Imperial use of Ch'ien Lung'. Unlike the Pittsburgh group, however, it does not have metal thread in the silk field. Although the practice of placing emperors' names on objects long after they were dead is well known from ceramics, it may be that the Ontario piece, differing as it does in technique (although not in style) may be a genuine early example. Regrettably, this point is not discussed, nor indeed is the Canadian carpet mentioned, in the otherwise excellent Pittsburgh catalogue.

194 The second group consists of carpets with overt religious symbolism. One carpet in this group is the extraordinary piece once in the collection of George de Menasce, and previously dated by most authorities as seventeenth- or eighteenth-century. It depicts full-length in the field the Amitabha Buddha seated in the lotus position on the lotus throne, his right hand in the *bumisparsa mudra* (gesture of touching the earth). Around the earth are scattered lotus blossoms and above the Buddha's head, there are two facing dragons and a flaming pearl. In the border are the Eight Buddhist Symbols and four of the Eight Precious Things – the painting, the book, the Artemisia leaf and the pearl. This rug was woven, according to the inscription, for the *Ch'ien-ch'ing Kung* (Palace of Cloudless Heaven).

The third group consists of rugs with pictorial fields; one shows the fabulous horses of Mu in a landscape dotted with trees and buildings. Another, according to its inscription, is a 'Complete View of the New Summer Palace'. Although built by the Emperor Ch'ien-Lung (1736–95), the complex was restored and added to by the Empress Dowager Tz'u Hsi in 1894–5. The word 'new' in the inscription and the depiction in the field of the Empress Dowager's famous marble boat, mean that this piece cannot have been woven before the last five years of the 19th century, and quite possibly is a twentieth-century piece.

The fourth group consists of a group of carpets either of medallion and corner design, or with rows of stylized peonies in stepped squares on a fretwork field. The Pittsburg exhibition catalogue illustrated carpets of the former design in the Metropolitan Museum and the Nessim Collection, Lausanne, which also includes one in the second design. All carpets from this group are considered to have been woven in East Turkestan, specifically in Khotan (Dimand suggests that all of the so-called Imperial carpets may have been woven there). The Metropolitan Museum piece has five Imperial dragons, one in the central roundel, and the other four in the corner pieces; the field has an allover pattern of scrolling tendrils and flowers. This is repeated in a more organized way in the field. The inscription says that it was made for the *Ning-shou Kung* (Palace of Eternal Heaven). Dimand points out in the Metropolitan catalogue that several carpets with very similar dragon medallions and corners exist, but with different field patterns. He quotes the example in the Warner Museum at the University of Oregon, and in a private Quebec collection. Lorentz illustrates another from a private collection which has a field and border pattern of angular fret and flowers more typical of Khotan weaving than the Metropolitan example; this piece, like the Menasce Buddha carpet, was woven for the Palace of Cloudless Heaven. Yet another example, this one

Right: the Menasce carpet. Woven in silk and metal thread with Amitabha Buddha seated on the Lotus Throne, Buddhist emblems and four of the Eight Precious Things. Woven with the inscription Ch'ien-ch'ing Kung Yu-yung (For Imperial Use in the Palace of Cloudless Heaven). Mid-19th century. 7 ft. 4½ in. × 4 ft. ¾ in. (225 × 124 cm.). Far right: Chinese silk and metal thread carpet woven with inscription Ning-shou Kung Yuan-ko (Woven for the Palace of Eternal Heaven). Mid-19th century. A hitherto unpublished addition to this group. 8 ft. 1 in. × 5 ft. 1½ in. (246.5 × 157 cm.).

Three Mongol saddle rugs, early to mid-19th century. Left to right: 4 ft. 4 in. × 2 ft. (132 × 61 cm.); 4 ft. 2 in. × 1 ft. 11 in. (127 × 58.5 cm.); 4 ft. 2 in. × 2 ft. 1 in. (127 × 63.5 cm.). All formerly in the McMullan Collection.

uninscribed, is woven on a background of fretted squares and cruciform motifs (the *ju'i* pattern), is also illustrated by Lorentz and is in his collection. The second design, the rows of peonies with fretted squares, is well-known in East Turkestan weaving.

We should not leave this discussion of Chinese weaving without mentioning the beautiful saddle-rugs which, although possibly of Mongolian origin, are always catalogued with Chinese weaving. The best-known group of these once belonged to Joseph V. McMullan, the majority of which are now in the Metropolitan Museum, while another fine selection belonged to H. A. Lorentz, some of which he illustrates in his book. McMullan, in the catalogue of his collection *Islamic Carpets*, illustrates eighteen of these pieces, which come in two shapes, with rounded ends or with square ends and cut bottom corners. All examples are woven in two pieces and joined in the middle; thus each side is a mirror image of the other. As McMullan noted, the Senneh-knotted pile slants downwards 'thereby shedding rain and dust and making a more comfortable contact with the thigh of the rider'. Each piece has four holes cut into it to enable it to be placed more securely under the saddle bosses.

These thick-piled artifacts are woven with field and border and in a variety of designs. Some have the crackled-ice pattern well-known from *K'ang-Hsi* blue and white porcelain; others have peonies and scrolling foliage, *Fo*-dogs, butterflies, bats – indeed, all the motifs of Chinese carpets. Others have allover geometric patterns more characteristic of Mongol design, while several have striped designs based upon animal skins, especially that of the tiger. One particular example now in the Metropolitan Museum has a peculiar irregular broken stripe which McMullan suggests may be based upon the antlers of a stag and thus relates back to Mongol Shamanist animal worship. Most saddle-rugs are datable to the 18th and 19th centuries. McMullan was of the opinion that they were woven in Mongolia but Lorentz, following Hackmack, felt that the traditional attribution to Kansu province and elsewhere in China was more probable.

Weaving in Tibet

As we have noted in our section on the history of East Turkestan, the Tarim basin was under Tibetan control during the 8th century A.D. The history of Tibet before the 7th century A.D. is undocumented, but it is known that, in the same century, peoples from what are now the eastern regions of Tibet moved down into the fertile Yarlung valley, on the present borders of Nepal, Pakistan and Bhutan, and formed a strong kingdom, the outstanding monarch being Songsten Gampo (*c.* A.D. 609–49). During the next two hundred years, Nepal, parts of northern India and west China as far as Kansu, and, of course, the Tarim basin, came under Tibetan control. It is thought that during this time, the Tibetans must have been on diplomatic terms with the Persian Sassanian dynasty, and even came into contact with the Arabs, who were bringing Islam steadily eastwards. It was at this time, however, that the Tibetans adopted Buddhism.

The empire collapsed around A.D. 850 and the Tibetans remained scattered, until the Mongol invasions of the 13th century brought some semblance of unity. From then until the Chinese communist invasion of 1959, Tibet was ruled by Buddhist religious orders and, from the 17th century, by the Dalai Lamas of the Gelugpa or Yellow Hat order. The majority of the population were farmers or pastoral nomads, raising sheep, cattle and yak.

According to Philip Denwood, who has written an authoritative book on Tibetan weaving (*The Tibetan Carpet*, 1974), pile carpets have been in common use in Tibet for at least 900 years. The two most common words for carpet in the Tibetan language are *gdan* and *grum-tse*. *Gdan* is not used to denote pile carpets specifically, but *grum-tse* almost certainly is. Its first recorded use is in the 11th and 12th centuries; the use of the word *gdan* goes back earlier, being found in eighth- and ninth-century texts.

Although examples of unusual Tibetan weavings are known (for instance, pillar rugs for wrapping round pillars, which were also produced in China) the Tibetans used their rugs most frequently for sitting and sleeping upon. They also slung them over donkeys, and like the Mongolians, made special saddle-rugs (*makden*); it was not unusual for there to be a saddle-rug under the saddle and a larger rug on top of it. Most Tibetan carpets, the earliest examples of which are dated by Lorentz to the 18th century, are square or oblong in shape, and rarely exceed about six feet in length. Since the Chinese occupation of Tibet, thousands of refugees have settled in the foothills of the Himalayas, and many of them

Tibetan medallion carpet. 19th or 20th century. 5 ft. 2 in. × 3 ft. (158 × 91 cm.).

weave standard 6 feet by 3 feet carpets, although they will produce pieces of different sizes if commissioned. These pieces, very coarsely woven on cotton warp and wefts and synthetically dyed, are of little interest.

Most of the surviving Tibetan carpets date from the last hundred years – Lorentz's dating of some examples illustrated in his book, *A View of Chinese Carpets*, to the 18th century is a little dubious. The Tibetans use a particular form of Senneh loop knotting, a descendant of the earliest form of U-loop weaving; the Tibetan version, which is also practised in Finland, has a single looped knot encompassing anything from two to five warp threads, thus resembling the *jufti* or false knot so prevalent in Persia today. The pile on Tibetan pieces is left long and shaggy, being up to three-quarters of an inch in depth of pile.

Lorentz distinguishes three basic forms of Tibetan carpet. The first was made in central Tibet, in the provinces once called Ü and Tsang, and has been sometimes referred to by European dealers as a *gyantse* rug, after the name of the trading town on the Lhasa road which organized the export of such pieces to the bazaars in Kalimpong and Darjeeling in north Bengal. Coarser versions were woven at Kampa Dzong on the Tibet-India border. The second type were woven by the peoples of what Denwood has called the Tibetan cultural influence, settlers in China in the two regions of Amdo in Kansu and Kham in Szechwan. Although coarsened versions of Chinese styles were produced, the Tibetans stuck to their traditional weaving techniques in most instances. It is possible, however, that the problematic silk rug in the Metropolitan Museum, discussed in the previous section on China, woven with dragons and clouds, may have been produced by Tibetans resident in China. In Kham and its environs, a coarse peasant rug was produced with long wool fringes on all four sides. Such pieces were called *tso*-rugs; they were usually woven with designs in blue and black, swastikas, flowers and wheels being the most popular emblems. According to the Tibetan scholar Lobzang Phunthsog Lhalungpa, pieces intended for the laity were usually woven with white grounds, and those for priests with yellow or red. The finest group of Tibetan rugs, which includes those of largest size, are called by the Tibetans themselves *gya-rum*. Even these, however, although based on Chinese prototypes, are coarse in comparison.

Both Lorentz and Denwood have commented upon the similarity between some Tibetan designs and those found on Caucasian pieces, a similarity which is undeniable. Sir Aurel Stein remarked upon the similarity between much Tibetan and Caucasian folk architecture. Denwood posits the theory that certain motifs once common stock in central and eastern Asia were trapped in remote areas like Tibet and the Caucasus (and in this context we could again mention Finland). This, however, seems unlikely, because the designs we are seeing in Caucasian and Tibetan pieces are not ancient patterns which have remained unchanged, but highly formalized and schematic renderings of what may once have been more representational symbols. More likely is Denwood's alternative suggestion that examples of Caucasian weaving were imported into Tibet by Armenian traders active in the area in the 17th and 18th centuries.

An interesting rug reproduced by Lorentz and attributed by him to the 18th century (plate no. 84) has a diamond lattice containing stylized cruciform motifs similar to those found on certain Turkoman and Baluchi pieces. His piece, albeit with a typical Chinese-East Turkestan running-T border, also has a colour scheme – brown, brown-red, buff and white – which is reminiscent of Turkomans and Baluchis. Furthermore, it emphasizes the diagonal nature of the design by making the cruciform motifs white and red in alternate rows on the diagonal axis. This method of handling the design is, as we remember from our Baluchi section, common to certain Baluchi carpets. As for the design, Lorentz suggests that it represents the *vajra*, the symbol of incorruptible virtue, which is usually represented by a design somewhat similar to a forked thunderbolt. Comparing its similarity to Baluchi pieces, the possibility arises that some of the designs on Turkoman and Baluchi pieces might well have an origin in Eastern cosmology, and not just in the Shamanist belief.

Later Ottoman Weaving

AS WE HAVE EMPHASIZED FREQUENTLY, Turkish weaving throughout its long history shows a remarkable consistency. Motifs and ideas of design which can be traced back to the Seljuk fragments of the 13th and 14th centuries reappear in easily recognizable form in late nineteenth-century village weavings. Concomitant with this historical progression is the notion of the individual design which appears, has a period of some popularity and then disappears or is transmogrified into another concept.

We are thus dealing with two distinct areas: the conscious creation of specific designs and the evolution of design through an ethnic cultural structure. In the first case, as we have shown in our section on early Ottoman weaving, there seems little doubt that patterns such as the Lotto, the star Ushak, the Cairene floral carpets, the bird Ushak and the balls-and-stripes Ushak were created by designers in well-appointed workshops for an aristocratic and Imperial clientèle. In some instances, such as the Holbein carpets, the designs as they appeared in the 15th and 16th centuries were certainly the culmination of a long history and it is probable that, whatever original significance the patterns may have had, it was unknown to the skilled designer working in the sophisticated urban milieu of a court workshop. The similarity between the geometrical ornament on these early Turkish pieces and that found on Turkoman and other tribal weavings suggests strongly that they evolved out of a common heritage of tribal symbolism. That many of these decorative motifs may have been current for at least three millennia is evidenced by the diamond lozenge diaper seen on Anatolian carpets depicted in fifteenth-century paintings, in particular those by van Eyck; an almost identical pattern is seen on a felt saddle rug excavated at Pazyryk by Rudenko in 1947, which dates from the 5th century B.C. (see Rudenko, *Frozen Tombs of Siberia*, plate no. 162).

However, the vitality of carpet design in Turkey is clearly shown by the adoption by village weavers of designs which originated in the court workshops. In the 17th century, the earliest time we are able to make distinctions between court and village weaving, it is not at all clear whether in fact village weavers saw the designs being produced in the towns and set about consciously adapting them, or whether, as seems more likely, they simply absorbed them into an already existing repertoire of motifs. Certainly, the characteristic simplification and formalization which occurs in Persian weaving when court designs are copied in more rural environments, occurs also in Turkish weaving. The most important example of this phenomenon is the prayer rug.

In our section on early Ottoman weaving, we discussed the prayer rugs produced either in Cairo or Anatolia for court use, and the early examples from Ushak. In eighteenth- and nineteenth-century Turkey, the production of prayer rugs is associated principally with village weaving, and in particular with the towns and surrounding areas of Ghiordes, Ladik and Bergama.

Ghiordes Prayer Rugs

The most prolific of these towns is Ghiordes in western Anatolia, which has given its name to a distinctive group of prayer rugs woven in the surrounding villages. There are two principal groups of Ghiordes prayer rugs, although the origins of one remain controversial. This group has a plain red mihrab, a horse-shoe-shaped arch from which hangs a schematic rendering of a mosque lamp and, in a few examples, columns which have been formalized into decorative bars with no architectural function. A number of these pieces, which date back to the early 18th century, are known; they include examples in the Metropolitan Museum, the St. Louis Museum of Art (ex-Ballard Collection), the Bernheimer Collection (illustrated in Erdmann's *Oriental Carpets*, plate no. 159), ex-Kevorkian Collection (Sotheby's, 5 December 1969, and again Lefèvre, London, 11 February 1977), the Museum of Islamic Art, Cairo (illustrated in *Prayer Rugs*, Textile Museum, Washington, 1974, fig. 10), etc. The most interesting, if the least attractive, example is illustrated by Kurt Erdmann in *Seven Hundred Years of Oriental Carpets* (plate no. 216), which is in the Evangelical Church at Rosenau in Transylvania. This is embroidered in the mihrab with the inscription 'M Hissen A.D. 1736'. It has been suggested that this inscription was added when the rug was presented to the church, a suggestion which implies that the name and date do not refer either to the rug's maker or to the year in which it was woven. It is more likely, however, that the

Eighteenth-century Ghiordes prayer rug. Approximately 5 ft. 9 in. × 4 ft. 6 in. (175 × 137 cm.).

inscription *is* the work of the weaver, and that she was Armenian. The 'M' before the name probably signifies *machdesi*, a title that Armenians who made the pilgrimage to Jerusalem were allowed to use throughout their lives. Iten-Maritz, in his book *Turkish Carpets*, a study largely of modern Anatolian weaving, illustrates another example of this usage on a nineteenth-century Turkish piece. It is certainly unlikely that an Armenian would have presented an already existing piece to a Protestant church, having first embroidered it with a defiant symbol of his Armenian orthodoxy.

The rugs of this group are so different in style from the more distinctive and prevalent type of Ghiordes prayer rug that scholars have found it difficult to reconcile them both to the same place of origin. Charles Grant Ellis, in his article, 'The Ottoman Prayer Rug', in the *Textile Museum Journal*, drew attention to the large numbers that are preserved in the Protestant churches in the Transylvanian Alps, now part of Romania, and suggested that they were woven in this area when it was part of the Ottoman Empire, or in nearby European Turkey. It seems fairly certain, however, that rugs of this design were being woven in Ghiordes in the late 19th century; Iten-Maritz illustrates a piece from his collection which he says is referred to in Turkey as a 'Kizil Ghiordes' (red Ghiordes) and which he dates to about 1875.

The finest examples of this type are dated to the mid- to late 18th century. Although all the village prayer rugs quite obviously evolved out of the court prayer rugs of the 16th century, these horse-shoe Ghiordes pieces are the closest link. The magnificent court rug in the Metropolitan Museum, for most admirers of Oriental carpets one of the finest, if not *the* finest, existing Ottoman prayer rug, has a triple-arch mihrab with columns. The outer two arches are red and the centre a dark blue-green. From the central arch hangs a realistically delineated mosque lamp, and from the base of each column grow realistic plants. The wide pale blue borders are woven with large palmettes, carnations, tulips, lilies and feathery lanceolate leaves. In the horse-shoe Ghiordes rugs, as in other village pieces, the realism and refinement of the drawing disappear, the columns, in all but a few specific instances, are reduced to decorative devices within the mihrab, and the lamp begins to resemble a bunch of flowers. In the borders, Ghiordes rugs, especially early examples, retain the palmette and lanceolate leaf pattern, but in a heavy schematic form, similar to the way the Herati pattern is changed in Kurdish and Caucasian weaving.

The second group of Ghiordes prayer rugs has been regarded traditionally as one of the classic types of Turkish village weaving; in saying that, however, we should note that Joseph V. McMullan, one of the most distinguished and successful collectors of Turkish carpets, remarked in his catalogue that 'the well-known prayer rugs called Ghiordes and Kula find no place in this collection. They deviate markedly from the mainstream of Turkish thought in both design and colour and they do not possess the robust character and spirit which is in the great tradition of Turkish rug-weaving.' Other authors have described the delicacy and femininity of these pieces, a style which certainly contrasts with the strength of the geometric ornament and boldness of colour – equal in intensity to the most vivid Caucasian carpets – which are found on the majority of the McMullan pieces and which their owner, with some historical justification, felt to be representative of the mainstream of Turkish rug weaving. However, the prayer rug occupies a particular place in Turkish weaving and it is obvious that the delicacy of detail, which is characteristic not only of Ghiordes pieces but of all other examples from the major weaving centres of Anatolia, was considered a desirable attribute; to suggest that such an idea is a marked deviation 'from the mainstream of Turkish thought' when it is obviously an important aspect of the mainstream of Turkish weaving is perhaps overly contentious. There is no evidence that the Turks themselves felt the same way.

The mihrab of the typical Ghiordes prayer rug is squarish, with shoulders and a V-shaped arch; it is usually dark blue, red, buff, cream or white. It is surrounded by an elaborate system of floral borders, the total width of which, on either side of the mihrab, is greater than that of the mihrab itself. It should be added that the format of the rug itself, especially the older examples, is unusually square, and the predominant colour scheme of the border system is usually brown-cream-yellow which gives the lacy effect which some authors have described as feminine.

The earliest of these pieces are now considered to date from the late 18th century (although Erdmann and others suggest that they can be dated to the beginning of the 18th century), with dated examples being known from the 1790s; however the majority are from the 19th century, and scholars have been at pains to distinguish features of design and structure which will help in dating both the examples which are considered to be from the Ghiordes region and those examples produced in great quantity in other parts of Anatolia and also in Europe – Bulgaria, Roumania and Italy being the most frequently mentioned countries. Perhaps the most detailed work has been carried out by Murray Eiland in his book *Oriental Rugs, a Comprehensive Guide*. He suggests that the earliest pieces are more curvilinear and the mihrab is more dominant in relation to the borders. The mihrab itself contains two columns (which do not, however, join the shoulders and are thus, even in the pieces generally considered to be the earliest, purely decorative devices) and a small lamp in the arch, which, again, has been converted into a floral motif even in the early pieces. Some examples, such as the white-ground piece illustrated by Eiland as no. 71a, have three free-standing plants at the base of the mihrab, a fact which further strengthens the link between these pieces and the court prayer rugs, such as the example in the Metropolitan Museum mentioned above. At either end of the mihrab is a transverse bar or panel (*takhta*) containing floral motifs. In structure, the earliest examples are woven on a wool foundation, with alternate warps depressed, and have a fairly fine knot count of between 120 and 200 to the square inch.

Thus, in determining whether or not a piece is late, the scholar will have several pointers: construction of the foundation; fineness of weave; size and shape of the mihrab; layout of the borders; nature of the ornament within the mihrab; and the nature of the ornament within the borders and *takhta*.

In examples from the early 19th century, the mihrab becomes more compact and the border system wider. The latter does not become more elaborate in design; if anything, the drawing is stiffer and the modelling of the floral motifs more schematic. The number of borders grows, however, and in some pieces there is a central system of seven narrow stripes which is called the *çubukli* (or *shobokhli*) border, supposedly symbolic of the seven steps of Paradise. Pieces exhibiting this motif are now considered to be fairly late, as are those in which the mihrab is squashed up into a rectangular shape. There is also an important structural

change in late pieces, the wefts being of cotton. On many later pieces, the mihrab lamp which, in contrast with the small schematic motif contained within the arch on pieces supposed to date from the 18th century, grows into a long design taking up most of the centre of the mihrab on the long axis. There is also an increased use of cotton for the white areas of the field, a material used only sparingly in early examples.

Thus far, we have considered rugs which may be considered as genuine examples of Ghiordes weaving. There seems little doubt, however, that the immense popularity of such pieces on the Western market, even during the 19th century, caused them to be copied in several Turkish weaving centres and in Europe. In Turkey itself, Ghiordes copies have been attributed to Panderma, Kayseri, Bursa, Istanbul and Hereke; according to Eiland, they can be attributed also to Corfu and as far afield as Tabriz in Persia. The examples from Kayseri are the most frequently encountered, these having a noticeably elongated mihrab. In the 20th century, the copying continued, with a marked degeneration in the interpretation of the design and in the quality of manufacture. A rug reproduced as no. 9 in the catalogue *Oriental Rugs from Canadian Collections* has several unusual features, not least of which is that it is woven entirely on cotton. This fact, and the rug's extraordinary mixture of motifs associated with both early and late Ghiordes weavings, aroused lively suspicions as to its origins and date. Weaving in Ghiordes all but ceased in the 1920s, but rugs similar to the Canadian piece appear in several books on modern Turkish weaving, are often attributed to Kayseri and are given dates within the last fifty years.

There are several other designs attributed to Ghiordes. These include two specific types of prayer rug: the Kis Ghiordes or betrothal rugs, and *mazarliks* or grave rugs. The former have a large cut-sided diamond lozenge (the mihrab) within a square field, the mihrab thus being double ended. It contains another smaller diamond medallion. Two examples are in the Metropolitan Museum and the Museum für Islamische Kunst, Berlin, respectively, being dated by Dimand and Erdmann to the early 19th century. Another, and possibly the finest of the three, is in the Iten-Maritz Collection (*Turkish Carpets*, page 149); this is dated 1863, and there is no reason why either the New York or Berlin pieces should be considered to pre-date this example. In all three, the white-ground mihrab is decorated with small hollow circular motifs, called *sinekli* or fly-specks, a decorative device found on many types of Ghiordes rugs and almost invariably on the Kis Ghiordes pieces. This design, and the field colour, are repeated in wide zig-zags in the main borders (these zig-zags are, in fact, large criss-cross patterns over which the square central field is laid, a device found also on Caucasian carpets). The diamond lozenge in the centre of mihrab has a blue ground; its shape, according to Iten-Maritz, is symbolic of eternity and its colour of fidelity.

The cemetery or grave rugs (*mazarliks*), of which there are two examples in the Metropolitan Museum (catalogue nos. 134 and 135), are usually woven on a pastel ground; the mihrabs contain realistically drawn symbols of mourning, including tombs, mausoleums, cypress trees and willows, together with floral motifs. They were woven by the whole family following the death of one of its members and were either handed on to the next generation or given to the local mosque, thus being sometimes called *turbeliks* (mosque rugs).

Large secular rugs were made in Ghiordes, usually of square format. A good example was included in the Sotheby's sale of 14 April 1976, lot 18. This had a large dark blue field, woven all over with a tight diaper of tiny flowers in a diagonal system. In the centre and at the four corners were large rectangular floral sprays. Inner and outer borders were decorated with the same alternate repeat pattern of sprigs and flower heads, whilst there was a central *çubukli* border, the stripes alternately black and white; these contained tiny floral motifs similar to those on the field. The design of this piece, an apparent adaptation of prayer rug design, should also be related to the early court carpets with medallion and corners and an allover field pattern, usually of ball and stripes (for instance, the McMullan piece now in the Metropolitan Museum and an almost identical example in the Berlin Museum). The regularity of the motifs, and the *çubukli* border, suggest a dating for the Sotheby piece in the mid-19th century, rather than the 18th century, as stated in the auction catalogue.

Ladik Prayer Rugs

The second of the major rug weaving areas is the northern town and surrounding district of Ladik. Like the horse-shoe arched mihrab prayer rugs of Ghiordes, the triple-arched prayer rugs of Ladik have a close stylistic link with the sixteenth- and seventeenth-century court

Nineteenth-century Panderma prayer rug with white cotton mihrab field. The style is derived from Ghiordes. 5 ft. 3 in. × 4 ft. 1 in. (160 × 124.5 cm.).

Opposite, top left: late eighteenth-century Ghiordes prayer rug with sinekli *decorated mihrab and* çubukli *borders. 4 ft. 7 in. × 3 ft. 7 in. (140 × 109 cm.). Opposite, top right: nineteenth-century Panderma prayer rug in the Ghiordes style. 5 ft. 4 in. × 4 ft. 1 in. (152 × 124 cm.). Opposite, bottom left: late eighteenth-century Kis Ghiordes prayer rug. 5 ft. 8 in. × 4 ft. 3 in. (172.5 × 129 cm.). Opposite, bottom right: late nineteenth-century Persian silk prayer rug from Tabriz in Ghiordes style. 5 ft. 6 in. × 3 ft. 11 in. (168 × 119 cm.).*

prayer rugs. However, in saying this, we are unintentionally avoiding one of the most controversial issues of modern carpet scholarship. There are, essentially, two types of Ladik prayer rug. The first has a tripled-arched niche supported by columns, six of which appear in the mihrab, the outer two running down the mihrab's sides. The large mihrab is surmounted by floral spandrels, above which is a transverse bar containing reciprocal trefoils or arrow heads (sometimes called 'Vandycks') and long slender tulips. The most usual field-colour is red. Although there are rugs with this basic design, but with differences in the border pattern or in the weave, which suggest that the type as a whole had a long history and possibly emanated from different places, we may, for the time being, consider it as homogeneous.

The second type of Ladik is generally considered more recent in date, although its history certainly goes back to the 18th century. The majority of scholars are satisfied in attributing it to Ladik. In these pieces, the mihrab still retains the suggestion of the triple-arch form, but in the examples where columns appear (this is not always the case), they are only two and they have been reduced to the same decorative status as those found on Ghiordes rugs. The most significant difference is in the size of the mihrab, which has shrunk in width, and in length is never more than half the total length of the rug, and in the majority of cases is only one third of the length. In these examples, the transverse bar of the earlier pieces has been enlarged into a square panel which has usually been moved to the base of the mihrab, but is still occasionally found at the top, as in the ex-Ballard example in the St. Louis Museum of Art (*Prayer Rugs*, Textile Museum, no. XVI). The contents of this panel, however, are the same as those found in the triple-arch Ladiks, namely a reciprocal trefoil pattern, and long-stemmed tulips which, when the panel is at the base of the mihrab, face towards the bottom of the rug, and the other way when the panel is above the spandrels. A number of examples bearing dates in the last two decades of the 18th century are known. It is probable that the pieces with the largest mihrabs containing decorative columns, and with three well-defined arches – that is those that remain closest in overall design to the first group – are the earliest.

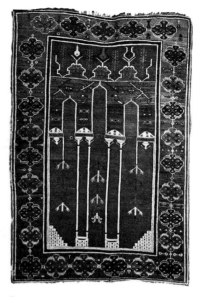

Late seventeenth- or early eighteenth-century triple-column Ladik prayer rug with three unusual candelabra motifs in the mihrab. 5 ft. 4 in. × 3 ft. 5 in. (162.5 × 104 cm.).

As we can see, there are many similarities, as well as obvious differences, between the two groups, and it might be thought that the second group obviously represents a degeneration of the design found in the first group. But here the controversy begins. The first group, which is generally considered to have the longest history, overlaps the second in time, and is itself a 'village-version' of the columned court prayer rugs of which, we repeat, one of the best examples is in the Metropolitan Museum.

Several fine examples of the first group are known; these include pieces in the following collections: the Textile Museum, Washington; Dumbarton Oaks; the Metropolitan Museum (two ex-McMullan); ex-Kevorkian (Sotheby's, 5 December 1969, lot 9), in the Bernheimer Collection (illustrated in Erdmann's *Oriental Carpets*, plate no. 160), ex-Davazanti Collection (illustrated by Bode and Kühnel, fig. 36), the Turk ve Islam Museum, Istanbul (illustrated by Iten-Maritz, p. 47). An odd piece is illustrated by Kendrick and Tattersall (plate no. 55); this has three long candelabra-like motifs in the mihrab between the columns, stepped squares in either base corner and more under the central pairs of columns. This piece appeared at Christie's on 13 January 1975, lot 28, as part of a distinguished collection of carpets sold anonymously, which included the fine star Ushak we have mentioned in a previous section, and another fine triple-arched Ladik prayer rug. The Kendrick and Tattersall piece was described by the auctioneers as Ushak. The field colour for the mihrab in these early pieces is usually red but can be fawn-yellow.

There is evidence from European paintings that such prayer rugs were reaching the West by the second half of the 17th century. The most significant of these pictorial representations is the still life by Nicolaes van Gelder, dated 1664, in the Rijksmuseum, Amsterdam; this shows clearly details of the mihrab and columns, the spandrels and borders, all of which are almost identical to the same features found on the majority of the rugs listed above. Nevertheless, despite the proof that such rugs were being woven in the mid-17th century, few scholars are prepared to admit that any of the surviving examples can be dated so early, and this has lead to a critical analysis of the rugs which is, for the layman, somewhat confusing. Thus, in the section under Ladik in the Textile Museum's *Prayer Rugs*, we read that 'a group of prayer rugs was woven during the eighteenth and nineteenth centuries in the town and district of Ladik, the ancient Laodicea . . . the earliest Ladiks, which can be dated to the first half of the 18th century, are known as column Ladiks'. Yet we know, without any doubt (and this can be rarely said of any Oriental rugs), that such pieces were being produced in the mid-17th century, and it is possible that the finest examples should be dated thus. The Metropolitan court rug is dated to the late 16th century, which would suggest that the concept of the design took less than a century to infiltrate the traditional culture of Turkish village weaving. It might be added that Murray Eiland, who demonstrated that the traditional association of Ghiordes with the ancient city of Gordium is false, also suggested that the same is true of the association of Ladik with Laodicea, which, he says, was probably on the site of the present city of Denizli.

As to where such pieces were woven, the traditional attribution to Ladik has been challenged frequently in modern scholarship. In an essay in *Oriental Art*, May Beattie suggested that the technical differences between the triple-arch or column Ladiks and the later small mihrab versions makes it difficult to believe that they were woven in the same place. In addition, one rug of this group, the Dumbarton Oaks piece, has a floral-geometric border, is a pale rust colour, has double arches on the side 'aisles' of the mihrab, and is heavier and thicker in construction than the other examples. These differences led Charles Grant Ellis to suggest that it, at least, may have been woven in Transylvania or European Turkey. The association with Transylvania cannot be lightly dismissed. Several of the rugs associated with the latter place exhibit the same borders and the same spandrel design of jagged lanceolate leaves enclosing stylized rosettes (for instance, the piece in the Metropolitan Museum illustrated in McMullan's *Islamic Carpets*, no. 89). It should be noted, however, that the Transylvanian rugs, which we will discuss in detail later, are now generally attributed to Bergama. The later group of small mihrab Ladiks post-date the triple-arch pieces by a century or more, so that the comparatively minor technical differences between the two are not wholly incompatible with a common place of origin. Certainly, the stylistic affiliations between the groups make it difficult to believe that they were not woven in the same geographic and cultural milieu. The Istanbul triple-arch Ladik has a gold-yellow and red colour scheme; it also has the usual cartouche borders, but with the double-crowned outer arches like the Dumbarton Oaks piece. It should certainly be considered among the earliest of such rugs, although the museum's dating of the 16th century is almost certainly too early. It might well pre-date the American piece by a century, however, thus providing an 'earlier model' unknown to the compilers of the Textile Museum's catalogue. Rugs of the later small mihrab design continued to be woven well into the 20th century, but with an increasing crudity of drawing and with a lot of synthetic dye.

Bergama Rugs
The Transylvanian rugs, which we have mentioned many times before, constitute another interesting, and at times controversial, group. As we have seen, many different designs of prayer rugs have been preserved in Protestant churches in the Transylvanian Alps, but one particular group, being the most prevalent, has been called after the region of discovery. As we noted above, these pieces are now thought by most scholars to have been woven in Bergama. In making this attribution, they acknowledge that the layout of the double-ended mihrab with its spandrels contained within a square is probably derived from late sixteenth-early seventeenth-century Ushak prayer rugs, although the date of the earliest Bergama pieces (from the evidence of European paintings, the second decade of the 17th century at the latest) suggests that 'derive' may be too strong a word. Both the Ushaks and the Bergamas may be independent but concomitant village adaptations of the Persian medallion and corner designs, and the Turkish court versions, of the late 16th century. The design of the double-ended Ushak mihrab with its central medallion, and the similar Bergama Transylvanian design, indicate only a peripheral connection with the normal unequivocal design of the prayer rug; in some instances there appears a rendering of a mosque lamp, more or less schematic, but in an equally large number no such motif appears. Early writers, such as Kendrick and Tattersall, did not even consider the possibility that such pieces as these were prayer rugs.

The region known as Transylvania was only under Ottoman rule between 1526 and 1699 and many of the existing Bergamas date from the latter end of this period. Something like a third of the various types of Turkish rugs found in the Protestant churches there are of the Bergama Transylvanian pattern. Their earliest appearances in European paintings, invariably in works of the Dutch school, date from the 1620s – for instance, *The Portrait of Abraham Grapheus* by Cornelis de Vos in the Royal Museum of Fine Arts, Antwerp, and the *Portrait of Constantijn Huygens* by Thomas de Keyser in the National Gallery, London; the carpet in the latter work has a most unusual green warp and field. The type continued to be popular and examples are found in paintings far into the 18th century. A particularly well-known representation of a later style of Transylvanian rug appears in the group portrait *Isaac Royall and his Family*, executed by the American painter Robert Feke in 1741, and now in the Harvard Law School.

The majority of these rugs have double-ended mihrabs, although a few, such as the fine example in the Metropolitan Museum (catalogue no. 89), which also has an unusually realistic mosque lamp, have conventional single-arched niches. The mihrab contains one of two designs: an angular arabesque of stems with large flowers, with a mosque lamp at either end which, within the context of the floral design, might also be subconsciously intended as vases, or a single large central medallion which in some cases can, with short poles at either end, take up the whole length of the mihrab. The mihrab itself is usually buff, red or cream.

In some of the floral mihrab designs (such as that illustrated in McMullan's *Islamic Carpets*, no. 86) there is no interconnecting angular arabesque between the flower heads. The spandrels usually contain large flower heads and lanceolate leaves rendered in stiff angular form; however, some pieces (for instance, McMullan, *Islamic Carpets* no. 85, or the piece in the Industrial Museum, Budapest, illustrated by Bode and Kühnel as no. 34) have a geometric arabesque related to the pattern of Lotto carpets.

Nineteenth-century Çanakkale (Bergama) rug, with a design which echoes that of some of the large pattern Holbein rugs of the 15th and 16th centuries. 5 ft. 8 in. × 3 ft. 3 in. (172.5 × 99 cm.).

The most consistent features, however, are the borders. The main border on the majority of pieces contains alternate square and rectangular stars. The square stars themselves contain other, more lace-like, eight-pointed stars, while the large rectangular stars contain angular open medallions, arabesques and flower heads related to the designs found in the mihrab and spandrels. An interesting feature of all old Bergama Transylvanians with this border is that the pattern is never satisfactorily resolved at the corners. A large number of the pieces have a guard stripe on either side of the main border with a reciprocal trefoil pattern.

We have described above the most typical form of this easily recognizable class of rug. There are, however, variations of motifs in many examples. In some versions of the border, there are only the rectangular stars; such borders tend to be found with rugs which have the central medallion and are assumed to be later than the floral lattice pieces. Still later examples, such as the rug depicted by Robert Feke in his group portrait, have the single rectangular star borders, but these rectangles contain a stiff system of six rosettes surrounding a central diamond. We have described also the cartouche and tulip border of the McMullan piece, an identical design to that found on early Ladik triple-arched prayer rugs. The early type of Transylvanian border resembles closely, of course, the star and cartouche borders of Mamluk rugs. Depending upon whether or not one considers the latter to pre-date or post-date the Ottoman conquest of Egypt, the Transylvanian border may be an adaptation by Anatolian weavers of the Egyptian design or, as Dimand would suggest, it is taken from Persian carpets, upon which it appeared from the beginning of the 16th century. As we have shown in our section on Mamluk weaving, the design was known from manuscript illumination and bindings long before its apparently earliest use on Persian carpets, and it may be that the Mamluk weavers developed it independently of the Persian influence which would have come to them via the Ottomans. Another Transylvanian variation, in the Bernheimer Collection (illustrated in Erdmann's *Oriental Carpets*, plate no. 162), does not have the cut-sided diamond mihrab, but one with zig-zag sides; this has the rectangular star border and is thus probably early eighteenth-century. Another piece also illustrated by Erdmann in the same book (plate no. 161) has a large central medallion which is hooked at the sides into realistic flower heads seen in profile, while the border contains a continuous system of large flower-head palmettes.

Also from Bergama and the surrounding villages came a variety of secular rugs with geometric ornament, the majority of which are attributed to the 19th century. In many instances, these are the direct descendants of the large pattern Holbeins which are assumed to have been produced between the 15th and 17th centuries in this same area. However, it is impossible not to note the similarity between many nineteenth-century rugs, both in design and colour, and those produced in the Caucasus, a resemblance due in some part to the presence of many pockets of immigrants from around Baku and other Caucasian regions.

Carpets very similar in style to those made in the nineteenth-century Bergama region, and even closer to the large pattern Holbeins, were also woven in the Dardanelles area around the town of Çanakkale; many of the pieces which have systems of large squares, which themselves contain geometric motifs, are now associated with this area, rather than with Bergama further south. This association with Çanakkale only began to be realized in the 1960s. When Kurt Erdmann examined the contents of the Turk ve Islam Museum in the 1950s, he noted, as he wrote later (*Seven Hundred Years of Oriental Carpets*, pp. 109–110), that many of the later variants of the large pattern Holbeins bore labels saying 'Chanakkale', which was, according to the author, 'a name unknown in Europe'.

Village Weaving

South and east of Çanakkale, there are several small towns and villages (Ezine, Manyas, Can, Avunya, Balikesir, Kirné, etc.) where weavings virtually indistinguishable in style from Caucasian rugs are produced, although the colouring tends to be softer and more mellow. Many of these pieces, including those of Çanakkale, have been marketed traditionally through Bergama, which thus tends to be used in the West as a generic term. It has to be said that

there is often very little difference either in style or quality between many of the products of these various villages, and the task of making accurate differentiations is a daunting one. On the finest examples, there is a thick heavy pile again reminiscent of Caucasian weaving.

Joseph V. McMullan, in his *Islamic Carpets*, illustrated an extensive group of such pieces, being one of the first to collect them systematically. He divided them into three groups; the first, which he called, after Bode, Holbein variants, loosely consists of rugs in which the field layout has a central square flanked at top and bottom by two smaller squares, which in some instances may have been turned into corner pieces, thus betraying an affinity with Ushak and Bergama double-ended prayer rugs with a central medallion. The second group are what McMullan suggests are highly schematic Anatolian versions of garden carpets. The design consists of interlocking panels of one colour forming a broad double arrowhead formation; the background colour of the field shows through in the channels and geometric areas between these panels. Several examples are known, mostly attributed to Bergama. McMullan no. 99 is now in the Metropolitan Museum; another example was in the Kevorkian Collection (Sotheby's, 11 December 1970, lot 1; Ian Bennett, *The Book of Oriental Carpets and Rugs*, p. 15); a third was sold at Christie's on 13 January 1975, lot 23. In these three examples, in which the field designs are almost identical, the panels remain separate. Subsequently, or concomitantly, rugs were woven in which only the outside outline of the total form created by the panels was retained and at either end, there appeared arrowhead indentations which McMullan, in discussing no. 100 in his collection, suggested were architectural features derived from prayer rugs. In a third example from his collection, no. 101, the arrowhead indentation has become an open-sided octagon at the end of a channel. This latter motif is well-known from sixteenth-century Anatolian prayer rugs and we mentioned specific examples in our section on early Ottoman weaving. It will be remembered that they are shown frequently in sixteenth-century Italian paintings; the German scholar Joanna Zick, in *Eine Gruppe von Gebetsteppichen und ihre Datierung*, has traced the earliest European representation back to 1469. We have instanced two works by Lorenzo Lotto (*Virgin and Child with Four Saints* in Treviso, painted in 1507, and *Virgin and Child Enthroned* in San Spirito, Bergamo, dated 1521). We can be certain, therefore, that the motif was common on Anatolian prayer rugs by the middle of the 15th century. We noted also that

Opposite, top: Robert Feke: Isaac Royall and Family, 1741. Harvard University Portrait Collection, Fogg Art Museum, Cambridge. Opposite, bottom left: Bergama Transylvanian prayer rug. Late 17th century. 5 ft. 9 in. × 4 ft. (175 × 122 cm.). Opposite, bottom right: Bergama Transylvanian prayer rug. Early 18th century. 5 ft. 8 in. × 4 ft. (172.5 × 122 cm.).

Below left: Bergama rug of garden design. Early 19th century. 8 ft. 9 in. × 5 ft. 4 in. (267 × 162.5 cm.). Below: Bergama rug with a field showing the influence of Transylvanian prayer rugs and border of Kufic inspiration. Early 19th century. 6 ft. 6 in. × 5 ft. 9 in. (198 × 175 cm.).

Top: Bergama rug. Note the similarity of the design to many Caucasian pieces. Late 19th century. 5 ft. 6 in. × 4 ft. 5 in. (167.5 × 134.5 cm.). Above: late nineteenth-century Ezine Bergama rug. 5 ft. 9 in. × 5 ft. 8 in. (175 × 173 cm.).

two single-ended mihrab prayer rugs in the Metropolitan Museum (ex-Ballard Collection), the earliest of which dates from the late 16th/early 17th century, have this motif at the base of the mihrab and there is another, similar to the earliest Metropolitan piece, in the Musée des Arts Décoratifs in Paris. This has the beautiful cloud-band borders found on some sixteenth-century floral court rugs of the so-called Cairene type, which are attributed to either Cairo, Istanbul or Bursa. Bode and Kühnel attribute the Paris rug to Ushak. Also in the Metropolitan there is a piece with the octagons facing at either end, which Dimand calls a prayer rug and dates to late seventeenth-century Ushak.

As to what the octagon and channel signifies, Joanna Zick suggested that it represented a niche within a niche, her colleague Volkmar Enderlein, drawing a comparison with a similar but less schematic motif found on a very early Mamluk rug, thought that it represented a bird's eye view of a canal and water basin, thus symbolizing the ritual ablutions undertaken by devout Muslims before prayer, while Charles Grant Ellis, in a note in the Textile Museum's *Prayer Rugs* catalogue of 1975 said that it represented a stylized mountain, 'such as may be found at the bottom of Chinese dragon robes and temple pillar rugs. The worshipper thus stands upon elevated ground.' Whatever view one wishes to take, the motif remained extremely popular, being used continuously on both prayer rugs and their secular derivatives throughout the 18th and 19th centuries.

We should note that very similar pieces were woven in the Caucasus. In the previously mentioned Textile Museum catalogue, a Kazak prayer rug of the 19th century has identical borders to the two McMullan Anatolian rugs, nos. 98 and 99, and similar interior motifs, including stylized cypress trees, to McMullan no. 100. Peter Bausback, in his 1975 catalogue, illustrates a nineteenth-century Bergama rug with octagonally indented field, which he relates to the designs found on Lori-Pambak carpets and we may speculate that the resemblance between the opposed arrowhead formations of separated bars in the first of the McMullan carpets and the similar format of early Caucasian dragon carpets may not be entirely coincidental. A fragment of an early prayer rug in the Staatliche Museum, Berlin, also has a diamond-bar and channel layout (Bode and Kühnel, fig. 37); a complete version illustrated by Murray Eiland and attributed by him to Bergama (*Oriental Rugs*, plate no. 82), shows the typical double-ended form and is dated by the author 'probably 18th century'. This piece, however, lacks the elegance of the Berlin fragment and is probably later in date. Iten-Maritz, in his book *Turkish Carpets*, primarily a study of modern Anatolian weaving, illustrates a twentieth-century Bergama prayer rug of related form to the Berlin piece, and a double opposed-octagon carpet of about 1875 which can be related to both the McMullan pieces and to the Kazak and Lori-Pambak rugs. This Iten-Maritz describes as a 'Kozak' and remarks that such pieces are frequently called Bergama in the West, the Turks referring to the design as *kalkali* (circular). Kozak, a corruption of Kazak, from whence its inhabitants originated, is a small town about fifteen miles north of Bergama, through which its weavings are marketed.

McMullan also illustrates (plate no. 102), a rug from his collection in which the double-ended octagon and square has become one huge medallion on a red field, a device often encountered on Caucasian rugs. The colours of this piece, primarily dark red and blue, led the owner to identify it with Anatolian Kurds. However, in Kendrick and Tattersall (plate no. 108a), there is a prayer rug with an open-ended hexagon and channel mihrab arch, which form is echoed by a similar indentation in the base. The colour scheme is much the same as on the McMullan piece, and the authors explain that it is called *jakshibehdir* or 'charcoal-burner'. Another example, of similar form and colouring, was included in the Christie's sale of 13 January 1975 (lot 8).

The third of McMullan's divisions for the village rugs of the 19th century is for pieces which 'continue the 15th century tradition of the dual medallion, or repeat octagonal patterns, both often represented in 15th century European paintings'. Of such pieces the most successful and well-known have a square red field containing two large octagons; these octagons have cream grounds, and in turn contain two smaller red octagons which are surrounded by eight thick radiating blue bars, each one of which contains a hooked geometric motif in red. In the spaces between the bars are single stars. In the triangular spaces on the outer edges of the field between the octagons are hooked triangles, which on some rugs (for instance, McMullan no. 106) are repeated in the corners. Surrounding the large octagons, there are single rows of geometric motifs or flower heads. The main border is either based on a diamond or square lattice, or has single floral medallions; such borders are brilliantly multi-coloured, giving an effect suggesting stained glass.

There were three such pieces in the McMullan Collection. One (no. 103), now in the Metropolitan Museum, another (no. 104), less bold, with smaller octagons, and the third sold at Christie's on 12 June 1975, lot 32 (an example close in style to no. 103, but in poor condition). This piece was erroneously catalogued by the auctioneers as being McMullan no. 103. A fourth example, also in the Metropolitan Museum (ex-Rose Collection, Dimand catalogue no. 93) has variations in colour; the central small octagons, for instance, are pale green and the border is a stiff octagon repeat, each octagon containing an eight-pointed star. A fifth piece, very similar to the McMullan rug now in the Metropolitan Museum, was sold at Sotheby's on 14 April 1976, lot 26. A sixth, very similar to McMullan no. 104, was included in the 1975 Bausback catalogue (p. 36). A seventh rug, in terms of both colour and condition the finest of those we have mentioned, was unillustrated in the Sotheby sale of 18–19 November 1976, lot 33, and is at the time of writing on the London market. Although described in the Sotheby catalogue as 'fair', the piece was in almost mint condition, with a thick, deep pile; the field colour was a rich madder-red and the rug retained its original wide rust-coloured kelim ends. Once again, its sumptuousness, both of pile and colour, reminds one of Caucasian pieces. (Illustrated opposite, bottom picture.)

Konya rug with an apricot field; archaic design. Late 19th century. 7 ft. 3 in. × 6 ft. 8 in. (221 × 203 cm.).

The rugs with the repeat pattern of octagons hark back, of course, to the Seljuk fragments of the 13th and 14th centuries, and are related to Caucasians, Turkomans and to the checkerboard Mamluks which, as we have noticed, are considered by many authorities to be of Anatolian origin. McMullan illustrates an example from his collection with six large joined octagons, each of which contains a cruciform geometric motif, which, he suggests, are the schematic birds of early Seljuk animal rugs rendered abstract by the passage of time. Such an interpretation, although worthy of attention, is possibly a little dramatic. A more direct connection with the purely geometric designs of the Seljuk fragments may be found in pieces housed in Turkish museums.

One particular example in fragmentary condition is illustrated by Erdmann in *Seven Hundred Years of Oriental Carpets* (plate no. 121); this has rows of eight octagons on the long axis, each octagon containing a geometric motif; between the rows are white bars, with arabesques in the spaces between each group of four octagons. This piece is attributed by Erdmann to 'Anatolia sixteenth to eighteenth century'. Two examples of the same design, but obviously much later, probably 19th century, appeared in the London salerooms of Lefèvre on 29 November 1974 and 4 February 1977 (lot 1). The compilers of the catalogue pointed out the relationship between these pieces and the early versions of the small pattern Holbeins found on a fragment from the mosque at Beyshehir now in the Mervlana Museum, Konya; Erdmann illustrates this piece (*Seven Hundred Years*, plate no. 44) and assigns it to the early 15th century. He remarks that the device of dividing the field into squares by the use of axial lines (as happens not only in the early fragment but in later variants) occurs in only one other group of early carpets – the checkerboard Mamluks which we mentioned above in connection with another Seljuk fragment. It is interesting that this pattern of interlocking octagons with axial lines is a prevalent motif in Anatolian kelims; two splendid examples appear in David Black and Clive Loveless's study *The Undiscovered Kelim*, illustrated as plate nos. 30 and 31.

Other Turkish Centres of Weaving

The characteristic Turkish prayer rug designs of Ghiordes, Ladik, Ushak and Bergama appear on rugs woven in several other towns and areas during the late 18th and 19th centuries. Those most frequently encountered are Konya, Panderma, Kula, Kakri, Melas, Mudjur, Kirshehir and the tribal versions known as Yuruks; all these names are associated also with secular rugs of geometric design, which look for their origins not only in old Seljuk pieces but also in Caucasian rugs and the designs made popular in the major weaving centres of Ottoman Turkey – principally Bergama and Ushak. It is difficult to make specific comments differentiating the prayer rug designs of these various centres. In many cases, they are derived, if not actually copied, from the rugs we have discussed. To be able to make accurate attributions with confidence requires considerable experience and any statement about, say, the design of Kula rugs, which often have triple-arched mihrabs and decorative columns, could as well be applied to any other group.

Top: striped Melas (Karaova Melas) prayer rug. Mid-19th century. 4 ft. 4 in. × 3 ft. 6 in. (132 × 107 cm.). Above centre: late eighteenth- or early nineteenth-century Mudjur prayer rug. 5 ft. 10 in. × 4 ft. 7 in. (178 × 140 cm.). Above: nineteenth-century Kirshehir rug. 5 ft. 8 in. × 4 ft. (173 × 122 cm.).

Melas Weavings

A distinctive group is that associated with Melas, a town in the south-west of Turkey; these pieces are especially admired by present-day collectors, and prices of late have been very high for good examples (which do not, it must be said, seem particularly rare). They have a distinctively shaped mihrab and an unusual colour scheme. The layout of the best-known type of prayer rug consists of a central rectangle. This has a series of narrow stripe borders which may contain different geometric motifs. Within this border system is the mihrab, which takes up about two thirds of the remaining length of the rectangle. The mihrab is nine-sided, the rectangular sides being pinched in at the top so that the arch is arrow-headed in shape. Above the arch is a large area of white, which has woven upon it angular floral motifs. Surrounding the central rectangle is a very wide border with a series of large palmettes separated by angular stems and smaller flower heads; there is then a guard with a reciprocal zig-zag. The colour scheme is predominantly yellow, rust-red, brown, aubergine and white, the aubergine colour, subtle and muted, being a particular hall-mark of Melas weavings of this type. Although Eiland remarks that the majority of such pieces are fairly coarsely woven, the close-cropped pile and soft wool give the best pieces a velvety sheen and a supple handle.

Other designs are also attributed to Melas. The so-called Ada-Melas prayer rugs are woven in the peninsular (*ada*) between the towns of Karaova and Bodrum. According to Iten–Maritz the name should be applied only to one specific type of rug characterized by its strange design and colour scheme of restrained brown-red (blue never being used). The design, an example of which he illustrated (p. 198), has two wide borders of geometric motifs; the field, a thin column in the centre, has, along its entire length, a comb motif like a giant centipede. Iten–Maritz remarks that no other type than this is ever made, but then proceeds to confuse the issue totally by illustrating, seven pages on, another rug described as an 'Ada-Melas' with a completely different design, the geometric borders surrounding a field which contains a pole medallion of two hexagons. This has a colour scheme of red, red-brown, orange, yellow and grey. In his 1975 catalogue (p. 69), Peter Bausback illustrates a prayer rug which he describes as Ada-Melas which has a central field which would be square but is pinched in at either side with a series of steps so as to form a flat-topped mihrab. This contains a tree-of-life motif with branches surmounted by comb-like leaves resembling large feathered *botehs*. A similar mihrab shape and a similar motif are illustrated on the next page of the same catalogue but this piece is described simply as Melas. This latter piece, from the McMullan Collection, was sold at Christie's on 12 June 1975 (lot 37). The tree-of-life

pattern with feathered *botehs* is also found on secular Melas rugs: for instance, the fine example sold by Lefèvre in London on 4 February 1977 (lot 14). In this same sale (lot 15), there appeared another small secular Melas, the field containing two squares, each of which contained rows of tulip heads, smaller squares and rows of star-like flower heads. Other nineteenth-century Melas pieces have a medallion and corner design in yellow, orange and grey on a vivid red field which, in style, relate to Ushak and Bergama prayer rugs and are descendants of Cairene court carpets. The last important design from this area is the striped Melas, in which the field is divided into vertical panels. In some cases, these are secular, but in others, the outline of the typical Melas arrowhead mihrab arch indicates a prayer rug.

Above left: mid-nineteenth-century Melas rug. 3 ft. 8 in. × 3 ft. 3 in. (112 × 99 cm.). Above right: late eighteenth- or early nineteenth-century Smyrna rug, possibly woven in Ushak. 6 ft. 10 in. × 6 ft. 3 in. (208.5 × 190.5 cm.). Ex-Kevorkian Collection.

Above, left to right: Yuruk carpet showing the influence of many different styles – Turkoman, Caucasian and Bergama, mid-19th century, 8 ft. 10 in. × 5 ft. 9 in. (269 × 175 cm.); late nineteenth-century Hereke silk prayer rug of double-niche form. 6 ft. 11 in. × 4 ft. 10 in. (211 × 147 cm.); nineteenth-century Koum Kapou silk rug of Indo-Persian inspiration, 6 ft. 3 in. × 4 ft. 3 in. (190.5 × 129.5 cm.).

Opposite, top left: nineteenth-century Koum Kapou silk rug of Persian animal carpet design. 6 ft. 10 in. × 4 ft. 4 in. (208.5 × 132 cm.). Opposite, top right: early twentieth-century Koum Kapou silk and metal thread carpet, based on a Persian tile pattern design. 9 ft. 8 in. × 6 ft. 11 in. (295 × 211 cm.). Opposite, bottom left: nineteenth-century Hereke silk and metal thread carpet, the design being of the same type as that of the Salting carpet. 6 ft. 7 in. × 5 ft. 4 in. (200.5 × 162.5 cm.). Opposite, bottom right: early twentieth-century Turkish (Hereke or Istanbul) silk rug of Indo-Persian inspiration. 10 ft. × 3 ft. 3 in. (305 × 99 cm.).

Smyrna Weavings

A type of carpet as distinct in style and colouring as those from Melas is the so-called Smyrna. Such pieces are known traditionally by the name of this port (now called Izmir), since they were almost certainly woven for export and left Turkey via Smyrna. It is thought that they were woven in Ushak. Carpets of this group are comparatively rare. Examples include one in the McMullan Collection (*Islamic Carpets* plate no. 95), another once in the Kevorkian Collection (Sotheby's, 10 December 1970, lot 7; Bennett, *The Book of Oriental Carpets and Rugs*, p. 99), and a third recently on the London market (Raymond Benardout, *Turkish Rugs*, 1975, no. 15). The Benardout piece, although possibly the oldest, was described as late seventeenth-century, which is too early. McMullan remarks that pieces of this kind are supposed to have been produced solely in the 18th century, while the Sotheby catalogue attributes the Kevorkian piece to the early 19th century. In decoration and colour all three are very similar. The field is orange-yellow; upon it are woven large peony blossoms in yellow, red and blue. In the Kevorkian and McMullan pieces, there also appear rows of quatrefoil motifs. The borders, in orange-red, have a system of ovoid cartouches separated by flower heads, a similar design to that found on early triple-arched Ladik prayer rugs, and on some Bergama Transylvanians. The designs of these pieces are almost certainly derived from the floral court carpets of the 16th and early 17th centuries, and they are woven with a fairly thick, heavy, pile. It seems unlikely that any should be dated from much before the end of the 18th century, and were produced throughout the 19th century.

Mejedieh (Mejid) Rugs

In the 19th century in many areas of Turkey were woven rugs with a particular type of decoration called Mejedieh or Mejid. It should be emphasized that this name applies to a style, not to the place of manufacture or marketing. Such rugs are woven in pastel shades, and are decorated principally with flowers in a style based on European, probably French, prototypes. They take their name from Sultan Abd ul-Mejid I (1839–61), who was extremely well versed in European culture, dressed in the European fashion and decorated his palaces in French style. This chronology is generally accepted, although some scholars have argued that the very odd prayer rug illustrated by Erdmann in *Oriental Carpets* (plate no. 166) which is dated 1760–1, suggests an earlier history for the type. This rug, previously in a Berlin private collection, is attributed by Erdmann to Kirshehir and the author remarks that the European influence is particularly strong on weavings from this area, which is south-east of

Top: late nineteenth- or early twentieth-century Hereke silk copy of the Ardabil Mosque carpets. 9 ft. 4 in. × 4 ft. 10 in. (284 × 147.5 cm.). Above: nineteenth-century Hereke silk carpet of Persian inspiration. 13 ft. 8 in. × 11 ft. 4 in. (417 × 340 cm.). Above right: mid-nineteenth-century Koum Kapou silk and metal thread carpet of arabesque design. 5 ft. 6 in. × 3 ft. 7 in. (168 × 109 cm.).

Ankara. It is true that in the 19th century, Kirshehir was well-known for the production of rugs in the Mejedieh taste, a taste which embraced not only secular pieces but also prayer rugs, particularly *marzaliks*. The Erdmann piece has neo-classic columns and a central cypress tree; in style, it reminds one not so much of French as Biedermeier taste. However, the stylized floral border is not untypical of Kirshehir weaving. Almost certainly the date as given in Erdmann is a hundred years too early. It would not be unreasonable to attribute such pieces to the mid-19th century. It would have been easy to have altered the date.

Yuruk Weavings

The word Yuruk, which means literally 'mountain nomad' is applied to weavings produced by Turkish nomads of no particular tribal association. They are a mixture of Kurds, Caucasians and Turkomans, and their shaggy-piled pieces, with strong geometric orna- 212 mentation, reflect their tribal heritage. They are made principally in the eastern part of Anatolia. As Murray Eiland has pointed out, the more modern Yuruk pieces are often very distorted in shape. However, little or no serious scholarly work has been done on Turkish nomadic weaving and the finest Yuruks, which often subtly change the well-known designs of established village weavings, are well worth attention and study and will almost certainly reward the discerning enthusiast.

Turkish Weaving in the 19th and 20th Centuries

212   We come now to the production of silk carpets in nineteenth- and twentieth-century Turkey.
213   It is believed that the Imperial looms were established in the town of Hereke in 1844, prob-
ably concomitantly with the revival of fine weaving at Bursa. What is not known is whether the looms of Koum Kapou, in the suburbs of Istanbul, were established at this time also or whether, as many writers have supposed, weaving did not begin here until about the last decade of the 19th century. What remains indisputable, however, is that in terms of sheer technique the silk rugs of nineteenth-century Turkey are supreme in the history of pile carpets. What stops them from being great works of art is the fact that the designs, although executed with almost miraculous precision and with an unrivalled beauty of colour, are almost

Below left: silk carpet based on a Hereke copy of a Persian animal carpet. Made by the Tossounian factory on the island of Corfu, c. 1930. 5 ft. 9 in. × 4 ft. 3 in. (175 × 130 cm.). Below: nineteenth-century Koum Kapou silk and metal thread prayer rug of the so-called Safavid type. 5 ft. 10 in. × 3 ft. 11 in. (178 × 120 cm.). Bottom: Hereke wool pictorial rug. Late 19th or early 20th century. 6 ft. 3 in. × 4 ft. (191 × 122 cm.).

Above: late nineteenth- or early twentieth-century Turkish silk prayer rug of Moghul inspiration. Probably a copy of the Pincket rug. 5 ft. × 3 ft. 3 in. (152.5 × 99 cm.). This rug was formerly in the Benguiat Collection and was catalogued by F. R. Martin as Moghul c. 1640. Above right: early twentieth-century Turkish silk prayer rug: the overall design is of late sixteenth-century Ottoman inspiration, and the field pattern of the mihrab and the Kufic borders are copied from one of the Seljuk carpets in the Turk ve Islam Museum, Istanbul. 6 ft. 6 in. × 4 ft. 5 in. (198 × 132 cm.).

completely derivative; hardly a spark of creative imagination illuminates them. The principal source of inspiration is Persian Safavid weaving of the 16th century, and in our section on Safavid rugs, we have discussed those pieces – the Salting group and the prayer rugs – which Erdmann and others have demonstrated, with little room for doubt, were woven in Turkey in the 19th century. We might add that pieces in the style of Cairene court rugs and Moghul rugs were also produced. Many examples, especially those rugs and carpets made at Koum Kapou, frequently use metal brocading, including multi-coloured gold in their brilliant and striking designs.

Perhaps the most graphic illustration of what we might consider to be a waste of brilliant technical ability is afforded by two extraordinary silk Hereke prayer rugs which appeared at Christie's on 12 June 1975, and again the following year. These had a triple-arched mihrab, the architectural features and spandrel decoration of which were clearly derived from the Metropolitan Museum Ottoman court rug. However, the field of the mihrab was woven with a tight diamond lattice containing stylized flower heads; the borders were woven with a large stylized Kufic pattern. The combination of field pattern and border gave one an uneasy feeling of *déja vu* until one realized that they were copied directly and very accurately from what is probably the best known of the fragmentary Seljuk carpets discovered in 1905 in the Alaeddin Mosque. This piece, first published by Sarre in 1907, and reproduced in colour by F. R. Martin in *A History of Oriental Carpets before 1800*, is also reproduced in Erdmann (*Seven Hundred Years of Oriental Carpets*, plate no. 25) and by other scholars who have had occasion to discuss the early history of weaving. To find its decorative motifs appearing on twentieth-century Hereke silk prayer rugs, the rest of the designs of which have been copied from a sixteenth-century piece, is peculiar, but to be expected. The designers of Hereke and Koum Kapou were nothing if not eclectic.

213
214

Tuduc Carpets

In conclusion, we should mention the existence in the early part of this century of an extraordinary Romanian workshop which, like its founder Tuduc (or Duduk), has acquired an almost legendary status. Its business was the production of rugs and carpets in the styles of the great weaving centres and cultures of the East. Whether or not it was the intention of the factory to deceive is a moot issue, but that it succeeded in doing so is unquestionable. Although most experts today would claim to be able to spot a Tuduc copy, it is my experience that the possible presence of one in their midst is the cause of considerable dissension and acrimony. The result can sometimes be more than a little ironic.

Kurt Erdmann, for instance, wrote a famous essay called 'A Carpet Unmasked', re-published in *Seven Hundred Years of Oriental Carpets*. In this, he writes of a group of Turkish and Caucasian copies by Tuduc, including the white ground balls-and-stripes Ushak which the Victoria and Albert Museum purchased in 1933. In the essay we are left in no doubt that such a piece would not now gain credence from any major museum, despite some unfortunate experiences in the past. The irony of it all is that in *Seven Hundred Years* Erdmann published for the first time another Ushak white-ground balls-and-stripes carpet, which he had been instrumental in purchasing for the Berlin Museum in the late 1950s, and which he considered to be an important seventeenth-century example of the type. This piece is now recognized by all scholars as being a Tuduc copy of the 20th century.

Similarly, it now seems probable that a not inconsiderable number of the Transylvanian rugs published by Schmutzler in 1937 in his classic *Altorientalische Teppiche in Siebenburgen*, one of the bibles of carpet scholarship, are in fact Tuduc copies; and at least one apparently important white-ground Ushak sold at auction in 1976 for a large sum of money emanated from the same Romanian factory.

Moroccan and Tunisian Rugs and Carpets

VERY FEW NORTH AFRICAN WEAVINGS, with the exception of those from Egypt, have found their way to Europe; even the most recent products, for the most part gaudy with synthetic dyes and very poorly woven, are rarely seen here. Thus the study of North African tribal weaving, like that of the applied arts from the same area, has been passed over by most writers on Islamic culture. Only the French with their territorial interests have given a degree of time and scholarship to the classification of the urban and nomad arts of Morocco, Algeria and Tunisia. In the context of weaving, we should mention P. Ricard's *Corpus des Tapis Marocains* (1923) and L. Poinssot's and J. Revault's *Tapis Tunisiens* (1950–7).

In the early years of the spread of Islam, the areas called the Maghreb and Ilfrikiya, which now comprise Morocco, Algeria and Tunisia, were backwaters of the Moorish empire of Spain, although the Moors were of North African descent. In the first half of the 8th century, the Moors founded an Emirate based on Cordoba, which was under the direct rule of the Damascus Umayyad Caliphate. In A.D. 750, when the Umayyads were defeated and the Abbasid Caliphate founded, the Moors remained faithful to the Umayyads, and in A.D. 929 founded their own anti-Abbasid Umayyad Caliphate at Cordoba. This city became one of the great cultural centres of Western Islam, reaching its apogee under Abd-ar-Rahman III (A.D. 912–61) and his successors Hakam II (A.D. 961–76) and Hisham II (A.D. 976–1009), spreading the influence of the Umayyad style throughout Spain and North Africa.

In the 11th and 12th centuries, North Africa, like Moorish Spain and Egypt, was under the rule of various Berber dynasties. The Sultanate of the Almoravids (1087–1147) established their capital at Marrakesh, the first and only time that Moorish Spain was ruled from North Africa. During this time, the Umayyad Caliphate of Cordoba having been defeated, allegiance was given to the Abbasid Caliphate, although the Moorish empire remained autonomous. The Almoravids had little interest in art, but under their successors, the Almohads (1147–1235), the first flowerings of the new Moorish style appeared. During this time, the Fatamid Caliphate, another anti-Abbasid group, who had been rulers in parts of North Africa since A.D. 909, gained control of Egypt. They, too, were Berbers, as were the Idrisids of Fez, in what is now the northernmost part of Morocco, who ruled from A.D. 788 to A.D. 974, the Aghlabids, who ruled in Kairouan, now in Tunisia, from A.D. 800 to A.D. 909, and their successors, the Zirids (A.D. 909–1150), who were related to the Fatamid rulers of Egypt. The Almohads unified much of North Africa and Spain. After their decline, the area broke into several groups, the Nasrids in Granada ruling from 1232 to 1490, the Merinids in Fez from 1216 to 1470 and the Hafsids in Tunis from 1228 to 1574; at about the same time, the Mamluks established their empire in Egypt. From the late 15th century, the Ottomans established either direct rule or strong influence over the whole of North Africa. This remained the case until the present century, when it fell subject to European, especially French and British, territorial expansion.

Although we have evidence that carpet weaving was carried on in Moorish Spain and Egypt from a very early period (existing Spanish carpets from the 14th and 15th centuries are representative of a long-established craft), there is no evidence that such an activity was carried on in North Africa, except for Egypt, at so an early a date, although we can presume that it was. No Moroccan or Tunisian carpets exist from before the 19th century; in the case of Tunisia, Jacques Revault, in *Designs and Patterns from North African Carpets and Textiles*, states that the most important carpets, those from Kairouan called *zerbiya*, were not woven in that city before the mid-19th century; their technique and predominantly Anatolian patterning were traditionally supposed to have been introduced by the daughter of an Ottoman Turkish governor. Other woven textiles dating from long before this time are, however, known from the area.

All North African carpets are somewhat barbaric versions of Anatolian weaving. They are produced predominantly by nomadic peoples, and in texture are coarse, the pile being long and shaggy. There can be up to seven wefts between each row of knots, giving examples a ridged appearance. North African carpets tend to have a fairly standardized design. Often up to fifteen feet in length (particularly true of the earlier examples), they have a square in the centre of the field containing a large diamond-shaped medallion with stepped edges. The diamond itself usually contains stylized floral and geometric motifs clearly derived

Moroccan carpet showing the typical format of large central stepped medallion. Compare this to the layout of the Safavid Portuguese carpets. Late 19th century. 12 ft. 10 in. × 5 ft. 5½ in. (385 × 166 cm.). Islamische Museum, Berlin.

from both Anatolian and Moorish designs, and the spandrels at either end of the diamond contain either a tight geometric pattern (as can be seen from the example in Berlin) or scattered motifs similar to those contained within the diamond (an example of this type is illustrated in Jack Franses's useful guide, *European and Oriental Rugs*, fig. 45). Surrounding the central square there are usually rows of flowers, often tulips, and multi-coloured rows of squares containing geometric motifs, like a patchwork quilt. As we have mentioned before, the overall decorative effect is not dissimilar to the Persian Safavid Portuguese carpets and to a group of related Caucasian pieces. The colours, the outstanding features of Moroccan weaving, are mellow shades of red, blue, mauve, green and yellow. On some examples, the field, a bright saffron yellow, has scattered motifs around the square, rather than a pattern of organized rows.

Moroccan and Algerian Carpets

The majority of Moroccan carpets were woven by the Kabylie and other nomadic tribes in the Atlas and anti-Atlas regions, and marketed initially in small towns such as Tiznit, Taroudant, and Tintazart. According to Jack Franses, there are made today rugs of good quality using browns and greys on natural coloured fields. These are woven in and around large urban centres, such as Marrakesh itself. In Algeria, the town of Sétif is particularly associated with the manufacture and distribution of carpets.

Tunisian Carpets

Tunisian pieces are generally in a different style to those of Morocco, although many do have the same layout of a central square containing a stepped diamond. The best-known pile-knotted pieces are those which have been made for about the last hundred years in the city of Kairouan, in the west of the country. The motifs found on these pieces, which are reasonably well-woven, are familiar from a study of Turkic urban and tribal weavings, although some of them have been given interesting names. A design similar to the Turkoman line is called 'roses in boats', a typical Anatolian star motif is called 'swallows', a diamond trellice containing cruciform motifs is called 'the Lord's tiles', and a large trelliced medallion of a type found on Persian, Anatolian and Central Asian weavings, is called 'Assembly'. A study of the derivation of some of these names might give a clue to the original meanings of the motifs, but it seem more likely that they were given such names as mnemonics to aid the weavers.

Bedouin Weavings

More interesting than these derivative urban pieces are the weavings of the nomadic Bedouin. According to Jacques Revault, such weaving has almost ceased today; in the past the tribes of central and southern Tunisia (the Hamama, Zlass and Mahadba) and a few in the north (the Drid and Ouled bou Ghanem) were well-known for their pile-knotted pieces. These, however, were made only on commission from a tribal chief or wealthy oasis owner, and were greatly outnumbered by flat-weaves. Such carpets (*ktif* or *ktifa*) were used as both mattresses and blankets during the winter, but were otherwise used only on ceremonial occasions or as part of the lavish hospitality afforded to guests. The fields of such pieces are made up of geometric ornament, obvious floral or animal motifs rarely appearing; the field is divided up into various large squares, or horizontal rectangles, each rectangle containing a different geometric repeat pattern. Stylistically, many of these pieces resemble some of the earliest Seljuk or Mongolian carpets. However, just as many seem to have typical flat-weave designs translated into pile, which is an unusual transposition; in Anatolian weaving for instance, kelims sometimes appear to be flat-woven versions of pile carpets (and are usually the worse for it), but pile carpets never imitate the more typical kelim designs.

Later Persian Weaving

IN 1722, following the Afghan invasion, the Safavid dynasty was overthrown. For about the next one and a half centuries, Persia was in a state of some political confusion. Following the intrusion of the Afghans, both the Turks and the Russians attempted to stake territorial claims, and the British looked upon Persia as being within their sphere of influence. In 1736, the Afghan leader Nadir Kuli ascended the throne, being known thenceforward as Nadir Shah; he extended the frontiers of his empire through Afghanistan and into India, capturing Delhi in 1738. In 1747, however, he was assassinated, and from 1750 to 1779 the country was under the regency of Kerim Khan Zand. He, in turn, was overthrown by Agar Muhammed Khan Kajar, founder of the Kajar dynasty which lasted until the revolution and ascension to the throne of Riza Khan, father of the present Shah, in 1925. Edwards, in his survey of modern carpet weaving in Persia, suggests that the real revival, or rather the conversion of weaving into a major export industry, began under the influence of Tabriz merchants in 1875, and was strengthened by the establishment of Ziegler and Company's offices at Sultanabad (now called Arak) in 1883.

In discussing weaving in Persia during the 19th and 20th centuries, the reader has to consider a number of somewhat confusing issues. Basically, there are two predominant groups: the tribal village carpets, and the urban factory pieces. Names for particular types of carpets do not necessarily refer to the place in which they were woven; they can refer also to the town in which they were marketed, to a particular design, or to a certain quality of weave; they can even refer to size. In other words, it has to be remembered that for the last hundred years, weaving in Persia has been a highly commercial affair, in the hands of dealers and merchants. Such dealers have classified carpets in terms of merchandise. This has caused a veritable babel of names which it is often difficult to sort out after so long a passage of time, especially as dealers in different countries have often used different names to describe the same carpets, and there has never been consistency in spelling.

Weaving Areas in Persia

It would be useless, in such a comparatively short survey as ours, to attempt a complete breakdown of the hundreds of different types of modern Persian weaving, many of which are, in any event, almost indistinguishable one from another. For the purposes of discussing the carpets in broad outline, however, it is feasible to divide the country into four principal areas: West, Central, East and South. Within each broad area, there are sub-sections.

West
1 *Far North-west:* weaving centred mainly on the town of Tabriz. This area also includes Herez and Gorovan.
2 *Central North-west:* the area around Hamadan, including Senneh.
3 *South North-west:* towns and villages of Saruk, Malayer, Jozan, etc.
4 *Central west:* area south of Malayer, around Arak.
In the above areas we also find nomadic rugs, especially those of the Kurds.

Central
1 *North Central:* Teheran.
2 *Central:* (i) the area around Kashan and Kum; (ii) the areas around Isfahan, Joshaqan and Nain.
3 *South Central:* environs of Kerman.
In the region south of Kerman is produced the tribal weaving of the Afshars.

South
South-west: environs of Shiraz, in the province of Fars. In this area are produced Kashgai and other tribal weavings.

East
1 *Far North-east:* the south-east shores of the Caspian harbour nomadic Turkoman weavers.
2 *North-east:* environs of Meshed, in the province of Khorassan. Here, and further south, there are also woven Baluchi and other tribal pieces.

Late nineteenth-century silk and metal thread carpet in the style of seventeenth-century Polonaise weaving. 10 ft. 2 in. × 6 ft. 4 in. (310 × 162.5 cm.).

West Persia

Tabriz Carpets

As we noted above, the far north-western area of Persia around Tabriz saw the conversion of what was left of Persian weaving in the late 19th century into a massive export industry. It was here also that the Kurdish tribes continued to weave carpets with themes developed directly from the designs of the golden age of the Safavids (for instance, the late garden and tree carpets) which, for the sake of continuity, we have discussed in the section devoted to Safavid weaving. Taken in conjunction with the Hamadan area to the south, this is now one of the principal rug producing regions of Persia.

Throughout the 18th and 19th centuries, Tabriz continued to produce carpets based on Safavid designs, but in a debased and coarsened form. Carpets for urban domestic use in the Middle East are woven to form a group; the central carpet is flanked by two strips and at the top end of this square construction of three pieces, there is a fourth carpet laid as a cross-beam. Edwards described the large central carpet as being called a *mina farsh*, with a length of about sixteen to twenty feet and a width of between six and eight feet. The side-pieces, called *kenarehs*, are of the same length, but 3 feet 4 inches (1 *zar*) or thereabouts in width; such pieces would be described as runners on the Western market, being used primarily as corridor carpets. The cross-piece (*kellegi*) is between 10 and 12 feet long by 5 to 6 feet wide. It should be added that many runners found on the Western market were actually woven as such.

The products of Tabriz over the last fifty years are usually woven with dense floral patterns, with large palmettes, vases, foliage and small flowers scattered in wild profusion. There are also animal carpets, some closely based upon Kashan pieces of the 16th century, and copies or adaptations of vase carpets. Even close copies of the Ardabil carpets are known. Edwards, in his book, castigates the Tabriz manufacturers of the 1920s and 1930s for having developed to a fine degree the art of being able to produce the largest woven area with the minimum possible means, so that many of the carpets were of the utmost coarseness. Since many of these were exported to the West, the reputation of Tabriz as a producer of

Opposite, top left: late nineteenth- or early twentieth-century Tabriz silk rug, the rust-red field is decorated with a dedicatory inscription to Shah Ismael in Nashki calligraphy, dated A.H. 926 (A.D. 1509). 6 ft. 2 in. × 4 ft. 8 in. (188 × 142.5 cm.). Opposite, top right: late nineteenth- or early twentieth-century Tabriz silk rug with an olive green field. 6 ft. 2 in. × 4 ft. (188 × 137.5 cm.). Opposite, bottom: detail of a nineteenth-century Tabriz tile pattern garden carpet. 20 ft. 7 in. × 13 ft. 10 in. (627 × 422 cm.).

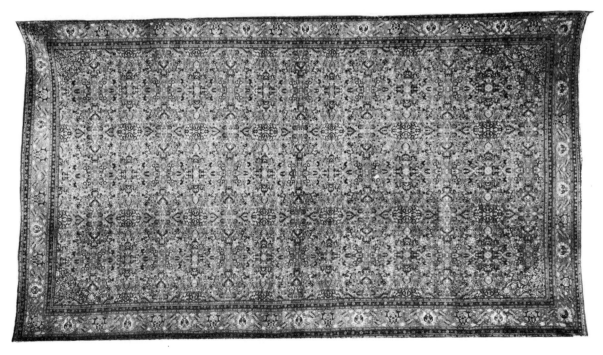

Nineteenth-century Tabriz floral carpet with grass green ground. 19 ft. 6 in. × 11 ft. 7 in. (592 × 352 cm.).

carpets was not a high one. However, as in most of the modern weaving areas, the manufacturers, being industrialists, produced carpets in a range of qualities. A Tabriz carpet of the finest quality – like similar pieces from Teheran, Herez, Kashan, Nain or Kum – is an example of extraordinary craftsmanship, even though its design is wholly derivative. It has to be said that modern factory-made carpets, whatever the quality of technical workmanship, have little to do with either art or instinctive culture; they should be classed as interior decoration and hold little interest for the serious student. In a way, one can admire them, while at the same time, being aware of their mechanical quality and aesthetic sterility.

Weaving around Tabriz

West and south of Tabriz are many small towns and villages which have been producing carpets for decades, if not centuries. In the area of Herez are Gorovan, Mehriban, Bakshaish, Bilverdi, etc. North of Tabriz is the village of Karaja which has given its name to the weaving produced in other nearby villages, and sixty miles south of Tabriz is the small town of Serab which likewise has become synonymous with all the carpets woven within its orbit. Herez, of course, is particularly well-known for the production of silk carpets of the finest quality. In his book, *Oriental Carpets*, published in 1966, Ulrich Schürmann remarked on the particular softness of Herez silk pieces, which he said was due to the 'horizontal insertion of the knots'. Tabriz was also a major producer of silk rugs in the 19th century, but in general those of Herez are considered of finer quality. Some writers have suggested that silk carpets were produced there before the beginning of the 19th century, but Edwards was of the opinion that there was no large-scale weaving industry (certainly nothing of the technical proficiency of the finest Herez pieces) before it was introduced by Tabriz merchants in the 1880s, although, surprisingly he makes no reference to silk weaving, only to the production of wool carpets. However, it is certain that silk and wool carpets were produced in Herez before Edwards' earliest dating. To the district of Serab are attributed some fine long rugs or runners with a characteristic camel ground and lozenge-shaped medallions.

Weaving around Hamadan

In what we have called the central and south north-west and the central west, there is a large and prolific weaving industry, centred principally on the town of Hamadan. This is also one of the main pockets of Turkish culture in Persia, and is also the marketing centre for many of the Kurdish weavings. Apart from Hamadan itself, the most important towns are Senneh, Bijar, Malayer, Saruk and Arak (Sultanabad). The main districts around Hamadan are Khamseh, Sard Rud, and Kabutarhang to the north, Kulayi to the west, Derghezin and Saveh to the east, and Tuisarkhan, Bozchelu and Malayer to the south. In the area south of Arak are the regions of Seraband, Japalak, Kezzaz, Kemareh, Dulakhor, Mushkabad,

Below: nineteenth-century white-ground silk Herez prayer rug. Note the similarity of the grotesque animal and bird heads to the Moghul fragment. 8 ft. 9 in. × 6 ft. 6 in. (267 × 198.5 cm.). Below right: nineteenth-century Herez silk rug with floral lattice design. 5 ft. 10 in. × 4 ft. 3 in. (178 × 129.5 cm.).

Nineteenth-century Herez silk prayer rug with four columns and hanging lamps. 5 ft. 9 in. × 5 ft. 7 in. (175.5 × 170.5 cm.).

Feraghan and Mahallet, and apart from Arak itself, the most significant weaving village is Lilihan. All these areas, towns and villages are contained within the large province of Kurdistan, overlapping slightly into the northernmost part of Luristan.

Hamadan, with the villages around, can lay good claim to being the most important centre of carpet production in Persia. The number of villages with significant weaving facilities is about fifty.

Khamseh and Derghezin

In the Hamadan area itself, the most important weaving areas are Khamseh and Derghezin. It would appear that rugs were woven here during the Safavid period, for Tahmasp is reported to have presented a carpet to Suleyman the Magnificent of Turkey which was woven in Derghezin. The rugs produced here during the last 150 years are characteristically rugged and hard-wearing. Although both the quality and the designs vary considerably from region to region, a particular pattern of those pieces known generically as Hamadans consists of a medallion and escutcheon design, or several such motifs joined by 'poles'. In this respect, they resemble the Afshar and Kashgai tribal rugs from further east and south, although the handle, with the shorter clipped pile, is different. This area is also well-known for runners, which usually have pole-medallion designs; some of the older examples have very beautiful camel fields and borders.

Above: early nineteenth-century Herez silk carpet of medallion and arabesque design. 14 ft. 10 in. × 11 ft. (427 × 335 cm.). Above right: nineteenth-century silk Herez rug, with arabesques and animals. 6 ft. × 5 ft. (183 × 152 cm.).

Opposite, top left: late nineteenth-century Zeli Sultan rug from the Hamadan region. The carnation and leaf border is characteristic of these carpets. 6 ft. 8 in. × 4 ft. 2 in. (203 × 127 cm.). Opposite, top right: Senneh rug with Herati border, late 19th century. 8 ft. 5 in. × 5 ft. 5 in. (257 × 165 cm.). Opposite, centre right: Senneh rug with plain lozenge centre. Late 19th or early 20th century. 6 ft. 4 in. × 4 ft. 2 in. (193 × 127 cm.). Opposite, bottom left: detail of an early nineteenth-century Bijar carpet. 13 ft. × 4 ft. 5 in. (396 × 134.5 cm.). Opposite, bottom right: late eighteenth- or early nineteenth-century Bijar carpet. 13 ft. × 4 ft. 5 in. (396 × 134.5 cm.). The last two carpets described were formerly in the Kevorkian Collection.

Senneh and Bijar

The two towns concerned above all with Kurdish weaving are Senneh (now called Sanandaj), the capital of Kurdistan, and Bijar. We should emphasize that the fine quality of weaving associated with these towns is exceptional by the standards of normal Kurdish production but that this has not been maintained in recent years. Previous generations were so impressed by the fineness of Senneh weaving that the name of the town was given as a synonym to the Persian knot, although the pieces were, in fact, woven with the Turkish or Ghiordes knot. The drawing of Senneh designs tends to be angular and stylized, and the favoured patterns are small, tightly drawn, floral repeats. One of the best-known designs consists of rows of *botehs* which, in some cases, can be quite large. Bijar (or Bidjar) carpets of some age, while not usually being of the same quality as the finest Senneh pieces, are most attractive. The most frequently encountered design consists of a plain field with arches at either end (somewhat akin to a double-arched mihrab); within the field is a large medallion with poles at either end which often finish in characteristic anchor-shaped escutcheons. The medallion, escutcheons and spandrels at either end of the field are filled with dense floral patterning.

227
228
232

Kurdish Weavings

The rugs woven by the nomadic or semi-nomadic Kurdish tribes (the Herki, Senjabi, Gurani, Jaffid and Kalhors, for instance) are more coarsely woven than those produced by the settled peoples of Senneh and Bijar, although they repeat many of the designs. Pieces are also found which are based loosely on certain Caucasian medallion designs (the same is true of pieces woven further north, near the Caucasian border, by the Shahsevan tribes), and there are also Kurdish pieces which adopt Turkoman designs: for instance, a fragment woven with the *tauk naska* gul illustrated in *Oriental Carpets from Canadian Collections*, 1975, no. 62, and another in the same exhibition, no. 63, woven with the continuous serrate-diamond and pole design, known particularly from small Yomut weavings such as *asmalyks*. Also associated with Kurdish weaving are amusing pictorial rugs, often woven with yellow grounds, with rows of historical and military figures (many copied from ancient ruins such as those at Persepolis). Although similar rugs are woven in many areas of Persia, the Kurdish examples, with their delightfully naive style of drawing, are the most attractive.

229

Feraghan and Seraband

230
231
The region around Arak further to the south is again well-known for certain specific types of weaving. From the areas of Feraghan and Seraband come finely knotted pieces, comparable both in style and quality to weavings from Senneh. They usually have a tight allover field pattern of tiny floral motifs, such as the Herati design. Early examples of Feraghan carpets, woven in the early and mid-19th century, are characterized by a distinctive greenish-yellow colour. From this region, as well as from Senneh, come some fine saddle-rugs, with semi-circular slits to accommodate the saddle-pommel, woven with the same tight patterns.

Top: nineteenth-century Feraghan floral rug with a dark blue field. 5 ft. 9 in. × 4 ft. 6 in. (175.5 × 137.5 cm.). Above right: nineteenth-century pictorial rug, possibly from north-west Persia, although an attribution to Anatolia has been suggested. 7 ft. 2 in. × 4 ft. (218 × 122 cm.). Above: Feraghan pictorial rug based on the reliefs at Persepolis. Mid-19th century. 6 ft. 9 in. × 4 ft. 3 in. (206 × 129.5 cm.). Right: an extremely rare silk saddle cover, probably Feraghan, c. 1850. 4 ft. 8 in. × 2 ft. 5 in. (142 × 73.5 cm.).

Saruk Weavings

The town of Saruk, about twenty-five miles north of Arak, has had a long history of weaving, although it is generally agreed that nothing of great interest has been produced there since the beginning of the First World War. In the last fifty years, the name 'Saruk' has been used as a trade description for carpets of poor quality woven in the area, which bear little resemblance to the earlier pieces. Genuine old Saruk pieces, however, are very beautiful; a variety of floral designs were used, the drawing style being angular and crisp. The colours of the older pieces are particularly rich; medallion designs on a blue or cream ground were often used.

Left: Feraghan rug with white ground with birds, second half of the 19th century. Approximately 8 ft. 6 in. × 5 ft. 4 in. (259 × 162.5 cm.). Jay Jones Collection, California. Top: late nineteenth-century Saruk rug with madder field. 7 ft. 3 in. × 4 ft. 4 in. (221 × 132 cm.). Above:

rug with madder field. 6 ft. 6 in. × 3 ft. 11 in. (198 × 119 cm.).

Top left: nineteenth-century Bijar carpet. 12 ft. 2 in. × 9 ft. (371 × 274 cm.). Top right: Herez silk rug, late 19th century. 9 ft. 3 in. × 6 ft. 2 in. (282 × 188 cm.). Above: an early to mid-nineteenth-century sampler (vagireh) from north-west Persia. 5 ft. 10 in. × 5 ft. 4 in. (178 × 162 cm.). Right: silk-embossed wool rug from Herez, late 19th century. 6 ft. 9 in. × 4 ft. 3 in. (206 × 129.5 cm.).

Arak Weavings

Arak, formerly called Sultanabad, was where the Manchester firm of Ziegler's opened an office in 1883. Originally importers of English goods, the firm realized the financial advantages of starting a carpet factory to produce pieces which they could then market in Europe and the United States. Edwards has estimated that by the turn of the century, Ziegler's controlled about 2,500 looms in Arak and the surrounding area. Initially, the weavers were given small mats showing details of the design, which they then transposed onto larger carpets. Such sample mats, showing often a section of different borders and field designs, could attain quite substantial sizes and were known as *vagirehs*. According to Erdmann, in *Seven Hundred Years of Oriental Carpets*, such pieces were used throughout the 18th and 19th centuries, although their employment seems to have been confined to north-west Persia, especially Bijar, and to the southern Caucasus. However, the pieces illustrated by Erdmann, which he attributes (as others have done) to Bijar, Herez, Kuba, Karabagh and even Ushak, are probably all late nineteenth-century, with the possible exception of one piece (which was sold at Sotheby's in London in 1976), which he attributes to the north-west Persian area of Garus and dates to about 1800, on the basis of its resemblance to the design of the Garus carpet dated 1794 given by Joseph V. McMullan to the Metropolitan Museum. This *vagireh* is described as eighteenth-century in the Sotheby catalogue; in fact, the design is neither so elegant, nor so refined as the dated carpet, and seems to be an adaptation of typical Kurdish motifs which appeared on weavings throughout the 19th century. Although it is difficult to be absolutely certain, it is possible that the majority of the *vagirehs* illustrated by Erdmann, including the example which he dates to about 1800, should be associated with Ziegler's operations in and around Arak in the last quarter of the 19th century. Ziegler carpets, as the

Two late nineteenth-century Saruk rugs. Below left: this piece shows a marked similarity in layout to the Safavid Portuguese carpets. 7 ft. 11 in. × 4 ft. 6 in. (241.5 × 137 cm.). Below: rug with an indigo field. 6 ft. 9 in. × 4 ft. 2 in. (206 × 127 cm.).

235
236
237
238

Above, left to right: Saruk pictorial rug with portrait of Riza Shah, dated A.H. 1250 (A.D. 1931); 6 ft. 5 in. × 4 ft. 8 in. (196 × 142 cm.); Ziegler tree-of-life prayer rug, late 19th century, 5 ft. 11 in. × 5 ft. (180 × 152 cm.); very rare mid-nineteenth-century Herez silk sampler (vagireh), 1 ft. 6 in. × 1 ft. 4 in. (45 × 40 cm.).

Below: Teheran rug showing 'The Map of Modern Iraq', c. 1920. 5 ft. 10 in. × 4 ft. 9 in. (178 × 145 cm.). Opposite: Isfahan carpet with medallion and floral arabesques. Late 19th century. Approximately 9 ft. × 6 ft. (284 × 183 cm.). Jay Jones Collection, California.

finished products are called, are sturdy, often beautifully coloured, and of fine quality. The best examples are highly regarded by collectors today.

We should note that the carpet trade described many of the weavings produced in the vicinity of Arak by three commercial terms, which denote quality of weave, and therefore market value. These names – Mushkabad, Mahal and Saruk – may or may not denote that the particular piece was woven in one of those areas, but if it does, it is coincidental. Certainly, the serious collector of nineteenth-century Persian carpets today does not have the same piece in mind when he says 'Saruk' as does the older generation of carpet importer when he describes a new, florid, carpet by that name. We should, perhaps, re-emphasize, without wishing to confuse the reader, that the nomenclature of nineteenth-century Persian weaving has to be treated with great caution, while that of twentieth-century weaving, both in the trade and among scholars, is little short of chaotic.

Central Persia

Moving east, we come to the central Persian area stretching from Teheran in the north through to Kerman in the south. In this last region are located some of the most famous Persian weaving cities: Kashan, Kum, Isfahan, Joshaqan, Nain, Yezd and Kerman itself. In the region south of Kashan are produced the tribal weavings of the Afshars. This large region, with its major cities, is now one of the major producers of Persian carpets, with large factories in Nain, Kum and Teheran.

Teheran Carpets

Scattered reports suggest that weaving may have been carried on in Teheran in the early part of this century, although according to Mumford in 1900, what the Tabriz merchants referred to as 'Teheran carpets' were probably woven in north-west Persia, around Feraghan. Edwards suggests that there was a minor rug-weaving industry there in the first two decades of the present century, producing pieces with floral designs, but that it ceased before the outset of the Second World War. In the late 1950s, however, Teheran became one of the principal weaving centres, both for domestic consumption and for export. Much the same is true of Isfahan, although this city has a weaving history which goes back to the 16th century. The modern products of Isfahan, like those of the 1920s, do not differ much from those of Teheran, Kum or Nain, although fine silk carpets began to be produced in the latter cities in the 1950s, the quality of which, like that of the elaborate pile-knotted pieces, has deteriorated in recent years (or at least the deterioration is apparent in those pieces which reach the West).

Bakhtiari Carpets

In the region outside Isfahan are woven the Bakhtiari carpets. These are woven either with medallions or with allover repeat patterns, often contained within a square lattice. There is some historical evidence to suggest that the Bakhtiaris, originally pastoral nomads, may have

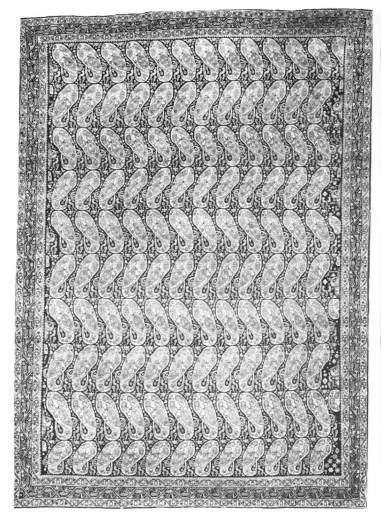

had a long history of weaving. From the 12th century to the middle of the 15th, the Bakhtiari country was semi-autonomous and ruled over by the Fasluyeh dynasty, with their capital at Idhej, now called Izeh. The empire stretched over two hundred miles, from Isfahan in the east to Shuster, beyond the Zagros mountains, in the west. According to Edwards, Ibn Batuta, travelling in the Bakhtiari region in the mid-14th century, reported that at Idhej 'a green rug was spread before him'. The drawing style of Bakhtiari pieces from the 19th and early 20th centuries has much in common with Kurdish pieces from the north-west around Hamadan and there are also structural similarities.

Joshaqan Weavings
The proper place of Joshaqan in the history of Safavid weaving remains to be explained satisfactorily by scholars. We remember that Pope associated it with many different designs, including examples of the lattice vase carpets and of some garden carpets. In more recent times, it has been associated with stylized geometric and floral ornament within a lattice design, and these seem derived from late decadent single-plane lattice vase carpets, some of which may have been woven there.

Kashan Weavings
Kashan, as we remember, was one of the principal rug-weaving cities of Safavid Persia, being particularly well-known for its production of silk pieces. Although there seems little doubt that the production of carpets continued throughout the 18th and early 19th centuries. Edwards, who knew the modern history of Kashan weaving well, tells in his book how, by the end of the 19th century, both the economy and the weaving of the city had become greatly impoverished. He suggests in a story which, despite its overt romanticism, cannot be dismissed out-of-hand, that the revival was due in large measure to the activities of a merchant

Above left: twentieth-century mochtachan (lamb's wool) Kashan rug. 6 ft. 6 in. × 4 ft. 3 in. (198 × 129.5 cm.). Above: late nineteenth- or early twentieth-century Kashan silk-embossed prayer rug. 6 ft. 6 in. × 4 ft. 3 in. (198 × 129.5 cm.).

Opposite, top left and right: two twentieth-century Kum silk rugs; the piece on the left has a tomato red field, 6 ft. 11 in. × 4 ft. 7 in. (211 × 140 cm.); that on the right has an indigo field, 6 ft. 10 in. × 4 ft. 9 in. (208.5 × 145 cm.). Opposite, bottom left: Bakhtiari carpet with boteh, c. 1900. 12 ft. 8 in. × 8 ft. 5 in. (386 × 257 cm.). Opposite, bottom right: modern Kum carpet. 10 ft. 3 in. × 7 ft. 9 in. (312 × 236 cm.).

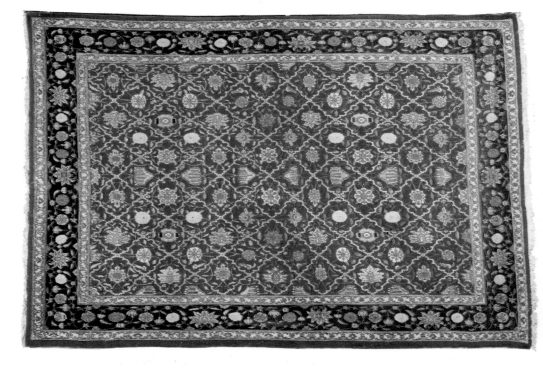

Above left: early nineteenth-century Joshaqan lattice carpet. Approximately 9 ft. × 6 ft. (274 × 183 cm.). Above: nineteenth-century Kashan wool prayer rug with tree-of-life. design. 6 ft. 3 in. × 4 ft. 5 in. (190.5 × 134.5 cm.).

called Hajji Mollah Hassan, an importer of Merino wools from Australia, whose wife had been a weaver in Arak. In terms of materials, Edwards remarks unequivocally that 'the Kashan carpets of the first two decades of the present century differed from the weaves of the rest of Persia in one essential particular; they were woven with imported Merino yarns', a practice which continued until the outbreak of the Second World War (by which time it was estimated that the area could boast some 12,000 looms). The favoured designs were, and continue to be, complicated floral patterns arranged in arabesques over the field, or with floral medallions, escutcheons and corners. The same holds true of the silk pieces, some of which are called raised silk Kashans, having the design woven in pile on a flat-weave ground, the latter often metal embossed. Also produced in Kashan are crude pictorial rugs, many of them illustrating Sufi religious subjects.

Kerman Weavings

Kerman, like Kashan, was one of the principal weaving cities of Safavid Persia, and it is probable that weaving also continued here after the break-up of the Safavid empire at the beginning of the 18th century. Certainly, three carpets in the Shrine Collection at Meshed, woven in the village of Ravar 100 miles north-east of Kerman, bear the date 1866, and are obviously representative of an uninterrupted tradition of weaving. In 1871, however, a report of Colonel Euan-Smith, quoted by Edwards, says that only six looms were operative in Kerman, but according to Major P. M. Sykes (*Ten Thousand Miles In Persia*), the city could boast 1,000 looms by 1895. Although most authorities consider this latter figure to be exaggerated, it seems certain that Kerman, like the other major cities we have mentioned, experienced a revival of weaving in the last quarter of the 19th century, a revival once again prompted by the activities of the Tabriz merchants and, additionally, by the growing demand for Persian carpets in the United States and Europe. Department stores in London and Paris were importing carpets in vast quantities to cater to the newly awakened taste for the 'exotic' and 'Moorish'. In the centenary exhibition of Liberty's of London at the Victoria and Albert Museum in 1975, three late nineteenth-century rugs imported from the Middle East and purchased by the museum from the store in 1878, were shown: a Persian Niris kelim, a Caucasian Kuba rug and a Turkish Ghiordes prayer rug. Such pieces were symptomatic of a new marketing attitude in Europe (although, significantly, all three rugs were described by the store as being far older than is now known, a description accepted at the time by the museum) which, under the influence of firms such as Ziegler's, was to have a tremendous impact on both the weaving and economy of Persia. The effect of this can be seen, for instance, in the growth of the number of looms in Kerman, and at the same time was to have a long-lasting influence on artistic taste in Europe and America.

During the 19th century, Kerman had been one of the leading producers of shawls,

Opposite: Bakhtiari carpet inscribed 'Made by the Bakhtiari' and dated A.H. 1302 (A.D. 1885/6). Approximately 7 ft. × 5 ft. (214 × 152.5 cm.).

Above, left to right: Kerman pictorial rug, late 19th century, 7 ft. 1 in. × 4 ft. 10 in. (223 × 147.5 cm.); Kerman pictorial rug, late 19th century, 8 ft. 8 in. × 5 ft. 9 in. (264 × 175.5 cm); Kashan pictorial rug depicting a Sufi prophet, late 19th century, 6 ft. 8 in. × 4 ft. 7 in. (203 × 140 cm.). Right: nineteenth-century silk hunting rug attributed to Kerman, of the type called Kermanshah. 6 ft. 3 in. × 4 ft. 2 in. (190 × 127 cm.). Below: Kerman oval portrait mat depicting President Theodore Roosevelt. Early 20th century. 2 ft. 11 in. × 2 ft. 3 in. (89 × 68.5 cm.).

decorated with variations on the *boteh* design, which became known in England as the Paisley pattern. It is not surprising, therefore, that many of the Kerman carpets, which in the early days were woven by former shawl-makers, had similar designs. There were also tree carpets, hunting carpets and garden carpets based upon classical originals of the Safavid period, and large carpets consisting of a square lattice of panels, each of which contained a miniature garden or hunting scene, or a single flowering shrub (such pieces were also woven at Tebily). After the Second World War, with the growing importance of the United States as a market, large carpets with vulgar floral borders and huge 'filigree' medallions on dark red grounds were made. Kerman was well-known for its silk carpets and also produced in the late 19th century a series of portrait rugs, numbered and inscribed, these being representations of famous historical personalities from Moses to Napoleon. Similar pieces were made in the 20th century, showing famous political, royal and military figures both of the Western world and of the Middle East.

Mid-nineteenth-century Afshar medallion rug. 6 ft. × 4 ft. 8 in. (183 × 142 cm.).

Afshar Tribal Rugs

In the region south of Kerman are woven the tribal rugs of the Afshars. Many of these rugs, with their angular medallions, resemble Kurdish work, and there are others which have rows of stylized motifs such as *botehs*, either free-standing or within a lattice, which resemble coarse versions of Senneh or Feraghan carpets. This is no coincidence, since the Afshars, originally a Turkoman people, were settled first in Azerbaijan before being forcibly moved east by Shah Ismael in the early 16th century. According to Edwards' experience of weaving in this area in the early 1950s, the Afshars proper accounted for only a small proportion of the weavings generally attributed to them, their designs and style of weaving having been adopted by many small villages in the area. However, it is impossible to agree with Edwards' assessment that Afshar tribal rugs are 'unlike the designs of any of the Persian tribal or village weaves'. We have pointed out their similarity to certain Kurdish products; Edwards himself, with a slight shift, admits their resemblance to some Kashgai weavings and we might add that, in their use of dark colours (blues, red, aubergines, greens), they may also be compared to some Baluchi weavings (although it seems more likely that the Baluchi copied ideas from them). We should also note the similarities between some of the geometric motifs on Afshar rugs and those found on Anatolian and Caucasian weaving. Edwards is correct, however, when he remarks that the Afshars were capable of original designs, drawing attention to the *morgi* or hen design, which consists of schematic renderings of birds within a square lattice.

South Persia

Kashgai Tribal Weavings

243
244
In the deep south-west of Persia is the province of Fars, home of the Kashgai tribe, who produced probably the most famous of all Persian tribal weavings. The Kashgai, like the other principal tribal groups in Fars, the Khalaj, with whom they are now amalgamated, are of Mongol-Turkoman descent. It seems that they take their name from Jain Agha Kashgai (often spelled Qashqa'i) who was made overlord of Fars by Shah Abbas. Tribes were settled in this area long before this, however, and are thought to be the descendants of the Seljuk Turks, who themselves were, of course, descendants of the Toghuz-Oghuz tribes from Mongolia who had moved west in the 8th and 9th centuries. In the 11th century, the Seljuks moved down into central Persia, becoming known as the Iraqi Turkoman (after *Iraq-i Ajam* = central Persia). It is interesting that an oral tradition among the Kashgai is that they are descended from Mongols who came west with Ghengis Khan, their name being a corruption of Kashgar, the city in East Turkestan in which they claim to have been originally settled. The Khalaj are considered to be descendants of the Hephtalites or White Huns, whom we mentioned in connection with East Turkestan. These White Huns are identified with the Choliatae, a central Asian people related to the Oghuz. In the 12th and 13th centuries, the Khalaj settled in Afghanistan, and established the Delhi Sultanate in India and the Ghilzai dynasty in Afghanistan, which overthrew the Safavids in 1722. They were settled in central and southern Persia by the beginning of the 13th century. A fascinating linguistic aspect of the Kashgai and Khalaj is that the former speak the western Turkish language and the latter eastern Turkish.

The tribal weavings of the Kashgai, no extant examples of which can be dated earlier than the second half of the 19th century, use a bright palette, predominantly red. The designs

An outstanding Kashgai rug with ivory ground. Second half of the 19th century. 4 ft. 6 in. × 3 ft. 6 in. (137 × 107 cm.).

have much in common with those of other Persian tribal weavings: those of the Kurds, the Afshars, the Baluchi, the Bakhtiari and the Turkomans. Again, many of the designs can be linked with Caucasian weaving. One of the most prevalent designs is a diamond medallion with a parallel zig-zag, a feature well-known from Caucasian weaving and found on some Turkoman pieces, for instance Beshirs. Other pieces may have rows of formalized *botehs*. Animals, usually highly stylized, are frequently included, and again resemble motifs found on Caucasian rugs. The pile of Kashgai weavings is long and the wool itself is of fine quality. The tribe weaves a variety of bags similar to those described in connection with Turkoman and Baluchi weavers, as well as beautiful embroidered or pile-knotted horse trappings.

Opposite: Kerman pictorial carpet depicting 'The Heavenly Ascent of Muhammed' from the Khamsa of Nizami, c. 1900. 10 ft. 7 in. × 7 ft. 2 in. (323 × 218 cm.).

Above, left to right: nineteenth-century Kashgai carpet with triple medallion, 8 ft. 10 in. × 5 ft. 3 in. (269 × 160 cm.); late nineteenth-century Niris floral rug, 8 ft. 3 in. × 4 ft. 9 in. (251 × 145 cm.); one of a pair of late nineteenth-century Kashgai saddle-bags. 2 ft. 2 in. (66 cm.) square.

Khamseh Tribal Weavings

The Kashgai, however, are not the only group of tribes in the area of Fars. There are also the Khamseh, a confederation of various different groups including the Basiri, the Arabs, the Ainalu and the Baharlu. Their weavings are perhaps not so fine as those of the Kashgai but the geometric layouts of the designs are very similar, in some cases being even closer to Caucasian prototypes. The weavings of the Mamassani and Hulagu tribes, and those of the Luri, are rarely encountered under such names in the West, and the designs, although similar to those of the Kashgai, are simpler and less successful. Edwards suggests that many of the Fars weavings attributed to the Kashgai are in fact the products of villages, rather than nomadic work. However, in the catalogue of the superb *Qashqa'i of Iran* exhibition held in England in 1976, Joan Allgrove writes that 'anthropological research since his time has demonstrated that the tribal situation is one of greater ethnic complexity, since most of the tribes include both nomadic and settled groups'. The cataloguer goes on to point out that much work remains to be done in the field of tribal identification, and the same is probably true of the weavings.

Shiraz: the Mille-fleurs Prayer Rugs

We now come to an interesting problem of Fars weaving, associated specifically, but almost certainly incorrectly, with the city of Shiraz. This city is known to have had active looms under the early Safavids but no weavings have ever been attributed to the place with any consistency or certainty. The problem concerns the so-called 'mille-fleurs' prayer rugs. We are discussing them here, rather than in the section on Moghul weavings, where the early examples belong, because the majority of books still refer to them as Shiraz carpets. It seems obvious that there are two groups of such rugs, one group far older than the other. The first group is almost certainly Indian, and the second Persian. It follows that the second group is a specific copy of the first, but why that should have happened is still a question which awaits a satisfactory answer.

The design of both groups remains remarkably consistent. The mihrab is formed on either side by a half cypress tree – that is to say, the body of the mihrab is the space between the trees – and has a scalloped arch. Within the mihrab is a fantastic flowering shrub (perhaps symbolic of the tree-of-life) with hundreds of multi-coloured flower heads radiating from stems growing from a central column. This peacock-spray bears an uncanny resemblance to similar bunches of flowers depicted by seventeenth-century Flemish painters such as Jan Breughel and Osias Beert, and it is possible that the peculiar treatment of flowers in vases seen in these prayer rugs may derive from the work of such European artists, whose colleagues are known to have visited both the Moghul and Safavid courts in the 17th century.

The spandrels contain scrolling foliage and more flower heads. In some cases, the cypress trees have decorated bands around the lower trunks, which may represent pots, and in others they grow unequivocally from the ground. The shrub within the mihrab grows, in the majority of cases, from a vase, but in at least one early example, that in Vienna, it grows from the ground (and the same is true of at least one piece from the later group).

The early group is obviously represented by fewer examples; the best-known are in the following collections: the Textile Museum, Washington; the Metropolitan Museum, New York (ex-McMullan); the Musée des Tissus, Lyons (very similar to that in the Metropolitan Museum); the Österreichisches Museum für angewandte Kunst, Vienna; the Fogg Art Museum, Harvard (ex-McMullan); the Art Institute of Chicago (ex-McMullan); the ex-Marquand-Benguiat-Kevorkian rug (Marquand sale, American Art Association, New York, 24–31 January 1903, lot 1285; Benguiat sale, American Art Association, 4 December 1925, lot 44; Kevorkian sale, Sotheby's, 5 December 1969, lot 8; again Sotheby's, 14 April 1976, lot 1; currently Peter Bausback, Mannheim).

Of the above pieces, the Lyons and Vienna rugs have been traditionally described as Indian; the Vienna piece is illustrated by Bode and Kühnel (*Antique Rugs from the Near East*, plate no. 121) and by Sarre and Trenkwald (*Old Oriental Carpets*, plate no. 37), all of whom follow the Moghul attribution. These pieces, and the others on our list, should be dated to the reign of Aurangzeb (1659–1707). The three McMullan rugs were attributed by their owner to southern Persia, and dated to the late 18th century, during the reign of Kerim Khan Zand (1750–1779). (McMullan specifically rejected the Moghul attribution.) This attribution is followed by Dimand in respect of the piece now in the Metropolitan Museum (although, without commenting on any ambivalence, he accepts the attribution of the Vienna piece to Moghul India). Charles Grant Ellis, in his 1969 article, 'The Ottoman Prayer Rug', in the *Textile Museum Journal*, was of the opinion that the Washington rug and related examples were of Indian manufacture, and so too are May Beattie and R. Ettinghausen, the former pointing out structural similarities between these rugs and known Moghul pieces and suggesting an attribution to Kashmir. The Kevorkian piece was considered by F. R. Martin to be Moghul (although it was mistakenly described as silk) and datable to about 1640, although those who now concur with the Moghul attribution would not date it so early. On both its appearances at Sotheby's, it was catalogued as eighteenth-century Shiraz, but is considered by its latest owner, Peter Bausback, in his 1976 catalogue, as seventeenth-century Indian. Arthur Upham Pope, who illustrated the McMullan piece now in Chicago, attributed it to Niris in Fars and dated it to the late 17th or early 18th century (once again, Pope strikes an idiosyncratic note).

The second group is well represented in carpet literature. John K. Mumford, in the fourth edition of his book *Oriental Rugs*, published in 1900, reproduced an example (plate XVII) which he described as 'antique Shiraz prayer rug'. Another example, illustrated by Charles W. Jacobsen in *Oriental Rugs, a Complete Guide* (plate no. 102) is almost identical to the Mumford piece. The author comments: 'It seems a very reasonable and very definite conclusion that these two rugs were made by the same weaver, somewhere between 1850 and 1890.' A third example, belonging to Franc Shor, is illustrated in the catalogue of the exhibition of Persian Tribal Rugs, organized by the Washington Hajji Baba in 1971 (no. 12). According to the owner, this piece was given to him by a Kashgai chief while he was visiting Fars. A fourth example was illustrated as no. 49 in *Oriental Rugs from Canadian Collections*, the catalogue of an exhibition held in Ontario in 1975. This was catalogued as 'Qashgai *circa* 1900(?)'; this example is related closely to the Mumford and Jacobsen pieces in design, although the mihrab has a white ground. The majority have blue-ground mihrabs, some red, and some yellow or white.

A fifth example is illustrated by Peter Bausback in his 1975 catalogue, *Antike Meisterstücke Orientalischer Knupfkunst*, page 207. The cataloguing of this piece is a little strange, in that it is described as 'Tabriz – south-central Persian', which could be said to be getting almost the best of all worlds. The author claims that the knotting is typical of Kashgai work; this piece, however, was purchased at Christie's, where it was catalogued as Malayer; although this attribution would probably not now be adhered to by the saleroom, John Siudmak, in a verbal communication with the author, said that in his opinion, the colour and the structure were both typical of Feraghan weaving. This rug also has some distinctive design features; all the rugs we have mentioned so far, with one exception, have the mihrab shrub growing from a vase. The exception is the Vienna rug, where the plant is growing from the ground. The same is true of the Bausback piece, the field of which is a close copy of the Vienna rug.

The six later pieces we have detailed above represent less than fifty per cent of known examples. The attribution to southern Persia seems rooted in dealers' traditions, and in one instance, the Franc Shor rug, there is a definite provenance to the Kashgai of Fars. Another significant design feature of these rugs is the main border which, in almost all examples, has, in McMullan's words, a system 'of a straight line trellis, forming octagonal sections, filled with floral shrubs alternating in pairs, and joined by alternating palmettes and rosettes'. A variation on this theme is seen in the Chicago piece which has a floral and meander border. Among the modern examples, we have discussed the Herati border on the Bausback piece, while the Canadian rug has an unusual inner border containing palmettes and birds (this feature of an extra inner border is also found in an example illustrated in the catalogue of the exhibition *Persische Teppiche*, held at the Kunst und Gewerbe Museum, Hamburg, in 1971, plate no. 93).

McMullan, in his catalogue *Islamic Carpets*, illustrates two rugs with allover mille-fleurs designs. One of these (no. 34) has the same border design as the majority of the prayer rugs and is extremely finely woven, with 700 knots to the square inch, a feature typical of the early prayer rugs, although the later group is more coarsely woven (the Canadian piece, for instance, has a knot count of 200 to the square inch). In contrast, the first of the two McMullan 'secular' rugs (no. 33) has different floral borders, has a diamond lattice in the field and is, by comparison, very coarsely woven, with only 178 knots to the square inch. Although assigned by Dimand in the Metropolitan catalogue (no. 51) to late eighteenth-century Shiraz, a later dating might well be more likely, while the finer of the pieces, with its very high knot count, is probably Indian, rather than Persian, and of an earlier date.

It has to be said that the dating and provenance of both groups is still a matter of considerable controversy. The attribution of the later group to southern Persia, and especially Kashgai weavers, has proved remarkably consistent, from Mumford in 1900, at a time when they were still being woven, until today (and there is, we should mention again, the documentary evidence of the Franc Shor piece). Against this, these pieces do not seem typical of Kashgai weaving, are mentioned by neither Edwards, who studied the weaving of Fars very carefully, nor by the compilers of *The Qashqa'i of Iran* catalogue, by far the most detailed study of its kind. We should also not forget John Siudmak's suggestion that the Christie-Bausback piece, based on an analysis of colour and structure, might be assigned to Feraghan. Nor should it be thought that such prayer rugs are necessarily confined to the two groups we have outlined. There are other Persian examples of the late 19th and early 20th centuries obviously based on the same models. In the 1975 Bausback catalogue an example with an even more ornate design is illustrated (page 269) and attributed to Kerman. Perhaps, this piece, like the so-called Feraghan example, should be considered as illustrative of the spread of the design from south Persia.

But even if we accept the attribution to the south Persia for the later group, there is no precedent for a tribal nomadic Persian people carefully copying, even down to small details, a highly complex design woven for Moghul rulers two hundred years before. Why and how this should have happened, why the design should have taken so long to travel, and who introduced it to southern Persia, are extremely puzzling questions. In the face of the later examples, one is tempted to suggest that the earlier pieces should also be assigned to Persia, perhaps, after all, to Shiraz; yet these early pieces are of brilliant quality – technically as well as artistically superb – and have many characteristics in common with Moghul weaving. To attribute them to late eighteenth-century Fars, when there is no evidence that pieces of such perfection were ever woven there, seems eccentric and illogical. We might add the compilers of the Canadian catalogue pointed out that the late mille-fleurs prayer rugs are woven with the Persian knot, which they felt was atypical of Kashgai weaving (following Edwards). However, more than half the pieces in the *Qashqa'i of Iran* exhibition in London are woven with the Persian knot, thus disproving Edward's statement that Kashgai weavers used the Turkish knot exclusively. Nevertheless, the whole question will no doubt remain open to scholarly exegesis.

Opposite: mille-fleurs Moghul prayer rug. Late 17th or early 18th century. 5 ft. 4 in. × 3 ft. 8 in. (163 × 112 cm.). Ex-Kevorkian Collection.

Fars Lion Rugs

Before leaving Fars, we should mention the strange group of rugs which feature depictions of lions, a subject, however, not exclusive to Fars, but also found on tribal pieces woven in north-west Persia. In the catalogue of the exhibition devoted to such pieces, *Lion Rugs from*

Above: nineteenth-century Herat floral carpet. 9 ft. 4 in. × 4 ft. 11 in. (284 × 150 cm.). Above right: mille-fleurs prayer rug. Late 19th century, possibly Feraghan. Approximately 5 ft. 8 in. × 3 ft. 11 in. (173 × 119.5 cm.).

Fars (a travelling exhibition organized by the Smithsonian Institute, 1974–7), Parvic Tanavoli points out that the practice of carving lions on the graves of soldiers had been known in Persia since ancient times (we might also mention the lion frieze of the north palace of Assurbanipal at Nineveh). The lion also has great symbolic significance in the ancient Mithraic religion, and later, under Islam, the fourth Caliph and the first of the twelve Shi'ite Imams, Ali ibn Ali Talib, was called 'the Lion of God'. In the 19th century, the Kashgai leader Darab Khan kept a pet lion, and also enjoyed lion hunting. Mr. Tanavoli also remarks on the Kashgai custom of using the Persian, Arabic and Turkish words for lion as first names for their sons. In the late nineteenth-century weavings, the rendition of the lion, surrounded by bushes, plants and other ornaments, was somewhat crude and schematic. Then, towards the end of the First World War, Indian blankets featuring more realistically drawn lions were imported into the area by the British and changed the local style. Latterly, according to Tanavoli, 'the British blanket lion, in undergoing a synthesis with the local lions, was remade into something most engaging and original and was fully assimilated into the local culture'.

East Persia

The eastern borders of Persia, like those in the west, are well-known for nomadic tribal weavings, specifically those of the Turkoman and Baluchi, which have been discussed in some detail in the chapter on tribal weavings. The major industrial weaving centre in the area is the city of Meshed, and its environs. The city itself, the capital of the province of Khorassan, is one of the most important historical and religious sites in Persia, containing the Shrine of Imam Riza (d. A.D. 818) and that of the famous Harun-al-Rashid, Caliph of Baghdad. Its place in the history of Safavid weaving is still a matter for discussion, although Edwards' suggestion that carpets generically referred to as 'Herat' may not necessarily have been woven only in that city (now, of course, in Afghanistan), but were also probably made in the area called the Kainat, along the western borders of Khorassan between the towns of Juymand and Birjand, and further north in the city of Meshed itself, is worthy of attention. Certainly, there is a tradition in the area that many of the carpets once housed in the famous Shrine Collection in Meshed were woven in the town itself (although less than 10 pieces from the Safavid period now survive there).

The Afghan invasion of 1722 effectively curtailed whatever weaving there may have been in Meshed, and there is no evidence that any was again carried out there, until the end of the 19th century, and even now, Meshed remains of prime importance as a centre for marketing rather than actual production. In the 1920s, the carpets made in Meshed were known to dealers as 'Farsibaffs' and 'Turkibaffs'; these were expressions which referred first to the weave – the Persian and Turkish knots respectively – and by extension to the quality, the Persian-knotted pieces being the finer of the two. Both types were woven with dense floral designs, which make some concessions to the old Herati designs, but generally reflect the importation of European concepts via Tabriz merchants. Much the same observations could be made of the carpets produced at Birjand and Dorukhsh in the Kainat, and at Kashmar, previously called Turshiz.

Persian Carpet Classification

Obviously we have been able to give little more than a general guide to the history of weaving in Persia over the last 175 years. However, probably more Persian carpets come onto the market in the West than any other type, and we feel it would be useful to append here an alphabetical list of names which the prospective purchaser is likely to encounter in visiting dealers. Even such a list as this cannot be comprehensive; we have not, for instance, given all the hundreds of small villages which can only be named as specific sources if there is an incontrovertible provenance, rather than the twenty or thirty other villages in the same area weaving carpets of identical design and quality. Nor have we broken down the tribal weavings into the many sub-groups now known, more of which are being discovered by ethnographers in the field every year. Our list contains only those named which are the most prevalent in the carpet trade today, and have been culled largely from auction and dealers' catalogues of the past few years.

Afshar Tribal rugs from south of Kerman.
Ainabad Kurdish rugs woven in this village in north-west Persia. Often referred to in the trade as Bibikabads (see below).
Arak (*Sultanabad*) Trade name for carpets marketed in that town.
Ardabil Rugs woven in the last thirty years in that town.
Bakshaish Rugs of a Kurdish type woven in this village near Herez.
Bakhtiari Tribal, semi-nomadic rugs, woven near Isfahan.
Bibikabad Kurdish rugs woven in this village near Herez; used also as a general trade name.
Bijar (*Bidjar*) Rugs of Kurdish type woven in this village in north-west Persia.
Birjand Trade name for coarse rugs marketed through Meshed.
Bozchelu (*Borchelu*) Kurdish village rugs woven in this district and marketed through Hamadan.
Derghezin Kurdish rugs woven in this district and marketed through Hamadan.
Dorukhsh (*Dorosh*) Fine early nineteenth-century pieces; modern pieces very poor; area in the Kainat in east Persia.
Feraghan (*Ferahan*) Generic name for fine Kurdish rugs woven in this and surrounding areas.
Gorovan Poor quality rugs woven in the villages near Herez.

Herat Town now in Afghanistan.

Herez Major weaving centre in north-west Persia.

Ingeles Rugs woven in this village and marketed through Hamadan.

Isfahan For modern pieces, this term can denote either rugs woven in the town itself or rugs of a certain quality marketed in Meshed, but not woven in Isfahan.

Jogan (*Jozan*) Rugs woven in this village, close to Malayer, in north-west Persia.

Joshaqan Rugs woven throughout the 18th, 19th and 20th centuries in this town, although in the trade the name is often given to rugs exhibiting particular designs.

Kabutarhang Small town near Hamadan whose weavings are marketed through the latter.

Karaja (*Karadia*) Rugs woven in north-west Persia showing Caucasian influence.

Kashan Major weaving centre in central Persia.

Kashgai Tribal and village rugs of south Persia (Fars).

Kasvin Trade name for a good quality rug woven in Hamadan.

Kerman Major centre in central Persia.

Kermanshah Trade name for a type of rug woven in Kerman. Also a town in the west.

Khorassan Generic name, much abused in the trade, for carpets woven in the eastern province of Persia.

Kum City of central Persia, significant modern weaving industry.

Kurdish Generic name given to weavings of a tribal type from north-west Persia, which do not lend themselves to a more specific nomenclature.

Laristan (*Luristan*) Generic name for the tribal rugs woven in the province above Fars in south Persia.

Laver Kerman Trade name for old type of Kerman rug. Corruption of 'Ravar', where they were woven.

Lilihan Kurdish rugs woven in this village near Arak.

Mahal Trade name for a quality of rug woven around Arak.

Malayer Village near Arak; fine Kurdish weaving.

Mehreban Area near Herez, but used in trade to describe rugs of a particular quality not necessarily woven there.

Meshed Capital city of Khorassan.

Mochtachan (*Mouchtasha*) *Kashan* Carpet from Kashan woven with lamb's wool.

Mosul Trade name for coarse rug of Kurdish type marketed in Hamadan.

Mushkabad Trade name for a type of carpet woven in and around Arak.

Nain City in central Persia; significant modern weaving industry.

Niris (*Neriz*) City in Fars connected with Kashgai weaving.

North-west Persian Generic name for carpets in Kurdish-Caucasian style which have no specific stylistic attributes.

Petag Abbreviation of Persian Carpet Company; active as manufacturers and exporters in Tabriz from about 1900 to 1930.

Ravar Kerman Village near Kerman; either refers to rugs woven there, especially when early, or is used as a trade name for good quality rugs marketed in Kerman.

Saraband Trade name for rugs woven in Arak, especially fine pieces called Mir Sarabands.

Saruk Kurdish rugs of north-west Persia. Used as a generic term. Also used in modern trade to describe new carpets of a floral type made in the area.

Senneh Town near Hamadan; fine Kurdish weaving; often mis-used in the trade.

Serab (*Sarab*) Rugs woven in this village near Herez. Now used as a trade name for certain types of Kashgai weaving, such as Mecca Shiraz.

Souj-Boulak Kurdish rugs from in and around this area in north-west Persia.

Tabriz Capital of Persian Azerbaijan, north-west Persia; important rug weaving and marketing centre.

Teheran Capital of modern Iran; modern rug weaving industry.

Veramin Made in this village near Teheran.

Yezd (*Yazd*) City of central Persia; there is a modern rug weaving industry set up by Tabriz merchants.

Zenjan Trade name for carpets woven in Khamseh district north of Hamadan.

Zeli Sultan Trade name for a type of floral rug woven in Hamadan. This expression can also refer to a particular pattern.

Ziegler Carpets woven for, and designed by, Ziegler's in Sultanabad (Arak) *c.* 1885–1930.

Flat Weaving

THROUGHOUT THE SECTIONS on Oriental carpets, various forms of flat-woven pieces have been mentioned. These alternatives to the pile-knotted rug are not confined to any particular region but are widespread throughout all the countries and tribal groups whose work has been discussed and, as we have mentioned in our opening section, there is considerable evidence to suggest that flat-weaving preceded the art of pile knotting.

There are various types of flat-weaving, differentiated by technique. The most common are tapestry-woven rugs, called *kelims* in Anatolia, *palas* in the Caucasus and *sarköy* in Thrace. *Soumaks* include the two types of rugs called *sileh* and *verneh* (the latter, however, not exclusively). Other types are brocaded rugs (which include some *vernehs*), embroidered rugs, compound-weave rugs, and those with mixed techniques; of the latter, pieces combining flat-weaving and pile knotting are most often encountered on Turkoman bag-faces and tent-bands.

In general, it is supposed that the majority of flat-woven pieces were not made for export. The exceptions are probably the late sixteenth- and seventeenth-century Persian silk kelims from Kashan, and nineteenth-century Caucasian *vernehs* and *silehs*. It is known also that many North African flat-woven articles for domestic use, pieces made specifically in Morocco and Tunisia, were woven for market trading, and it is obvious that such pieces were not made with the same degree of craftsmanship as those produced solely for use in the weavers' own homes. With the exception of the Safavid kelims and those associated with nineteenth-century Senneh, the majority of flat-weaves are geometric in design, which bespeaks their essentially nomad or village origin. The Senneh kelims, with their fine, intricate, floral designs and blending, harmonious colour, are unlike the flat-weaves of any other area; they relate closely to the pile-knotted pieces produced in the same region.

Of all the various types, the most common are the slit-tapestry kelims. In this technique, one block of colour formed by the wefts is separated from the next by the wefts turning back over the last warp in a particular block, thus creating gaps or slits between each area of colour.

Anatolian prayer kelim. 19th century. Approximately 6 ft. × 3 ft. 8 in. (183 × 112 cm.).

Anatolian Kelims

Anatolian kelims are often long and narrow and woven in two halves. They have the usual carpet layout of field and borders, the field containing large medallions on the long axis, surrounded by scattered geometric or stylized floral motifs. The effect of the design is similar to that of certain village-woven pile carpets, such as those of Bergama, but the sheer size of the kelims makes their impact, if anything, more dramatic. There is, however, no question of such pieces imitating pile-knotted carpets; they have their own style, with a use of bold primary colours which complement the powerful geometric medallions.

A second group of Anatolian kelims are the prayer rugs, one example of which, in the Metropolitan Museum, is dated 1774/5. In general, these pieces follow the designs of the pile-woven prayer rugs, being closest in style to those of Konya and Ladik. A few have metal thread, and some rare examples are woven in silk with silver thread. In a sense, these prayer kelims, although highly regarded by collectors, are less successful than the large pieces with their bold abstract decoration, simply because they adhere too closely to the established format of the pile-knotted pieces. It must be admitted, however, that prayer rugs, whether flat-woven or pile-knotted, exist to serve a functional purpose as the adjuncts of prayer and their representation of the pulpit or mihrab is therefore invariable, giving the flat-weaver less scope to use the unique properties of the medium. In other words, the prayer rug does not admit of much stylistic innovation.

A few flat-woven pieces, however, such as the fine old example with multiple vertical niches belonging to David Black and Clive Loveless (*The Undiscovered Kelim*, plate no. 12), manage to use the bold geometricity of kelim design to good effect within the prayer rug format, but such pieces are exceptional. More interesting are some of the kelim saphs which, because of their larger size and abstraction of motifs, are perhaps more suitable to the schematic simplification of flat-weaving, which is more successful on a large scale.

Caucasian Palas

The kelims or *palas* of the Caucasus are divided usually into two groups – those from the north, generically called Kuba kelims, and those from the south, called Shirvan kelims. The northern pieces have borders; the field pattern consists of either a repeat pattern of stylized animals or large medallions of escutcheon form similar to those found on pile carpets. The Shirvan kelims are closer in style to the Anatolian pieces.

Soumak Weaving in the Caucasus

As widespread in the Caucasus is the flat-weaving technique called Soumak, a system of progressive weft-wrapping close to stem-stitch embroidery. Experts differentiate two principal types of Soumak weaving, called Soumak wrapping and Soumak brocading; in the first there is no ground weave between the wrapping wefts, while in the latter the wrapping wefts are supplementary to ground weave and are usually discontinuous, as in the slit-tapestry technique described above. The wrapping may be in the same direction, i.e. 'plain', or reversed in direction from row to row, i.e. 'countered'. When the back of the piece may equally well be used as the front, the technique is called 'reverse' Soumak. In some examples, for instance those from Lenkoran, the threads forming the design are left long on one side, thus creating a definite front and back.

Such Lenkorans are, according to Schürmann, called *djidjims*. This word, spelled variously *jijim*, *jimjim*, *cicim* or *dyeddyim*, has been the cause of some controversy. In Western rug literature, it was first used by Mumford to describe Turkish kelims woven from thin strips and used as *portières* (i.e. hangings used at the entrance of a room in place of a door). Subsequent authors suggested that Mumford had mistaken the Turkish word *cici*, which is vernacular for 'a little beauty', used by the merchants to describe pieces they were trying to sell, as the proper name for a particular type of weaving. However, according to Hony's Turkish-English dictionary of 1967, *cicim* means 'light carpet for hanging as a curtain or on walls'. Landreau and Pickering, in *From the Bosphorus to Samarkand*, *Flat Woven Rugs*, suggest, therefore, that the word should be applied only to those pieces obviously intended for use as *portières*, but as to whether such pieces must also be woven in strips or sections, as Mumford thought, they are not certain. Such a narrow definition certainly does not accord with Schürmann's interpretation nor with Sotheby's catalogue of 18 November 1976, lot 66, where a Kashgai embroidered kelim horse-cover was described as a *dyeddyim*. Iten-Maritz, in *Turkish Carpets*, says that the word *cicim* applies to a specific technique used to produce curtains and blankets (although he illustrates a prayer rug which he describes as being in the *cicim* technique). The method was to embroider the coloured motifs onto a background of undyed wool or, occasionally, canvas. The most usual way (and here the author comes back to Mumford's original suggestion) is to stitch together several thin strips around one foot in width and between $9\frac{1}{2}$ and 13 feet in length; this 'strip' method is not, however, invariable.

According to Schürmann, the majority of Caucasian Soumaks were produced in Daghestan, with poor examples being made in Derbend and very fine ones in Sejshour. There are in addition the Lenkoran *djidjims* mentioned above. Two particular groups of Soumaks are the so-called 'Kuba dragon' and 'Kuba blossom' Soumaks, which, as their names imply, are thought to have been woven either around Kuba itself, or further north in Daghestan (the latter, according to Schürmann).

254

The Silehs

Schürmann also attributes the dragon *silehs* to Daghestan (presumably Sejshour) and the *vernehs* to Shirvan, slightly to the south. He is, however, a somewhat confused authority, since he remarks in the English edition of his book on Caucasian rugs that the origin of both types is 'probably Karabagh', which is even further south-west. Dimand, in the Metropolitan Museum catalogue, agrees with the Kuba attribution of the dragon Soumaks, but attributes the *silehs* to Shirvan.

Dimand, however, has a particular theory about the *silehs*. This concerns the interpretation of the motifs found on these pieces. In the majority, the design consists of rows of large S-shaped motifs in two basic field colours, which alternate. At one end of the S, on the outer long side, are usually two but sometimes three comma-like extrusions, and at the other end, a thin parallel line. The large S has most commonly been interpreted as a highly stylized dragon, or rather the formalized but recognizable dragon of old Caucasian weavings degenerated into an abstract form with only the vestiges of its original zoomorphism.

It has been assumed that even the weavers of the nineteenth-century pieces were unaware of the animal motif which lay behind the S-pattern. The comma-like extrusions have

Two so-called dragon silehs, *possibly Shirvan. Above left: probably dated A.H. 1258 (A.D. 1843). 9 ft. 3 in. × 6 ft. 2 in. (282 × 188 cm.). Right: second half of the 19th century. 7 ft. 8 in. × 6 ft. 8 in. (234 × 203 cm.).*

Kashgai embroidered horse cover. Late 19th century. 5 ft. 9 in. × 5 ft. (175 × 152 cm.). Ex-Akeret Collection.

Right: nineteenth-century medallion and jewelled Soumak. Probably Kuba or Daghestan. 10 ft. 8 in. × 6 ft. 4 in. (325 × 193 cm.). Far right: south Caucasian (Shahsevan) verneh brocaded rug, similar in style to pieces from Akstafa. Mid-19th century. 7 ft. × 4 ft. (214 × 122 cm.).

Below: dragon Soumak. Probably Kuba or Daghestan, dated 1806. 11 ft. × 7 ft. 6 in. (336 × 229 cm.). Below right: so-called dragon sileh dating from the mid-19th century. Probably Shirvan. 12 ft. × 6 ft. (366 × 183 cm.).

been interpreted as ears by one school of thought; this seems unlikely, as some pieces have three, not two, extrusions, although it could be argued that since the weavers were not aware of what they were representing, they would have been as likely to weave three as two. The thin parallel line at the other end thus becomes a tail. The second interpretation, which at the present time seems to represent the majority view, is that the extrusions represent feet and a tail and that the thin line is the jaw of the dragon.

There is, however, a drawback to this latter interpretation, that drawback being the extraordinary embroidered rug once in the McMullan Collection and now in the Metropolitan Museum. This piece represents a considerable problem. In date, it is almost certainly early nineteenth-century; yet the forms found on it are more obviously of animal derivation – if not dragons, then horned snakes or some other vast and powerful mythological beast. The comma-like extrusions and parallel lines are, in this case, most obviously ears and tail. Nevertheless, it affords no easy solution to the interpretation of the motifs on the *silehs*, for the simple reason that it is of the same date. Had it been a century or two earlier, the transition from recognizable formalism to abstraction would have been simple to follow and explain, but it is not so easy to comprehend why rugs of the McMullan type and the *silehs* were being made at the same time. Dimand, without admitting that such a problem exists, attributes the McMullan piece, which he describes as a 'dragon rug', to Kuba, but attributes the S-pattern *sileh* in the Metropolitan to 'probably Shirvan' and describes it as a 'bird rug'; he interprets the comma-like extrusions as birds' heads. In other words, Dimand suggests that the motifs of these so-called dragon *silehs* are not dragons at all, but simply abstract motifs. Although this idea is difficult to accept, if only because the sticking of two birds' heads on to an abstract motif seems illogical and pointless, the McMullan rug, with its clearly recognizable animal forms certainly indicates that the old dragon motifs had not become so abstract by the 19th century as the S-pattern suggests. One might also add that the nineteenth-century dragon Soumaks of Kuba closely follow in style and colouring the sixteenth- and seventeenth-century pile-knotted carpets of the dragon type. The nearest parallel to the nineteenth-century S-pattern *silehs*, however, is a rug like the sixteenth- or seventeenth-century 'Hitler' carpet destroyed in Berlin in the Second World War (Erdmann, *Seven Hundred Years of Oriental Carpets*). This had rows of swastikas in squares, and it is possible that the S's derive from such a motif.

Attribution of Caucasian Soumaks

The attribution of the dragon Soumaks to Kuba or Daghestan rests on the assumption that the earlier pile-knotted carpets were woven there. This, of course, is an attribution no longer accepted by many scholars. Apart from the fact that Kuba did not become a major town until the 18th century, the dragon rugs, while bearing no resemblance to the nineteenth-century pile carpets from Kuba, are obviously close to nineteenth-century Karabagh products. Modern scholarship, therefore, is of the opinion that the dragon rugs should be associated with the south-west Caucasian region of Karabagh, and specifically with the town of Shusha. The later dragon Soumaks would thus originate from the same area.

Apart from rugs, often of large size, the Caucasian Soumak technique is frequently applied to small pieces such as cot hangings, saddle-bags, and other receptacles. The quality of these pieces, especially the saddle-bags, is often brilliant and there are many students of weaving who would suggest that a fine Soumak bag-face is more representative of the qualities of design and colour inherent in the technique than the larger rugs.

The Vernehs

Vernehs, which are either Soumak or embroidered, are usually attributed to the south-east Caucasus, and like the *silehs*, it is thought that they may have been woven for export. Certainly, large quantities of fairly recent manufacture were still reaching the West in the 1920s and 1930s. The most usual design consists of a madder field upon which is an open blue rectangle; both field and rectangle are divided into squares by white strips, each square containing geometric motifs and highly stylized birds (usually described as peacocks) and animals. In some rare cases, the design may be wholly abstract, with rows of squares containing geometric motifs. The colour scheme is almost always sombre – madder red, dark blue and white. The motifs on these pieces, especially the long-tailed birds, relate them to the animal rugs from Akstafa, a village in Shirvan.

256

Above: mid-nineteenth-century Shirvan Soumak carpet from the village of Bidjof. 8 ft. 6 in. × 3 ft. 4 in. (259 × 101.5 cm.).

Below: pair of Soumak bag-faces. Second half of the 19th century. Approximately 2 ft. (61 cm.) square.

Moroccan and Tunisian Flat-weaving

Several flat-woven articles were produced in Morocco and Tunisia, although fine old examples seem for the most part to be in museums and are rarely, if ever, seen on the market. From Gafsa, an oasis in southern Tunisia, located at the cross-roads of the main caravan routes across the country, came flat-woven rugs or blankets, called *fras* and *ferrasiya*. In style, these pieces are similar to Shirvan kelims, having horizontal bands of motifs, some wide and some narrow, but not strictly alternating, as in the Caucasian pieces. The patterns within the bands consist not only of abstract geometric motifs, but also stylized animate subjects, such as humans, camels, fish, etc. The colours are fairly subdued, usually red, blue, green, yellow and black, and in mellow shades which resemble Thracian kelims.

Other flat-woven textiles are produced in the Tunisian town of Kairouan to the north-east and in several villages – El-Djem, La Chebba, Bou-Merdas, Djebeniana, etc. – in the Sahel region to the south of Kairouan. Pieces include shawls (*mendil*, *mustiya*), cushion covers (*usada*), blankets (*wazra*), wall-hangings or *portières* (*ksaya*), prayer rugs (*klim*) and saddle-rugs (*best*). Rugs with ornamental design similar to the Gafsa pieces are called *mergum* and those with a decorative scheme partly of thin bands and of colour but with some pictorial elements are called *klim-mergum, klim* presumably being a corruption of kelim. Most of these weavings have horizontal bands of soft colour containing lateral repeat patterns .

Tribal Flat-weaving

Flat-weaving was common among the major tribal groups – the Turkomans, Kashgai and Baluchi. The Turkomans and Baluchi also produced mixed technique pieces, partly piled in either wool or cotton and partly flat-woven. The flat-weaves of all these groups bear little resemblance to their pile-knotted fabrics, although in Turkoman flat-weaves, madder-red is still the predominant colour. The patterns are usually woven in horizontal bands or in a tight allover diaper. Jon Thompson, in an essay in *The Undiscovered Kelim*, remarks that certain twentieth-century Turkoman piled rugs from north Iran were obviously derived from the designs of flat-woven carpets, a most unusual transposition, and one which was as unsuccessful as the instances where kelims copy pile carpets. Indeed, it was one of the most remarkable features of the Caucasian dragon and blossom Soumaks that, although they follow closely the designs of pile carpets, they are successful as flat-weaves.

Below: south Caucasian (Shahsevan) verneh rug, similar in style to pieces from Akstafa. Late 19th century. 5 ft. 11 in. × 4 ft. 6 in. (180.5 × 137 cm.). Below right: nineteenth-century verneh brocaded rug. Possibly south-east Caucasus. 5 ft. 7 in. × 5 ft. 2 in. (170 × 157.5 cm.). Ex-McMullan Collection, illustrated in Islamic Carpets, *no. 60.*

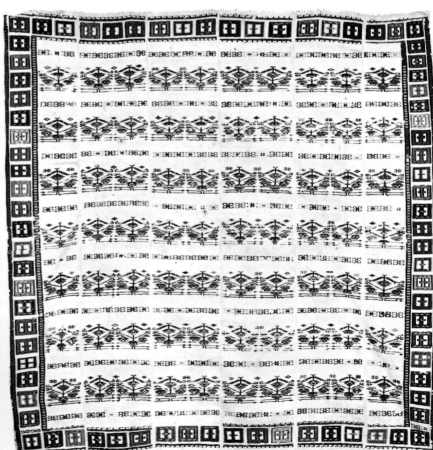

Embroideries

Although embroideries should not, properly, find a place in a book on weaving, being needlework, a number of examples are sufficiently interesting and closely related to carpet weaving to merit inclusion. In Turkey and the Caucasus, embroidered pieces were often produced in the same style as pile or flat-woven rugs. Thus, there are embroidered Ghiordes prayer rugs from Turkey and some exceptionally beautiful small silk petit-point embroideries from the Caucasus in the style of the dragon and blossom rugs. Schürmann also illustrates, in *Caucasian Rugs*, small flat-stitch silk embroidered panels from Chila, Schemacha and Surahani. From central Asia, and specifically from Uzbekistan, come *suzanis* (*suzani* being Persian for needle) which are large panels embroidered in silk on cotton with floral and geometric motifs. These were, apparently, made as part of a bride's dowry, and in their use of simplified shapes, which appear cut-out from the field, they resemble the finest American patch-work quilts.

The majority of flat-woven rugs, bags and other items represent a taste among Western collectors which is relatively new. Like the Baluchi rugs which were given away as gifts, fine old kelims were, apparently, used as wrappings for bales of pile-knotted carpets. The majority were not, as we have said, woven for export and in any case, their technique and thinness made them unsuitable for a functional use in a Western home. Only in recent years has serious interest been taken in nineteenth-century village and tribal weavings. Flat-woven pieces, which are, by comparison to pile-knotted carpets, two-dimensional, have a splendid individuality and their often unique vocabulary of design and colour now seems self-evident and a crucial aspect of Oriental weaving.

Above, left to right : Bokhara suzani *panel, mid-19th century, 8 ft. 10 in. × 7 ft. (269 × 213 cm.) ; south-west Persian (Fars) kelim, mid-19th century, 8 ft. 6½ in. × 4 ft. 10½ in. (260 × 148 cm.) ; late nineteenth-century Kashgai kelim, 10 ft. 2 in. × 5 ft. 6 in. (310 × 167.5 cm.).*

Nineteenth-century Romanian kelim. Victoria and Albert Museum, London.

EUROPEAN RUGS AND CARPETS

Origins of European Carpet Weaving

THE ORIGINS OF CARPET WEAVING in Europe are obscure, although there is evidence to show that Oriental carpets were imported from early times, so that the technique of pile-knotting would at least have been known if not immediately imitated. The spread of pile carpets over Europe must have been due to the presence of the Moors in Spain, the Crusades (11th–13th centuries), the travels of Marco Polo (1254–1324) and the embassies to Venice from the 13th century onwards. It was also helped by the colonial expansion of Portugal which began in the 14th century, with later settlements in the Persian Gulf (1509), Goa (1510) and Japan (1542), before the country was conquered by Philip II of Spain in 1580.

One of the oldest fragments of pile carpet is preserved in the Schlosskirche at Quedlinburg in the Harz mountain region of what is now East Germany. This is a portion of a panel, which must have measured 24 feet high by 20 feet wide, representing rows of scenes from Martianus Capella's *Marriage of Mercury and Philology*, and is known to have been made in the time of the Abbess Agnes (1186–1203). The portions were woven using the single knot, like Spanish carpets, although no connection with Spanish weavers has been shown.

In England rushes and hay were strewn as floor covering until the early 17th century, although there is a record of the use of woven rush matting in France in a picture in the early fifteenth-century *Book of Hours* in the château at Chantilly, showing the Duc de Berry seated at dinner in a chamber, the floor of which is covered with rush matting, but it was not used in England until later. A German traveller, Paul Hentzer, said that he personally saw hay strewn on the floor of Queen Elizabeth's presence chamber at Greenwich Palace in 1598, although, in the *Dictes and Sayings of the Philosophers*, a book translated from the Latin by Earl Rivers in Lambeth, there is an illustration of Edward IV in a room strewn with rushes, with some kind of carpet for the King himself.

Many account books for big houses have entries for floor rushes up until the early 17th century. This practice could hardly have been hygienic, although it is recorded that the enlightened Cardinal Wolsey had the rushes at Hampton Court changed every day. In 1255 Eleanor of Castile, on her marriage to Edward I of England, brought over many fine Spanish rugs, which are said to have come from Cordoba and Granada, and to have displayed them in the street and at her lodgings in the Temple after the Spanish custom.

There is no other evidence of pile-knotting in Europe at such an early date; almost all the examples which appear in paintings were Oriental carpets. There are some depictions of what would appear to be flat-weaves which could have been produced in Europe. At first, carpets would obviously have been considered too precious to be laid on the floor and would have been used as table cloths or ceremonial coverings such as altar cloths, but by 1600 the distinction had been drawn in England between 'table carpets' and 'floor carpets'.

It is said that Venice imported rugs from Asia Minor in the 15th century and that it was the custom to decorate the gondolas and balconies with them during festivals. When Venice lost her possessions in the eastern Mediterranean, as the power of the Ottoman empire spread after the conquest of Constantinople in the mid-15th century, carpets were brought into Europe from Constantinople.

The rugs imported from Turkey were brilliantly coloured and boldly patterned; some from Ushak had Italian coats of arms incorporated in the designs. They probably would not have been used on floors. Those most often portrayed in the paintings of the Renaissance show geometrical ornament in square fields and were probably woven in the Bergama district of north-west Anatolia; some were also brought from Cairo.

At the start of the 17th century Persian carpets were brought into Venice as gifts from political embassies, including five Persian silk carpets in the Basilica of St. Mark.

Holland established trading relations with Persia and India at the time when Venice was flourishing. The Flemish weavers had been famous since the 12th century in the towns of Ghent, Bruges, Ypres and Courtrai. They imported the wool via Antwerp, which was then one of the richest seaports in the world, from England at a time when Ghent was five times the size of London. Arras, which was famous for its tapestries in the 13th and 14th centuries, was captured by Louis XI of France in the 15th century.

The influence of the Italian Renaissance reached the Low Countries in the first decade of the 16th century; the Netherlands came under Austrian and later Spanish domination

Opposite: Empire period tapestry technique Aubusson carpet, with central rosace. Mobilier National, Paris.

when Mary of Burgundy, at the time when the Dukes of Burgundy held sway over these feudal states, married Maximilian of Austria who was elected Holy Roman Emperor in 1494. The southern provinces formed a league in 1597 to defend Catholicism after the religious strife of the earlier part of the century, and so retained the Spanish and Moorish influence in their designs.

The northern provinces united in 1609 and became a maritime power, also famous for tapestries. Despite this long history of weaving skill, it is not known when pile-knotting first started. In Belgium the Brussels carpet was known and copied by 1749, but its earlier history is difficult to trace. In Holland the first factory for floor carpets was at Amersfoort and the Royal Deventer Factory was founded in 1797. In their early designs the influence of earlier imported Eastern carpets can be seen and this Oriental influence was continued as contact was maintained during the period of colonial expansion in the early 19th century.

Weaving in Germany had been largely developed in the monasteries, but by the end of the 11th century the first weavers' guilds had been started. However it was not until the 19th century and the industrial boom that Germany became a major producer of carpets. There are Indian carpets in Düsseldorf and also Shah Abbas Turkish carpets have been found.

In Austria an inventory of 1596 of the Archduke Ferdinand lists a Turkish carpet 'mit dem Österreichischen Schild', which shows that he too had established relations for the practice of sending designs to be incorporated in carpets woven in Turkey. The Emperor of Austria also received a carpet as a present from Peter the Great of Russia, which is sixteenth-century Persian and depicts a vivid hunting scene. It is always difficult to trace the influence of one culture upon another, especially where the evidence, the carpets themselves, are perishable goods at a time of war and disorganization, but these few facts show that the art of pile-knotting was known, at least from examples, in Europe, and we can only chart the emergence of the actual practice of the art.

Spanish Rugs and Carpets

SPAIN IS THE OLDEST European producer of pile rugs. The earliest surviving document which discusses rug weaving dates from the 12th century. It indicates that at that time there was already a well-developed industry and even that rugs were then being exported to Egypt and the Near East. By the 13th century the industry was highly developed and had reached a peak in sophistication and technique under the Moors, who also imported rugs from Anatolia and the East.

The Moorish domination of Spain lasted from their conquest in A.D. 710–12, when they came over from North Africa, until the late 15th century, and they were finally expelled in 1609. Their first great city was Cordoba, in Andalusia in southern Spain, and records note that their palaces there were strewn with some of the richest carpets in the world. The last Muslim dynasty was that of the Nasrids, who built the Alhambra in their capital city of Granada, where the official colour, red, and the insignia of the city, the pomegranate, were often found in their designs, incorporated in simple colour schemes of green and white.

Granada was finally conquered by Ferdinand and Isabella in 1492. The best period of carpet production therefore coincided with the Moorish domination, although as the Moors were gradually assimilated, as Mudejars working for Christian patrons, into the Christian population under the growth of Catholic power, they increasingly adopted European decorative elements and combined them successfully within their Islamic tradition. In the 12th century there were 800 looms for weaving silk in Almeria alone and the major rug-producing centre at this time was Alcaraz in the province of Murcia and it remained so until the late 16th or early 17th century. In the 11th century Cuenca was also famous for the manufacture of woollen rugs, which formed the town's chief industry.

All the Spanish rugs were woven with a single warp knot peculiar to Spain, which may have come from Egypt, as a similar single knot was used in cut loop weaving by the Coptic weavers of the 7th or 8th centuries and also by Arab weavers in the 9th; it is known that Coptic weavers were active in Spain in the 10th century. The use of this knot shows that the knowledge of the techniques of carpet-knotting could not have been derived in Spain from Persia or Turkey for then the double warp knot would have been adopted. The single warp

Opposite: sixteenth-century coarsely woven Cuenca carpet.

6

Sixteenth-century woollen Spanish carpet copied from contemporary textile designs; probably made at Alcaraz.

knot is one where the yarn is tied around every other warp thread and on alternate warp threads in succeeding rows, and it is by this characteristic that Spanish carpets can often be identified. The Ghiordes, or Turkish knot, which was used throughout the rest of Europe was first used in Spain at Cuenca in the mid-17th century.

Some of the oldest examples of Spanish carpets known today can be dated by the heraldic arms and devices they bear. These date from the first half of the 15th century, although they could be earlier. In a manuscript Bible, now in the Vatican library, called the Bible of Manfred, is a miniature illustrating the presentation of the book to a figure, who could be Manfred himself (he was crowned King of Sicily in 1258). The action takes place upon a brown and white fringed carpet with a band of Kufic script, eagle heads and shields. The carpet may be of Spanish origin, or perhaps Sicilian, but in either case it shows the early practice of incorporating armorial devices into designs.

There is documentary evidence that Pope John XXII (1249–1334) bought rugs for his palace at Avignon with coats of arms woven into the pattern which had been made by the Moors in Spain. Two examples of armorial carpets are from the Convent of Sta Clara in Valencia, Old Castile, dated 1405 and 1473, and made for the Enriquez family who founded the convent. Alfonso Enriquez, who died in 1429 and was buried in Sta Clara, was admiral of Castile and on one of the carpets two pairs of anchors attached by ropes twisted in loops are depicted at the sides of the arms.

There is also a large group of carpets bearing the arms of Castile and Aragon, probably commissioned by Maria of Castile who became Queen of Spain in 1416 after her marriage to Alfonso of Aragon. The armorial carpets were mostly made by the Moors for Christian patrons and often combine both the traditions of Islam and European influences. The arms are usually shown on fields of small repeated polygons which still reveal the Islamic influence, sometimes decorated with a star or cross motif, stylized birds, animals or human figures. One distinctive feature is that they are long and narrow, perhaps to complement the long tiled halls of Spanish architecture, with borders, often bands decorated with geometric designs, figures or Kufic inscriptions. The use of representational figures was forbidden by Sunni edicts but, where they are used, they are generally crudely drawn, for where figure design is a European standard of art, decoration was the Moorish criterion. This use of figures could be derived from contemporary armorial devices or ceramic and lustreware designs, which the Moors also produced, especially in Valencia.

In 1492 Christopher Columbus, incidentally the son of a weaver from Genoa, had set sail for the New World and in the following century, in 1519–22, Cortez had conquered Mexico, and between 1531 and 1534 Pizarro took possession of Peru. One of the most important discoveries in the New World was the finding of new dyes, which led to new uses of colour in patterning. Previously the predominant dyes had been red and dark blue, with some green, yellow and light blue, but new varieties of red were introduced from Mexico, for example one dye made from dried insects (*Dactylopius coccus*).

Many of the Islamic secrets of dyeing and fixing were lost when the Moors left Spain during the Catholic domination of Isabella and Ferdinand. Throughout the 16th and 17th centuries there was a progressive reduction of the number of dyes used. A two-colour scheme was consciously sought as new patterns of a more pronounced European character were adopted, following the importation of Venetian velvets and tapestries from France and the Low Countries which gave new inspiration for designs.

From the early 15th century Anatolian rugs and also silks from Baghdad were imported and copied, and there is a strong Anatolian influence on the early Spanish carpet designs. This can be seen in the use of the tree-of-life symbol and of the Kufic script as a pattern for the border. This gradually became more debased, especially as it was adopted for use in Spanish silk weaving.

One pattern was particularly popular and is known as the large pattern Holbein, due to the fact that this design was often seen in carpets portrayed by European painters. It consists of rows of octagons enclosed in squares and decorated geometrically. The borders often show a stylized floral motif, also Anatolian in origin, which was known as the scorpion in Spain, and also as the Persian endless knot motif, which is depicted in numerous fifteenth-century Persian paintings. This pattern could have been introduced by the Persian potters who settled in Spain in the 13th century and whose influence can be seen in the Alhambra. Many of the large pattern Holbeins were made at Alcaraz. There is also a design called the small

IOANNES XXII PAPA NEPOLITA
NVS CREATVS CARDINALIS A BONIFACIO
IX SEDIT ANIV DIES XV VACAVIT SEDES

Pope John XXII (1249–1334) bought Moorish carpets for his palace at Avignon.

267

268

Sixteenth-century Spanish woollen pile carpet made at Alcaraz; wreath design with the arms of the Dominican order at the corners. Hispanic Society of America, New York.

pattern Holbein which is based on a design of alternate octagons and small cross-shaped diamonds in offset rows. This motif was perhaps more successfully adapted and it is sometimes difficult to see clearly the underlying geometric shape of the pattern.

At Alcaraz in the 15th century Western elements were increasingly adopted, which followed the Gothic style of architecture prevailing in Europe at that time. One Gothic floral decoration which was adapted was the pomegranate, which had previously been used in Granada and was also popular in Italy. There is a carpet in the Victoria and Albert Museum, London, showing this motif with a Kufic border like the earlier armorial rugs.

Many of the Gothic and Renaissance patterns were copied from Spanish and Italian textiles, with limited colour schemes, and must have been introduced by Christian, not Moorish weavers. A favourite motif was the wreath, used in a more angular fashion than its Italian counterpart, and often arranged in rows which reflect the earlier large pattern Holbein design, but still showing a move away from the Islamic tradition. Arabesques made from the bodies of winged animals or dragons were also used in designs.

In the 16th and 17th centuries Turkish rugs were imported from Ushak and the angular arabesques in yellow on a red ground of these rugs were frequently imitated. After the Ottoman conquest a new rug pattern, no longer so geometric, was introduced, with naturalistic floral designs placed around a central medallion, and this became a basic form for many subsequent designs. Some of these later rugs were made using the Turkish or Ghiordes knot, replacing the single warp knot which had been used for so long.

There was a steady decline in quality after the Moslem departure, however, and after the mid-17th century, Western styles were more and more frequently copied. In the 18th century, at the time of the Spanish Bourbons, the Islamic influence finally died out as copies of English, Aubusson and Savonnerie carpets were made, using the Ghiordes knot. The Spanish Aubussons made in the 19th century are largely the same as the French, but used bolder colours, with black or bright red used to emphasize the outlines of the designs.

At Alpujarra, in the province of Granada, a local craft of weaving had grown up which

Spanish armorial carpet, showing the arms of La Cerda of Medinaceli, an elder disinherited branch of the Kings of Castile, invested by Pope Clement VI with the Isles of Azores. Victoria and Albert Museum, London.

294

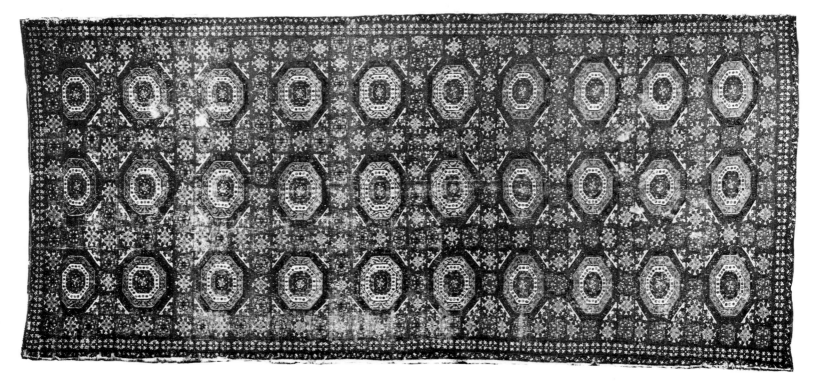

must have been influenced by the Moorish domination of the area. It is not known exactly, as with any peasant art, when the first rugs were made, but it was probably late in the 15th century or early 16th. The Alpujarra rugs are of a thick, coarse carpet weave with uncut loops, made on hand looms with the loops and the weft woven into the warp, in a manner slightly similar to the Brussels technique, with between nine and twenty loops per square inch. Many have a fringe on all four sides, which would be woven separately, unlike the Oriental fringe which is made of the long warp threads. The fringe, which would be impractical for use on the floor, indicates that these rugs were woven for use as bed covers.

The designs are much simpler than the Moorish rugs, often using only two colours, favourite combinations being blue and off-white, red and black, or red and green, although some employ between three and six, or eight to ten, colours, often blues, red and white, or blues, yellow and a popular honey colour. Some rugs are similar to the Italian peasant rugs in that the loops are omitted in places to leave the flat-woven background to form the pattern. The commonest motifs are the tree of life, vases of flowers, birds, animals, especially the lion, the pomegranate, which was the emblem of Granada, and bands and borders of vine leaves and grapes.

After the Moors were finally expelled from Spain in 1609 other motifs were used, such as church symbols, coats of arms, the double-headed eagle of Charles V, names, initials or dates, but on the whole the domestic weavers stuck to the Moorish-inspired designs. This local practice continued in the 19th century when rugs were made with floral and animal designs in bright folk colours, still using the loop knot rather than a knotted pile.

Spanish carpet made with looped pile, dated 1797. Victoria and Albert Museum, London.

Polish Rugs and Carpets

ON THE OTHER SIDE of Europe, in Poland, Romania and the Austro-Hungarian Empire, carpet weaving was also developing, with influences from both East and West. In Poland there were the influences of both Islamic and Russo-Byzantine art and also a long-standing friendship with France. In the 16th century Poland was one of the most important markets for the sale of Turkish and Persian merchandise. In 1601 King Sigismund III sent an Armenian, Sefer Muratowicz from Lwow to Isfahan and Kashan in Persia to buy rugs for the palace. This is part of the account presented to the Polish treasury on 12 December 1602:

Exceptionally rare and important Bessarabian rug, finely woven in the style of Louis-Quatorze Savonnerie designs, c. 1850. 13 ft. 2 in. × 12 ft. 10 in. (401 × 391 cm.).

'Price of objects which I bought in Persia in the city of Kashan for his Majesty our gracious King.

2 tents	360 crowns
2 pairs of carpets at 40 crowns, together	160 crowns
2 carpets at 41 crowns, together	82 crowns
For the execution of the royal arms extra	5 crowns
2 carpets at 39 crowns, together	78 crowns
(other items follow).'	

Below: Polish flat-weave kelim,
c. 1800, with stylized flowers and
ribbon border. Below centre:
flat-weave Bessarabian kelim,
c. 1870. Bottom: knotted pile
Ukrainian rug, c. 1810.
Below left: eighteenth-century
Polish carpet with date and crest,
probably made in Lwow. 10 ft. 2 in.
× 6 ft. 6 in. (310 × 198 cm.).

These eight carpets are probably the ones now in the Residenz Museum in Munich. T. Mankowski has established that the cost of these carpets would be equivalent to 81 cwt. of wheat and, including the cost of travelling and the customs due at four different places, these carpets would have been expensive items. It is therefore more likely that Poland would have preferred to use workshops nearer home, such as those in Ushak in Turkey. Many Turkish carpets were obtained by King Jan Sobieski as the spoils of war after the Battle of Vienna in 1683.

The Polish carpets are of silk, interwoven with gold thread and some bear coats of arms. There were also some sixteenth-century Polish tapestries which were woven in the tufted Savonnerie manner, although most are in a flat-weave, like kelims. In 1643 there was an

Late nineteenth-century Romanian rug with geometric tree-of-life design.

Bessarabian rug c. 1860, with stylized bunches of flowers. 12 ft. 6 in. × 8 ft. 2 in. (381 × 249 cm.).

attempt by the hetman, Stanislaw Koniecpolski, to bring weavers from the west, from Flanders, to weave silk and wool after the Italian style. However, it proved too difficult to import the raw thread required from Italy and Spain, so once again Poland turned to the East and a factory was set up in Brody with Greek workers to make carpets in the Persian style.

In 1649 there was a decided change in taste in favour of the Oriental styles evidenced by the fact that in Lwow all the vendors of Italian fabrics went bankrupt. From this time onwards the Poles developed their own style, using different wools from the Eastern rugs, sometimes with a linen warp, and using different colours – more blues and greens and less red. The designs are mainly floral, naturalistic and abundant flowers and leaves, which constitute an individual Polish style.

Carpet Weaving in South-eastern Europe

IN ROMANIA three distinct styles evolved in the three areas of Moldavia in the north, Oltenian in the south and the central district of Transylvania, again influenced by both East and West. The Romanian rugs are based on the Bessarabian kelim, which is a strong reversible tapestry weave, first used for wall hangings or blankets. The Romanian word for these rugs is *scoarta* which means tree bark, as the earliest peasant houses had the inside walls lined with bark, and when this was replaced by woven wall-hangings the word was retained.

271

These early rugs, which were used as covers or hangings, were woven, not knotted, on narrow horizontal looms so that often several narrow strips would be sewn together. Wool was used exclusively until the 19th century, when a cotton, hemp or flax warp was introduced. The dominant colours were black, which was derived from alder bark or marjoram, red, from madder, green, brown, and yellow, from saffron. Blue was an expensive colour, as it had to be imported from the Orient.

The development of the designs grew from horizontal stripes of two colours (brown, yellow, pale green and blue in Moldavia, green, red, black and several shades of orange in Transylvania, and in Oltenian, which also had wider looms, blue, white, cherry or purple-red) to the division of the stripes by narrow hems, usually in white, and then different geometric patterns, which all had names, such as 'chain mail', 'little corners', 'tablets', 'double crosses', 'little mouth', 'eyelets', 'starlets', etc. At this stage there is a strong resemblance to some Norwegian fabrics, such as the ryiji rugs. Later developments brought representational figures and animals and also borders.

The carpets of Oltenian, which often have a black or green background, depict figures and scenes, such as hunting parties, reminiscent of Persian miniatures. The floral patterns of that area are more freely flowing, often impinging on the borders. In Moldavia the sense of design is totally geometric, often showing the symbol of the tree of life, which is originally attributed to the Babylonians, with snakes at the base and birds in the branches, or flowers and sometimes female figures with lifted arms. The colours too are more subdued.

The carpets from the district of Transylvania are the most influenced by Oriental rugs, with firm borders and small stylized flowers, often diapered, and sometimes birds and animals. All over Europe the fact that folk rugs are largely made with borders, or with the field divided into two with narrow inner and outer guards, would suggest that the influence of Eastern carpets was inherent in their production.

Italian Rugs

IN ITALY A PEASANT PRODUCTION of rugs existed which was relatively independent of the importation of Eastern carpets and was perhaps begun after the isolated activity of some immigrant weavers in southern Italy and Sardinia. The 'tappeti abruzzesi' were not real rugs, but were used as table, bed or bench covers, woven in long strips using a flat double-face tapestry weave. Threads of different colours are inserted between the regular weft threads to form the pattern and then carried along on the underside of the fabric, not cut away, and picked up again when required by the design. These rugs remained largely uninfluenced by the changes of style in the Italian city states and also by the Renaissance; the designs are mainly heraldic, showing a two-headed eagle, or religious, often the symbol of the Lamb, stylized flowers, trees, vases or birds and animals, such as horses. The zig-zag line was especially emphasized and also a star motif.

274

274

There are some examples of rugs made with the Persian knot and there is a hypothesis that Turkish or Cyprian slaves who were interned at Pescocostanzo around 1600 could have taught the techniques to the local population, although perhaps it was that the imported Oriental rugs could have been a stimulus to imitation. The rugs which do bear Chinese or Oriental motifs can be identified as of local manufacture by the poor quality wool and the primitive method of knotting and also by a detail in design, that the local rugs seldom show the border as a separate colour from the centre as in Eastern practice. Only the knotted rugs show any Oriental influence and among the flat-weave rugs the Abruzzi are on the whole of finer quality than the Sardinian, which are slightly wider and use paler colours.

Carpets and Rugs of Northern Europe

IN NORTHERN EUROPE too the influence of the East can be seen. An Anatolian carpet found in a village church in Marby (now in the Statens Historiska Museum in Stockholm) proves that Oriental carpets had reached the Baltic in the 15th century. Four different weaving techniques are found in the Baltic states: a flat tapestry weave like the Ukrainian rugs of Moldavia, the ryiji rugs, which use a knot similar to the Ghiordes knot, a double-weave and the loop knot.

    The ryiji, or rya, rugs of Norway and Finland are similar to the Bessarabian kelim and could have resulted from flat tapestry carpets being brought back by the Goths and Vikings who traded across Russia and down the rivers to Byzantium (Istanbul). From the 15th century a type of kelim tapestry carpet was woven in the thirteen provinces of Sweden, although the earliest ryijis would have been plain and shaggy, of undyed yarn with a long nap, often piled on both sides for use as bedcovers. The Lässne ryijis had a shorter pile.

    At this time the Finnish rugs were of finer quality than the Swedish, although rug-making in Iceland and Norway followed similar patterns, and it is known that Queen Margareta of Sweden bought several Finnish rugs in 1544. The first evidence of rugs in Finland comes in an inventory of 1495 from a convent near Naantali. The next reference, from the same district, is in 1549.

In Sweden, the first reference is found in the convent regulations concerning bedclothes at Vadstena in 1451–52. These rugs, woven in the Finnish castles, formed an important means of payment in trade and were often given to the daughter of the house as a part of her dowry and used to cover the marriage bed, as well as being used as a wedding rug – a custom that has now been revived – on which the couple stood while the ceremony was

Eighteenth-century Dutch table carpet.

276   performed. These often have a boy-and-girl design in the centre, holding hands. The rug would revert to the wife on the husband's death as part of her widow's portion.

The first ryiji were woven in plain colours, mainly black, white and grey, with slight variations. Yellow was occasionally used and red was introduced later, although it was not until the 18th century that more natural dyes were introduced: blue, yellow, red and brown. Around 1600, following European custom, the nobility began using counterpanes instead of rugs as bedcovers and the decorative and picture rugs began to develop, woven in the homes of the prosperous bourgeoisie and farmers. The earliest motif in the ryiji rugs was
276   the tree of life, with borders and geometric motifs. The tulip also figures as a popular representation, though whether this can be ascribed to the Turkish tulip motif is doubtful and it is perhaps more likely that it is derived from the Dutch tulip. The rugs are brightly coloured with flowers, pots of flowers, figures and animals, all geometrically represented.

In the 18th century, and possibly before, a long pile rug evolved, made with the Turkish knot, but using the Spanish method of several weft strands in between each row of knots.

Right: ryiji bedcover, dated 1740, and made in the Finnish province of Småland, with knotted pile and a design of a pot of flowers. 6 ft. 4 in. × 6 ft. (193 × 182 cm.). Far right: ryiji bedcover woven in two pieces and showing the traditional boy-girl motif. 5 ft. 11 in. × 4 ft. 6 in. (181 × 139 cm.). Both pieces: Röhsska Konslöjmuseet, Gothenburg.

Finnish rug dated 1799, with a design of tulips and lions; a linen warp woven with wool and flax.

The designs are again semi-geometrical, floral or plain, sometimes with many parallel borders, the fields decorated with flowers or figures; favourite motifs were the lion and deer, the double heart or pots of flowers. The Norwegian rugs more often had religious motifs and many were obviously influenced by prevailing European styles.

Early English Carpets

ACCOUNTS EXIST of certain transactions between Cardinal Wolsey, when Chancellor of England, and Sebastian Guistinian, the Venetian Ambassador, concerning the taxes levied on the importation of Venetian traders' wines and spices. The traders had a monopoly, so when Wolsey imposed a crippling tariff on the Candian wines, Guistinian tried to bribe Wolsey with an offer of seven carpets in an attempt to get the tax repealed. In June 1518, Guistinian wrote from Lambeth to the Signory saying that Wolsey had demanded one hundred Damascene carpets in return for taking the Ambassador before the Council and obtaining audience for his arguments. The traders themselves were willing to take on much of the expense of obtaining these carpets, and it was decided to sell the chain given to

Guistinian by the King of England, worth 500 ducats, and also two cups given to the Ambassador Bon by the King of Hungary, which were worth about 200 ducats. In fact it was later necessary to pawn the surplus of Rhenish Guilders belonging to the Signory as a security for the balance needed to complete the purchase.

English Elizabethan carpet belonging to the Earl of Verulam. Gorhambury, Hertfordshire.

In October 1520 'there arrived from Antwerp the sixty carpets destined as a present for the Cardinal Wolsey . . . These were accepted graciously, and the Cardinal inspected them one by one. They were very beautiful, and pleased him much; and he saw the present was worthy of a much greater personage than himself.' In return, he promised the Signory that he 'would do everything and anything' in the future to help. Unfortunately none of these carpets from Hampton Court now exist and they were listed on British records merely as Turkish carpets, with no description or size.

Cardinal Wolsey, who ordered Oriental carpets for Hampton Court in the early 16th century.

The oldest example of carpet knotting in England is probably the carpet which is the property of the Earl of Verulam. In the centre it bears the royal arms of England, with the initials of Queen Elizabeth and the date 1570. On the left are the arms of the Borough of Ipswich and on the right those of the family of Harbottle. The rest of the pattern is thoroughly English, with borders of honeysuckle and oak stems, gaily coloured, and typically Elizabethan. The warp is made of hemp – one indication that it was made in England, although C. F. Kendrick said of it that 'it might be argued that it would be as easy to send out to the east designs for the whole as for the heraldry only (a favourite practice of the time), but all evidence tends to show that this was not done. The Anatolian weaver would not work freely and successfully under such restraint.'

With the setting up of the Muscovy Company in 1555 for trade along the shores of the White Sea and to Moscow, traders must have crossed the Volga and the Caspian to reach Persia. The Turkey Company had its chief depot in Ushak, in the Anatolian Hills, not far from Smyrna, which had for long been a famous carpet-weaving centre. It became

popular to send out drawings of a customer's shield of arms to be woven into the fabric. There are two carpets made for Sir Edward Montagu, now the property of the Duke of Buccleuch at Boughton House, two of which are dated 1584 and 1585 (an earlier generation of scholars considered these to be Turkish, but they are now thought to be English). At this time however, there were no Persian carpets in England, only 'Turkey work', but there is a chapter in Hakluyt's *Voyages* which is entitled 'Certaine directions given . . . to M. Morgan Hubblethorne, Dier, sent into Persia, 1579.' This includes the following passage:

'*In Persia you shall finde carpets of coarse thrummed wool, the best of the world, and excellently coloured: those cities and towns you must repair to, and you must use means to learn all the order of the dyeing of those thrums, which are so dyed as neither rain, wine, nor yet vinegar can stain . . . If before you return you could procure a singular good workman in the art of Turkish carpet-making, you should bring the art into this realm, and also thereby increase work to your Company.*'

('Turkish' was the term then used to designate any carpet made by the knotting technique.) There is no evidence to show that Hubblethorne ever secured his Persian workman.

During the latter half of the 17th century many carpets were brought into England via the East India Company which had been chartered by Queen Elizabeth in 1601. For example, the Girdlers' carpet was obtained through the East India merchants in 1634 by Sir Robert Bell; it had been made at the factory in Lahore which had been established with Persian workers under the Moghul Emperor Akbar and decorated with the Company arms. Hand-knotting in England declined in the 17th century because of this established importation from Turkey, Persia and even India. These carpets must have been cheaper because of the increase in general trade owing to safer sea travel.

The carpets known in England at this time were of two main types. Firstly, there were those made either on looms, with a Turkish knot in a linen ground, depending largely on the motifs of Oriental carpets, sometimes woven on Chinese influences, often with coats of arms and dates incorporated. Secondly, there were embroidered carpets made on frames with a needle on a canvas ground, where the influence of medieval English embroidery, can still be seen in the floral and abstract designs. During the Jacobean period there was a great advance in architecture and all aspects of the decorative arts and, although this vanished again under the Puritanism of the Commonwealth, with the Restoration came an even stronger resurgence of interest. During the first half of the 17th century 'Turkey work' was much in vogue, when small pieces of fabric knotted according to the true Turkish technique were made for chair-backs and seat covers.

The Great Age of French Carpet Weaving

IN THE 17TH CENTURY carpet weaving took root in France, which subsequently became the centre of carpet manufacture in Europe. Carpets had apparently been woven in France since the Crusades, when Louis IX brought 'sarrasinois' rugs back from the wars. A guild of carpet makers existed at that time, but the terms 'tapis sarrazinois' and 'tapis nostrez' which appear in medieval documents are used ambiguously and it cannot be known whether these woven products were for the floor or for use as wall hangings.

No carpets from this time survive. However, when Henri IV came to the throne, his first aim was to re-establish order and to promote national industries after the wars and religious troubles of the previous decades. Peace was reached in 1598 with the Edict of Nantes, which may have encouraged Protestant weavers from Flanders to stay in France, and in 1601 he started a Consultative Commission to establish trades in the kingdom. In 1604 the suggestion was put to the Commission, by Jean Fortier from Melun, that factories should be set up to make carpets 'à la façon de Perse et du Levant'.

In 1608, following Fortier's idea, one Pierre Dupont, a former illuminator, now aged thirty-one, received royal patronage and obtained a licence to use a workshop in the Louvre for the manufacture of carpets. Dupont was the son of a treasurer of the Gendarmerie de France and also had the helpful influence of the powerful Madame de Chasteauneuf.

Savonnerie carpet, c. 1660; note how the area folded over has retained its freshness of colouring, probably because it has been concealed from the light by an article of furniture. Musée Nissim de Camondo, Paris.

Savonnerie carpet in the Louis-Quartorze style.

Savonnerie carpet designed by Charles Lebrun for the Grande Galerie du Louvre, c. 1675, showing the monogram of Louis XIV in the centre, surrounded by quivers and trophies. Mobilier National, Paris.

In 1623 he published a treatise, which he presented to the King, entitled 'De la Stromatourgie ou de l'excellence de la Manufacture des tapis de Turquie nouvellement établie en France, sous la conduite du noble homme, Pierre Du Pont, tapissier du Roi des dites ouvrages', in which he affirmed, with many ponderous Latin quotations, that he had discovered the Eastern technique for making pile carpets in silk and wool with grounds of gold thread, similar to the so-called Polish carpets.

In 1627 Dupont took Simon Lourdet, a former pupil, as a partner and installed himself in buildings acquired by the Crown near the Colline de Chaillot, in a former soap factory – hence the name Savonnerie – and undertook, in return for financial help, to train orphans from the Hôpital de Bon Port. The workshops in the Louvre were still maintained as well. The looms set up in the workshops were large high warp looms which had to take a pull of several tons. Not only carpets were woven there, however, but also screens, seat covers and wall hangings.

By a decree of the Conseil d'Etat of 17 April 1627, the ateliers were given their own constitution. The output of the Savonnerie workshops was reserved exclusively for the King as part of the furnishings for his palaces and as presents for visiting dignitaries. It was from this time that the name Savonnerie was attached to their carpets instead of 'tapis à la façon de Perse et du Levant'.

Relations between Lourdet and Dupont deteriorated during this time and Dupont had recourse to Parliament to enforce his right to enter the Chaillot buildings. Some apprentices took advantage of these troubles and escaped to England where they set up a rival establishment and started importing carpets into France. To safeguard the Savonnerie the government had to pass an edict that no such carpets might be imported except those specifically allowed by the King.

Dupont died in 1640 and was succeeded in the business by his son Louis. Letters patent of 1650 mention that the products of the Louvre and Savonnerie workshops had become so famous that they were no longer known as 'tapis façon de Turquie' but as 'tapis façon de France'. The carpets produced were of excellent quality. One panel, which was woven by Dupont at the Louvre and is now in the Mobilier National, shows portraits of

Empire period Savonnerie carpet with central floral medallion. 29 ft. 8 in. × 18 ft. 2 in. (904 × 553 cm.).

Louis XIII and his family. There is another description of a carpet in the 'Inventaire de Tous les Meubles du Cardinal Mazarin' of 1653:

'*Un grand tapis de Savonnerie à fonds noir, dans le milieu duquel il y a une cartouche en ovalle, remplie de fleurs et de fruits, à l'entour de la quelle sont plusieurs branches de feuillages liées ensemble d'ou sortent quantité de fleurs, et entre les dites branches il y a pots remplis de fleurs, de pots et de panniers plains de fleurs entre deux petites bordures, l'une ornée de coquilles blanches, et l'autre de rozettes bleües et feuilles vertes, le dit tapis long de cinq aunes un seizième, et large de trois aunes trois quarts.*'

Watercolour study for a Louis-Quinze Savonnerie carpet after Chevillon.

Eighteenth-century Savonnerie carpet. Probably made at Versailles. 15 ft. × 13 ft. (457 × 396 cm.).

This shows that the carpets now produced were of entirely European design and no longer owed their influence to the Eastern models.

In 1663 Colbert conferred a new constitution on the Savonnerie, to Simon Lourdet and his son Philippe, a year after he had bought up the 'hôtel' of the brothers Gobelins outside Paris and had started workshops there. In 1667 the Gobelins became the 'Manufacture Royale des Meubles de la Couronne' and was to furnish royal residences and pave the way, under supervision, for the development of a new national style, although the Flemish and Italian craftsmen there were encouraged to remain.

At the Savonnerie the new constitution meant that administration was no longer the concern of the master weaver; his role was confined to the training of apprentices, who now included sixty children a year from the Hôpital Général, of between ten and twelve years of age who were to serve an apprenticeship of six years, and to the running of the workshops. In addition, every month a painter from the Royal Academy was to inspect the designs and to teach some drawing to the staff. The Manufactory continued in this way until the end of Louis XIV's reign.

At this time Colbert was concerned to extend the wealth and power of France and to help develop some national style which would reflect this new position in the world. He advocated exploration to uncover the rich territories and treasures in lands beyond the seas. When he was made Surintendant des Bâtiments in 1664, had created an Academy of Architecture where every new project had to be submitted for approval.

Versailles was the epitome of this new movement, both in style and as representing the absolute centre of power of the divine right of kings. The court was installed there in 1682, with many carpets supplied by the Savonnerie workshops and tapestries from Aubusson and the Gobelins. However, the country as a whole did not reflect this show of wealth, as Fénelon wrote in 1699: 'While you (Louis) had abroad so many enemies who threatened your still unstable kingdom, you thought of nothing but adorning your new city with magnificent buildings. You exhausted your wealth; you never thought to better your people, or to till the fertile soil . . . By trying to appear great, you have all but destroyed the foundations of substantial greatness.'

A tapestry commemorating the visit of Louis XIV to inspect the Gobelins factory.

Both the Gobelins and the Savonnerie workshops were placed by Colbert under the supreme direction of the 'premier peintre du roi', Charles Lebrun. Lebrun was responsible for the carpets made at the Savonnerie for the Tuileries and the Louvre, and there his preference for classical forms prevailed. The Savonnerie received a large commission of thirteen carpets for the Galerie d'Apollon and for one hundred carpets for the Grande Galerie à Bord de l'Eau in the Louvre. The designs were begun in 1665 and the first carpets were on the looms in 1668. The work kept the factory occupied for the next twenty years. In 1680 alone 14,449 livres were paid by Louis XIV for work on these carpets, and also at this time other carpets were woven as presents for foreign ambassadors and princes. Lebrun's designs for the Grande Galerie du Louvre reflect the glories of the age. Many show a uniformity of composition, but with much variety between individual carpets, and most show coloured garlands of flowers and bold leafscrolls against a black background – purely ornamental motifs such as acanthus leaves or scrolls are used side by side with naturalistic flowers – with tableaux at each end representing a landscape or allegory with the appearance of bas-relief. In the centre are symbolical images such as the terrestrial globe, military trophies, the sunflower or Louis XIV's emblem of the sun, the King's cipher interlaced or the head of Apollo. There is much classical ornamentation, a favourite image being the head of Hercules with a lion skin, flanked by cubs, or trophies of the chase, monsters and female sphinxes.

At the end of the 17th century there were financial setbacks; the Gobelins closed between 1694 and 1699 and the Duc d'Antin, the new Surintendant des Bâtiments, wrote to Louis: 'Je fus à la Savonnerie, cette belle Manufacture est sur le point de sa chute.' In 1712 the King commanded new orders for furnishings for the Palais de Versailles, which evoked the Baroque manner of Roman palaces adapted to create a French style, and the Savonnerie became the 'Manufacture des Meubles de la Couronne de tapis façon de Perse et du Levant'. However, the factory did not thrive, and it suffered at the hands of the Revolution, if only because the old royal insignia had to be removed from the carpets as such emblems as crowns or the fleur-de-lys were no longer acceptable.

In 1797, in an effort to raise money, the carpets were offered to the public for sale at a heavy loss, but already the new bourgeoisie preferred the even cheaper Aubusson carpets. In 1805 there were only nineteen workers at the factory, but a few commissions came in. For example, Napoleon presented two large Savonnerie carpets to Pius VII after he had performed the coronation ceremony at Notre Dame in 1804, and by 1812 the number of workers had risen to forty.

In 1780 there had been a suggestion to move the Savonnerie to the Gobelins workshops and this finally took place in 1825 after the Savonnerie had been all but abandoned during the poverty-stricken period of the Restoration. This meant that the designs were even more closely linked to contemporary tapestry designs. Under Louis-Philippe some important Savonnerie carpets were ordered, including a large one for the choir of Notre Dame which was commissioned in 1833.

Manufactory of carpets at Gobelins.

The practice of having an artist to control the designs in the manufacture continued throughout the 18th century, most of the designers coming from the Gobelins. Lebrun was succeeded by Belin de Fontenay in 1667, who had been a flower painter at the Gobelins, and his models begin to show a lighter form. In 1715 his son, collaborating with Pierre Josse Perrot, who was one of the best tapestry cartoon painters, took over until 1749.

From 1760, Perrot worked with a former pupil, Chevillon, who was a painter of the Menus Plaisirs du Roi. Together they introduced more floral elements into the carpet designs and new rococo devices, such as green palm trees, bat wings, shells and the fleur-de-lys, replaced the former baroque scrolls. Lighter colours were also used: pink, yellow, pale blue or white replaced the earlier deep browns and blacks as background colours. During Louis XVI's reign the fashion of weaving portraits in pile carpeting revived for a short while. Perrot and Chevillon were succeeded by Maurice Jacques, a painter and designer from the Gobelins, who introduced the new fashionable style, 'à la grecque'.

Under the First Empire a new style evolved heralded by Percier and Fontaine and also La Hameyde de Saint-Ange, who was appointed designer to the Mobilier Impérial in 1810. New designs for carpets were required for the Palaces which were devastated during the Revolution. The new carpets were enormous and the decorative elements were usually warlike emblems such as helmets, swords, shields, Roman spoils of war, lictors' fasces, eagles and heavy wreaths of laurel and oak. More simple designs were also carried out,

280

282

with cornucopias, garlands of roses and marguerites, often influenced by formal gardens. Strong colours, with bold combinations, were used on light backgrounds.

With the Restoration came more romantic images of plumed helmets of medieval knights which tended to replace the earlier Roman spoils of war.

In the second half of the 19th century, under the Second Empire, many mixed styles were adopted and copies made of all sorts of styles. In 1850 Viollet-le-Duc, chief architect of the Gothic revival in France, brought out a Gothic model which was extremely popular. Throughout the history of the Savonnerie, however, there was a very conservative attitude to design, and it is known that the models of Lebrun and Perrot were used again in the reign of Louis XVI.

Today the Manufactory is divided between reproducing copies of ancient carpets and making new ones by modern designers.

In 1665 Colbert granted letters patent to the private workshops already in existence at Aubusson, on the Creuse River in La Marche, giving them a private charter. It is claimed that weaving began there when the area was invaded by Saracens in the 8th century, but it is more probable that the workshops had been started by Flemish tapestry weavers in the 13th century. The new charter enabled the workshops to maintain their own freedom of management but conferred on them the overall title of 'Royal Manufactory'. Apprenticeship and guild membership were both subject to certain rules and regulations and tapestries were to be woven with the Aubusson mark and the initials of the manufacturer.

In 1743 the King's Council decided to establish a carpet factory at Aubusson, and this was carried through by Orry de Fulvy, the Inspecteur-Général des Finances, who had also started the Vincennes porcelain factory which later moved to Sèvres. Women workers were employed and samples of Turkey carpets were sent from Paris with precise instructions on how they were to be woven. By the end of 1774 there were eight vertical looms.

Two methods of weaving were employed, the first was practically the same as that practised at the Savonnerie, making thick pile carpets on vertical high warp looms, and the

Empire period Aubusson carpet made for the château of Malmaison.

other was the tapestry technique using a horizontal low warp loom to make close or short pile carpets which were worked from the wrong side. The pile or velouté carpets were the first to be produced there. In 1746 two Paris merchants, Pierre Mage and Jacques Dessarteaux, gained, by decree, exclusive privilege of manufacture, beginning the successful tradition of the entrepreneur.

The first designer and painter at Aubusson was Jean-Joseph Dumons. His first models were straight copies of carpets from Smyrna and other Turkish centres. One carpet was made to order for the Cardinal de Rohan for his palace in Strasbourg in 1745, and is still there. It is an awkward interpretation of a Smyrna carpet, showing the Cardinal's arms in the centre, surmounted by his hat. Copies were made for several years, and the report left by the inspector who supervised the work praises the workmanship, the precision of the designs, the harmonious colours and the likeness to the work of the Anatolian weavers of Smyrna and Constantinople.

The designs at Aubusson were much simpler than the Savonnerie. The carpets were also far less expensive and reached a less exclusive clientèle, fulfilling the needs of the growing bourgeoisie, while the Savonnerie supplied royalty and nobility. In 1748, however, Louis XV ordered two carpets for the château of Choisy: one small one for the chapel, which was described as 'imitation Persian', with a red background with flowers and blue arabesques touched with yellow, and a larger one of similar design for one of the first floor apartments. The inventories for Versailles show a large number of Aubusson carpets in the secondary apartments and the workshops continued to supply the Garde Meuble until the fall of the monarchy and the Revolution.

Dumons was succeeded, at his request, by Roby as painter and designer of cartoons in 1751 and in that year carpets and bench and stool coverings were produced for the Marquise de Pompadour based on a model in the Persian manner. One of the difficulties recorded at this time was that of making cartoons, which had to be drawn out on special squared paper, 'papier maillé', and coloured to show all the shades of the finished carpet, and also on cloth foundations, again squared, on the same scale as the finished article. Roby's cartoons were criticized for having asymmetrical motifs, thin and indistinct outlines and hand drawn

*Detail from a Charles X
Aubusson carpet. 22 ft. 4 in. ×
16 ft. 3 in. (681 × 495 cm.).*

*Nineteenth-century tapestry-
woven Aubusson carpet. Victoria
and Albert Museum, London.*

lines which were not straight. One of the main preoccupations was to simplify the designs to lower the price of production.

It was felt, however, that a new style was needed and Perrot, the designer at the Savonnerie and Gobelins, was asked to make a model for Aubusson. The King also gave three Savonnerie carpets from his Garde Meuble to serve as models. In 1753 the painter Louis-Joseph Le Lorrain produced a real innovation in design with a model called 'à la grande mosaïque', which was praised as being less striking and therefore less inclined to detract from the charms of the other furniture in a room. It was a popular circular motif or rosette, also called the 'rose mauresque', repeated on the ground colour.

A new style of a central motif surrounded by garlands or a scattering of flowers was gradually developed, with a design for the ground known as 'en camaïeu', similar to contemporary Gobelins tapestries, composed of shades of one colour in gradation. This was also helped by the fact that the techniques for dyeing wool at Aubusson were far from perfect, although documents of this period show constant attempts to improve them. In 1767 there is mention of a 'carpet design composed of different animal skins painted from life' which was made for the Controller of Finances. This new model, which portrayed 'skins of tigers and other wild animals', was a great success and marked the beginning of a fashion which was extremely popular under the First Empire. In 1770, a similar design was produced at the Savonnerie workshops.

From the end of the 18th century the designs became more linear, with a mosaic tessellated ground, after the new Greco-Roman taste. During Louis XVI's reign there were more royal orders for the Aubusson Manufactory: in 1780 a carpet was made for the Queen's 'cabinet' at Versailles; this was large with a grey and white mosaic ground with small blue flowers for the border and decorated with garlands of flowers and other motifs. The characteristic designs during this time were garlands, cornucopias, bunches of flowers, ribbons or laurel and oak branches, although the weaving of imitation Persian carpets was still continued.

286

261

At the time of the First Empire the fashion for wall tapestries declined and Aubusson survived on its carpet production. One of the most successful entrepreneurs at Aubusson during this period was Sallandrouze de la Mornaix. Before 1800, he set up a store in Paris from which he sold Aubusson products; he managed to survive the Revolution, and in 1801 he set up his own workshop in the capital for making thick pile carpets with workmen recruited from the Savonnerie.

Using these two outlets, he became one of the most important suppliers of carpets for the palaces of the Emperor and princes at Compiègne, the Tuileries, Fontainebleau, Trianon, Saint Cloud, the Elysée and Rambouillet. His greatest rival was a merchant named Bellanger who also had a warehouse in Paris and workshops in Tournai. The new Empire style, which was created by Percier and Fontaine, inspired carpet design. The bills Sallandrouze sent to the Garde Meuble mention carpets 'decorated with lyre and swans', 'with a pattern of peacocks', 'a design with nine Muses', 'grasslike mound' and 'brown mosaic ground called Etruscan' (although the *Style Etrusque* had begun to appear in furniture during the latter part of the reign of Louis XVI).

In 1809 orders came to Aubusson for carpets for Versailles and the Petit Trianon, including one for the Salon des Princes, a close pile carpet of Bonaparte pattern, with mosaic ground in two tones of purple, and a star in the centre against a flaming red ground; for the Emperor's Salon, a thick pile carpet with a design incorporating the Nine Muses, poppy-red centre, eagles on a purple ground in the corners; for the Emperor's Grand Cabinet, an extra fine quality Savonnerie carpet, with thick pile, design of poppies, yellow border, white centre piece on a brown mosaic of ground, border of laurel leaves, the centre piece in a surround of oak leaves, pattern swans. Sallandrouze continued to prosper until the end of the Second Empire although it was clear that the Savonnerie carpets would always be more hardwearing and of finer quality.

In 1810 La Hameyde de Saint-Ange, a painter, became the designer for the Mobilier Impérial, and he provided rough sketches for both Aubusson and the Savonnerie. The drawings for the Savonnerie were slightly pompous and official, incorporating emblems and weapons, but the Aubusson cartoons were simpler, with cornucopias, garlands of roses and daisies, and scrollwork in rich colours, all with light grounds, white or pale yellow, and sometimes crimson. By this time the demand for Oriental copies had ceased completely

Below: Empire period Aubusson carpet using tapestry technique. Mobilier National, Paris.
Bottom: Louis-Philippe tapestry technique Aubusson carpet; a garland of flowers on a brown background.

Nineteenth-century Aubusson carpet with central floral medallion. 6 ft. 5 in. × 5 ft. 5 in. (195.5 × 165 cm.).

and only French designs were used. Saint-Ange continued to supply designs through the reigns of Louis XVIII, Charles X and Louis-Philippe.

However, in 1810 Sallandrouze had to dismiss half the Aubusson workers and all of those in Paris, and could only keep the Aubusson workshops running by gaining the help of various influential people and by writing directly to the King to ask for orders. He soon realized that with the importation of the power loom from England the market for expensive handwoven carpets would shrink; already there was hardly any market for the Savonnerie carpets. So he installed himself in new premises at Aubusson and started making cheaper 'tapis jaspé' or mottled carpets, at his workshops in Felletin. After the revolution of 1830 he began to import cheap carpets made on English moquette power looms. Even the Grande Galerie in the Tuileries, in the reign of Louis-Philippe, was furnished with one of his machine-woven carpets.

Sallandrouze adapted the Aubusson workshops to cope with the competition from Amiens, Abbeville and Lille, bringing over workers from Kidderminster, at great expense, to show them how to set up the looms for English moquette carpets. Carpet designs were now overburdened with mixtures of styles and motifs, with Louis-Quinze designs combined with arabesques, fantastic animals and vulgar Oriental decorative motifs. Sallandrouze offered machine-made carpets with names such as 'branches design', 'Gothic', 'Chinese', 'Scottish', 'cashmere' or 'leaf design'. In 1848, with the overthrow of the monarchy, all the factories in Aubusson closed down, but eight years later there were fifteen workshops at Aubusson, and eleven at Felletin. By the war of 1871 there were only ten remaining in Aubusson, and Sallandrouze had been declared bankrupt.

Like England, the French had purchased a town in India, Pondicherri, at the beginning of the 18th century, and cheaper carpets were produced there, on a small scale, using French designs. India was still a source of cheap labour and materials in the 19th century.

English Carpet Weaving in the 18th Century

TO RETURN TO THE DEVELOPMENT of carpet weaving in England, the influence of the Savonnerie was felt across the Channel in the 18th century. The Revocation of the Edict of Nantes in 1675 drove many French Huguenot and Walloon artisans to flee the country for England and other Protestant European countries. Within a few years 250,000 Protestants had left France to escape religious persecution and government restraint on industries.

In 1750 two workmen left the Savonnerie workshops, complaining of ill-treatment, and sought refuge in England. Two years earlier, Pierre Norbert of Lorraine, a French priest who had become anti-Jesuit, took refuge in London and changed his name to Peter Parisot. He wrote in his account of the state of carpet weaving in England at this time, *An Account of the New Manufactory of Tapestry and of Carpets*:

'Two Workmen, who, upon some Disgust, had quitted Chaillot, came to London, in the Year 1750, to try to procure Employment. After they had been here some Months, and brought themselves into great Streights, they applied themselves to me.

'By the help of some Money which had been rais'd by Subscription, they had begun a carpet in a Room in Westminster; but they soon run themselves into Debt, and had to stop the Pursuits they apprehended on this Account, they made a sort of an Agreement of Partnership with a Tradesman in London; and, at their Request, I drew up the Articles between them But the Man not finding his Account in this Partnership, dropt it.

'They then began to be sensible of what I had before told them, that, to form an Undertaking of this Kind, it would be necessary to procure the Protection of some Person of Fortune, who, actuated by the Motive of Public-spiritedness, might be both able and willing to sacrifice a Sum of Money, to procure to the Nation the Advantage of such an Establishment.'

With this in mind, Parisot, who was a little sycophantic where nobility were concerned, managed to obtain the interest of the Duke of Cumberland and Articles of Agreement were signed in May 1751 and a factory started in Paddington. The first carpet was completed in December of that year and was presented by the Duke to the Princess of Wales. Following this successful start, however, Parisot writes of the two Frenchmen that:

'... yet they began to make very extravagant Demands; and at last they refused to work, unless those Demands should be comply'd with. Upon this, they were taken at their Words, and dismiss'd.'

A few months later Parisot hired new workmen and moved the factory to new larger premises in Fulham, next to the Golden Lion Inn. By 1753 he had a hundred weavers and many apprentices and work flowed in, but in 1755 the entire works were sold by auction at the Pisa Saleroom in Covent Garden. The reason for this is given in Thomas Whitty's record of the Axminster Carpet Factory, written in 1790:

'Whilst I was in London I saw an advertisement from Mr. Parrisot, who carried on a manufactory of carpets at Fulham (which had been lately introduced from France under influential patronage), complaining of the want of due encouragement from the public, and saying that if he was not better supported he must decline the manufacture, and the youths who were apprenticed to it be returned to their parents.

'The reason of this I afterwards found to be that his carpets, though deemed handsome, were sold at such an exorbitant price that few cared to buy them. This afterwards turned to my great advantage when I could serve them much cheaper.'

Peter Parisot, the Huguenot emigré, was obviously a good public-relations man, but must have been motivated more by a love of money than an enthusiasm for carpets. Thomas Whitty, however, the founder of the Axminster Carpet Factory, who had been a woollen cloth weaver and was a devout Congregationalist, was inspired to turn to carpet weaving when he first saw some Turkish carpets which had been imported by an acquaintance, Mr. William Freeke of Ironmongers Lane, in 1754. Whitty was mystified as to how such a large piece (the carpet he saw measured 36 feet by 24 feet) could be woven without seams. In his own words again:

'After I had seen this carpet I could never keep it out of my mind long together, without being able to form the least idea of the method of doing it.

Opposite: English eighteenth-century needlework rug.

Lady Betty Germain's room at
Knole, showing an early English
carpet, c. 1650.

*'After this my mind was almost constantly employed about it and my spare time in making
some little trials in one of my broadlooms. At length on the 25th April 1755 (being our Fairday,
while our weavers were at holiday) I made in one of my looms a small piece of carpeting, about
7 or 8 inches square, resembling as near as I could the Turkey carpet.'*

It was after this first experiment that Whitty managed to procure a visit to Parisot's
Fulham factory:

*'Accordingly, I obtained a view of everything I wanted, by which all remaining doubt was
removed from my mind, and I was thoroughly satisfied I could go on with the manufacture, only
the Fulham carpets were so much finer than I had formed any idea of, that I had not at that
time the least idea I should ever rival them.*

*'When I came back to Axminster I immediately began to prepare a loom and materials for
making a carpet, and on Midsummer-day, 1755 (a memorable day for my family), I began
the first carpet I ever made, taking my children and their aunt Betty Harvey to overlook and
assist, for my first workers.'*

Whitty's family of daughters was trained to weave the Ghiordes knot and in 1756 he
produced a carpet 16 feet by 12 feet in a linen weave tufted with a soft worsted, and after
that produced carpets which he sold for £15 each. Incidentally, women and children were
mainly employed as weavers for carpet looms, partly because of their smaller, nimbler hands
and also, obviously, because they were a cheaper source of labour; women had not previously
been greatly employed as weavers in Europe for it was thought that bending over the looms
was injurious to the female organs – the same reason given for their employment on the
vertical looms at Aubusson – but with the carpet loom the women could safely sit to do their
work without danger to their persons:

*'When the manufacture was thus begun many gentlemen came out of curiosity to see it, and
professed their desire to encourage it by ordering carpets. Among them one of the first was Mr.*

Cook, of Stape, near Beaminster, who ordered a carpet from the first pattern. When I took this carpet home I met Mr. Cook at Beaminster, and he desired me to open it to show to a gentleman then with him. It was Mr. Twiniker, of the Temple, London, Steward to the Earl of Shaftesbury.'

That first carpet was eventually purchased by Lady Shaftesbury:

'Lord and Lady Shaftesbury were so well pleased with that carpet that they and their family have been since some of our best customers.'

In 1756 the renewed interest in carpet weaving gained official recognition when the Royal Society of Arts offered a premium for their manufacture. The minutes of the Society for the relevant meeting read:

'14. Turkey Carpets for their Strength and Wear being most useful to the Publick, and the Value of them, annually imported, amounting to more than £16,000. Could such Carpets be manufactured here, it would cause a great consumption of our Wool, a considerable Increase in the Dying trade, and employ a number of Men, Women and Children; therefore a Premium of £30 is proposed to be given to the person who shall make the best Carpet in one Breadth, after the manner of Turkey Carpets, in Colour, Pattern and Workmanship; to be at least 15 Foot by 12 Foot; and to be produced on or before the last Wednesday in March 1757.'

Thomas Whitty heard of the premiums offered:

'Accordingly, in March 1757 I produced a Carpet to that noble Society, about 16 feet by 12 feet 6, which I valued at £15. Mr. Thomas Moore of London produced another of about the same dimensions, which he valued at 40 guineas. The Society were convinced, on examining both carpets, that although Mr. Moore's was made of the finest materials, and therefore cost him more money in making, yet that mine was the best carpet in proportion to its price. They therefore recommended it to Mr. Moore and me, to take the fifty pounds, and divide it equally between us: which we agreed to do.'

The following year Whitty shared the prize with Passavant of Exeter, a Swiss from Basle who had bought up Parisot's works and moved them and the weavers to Exeter, where they prospered. In 1759 the premium was increased, and Whitty was awarded £30, sharing the premium with William Jesser of Frome, who received £20.

Carpet Weaving in Ireland

AT THIS TIME carpet weaving was also beginning to take root as an industry in Ireland, supported by the Royal Society of Dublin. The first reference to pile carpet making in Ireland came in 1525 when Piers Butler, Second Earl of Ormond and his wife Margaret, daughter of the Earl of Kildare, brought artisans from Flanders and the neighbouring provinces, and employed them at Kilkenny to make 'diapers, tapestries, Turkish carpets, cushions and other like works'. There is no further documentation to show that a new industry developed and, as in England, there is no evidence to show that carpets were produced again until the 18th century, when, in 1740, the Dublin Royal Society offered premiums for several varieties of carpet weaves. The first premium, in 1741, was of £5 for 'the best carpet in imitation of Turkey carpets' and was won by Mr. Richard Hogarth of Chamber's Street, Dublin. The following year the premium was raised to £10 for 'Turkey or Persian Carpets' (the only time that Persian carpets are mentioned) and was again won by Richard Hogarth.

As there were so few competitors no premiums were offered again until 1752, when in April a Mr. William McCreagh received a special award of two guineas for 'a carpet of his own making in imitation of Scotch carpets', which probably refers to a type of machine-woven pileless and reversible material then produced in England. In June 1752 £10 was offered for Turkey carpets and £5 for Wilton or Tournai. Wilton carpets, with cut loops, had just begun to be produced in England and were like a coarse velvet, and Tournai, or Brussels carpets, which had been introduced into England from Belgium in about 1745, were similar to the Wilton weave but with uncut loops.

For the next few years there were few claimants for the Turkey carpet premium, probably because they were very expensive to make, needing an expensive loom; the premiums would not be of much use to the small struggling manufacturer who would most benefit from the money. In 1756, however, the Society advanced £45 to one Patrick Brady to purchase a loom to make carpets, but either he was unlucky or he ran off with the money, but there is no further mention of him in the Society's transactions. But standards gradually rose, and in 1760 the premium for Turkey carpets was won by Mr. William Reed, originally a linen weaver, who was also lent money by the Society to buy looms and was encouraged by Lady Arabella Denny. His first carpet, produced for the Society in 1759, used the tapestry technique: 'Mr. Reed exhibited a beautiful rich carpet, after the manner of the Gobelins in France, and the same of that purchased from him by her Grace the Duchess of Bedford which gave the Society great pleasure, and may be viewed at his Manufactory on the Comb'. In 1760 he shared the premium for Turkey and Scotch carpets.

In 1761 French or Gobelins carpets were added to the list of premiums, but after 1762 the premiums ceased until 1780 when they were renewed on a different basis.

The carpet which Reed made for the Duchess of Bedford no longer exists, but was famous at the time. Reed continued to prosper until his death in 1772. In 1762 he appealed to the Irish Parliament for money and support, saying that since he had started his manufacture, less than half the previous number of carpets had been imported into Ireland. In June 1764 he advertised in the Freeman's Journal: 'Royal Charter School (he employed the boys of the school), on the Strand, Carpeting and Worsteds, etc. The first and finest made in this Kingdom are making at said School, per William Reed, Master. N.B. – His curious Shades may be viewed, and sold at 4/- per Pound, and no where else in this Kingdom.' He was undoubtedly the most important figure in the carpet industry in Dublin at the time and produced the greatest variety, if not the largest quantity, of carpets. As none of them can now be authentically traced, their quality remains unknown.

Of the other contemporary manufacturers, such as Samuel Lapham of Cork Street, Henry Lapham (no relation) of Cambre Street, Benjamin Bowes of Marybone Lane, the most important was John Long of Dolphin's Barn Lane who, also helped financially by the Society, produced Turkish, Scotch and Wilton weaves. There were other attempts by Huguenot weavers at Innishannon in Co. Cork and by Denis Duffy in Limerick in the 1770s. The most successful manufacturer in Cork was William Hutchinson who was well-known by 1771. Judging by the advertisements at this time the sales of Irish-made carpets between 1750 and 1800 must have been considerable, although probably mainly of rather poor quality due to the lack of money and the absence of a distinctive Irish style which would have encouraged artists to compete with, say, the Adam style in England. The best carpets were probably produced between 1755 and 1775.

When the Society awards were revived in 1780, the first premium was for an 'Irish carpet 28 feet long, 18 feet wide in imitation of ancient Mosaic with a foot border round it, to be made of the Wilton kind', which was probably to encourage angular Oriental designs rather than the earlier 'flowers or foliages'. From the later Society premiums it would seem that Wilton was more often made than any other weave and probably formed the bulk of goods advertised as 'Irish Carpeting'. Neither Turkey nor Tapestry weaves really prospered.

British Carpets in the 18th and 19th Centuries

CARPET WEAVING IN ENGLAND was now flourishing and around this time Kidderminster was also beginning to become a centre for carpet making. The town had had a weaving industry since the 16th century and Kidderminster carpets are mentioned as early as 1635 in an inventory of a bedchamber of a Lady Lettice, though the precise meaning of the word cannot be clear.

In 1751 Richard Pococke, in his *Travels through England*, mentions that the town was famous for carpets and by 1800 the carpet industry had become the town's major employer, although the trade was threatened by the Earl of Pembroke's Wilton Carpet Manufactory. It is known that one manufacturer, John Broom, went to Brussels and Tournai to learn the new techniques, although only two of the many original firms were to survive the technical innovations of the Industrial Revolution later in the century. In 1760 the Royal Society held an exhibition in their Great Room for a fortnight, showing two carpets from each of their

Top: Robert Adam, who collaborated with Thomas Moore during the latter part of the 18th century to supply carpets for the houses he designed. Above: George IV, who was responsible for the furnishing of 'Prinnie's Folly', or the Royal Pavilion at Brighton.

leading premium winners – Whitty, Moore and Passavant. Whitty wrote of his success:

'*These repeated Successes so advanced the reputation of my carpets, that I had a constant and almost uninterrupted demand for many years.*'

Whitty had also formed a London outlet through a London merchant, Mr. Crompton, who showed many carpets in his warehouse, which also brought in orders from America. In 1768 is this entry in Lady Mary Coke's journal:

'*Went by the new road to Moorfields to the carpet manufactory. (Thomas Moore's factory in Chiswell Street.) They make several different kinds, and some remarkably fine. We saw one that was making for Lord Coventry that he had agreed to pay 140 guineas for; it is indeed excessively fine. There are other kinds like the Persian, and looked quite as well. I believe I shall afford myself one of them for the room that I am furnishing.*'

In the first volume of the Royal Society's Transactions, 1783, there is a note that by that time the manufacture of carpets 'is now established in different parts of the kingdom, and brought to a degree of elegance and beauty which the Turkey carpets never attained.' This judgement reflects the tastes of the time and may well be disagreed with today, but home manufacture had become more important than importation, as Oriental designs did not suit the scrolls, plaster work and cameos of the lofty Adam style. Vanbrugh had been followed by the Adam brothers, Leverton, Chippendale, Wyatt and, eventually, John Nash, in the age of elegance, of gracious living, at a time when the country was comparatively peaceful and prosperous, with a wealthy aristocracy who had the time and means to give thought to their surroundings.

The fashion of the time was to have the pattern of the carpet reflecting the painted 295 ceiling. Thomas Moore, Whitty's main competitor, was a friend of Robert Adam, who directed business to Moorfields where he could personally supervise the production of his designs, as in the carpet in the Red Drawing Room in Syon House, designed by Adam and with the mark 'Thomas Moore 1769' woven into the border. Moore's factory declined when Adam died in 1792 and was sold for other purposes in 1795.

The other premium winners did not survive either: Passavant does not seem to have made much after 1760 and went bankrupt the following year. Jesser of Frome must have had a very small business and none of his carpets have survived. However, Whitty's Axminster factory continued to prosper. Within five years Whitty had established his factory as a leading concern in the town's economy, employing women and children as cheap labour, though apparently well-cared for. It became the custom for the finer completed carpets to be taken to the Congregationalist Church to be spread over the pews for all to admire and for thanks to be offered for their completion before they were sent to their destinations.

Whitty was a keen botanist and an expert dyer and a mastery of floral forms and use of colour characterize his carpets, though unfortunately he used no mark, so it is often difficult to identify the early Axminsters. Often he would use the same designs, with slight variations in size and colour, for different carpets and customers. When the third Thomas Whitty took over the factory, after the death of the first Thomas's son in August 1799, this mastery of floral pattern declined and was replaced by more classical motifs; for example, the accounts of 1808 for Crawley House, Bedford, record the sum of £65.12s.6d. paid to Drury, a carpet merchant, for an Axminster carpet in Egyptian style in yellow and black.

On 13 August 1783 George III and the Queen had visited the factory, which had resulted in a flood of orders. The Crown Prince, later George IV, ordered several carpets, including one for the Throne Room at Carlton House, and he obviously remembered the factory when he came to furnish Brighton Pavilion. There is a great difference between the elegant carpets made for the Adam style houses and those made for the Royal Pavilion, with its incredible mass of chinoiserie and exuberant decoration. The Pavilion was begun in 1748 when Henry Holland designed it as a pleasant seaside residence and in 1802 P. F. Robinson introduced Chinese paper to the walls of the Eating Room and Library and transformed the Corridor into a Chinese Gallery. In 1817 John Nash took over and the Pavilion became a Royal Palace on the accession of George IV in 1820. Huge sums were spent on the furnishings and decoration – £2,119.9s. was paid to Whitty's firm for the three carpets Axminster supplied and was only a small proportion of the total cost.

The three carpets made for the Pavilion were for the Music Room, the North Drawing 298

Room and the Banqueting Room. The first measured 61 feet by 40 feet and was the largest in the kingdom, weighing 1,700 lb., and the other two were designed by Robert Jones, one a circular carpet and the other made in one large square and two end pieces to fit the recesses of the room and was of similar size to the Music Room carpet. We have John Nash's own description of the carpet for the Banqueting Room, of the centrepiece of a dragon coiled around with three serpents 'surrounded by circles of interlacing scrolls, diversely wrought and increasing in diameter towards the border'. All three reflect the colour and decoration of the rooms, depicting serpents and dragons in the Chinese style with gold stars, insects, birds and lotus flowers, with blue or rose-pink grounds.

On 23 January 1828 the Axminster factory burnt down. New buildings were erected on the site, but the firm never recovered from the subsequent loss of orders and drifting away of skilled workmen during the interim period. In 1835 Samuel Whitty was declared bankrupt and the whole place sold on 31 August 1836. The carpet stock, looms and machinery were bought up by a Mr. Blackmore who moved everything, including many of the weavers, to Wilton where he continued production. Supported by a steady production of machine-made products, Blackmore was able to rebuild the old Axminster business despite encroachment by other firms. His main competitor was Jackson & Graham of Bond Street who had re-started Parisot's venture in London in the late 1840s. Mr. Peter Graham was on the committee of the 1851 Great Exhibition and also exhibited in 1862 at South Kensington, which was obviously a boost to their business, but little was subsequently heard of that firm.

Despite opposition, however, Blackmore was commissioned to weave five carpets for Queen Victoria at Windsor Castle and all were exhibited at the 1851 Exhibition; they were in a typically mid-Victorian mixture of styles: Renaissance, Louis-Quatorze, Italian and Persian. Blackmore increased the manufacture from employing thirty or forty weavers in 1836 to over 200 in 1860, when he sold out to Alfred Lapworth, a London carpet maker.

Detail from a tufted carpet designed by Robert Adam and made by Thomas Moore at Moorfields c. 1770. It comes from Ingestre Hall, but is identical to the carpet made for the Red Drawing Room at Syon House.

The Banqueting Room, the Royal Pavilion, Brighton.

We have the account of an American, Elihu Burritt, who visited the Wilton factory in 1864 and recorded his impressions of the place at this time in his *Walk from London to Land's End and Back*:

'There are two or three peculiarities that distinguish this carpet (Axminster) from all other kinds manufactured in different countries. In the first place, it is made whole, without stitch or seam. There are twenty Axminster looms in the factory, the longest of which is forty-five feet. (In fact the widest loom was forty feet.) *That is, on this loom a carpet may be wrought forty-five feet in width, and in length ad infinitum. No private apartment in the world has ever been carpeted of a greater breadth than this without seam.'*

Lapworth died in 1871 and his executors sold out to Yates & Wills, later known as Yates & Co., and the factory continued for thirty years. In 1891 Yates opened an American branch in New Jersey as well as extra premises in Southampton and Bemerton, all of which eventually failed. In Wilton Yates was known as an extremely pious man, a teetotaller, but when he died it was discovered that in fact he had been squandering company money on gambling, drink and chorus girls in London and Chicago. The factory again went into liquidation in 1905, but was saved by private subscription, mainly to save jobs in the area, under the patronage of the Earls of Pembroke and Radnor. In 1946 there were 102 looms, but by 1956, despite an excellent recovery after the Second World War, there were only six hand looms. Hand work was no longer economically viable and many of the hand weavers wanted to move to the less demanding machine jobs, and in 1957 the last hand carpet factory in Britain closed down.

To understand the development of carpet making in the 19th century it is necessary to give an outline of the innovations in machine production. Machine-weaving stemmed from the inventions of Arkwright which had been applied to the woollen and worsted industries during the last quarter of the 18th century. Boulton and Watts had given their steam engine a practical application and Cartwright had made a power-loom for weaving calico as well as patenting a wool-combing machine.

By 1825 the French Jacquard mechanism, which was a device for selecting and raising the threads required to form the pattern, had begun to replace the old and complicated harness of the hand loom. However, although the introduction of the factory system led to an increase in production, trade and wealth, the new weaving and dyeing techniques required a capital investment for machinery and reorganization which many of the smaller companies could not afford. Out of the many carpet industries existing in Kidderminster at the beginning of the 19th century only two now remain: Brintons, which was founded about 1783, and Woodward Grosvenors, now part of Guthries, which began around 1790, although several have started since the time of industrial expansion.

The Brussels weave was the first to be adopted by most factories, as it could be produced using cheaper materials, linen and later jute, for the back, while the more expensive woollen pile was brought to the surface, so that only the more expensive material was visible. The pile is brought up and raised over the other warps in a loop over a wire, with extra warp threads, usually five in all, raised either by hand or by Jacquard, to form the pattern. The loops could

Below: the North Drawing Room, the Royal Pavilion, Brighton. Right: the Music Room, the Royal Pavilion, Brighton.

An interior of Strawberry Hill, built in 1754–76 by Horace Walpole in the Gothick style.

be cut to achieve a velvet pile finish. The quality of such carpets is measured by the number of wires to the inch. Also, if the size of the wire is increased, then the pile is thicker. The coloured worsted is wound around the wire, which has a groove in it, and when a sharp knife is drawn along the groove the wire is liberated and the cut worsted forms the pile.

A Brussels carpet usually has nine wires to the inch, a Wilton ten. In 1830 Mr. Whytock of Edinburgh and Glasgow patented the tapestry process of weaving using a complicated drum system in which just one strand of yarn is dyed the requisite colour in different places according to the eventual pattern. This meant that a saving was made on the other four yarns previously needed for the pattern which had remained concealed in the web and also that a wider range of colours could be used, and yet the fabric produced more cheaply.

After initial protests the process was developed in Scotland and, after 1842, in Halifax. By 1850 there were 1,299 tapestry hand looms in England and Scotland compared to 2,500 ordinary Brussels looms.

In 1839 James Templeton of Glasgow patented a device for the manufacture of Axminster carpets known as Chenille Axminsters. By this method the pile was woven separately with tufts inserted of the right number and colour to form the pattern before it was attached by hand to the weft. This again saved money on wool but made a weaker fabric, as under stress the top could come loose from the linen or jute base. Also at this time the

Detail of a sample made by Templeton & Co., designed by Owen Jones.

English patent on the American Brussels power-loom, perfected by Erasmus Bigelow, was taken up by Crossleys of Halifax, and Britain once again began to complete with the growing American market.

In the 1870s, the moquette or Royal Axminster loom, developed by Alexander Smith & Sons of Yonkers, New York, was first used in England by Messrs. Tomkinson & Adam of Kidderminster. In the 1890s, Alexander Morton & Co. of Carlisle, a textile company, decided to branch out into manufacturing carpets, using Templeton's Chenille Axminster process. By 1895 carpets constituted nearly a quarter of the company's total sales.

In 1897 Alexander Morton visited America and investigated the Crompton Knowles spool Axminster loom then being developed. In order to produce a less expensive carpet they made a flat-weave tapestry carpet using ordinary yarns rather than figured chenille, buying looms from Brintons of Kidderminster. The carpets produced were called 'Caledon' and were derived from the old hand-woven 'Scotch' carpet.

Also in the 1890s Alexander Morton saw, in an exhibition in Brussels, a Donegal weave, and his son James, who had been influenced by the writings of William Morris on the need to reassert hand crafts, went over to Ireland and set up a factory producing hand-woven Donegal carpets; by 1906 the total annual sales of these hand-tufted rugs had reached the considerable sum of £25,000.

Many of the manufacturers so far mentioned exhibited at the Great Exhibition of 1851 – Messrs. Templeton of Glasgow, Messrs. A. Lapworth & Co. of London, Messrs. Watson Bell & Co. of London, Messrs. J. Bright & Co. of Craig, near Macclesfield. It was this exhibition which sparked off much of the Victorian discussion of the principles of design, although there had been an acute awareness since the 1830s that English design left a lot to be desired when in competition with European trade, especially French. In 1836 there had been a Government Select Committee to report on the state of design in British industry, with witnesses called from other countries: 'According to the evidence of M. Guillotte, a maker of Jacquard looms . . . a French capitalist employs three or four artists, where in England one artist would supply eight or ten manufacturers.'

Many of the designs of the 1851 Exhibition were condemned by its commentators, Sir Matthew Digby and others, as being 'indolent and servile', and in accordance with the feeling that a poor national architectural and decorative style represented a moral decline within the country, as voiced by Ruskin and the writers of the Gothic Revival, as well as critics such as Carlyle and Matthew Arnold, a new style of 'an intelligent and imaginative eclecticism' was now called for. What was particularly criticized was the incoherence of the adaptation of

Right: an example of the profusion of scrollwork, giving the impression of depth and relief condemned by the critics of the Great Exhibition, from the Art-Journal Illustrated Catalogue of the Great Exhibition of 1851. *Below: two examples of naturalistic patterns for carpets from the* Art-Journal Catalogue.

299

different styles and the florid profusion of naturalistic details, often giving the impression of a third dimension, with scrolls, wreaths, bouquets, roses, ferns and plentiful acanthus leaves, which was particularly unsuited to flat surfaces:

'The style is now utterly condemned by the taste of the present day, the opinion being all but universal that nothing is suitable for the ornamentation of a flat surface – like a floor, which is to be walked upon – but that which is in itself flat, and that carpets should not vie in brilliancy with works of art, ladies' dresses, or even furniture.'

The dining room at Kelmscott House, Hammersmith; where William Morris first began carpet weaving, showing a seventeenth-century Persian vase carpet, now in the Victoria and Albert Museum, London.

A bedroom at Wightwick Manor with wallpaper and carpet designed by William Morris.

The new style then, was for totally flat, conventionalized designs and was perhaps best expressed by Owen Jones, who was greatly influenced by Persian designs. Persian carpets once again became popular and their smaller, neater borders, subdued colours and conventionalized flower motifs replaced the sprawling, flamboyant and highly coloured roses, foxgloves or ferns.

A carpet designed by Owen Jones and made by Messrs. Jackson and Graham, was exhibited at the South Kensington International Exhibition in 1871 and his mastery of Persian forms and use of colour were praised; the carpet was reckoned 'the most successful exhibited'. Digby Wyatt, another spokesman for reform, also designed Patent Axminsters for Templeton's of Glasgow which were exhibited at the 1871 Paris Exhibition. These new designs also showed an understanding of the requirements of machine production.

At this time a central art collection was being assembled at what is now the Victorian and Albert Museum which included a sizeable number of Persian and other Oriental carpets. An interesting note on the influence of this collection is that there is a carpet made for Carminow, a house in Mount Lofty, South Australia, by Templeton's in 1885 which combines exact copies of the border and centre of two Persian carpets which had been purchased by the Museum shortly before that date.

One of the Examiners at the South Kensington Science and Art Department was William Morris, and it was there that he studied the recently acquired collection of Persian carpets, textiles and ceramics. In his lecture, *The History of Pattern-designing*, Morris wrote:

'*To us pattern designers, Persia has become a holy-land, for there in the process of time our art was perfected, and thence it spread to cover for a while the world, east and west.*'

In another lecture, in 1880, however, he criticized the art in India, saying that Indian carpets, as a profitable export commodity, were now manufactured in prisons under Government direction and that, this being the case, there remained little hope for Eastern art:

'*In this case the Government . . . has determined that it will make its wares cheap, whether it makes them nasty or not. Cheap and nasty they are, I assure you; but though they are not the worst of their kind, they would not be made thus if everything did not tend the same way. And it is the same everywhere with all Indian manufactures . . . One thing is certain, that if we don't get to work making our own carpets it will not be very long before we shall find the East fails us: for that last gift, the gift of the sense of harmonious colour, is speedily dying out in the East before the conquests of European rifles and money-bags.'*

In fact the carpet in the Waterloo Chamber at Windsor, reputedly the largest seamless carpet in Europe, was made for Queen Victoria in the prisons at Agra, in India.

Morris himself is undoubtedly renowned as the greatest pattern designer of the Victorian

age and it was only to be expected that he would turn his attention to carpet design and the techniques of weaving. On 13 April 1877 he wrote to George Wardle:

'I saw yesterday a piece of ANCIENT Persian, time of Shah Abbas (our Elizabeth's time) that fairly threw me on my back. I had no idea such wonders could be done in carpets.'

After moving into Kelmscott House he had a tapestry loom installed in his bedroom and during the winter of 1878–9 he turned his interest from dyeing to weaving. He made an intensive study of Persian work before he felt that he could begin weaving carpets in the same manner himself, though between 1876 and 1883 Morris made twenty-four designs for machine-woven carpets as well as designs for the Hammersmith hand-woven carpets and rugs. The machine designs were for the Wilton Royal Carpet Factory and the Heckmondwike Manufacturing Co. in Yorkshire.

The first hand-tufted carpets were made in 1878; Morris would make a one-eighth scale drawing of the design, colouring this himself by hand, which would then be enlarged on point paper for the pattern to be copied by the weaver. Lewis F. Day wrote in 1899:

'With carpets he began modestly, by designing cheap Kidderminster, Brussels, Wilton pile and patent Axminster, machine-made varieties all, not produced in his own workshops, but woven for him. But apart from the objection that these were machine made, the conditions of the loom were irksome to him as a designer; he did not like being restrained; and, the beauty of the Oriental carpets imported into this country inciting him, he eventually set about weaving "real" Axminster, i.e., carpets of soft close pile, all in one piece, after the Eastern fashion . . .Carpet weaving of this description he himself describes as a "mosaic" of small woollen squares; the designer has only to observe the size of the squares, and he is free to let his fancy spread itself over the carpet . . . He did not approve of the gradation of tint so much sought after in modern carpets, preferring a pattern which lay "absolutely flat upon the ground"; and he contrived to get wonderful variety and beauty of tint by juxtaposition of contrasting colours (red and blue by preference), bounded by judiciously chosen outlines. A carpet, he held, should be not only a passable but an exquisite piece of colour. And, of course, it should have something to say for itself.'

The derivation of many of his designs from Persian models is clearly seen, but his absolute mastery of showing growth among floral forms is always present, although never in

Below: the workshops of Morris & Co. at Merton Abbey: the dyeing vats. Centre: an original design from the Morris workshops for a carpet 'with peacocks and dragons', which was never put into production. Right: Bullerswood carpet by William Morris. William Morris Gallery, Walthamstow.

the carpet designs, as in his textile and wallpaper designs, is there the impression of depth and relief, a rule of the time to which he did not generally conform.

The first pile carpet squares were woven on a loom in a back attic of Queen Square, but when production increased the loom was moved to the coach house at Hammersmith, where women were employed as weavers. In May 1880 he held an exhibition of the Hammersmith carpets and issued a circular in which he said that he wanted 'to make England independent of the East for carpets which may claim to be considered as works of art.'

The Naworth carpet, made for George Howard, which was the largest carpet produced by Morris & Co., was woven in the coach house at Hammersmith, and took nearly a year to weave. Some of the Hammersmith carpets are marked with the device of a blacksmith's hammer, a large M, and a waving line, representing the river, woven into the border. In November 1881 the loom was moved to the Merton Abbey works, where production continued. Although Morris had based his socialist views on a hatred of the machine, his designs added greatly to the change in style of machine-made carpets.

As this original impetus in design gave way to more concrete movements in style, other designers turned their hand to carpet design. At that time a particular designer would take responsibility for a complete interior, making the designs for manufacturers to make up for all aspects of a house, so that it is likely, even if no designs can be traced today, that most of the great names of the Arts and Crafts Movement and Art Nouveau would have produced

306   carpet designs. Many names can be traced: Walter Crane; C. F. A. Voysey, who produced many wallpaper, fabric and carpet designs, worked for Tomkinson & Adam, Heal & Son, and Alex. Morton of Carlisle with whom he signed a five-year agreement for the minimum fee of £120 for ten original designs and exclusive use of his services for designs for woven textiles

306   other than carpets. Christopher Dresser designed for Crossleys and Brintons, Archibald
307   Knox for Morton & Co. and for Liberty's. Templetons are known to have made rugs to C. R. Mackintosh's designs for Hill House, Helensburgh.

The preference for small, Oriental-style designs still held, although the Art Nouveau style brought larger, more swirling patterns and new colours. But although designs for wall-fabrics and tapestries were numerous, carpet designs were relatively uncommon, as they presented greater difficulties to the designer in being two-dimensional and as surfaces which had to be viewed from all angles.

Beam rug weaving at the Royal Wilton Carpet Factory c. 1900.

Hand-knotted rug made for the Century Guild c. 1884, probably by Morris & Co. William Morris Gallery, Walthamstow.

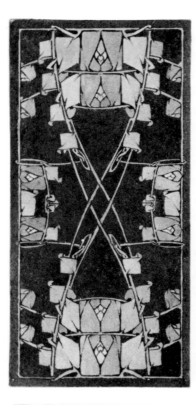 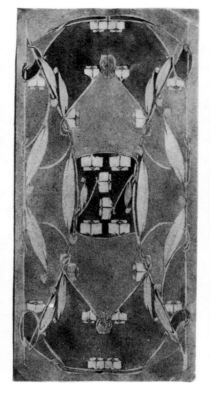 

Three watercolour designs by Archibald Knox for hand-woven rugs, probably intended for production by Alexander Morton. Manx Museum, Isle of Man.

Right: the 'Wykehamist', designed by C. F. A. Voysey for Tomkinson & Adam, 1897 (detail). Above: 'Green Pastures', also designed by Voysey for Tomkinson, 1896. Victoria and Albert Museum, London.

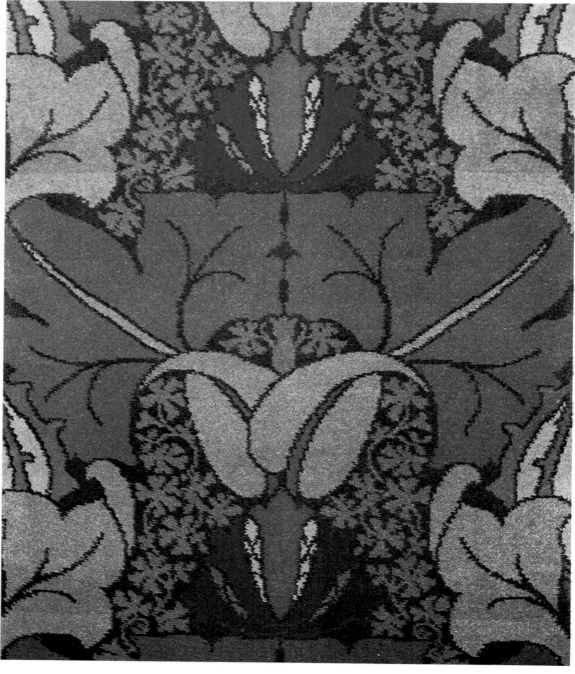

In England, Voysey's carpets were perhaps the most successful; the rugs which Archibald Knox designed for Liberty's seem to have tried to hold too much movement within a contained space for a floor-covering, and Mackintosh went to the other extreme with plain, pale colours and small chequer patterns. Many of the Liberty designs were plain with decorated borders, such as the Kildare carpets, founded in 1903 with the support of the Countess of Mayo, hand-woven and dyed with natural native dyes.

Most of the photographs of contemporary interiors by architects such as George Walton, Lutyens or Norman Shaw show Oriental rugs. The Art Nouveau movement was contemporary with a Jacobean revival which encouraged the sale of Eastern carpets. On the Continent, more designers did produce rugs; Horta, for instance, designed a number for the Solvay Residence in Brussels. John Betjeman, in 1930, wrote that:

'The date 1900 gave impetus to the artists. They thought they would evolve a new twentieth-century style. And they did.'

In Europe Jugendstil held sway, with the Darmstadt Exhibition of 1901 as an example of the new enthusiasm for the work which had been sparked off by such as Mackintosh and the Glasgow school, but Le Corbusier and Dufy were later to rationalize the work of Morris and Mackintosh and a new style evolved which eventually totally rejected the 'unwholesome stuffiness of the Victorian house with its musty atmosphere of a third-rate museum.'

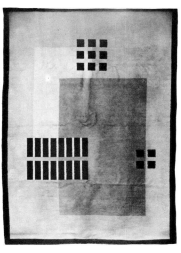

Above: Glasgow school carpet, the underside of which bears the label 'Templeton Romney', c. 1910. Left: an interior of C. R. Mackintosh's Hill House; the carpet is designed by Mackintosh.

The Modern Movement in European Carpets

Scandinavia

It is impossible to say how far and in what respects William Morris was influenced by his visits to Iceland, but in Finland his influence was felt. In 1879 an artist, Fanny Churberg, founded the Friends of Finnish Handicrafts with aims similar to the ideals of Morris. This society had a great effect on Finnish textile art, which had declined during the mid-19th century due to industrialization. In Sweden too, in 1874 a similar association had begun, and in 1878 Johanna Brunsson founded a practical weaving school, both of which still exist today.

In 1902 Herman Gesellius, Armas Lindgren and Eliel Saarinen, influenced by 'Kallela', the house that Akseli Gallen had built for himself in Ruovesi, in the style of the log cabins of Karelia, built 'Hvitträsk', a house near Helsinki. Akseli Gallen himself designed carpets and was concerned with reviving the native arts of his country, which started a new national romantic current in style. 'Hvitträsk', where the architects designed all the furniture, was both a reinforcement of Finnish art against the Russian panslavism of the period and a reflection of the Jugendstil in Finland. Saarinen's wife was a weaver and designed rugs for Frank Lloyd-Wright in America.

The Finnish folk-style rug patterns came into fashion again in the 1920s, but by the 1930s this trend gave way to Cubism and functionalism, in keeping with trends in the rest of Europe. In the following decade came the toned rug, where the design was no longer starkly geometrical, but the outlines of the patterns merged softly into each other. The pioneers of the new rug were Impi Sotavalta and Eva Brummer and their work was followed up by many good artists. The number of rug designers, almost all of them women, grew considerably after 1950, encouraged by competitions run by textile firms, and many modern rugs were made, still using a woollen yarn and the Ghiordes knot, but with the rows of nap more widely spaced and with longer tufts – from three to five centimetres – in an attempt to reflect, in modern expressionistic form, the snow and ice of the Icelandic countryside. The new emphasis placed texture above design.

Left: knotted pile linen ryiji from Sweden, designed by Märta Måås-Fjetterström, 1923, called 'Silverryan'. 8 ft. 3 in. × 5 ft. (250 × 153 cm.). Right: knotted pile Swedish carpet by Måås-Fjetterström 1918–19. 10 ft. 4 in. × 7 ft. 2 in. (315 × 220 cm.). Both pieces: Röhsska Konstslöjdmuseet, Gothenburg.

*Eighteenth- or nineteenth-
century Norwegian rug. Victoria
and Albert Museum, London.*

Top: tapestry-woven wool rug from the Båstad studio of Märta Måås-Fjetterström, Sweden, c. 1930. Right: tapestry-woven woollen rug designed by Barbra Nilssen, Sweden, c. 1955. Both pieces: Victoria and Albert Museum, London. Above: tapestry-woven linen, cowhair and wool rug, designed by Inga-Lill Sjöblom for the Handicraft Centre in Gothenburg, Sweden, 1968; called 'Popocatapetl'.

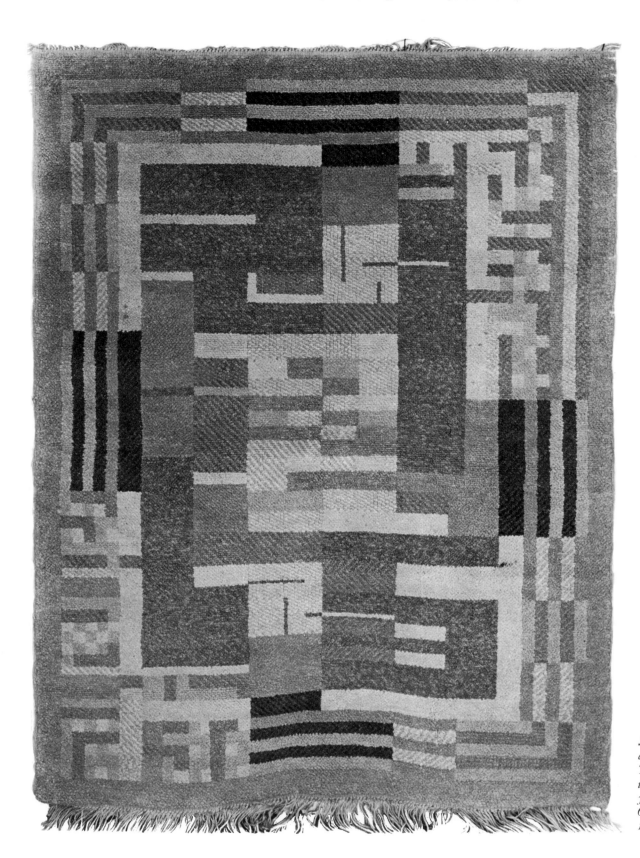

Small woollen carpet designed by Benita Otte, 1923. This rug is brightly coloured in shades of blue, green, yellow, red and violet. 6 ft. 9 in. × 5 ft. (205 × 152 cm.).

Germany

In Germany the Bauhaus movement was taking root under the guidance of Walter Gropius, and the architectural impetus led outwards into all forms of the decorative arts. Gropius had distributed his manifesto in Weimar in May 1919, influenced by the earlier Deutscher Werkbund founded in 1907 by Hermann Muthesius; the aim of the Bahaus was to train artists and craftsmen on the basis of a craftsman's apprenticeship, but within the spirit of machine technology, so that their designs would be directly relevant to mass production. The first Lehrmeister of the weaving workshop was Hélène Börner, who had previously worked with Van de Velde, and in 1920 the painter, Georg Muche, was appointed Form-meister, with such students as Hedwig Jungnick, Benita Otte and Gunta Stölzl. Paul Klee did many designs for them.

Cotton carpet designed for a nursery by Benita Otte of the Bauhaus, in 1923; it has a predominantly grey and green background, with bright squares of red, yellow and blue. 5 ft. 10 in. × 3 ft. 4 in. (177 × 101 cm.).

When the Bauhaus moved to Dessau the emphasis of the training changed to a more systematic approach to the mechanics of weaving and dyeing, but there was a split between Georg Muche, who supported this emphasis on machine-weaving, and Gunta Stölzl who claimed that the machine techniques were not yet sufficiently flexible to adopt the revolutionary advances she and her students had made on the hand-looms and she insisted that the hand-weaver should be given the freedom to continue experimenting.

In 1926 Muche left the workshops and Gunta Stölzl took over, with Otti Berger, Anni Albers and Lies Beyer as students. Her approach was practical and under her direction the workshops continued to experiment with new ideas, many of which were successfully used by German manufacturers who put their designs into production using new mechanical techniques in collaboration with the Bauhaus.

France

In France the Cubist painters also had their effect on the decorative arts, which perhaps proved to be stronger than the Bauhaus teachings when it came to carpet design. In 1925 the Paris Exhibition was held where several modernist-style rugs were shown. These were revolutionary in design in that they did away with the border, leaving a free space for a more

314   outward movement of form and line. The use of a white, or natural off-white, background was also a great innovation with far-reaching effects.

Great Britain

Although England at this time was criticized for provincialism and a tendency to copy rather than develop incoming ideas, a new interior décor was evolving, with an emphasis on plain, light surfaces, space and light and also the avoidance of incongruity. *The Studio* of 1930 said:

> *'The easel-picture has already lost something of its predominance in the house. It has too often in the past been a feature of incongruity, and now that a more unified arrangement is being demanded in interior decoration, its pride of place is being seriously imperilled.'*

Its most serious rival was to be the designed rug. Cubism, 'un style purement décoratif', provided an abstract style which would really furnish and no longer merely decorate a room; it would also show a certain 'élan' after the Victorian clutter then so despised.

In London at this time many ideas for new interior design were being discussed, such as the 'all white room', which would have been totally impractical in the smog-bound London of the time. The first real impetus in rug design, however, came from two Americans,

315   the Vorticist poster-designer E. McKnight Kauffer, who was responsible for introducing Cubist abstraction into advertising art in England, and the textile designer, Marion Dorn, who probably first suggested the possibilities inherent in the medium to McKnight Kauffer, who promptly applied them to rug design.

Their first rugs were woven by an Irish woman who lived in Chelsea, Mrs. Jean Orage, who later also wove rugs for Ronald Grierson. On the whole, the major manufacturers were wary of producing such original and unexpected designs so that most rugs were woven by the

Below: a design by Marion Dorn for a Wilton hand-tufted 'Wessex' carpet. Left: a design, also for Wilton, by Marian Pepler.

artist himself or by small firms, which obviously meant that manufacture was limited and costly. As many of the designers were in any case graphic artists the rugs were sold as individual works of art, with a status as a fashionable one-off item.

During the mid-twenties, many French designers had sold their designs, without copyright, in unbound folders which were sold in London, Berlin and New York. It is likely that some of these designs were later produced in England, often sent out to India or China to be woven cheaply, and many good, unsigned designs were sold by Heal's and Fortnum and Mason's. In France, designs by Da Silva Bruhns were made by the Savonnerie; in England in the thirties the Wilton Royal Carpet Factory commissioned designs by Marion Dorn and later by Marian Pepler, Ronald Grierson, John Tandy and others. As a reaction to the economic slump of the 1930s the Carlisle carpet and textiles firm of Morton Sundour started producing modernist designs through a separate company called Edinburgh

313

Right: hand-tufted rug designed by Ronald Grierson, made in India in 1936, and exhibited at the Redfern Gallery, London. Far right: 'Orpheus' design by Ashley Havinden for Wilton, 1930. Below: modernist rug, possibly French. Bottom right: carpet designed by John Tandy, c. 1932. Bottom: Chinese rug by Betty Joel, c. 1935.

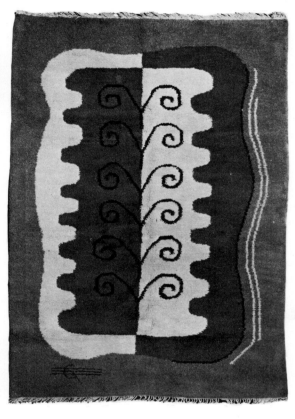

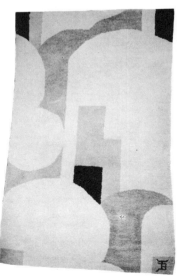

Weavers, run by Alastair Morton. His father, James Morton, later wrote about the period at this enterprising Scottish concern.

'*I had felt for many years that manufacturers of textiles were not making headway commensurate with the developments in kindred industries, and that while chemistry, for example, was giving us beautiful new fibres, and colours with wonderful new properties, in so far as the conversion of those into fabrics was concerned we were breaking little new ground, and were remaining content with old ideas and methods.*'

Edinburgh Weavers therefore was a conscious attempt to evolve decorative fabrics suited to modern taste and to bring weaving into line with architecture, as taught by the Bauhaus. In London Alastair Morton, a painter, came into contact with many artists whom he later involved in designing for the company, and in 1932 he met Hans Aufseeser (later

Below: Royal Wilton 'Wessex' carpet, designed by E. McKnight Kauffer. Bottom left: French modernist rug.
Bottom right: rug designed by Terence Prentis for the Edinburgh Weavers, 1936–7.

Tisdall) in Düsseldorf, who encouraged his ideas and did many designs for him. Showrooms were acquired in Hanover Square and later in Bond Street, from where carpets and fabrics designed by Marion Dorn, Hans Aufseeser, Marion Pepler, Ashley Havinden, McKnight Kauffer, Terence Prentis and Paul Nash were sold.

They also encouraged pure artists, such as Ben Nicholson, Jean Varda and John Tandy, who derived his designs from his wood cuts, who had previously had little or no contact with applied art. Duncan Miller, who had showrooms in Lower Grosvenor Place, had a strong connection with the Edinburgh Weavers and there the rugs were shown beside the furniture of Marcel Breuer, Wells Coates, Serge Chermayeff and Denham McLaren.

One of the first exhibitions of the modernist rugs was at the Picture Gallery of point-noué carpets and rugs by Da Silva Bruhns, which were described thus:

'*These were early and, in some cases, brilliant interpretations of abstract compositions. A few of his carpets seemed to be influenced by rather primitive Moorish patterns, but the colours were delightful.*'

Marion Dorn did special 'off the peg' collections for Fortnum and Mason's, who at one time devoted an entire floor to Modern Movement designs, and in 1932 she designed carpets, in tones of black, grey and cream, for Claridges. Simpsons sold carpets by Ashley Havinden; Betty Joel sold her own rugs, made at Tientsin in China, from her own showrooms, Betty Joel Ltd., at 25, Knightsbridge; in 1935 the Dorland House Exhibition was held. Ronald Grierson held a one-man show of rugs at the Redfern Gallery, Cork Street, in 1936; it opened on the day King Edward VIII abdicated, but sold out nevertheless; the rugs were priced at £12 and measured about nine feet by six feet, and were mainly woven in India.

The designs of Duncan Grant and Vanessa Bell, both painters of the Bloomsbury Group, woven by the Blind Employment Factory, were sold through Alan Walton Fabrics Ltd. Another designer, who wove all her own rugs and whose weaving was even praised by Mrs.

The sitting room of Ronald Grierson's house in Hampstead, London, in the 1930s. The rug was woven in India in 1933.

Opposite: the interior of Claridges Hotel, London; the carpets are by Marion Dorn.

314

314

Orage, was Evelyn Wyld, an Englishwoman who lived in Paris, and who exhibited at the Curtis Moffat Gallery in Mayfair. Other designers were Michael Heulen, who designed for Tomkinsons of Kidderminster, and Mrs. Pindar Davis, for Crossleys of Halifax.

The Post-war Years

AFTER THE THIRTIES, however, this movement in design began to wane and hardly survived the war. Betty Joel retired from business in 1937; John Tandy, Terence Prentis and Ashley Havinden moved to advertising and design consultancy, and Marion Dorn and McKnight Kauffer both returned to the United States. Ronald Grierson did continue to design textiles and carpets, made by S. J. Stockwell's and sold through Liberty's, and for Crossley's. A new impetus came with the Festival of Britain in 1951, but the fashion in rugs had changed, influenced by Scandinavian designs, where the emphasis was on texture rather than design, such as sculpted pile or tapestry and tufted rugs. Edinburgh Weavers also continued to prosper after the war, but the time of creative rugs was over. Royal Wilton, who had supported the creative trend of the 1930s, closed their hand looms in 1957.

The individually designed rugs of the Modern Movement had shown great daring in their abstract forms, new treatment of classical themes and their freedom from the restraints of the traditions of floor-design. They were characterized by a carefully controlled use of space, line and colour, with transitions of tone against lighter backgrounds. There were also many debased jazz motifs produced with American Art Deco or 'Cunard' lines, influenced in part by Hollywood cinema, which found their way onto the market, but the demise of interest after the war in the innovations of the twenties and thirties has not since been replaced by any new individual style, despite the resurgence of interest in Persian and Oriental rugs and the consequent effect on their value.

A late nineteenth-century Navajo saddle blanket. 2 ft. 8 in. × 2 ft. 6 in. (81 × 76 cm.).

NORTH AMERICAN RUGS AND CARPETS

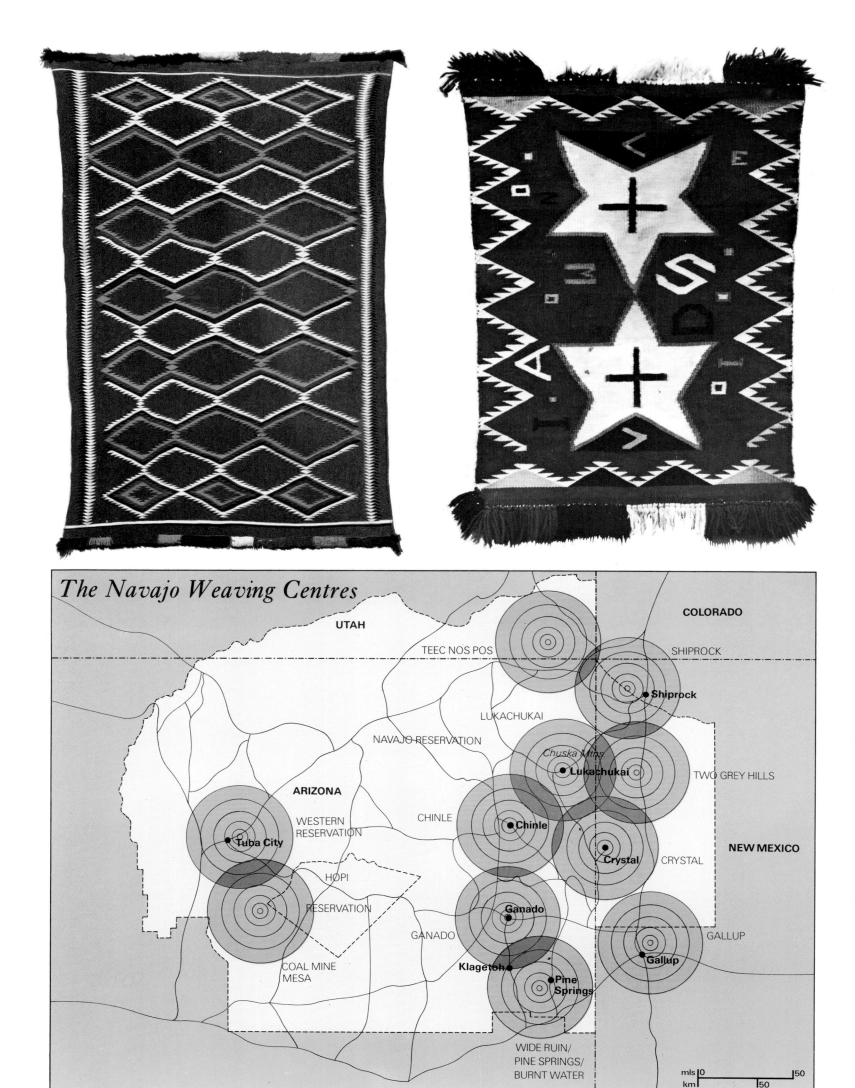

The Navajo Weaving Centres

Navajo Rugs

THE WEAVING OF THE NAVAJO RUG is the continuation of a long tradition of excellent craftsmanship that dates back nearly three centuries. The Navajos learned the craft from the Pueblo Indians around 1700, and early examples of Navajo weaving show the close parallels between the two groups. The principal difference between Navajo and Pueblo weaving is the use of wool by the Navajos, and cotton by the Puebloans. The Spanish introduced sheep into the Southwest in the early 1600s and the nomadic Navajos quickly adopted the animal as the mainstay of their economy.

Before 1890, the Navajos wove primarily blankets for their own use as clothing and for bedding. The 'Classic Period' of weaving, when the Indians acquired European yarns and commercial yarns from Germantown, Pennsylvania, lasted from about 1850 to 1875. During this period a few native dyes were employed and natural undyed wools in shades of black, white and brown, as well as the commercial yarns. It is probable that the Navajos produced fine weaving as early as 1800, but material examples are scarce. The Navajos acquired their first commercial yarns, such as Saxony from Germany, towards the end of the Classic Period.

Indigo dye from Europe arrived in the Southwest in the early 1800s, and by 1850 vegetal yellows and greens were occasionally used along with the natural white, brown and black wool. The single most striking colour in Navajo weaving was undoubtedly the so-called Bayeta red. The Spaniards imported bolts of English-made baize, and the Indians would unravel the treasured cloth strand by strand.

Probably the most famous examples of Classic weaving are the 'Chief blankets', for the most part export items that were highly prized by the Plains Indians. The Chief blanket, similar to the *manta*, was worn about the shoulders. The great majority of wearing blankets were traded to southern Plains Indians such as the Cheyenne, Arapaho, Sioux, Comanche and Kiowa. Other garments of the Classic Period included the Bayeta serape and the *moki* blanket, *moki* being a term used for the Hopi Indians.

Above: a serape (clothing blanket) from the Classic Period, c. 1870. 5 ft. 4 in. × 3 ft. 7 in. (162.5 × 109.22 cm.). Opposite, top right: Germantown rug. c. 1890. 6 ft. 9 in. × 4 ft. 5 in. (206 × 134.5 cm.). Opposite, top left: Germantown pictorial rug, c. 1890. 2 ft. 1 in. × 1 ft. 7 in. (63.5 cm × 48.25 cm.).

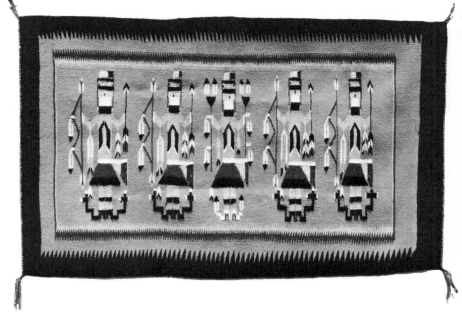

Navajo weaving changed radically in the last twenty years of the 19th century. The sheep population was greatly reduced, and trading posts and the railroad came to the reservation. Commercial, ready-to-weave yarns predominated in a veritable kaleidoscope of colours, and by 1890 the Indians were weaving for the trading posts and the early white tourists.

Until the 1870s, the Navajos wove blankets for their own use, both for wearing and trading with other Indians, but by the 1880s the white traders, whose stores were springing up across the reservation, were exchanging clothing, utensils and food for Indian weavings which were then sold to the tourists.

The traders were a great influence on the weavers, and the requests for pillow covers and bed covers to decorate white homes resulted in a proliferation of quickly woven, inferior pieces. There was less need or use for homespun yarns as commercial, ready-to-weave

Above left: a contemporary yei *rug. The* yeis *were the supernatural beings of the traditional Navajo religion. 3 ft. 10 in. × 2 ft. 5 in. (117 × 73.5 cm.). Above: a contemporary* yeibichai *rug. The* yeibichai *rugs are related to the* yei *rugs, but instead of showing the spirits themselves, they show the Navajo dancers impersonating the* yeis. *5 ft. 7 in. × 4 ft. 8 in. (170 × 142 cm.).*

Germantown yarns were easily imported by the traders. Vivid multicoloured blankets, such as the 'Eye Dazzlers', created intense optical effects.

Inexpensive aniline dyes were introduced in the 1880s and this resulted in a lessening of the popularity of the expensive Germantown yarn.

By 1890 there was demand from the white consumer for a Navajo tapestry that could be used as a floor covering. The traders and Indians were quick to oblige, and the Navajo rug was born. Borders were introduced, and the proportions and dimensions of tapestries changed to fit the requirements of a floor.

In a marked contrast to their long tradition of abstract design, the Navajo began to weave pictorials; these were often highly elaborate tapestries embellished with American patriotic designs, animals, railroad scenes, houses and bows and arrows. The *yeis*, the Navajo supernatural beings, were also included in tapestry designs.

By 1890 the Navajo sheep flocks had multiplied, local wool was abundant, and there was a marked reduction in the use of commercial yarns. The quality of weaving deteriorated greatly and it was left to a few dedicated traders to revitalize the art of weaving. J. B. Moore of Crystal and Lorenzo Hubbell of Ganado were among the first traders to champion the cause of quality Indian weaving, and the traders have continued up to the present day to play a vital role in the development of the Navajo rug.

Teec Nos Pos

Teec Nos Pos, which in Navajo means 'circle of cottonwood trees', is the most northern of the Navajo weaving regions, and its tradition of rug making dates back to the latter years of the 19th century.

The Teec Nos Pos style is very reminiscent of Middle Eastern designs, and could have been inspired by early traders who showed the Indians photographs of the then fashionable Persian rugs. The borders of the rugs are wide with elaborate interlocking geometrics, and the central motifs are often similar to those of the Two Grey Hills rugs. One sees connected diamonds, fret and zig-zag designs, with occasional arrows and feathers, and most of the design elements are outlined with contrasting colours.

The origins of most of the designs used in Navajo weavings are lost in antiquity, and few Indians are aware of the meanings behind the majority of the symbols that they weave.

Aniline dyes are usual in Teec Nos Pos rugs, and commercial yarn is being used in increasingly large amounts.

Important Teec Nos Pos Weavers
Hilda Begay/Dee Etsitty/Mary Moon/Alice Nelson/Esther Williams/Emma Yabeney

Shiprock

The volcanic neck of Shiprock in the north-eastern corner of the Navajo reservation is the centre of *yei* weaving.

At the beginning of this century, Will Evans of the Shiprock Trading Company persuaded the local weavers to portray *yeis*, the Navajo supernatural beings who act as intermediaries between the Indians and their gods. At first there was much tribal opposition to the weaving of *yeis* as the figures are taken directly from the sacred sand paintings. However, the rugs serve no religious function and are not used in Navajo ceremonials, and today the Navajos accept the secular *yei* rug with minimal objection.

A typical *yei* rug from the Shiprock region has a pale-coloured ground, often white. Tall, slender *yei* figures carrying arrows, plant stalks and other symbolic motifs extend across the rug in rigid postures. The exaggerated and attenuated body of the 'Rainbow Goddess' sometimes lies along three sides of the rug. *Yeis* are usually woven in vivid colours similar to Germantown hues, and commercial and aniline dyes are much in evidence.

Associated with the *yei* rug, but markedly different, is the *yeibichai*. The *yei* rug depicts the *yei* spirits themselves, while the *yeibichai* depicts the Navajo dancers impersonating the *yei* spirits. The figures on *yeibichai* rugs resemble human beings much more closely and often seem to be dancing with uplifted feet.

323
331

Important Shiprock Weavers
Anna Funston/Edith Johnson

Two Grey Hills

Two Grey Hills lies just over the Chuska Mountains on the eastern edge of the Navajo reservation, and the rugs from this region are some of the most tightly-woven of all Navajo products.

The natural coloured rugs produced prior to 1915 were coarse and without distinction, but the area did begin to produce good rugs in about 1920, developing partly from J. B. Moore's Crystal designs. Two competing traders, George Bloomfield and Ed Davies, were in part responsible for the inspiration and instruction with which the weavers turned their poorly-made, early rugs into great weaving by the 1920s.

Aniline dyes and Germantown yarns were avoided and the weavers were encouraged to use only handspun wool. The finely spun native wool is woven into weft counts of up to 150 per inch, and many of the finest weavings are quite small and are hung as tapestries.

The predominant Two Grey Hills colours are white, black, tan and grey, with subtle shading created by the inter-carding of colours. Occasionally native-dyed yellow is used, or a little commercial turquoise blue.

The rug designs from this area are complex, most having a black border, perhaps as many as three inner borders of a lighter shade, and an elaborate central panel of stepped diamond-shaped motifs, frets and zig-zags. Swastikas, often used as design motifs before the Second World War, are rarely woven nowadays because of the non-Indian significance of the symbol. It is possible that the weavers received inspiration for some of their geometric designs from the prehistoric black-on-white potsherds dug from the Chaco ruins.

Important Two Grey Hills Weavers
Donna Marie Cohoe/Ramon Curley/Mary Gilmore/Mary Joe Gould/Mary Louise Gould/Julie Jumbo/Dorothy Mike/Elizabeth Mute/Mildred Natoni/Daisy Taugelchee/Esther Taugelchee/Priscilla Taugelchee/Julia Theadore/Stella Todacheenie/Mary Tom

Lukachukai
The Lukachukai Trading Post region, that includes Upper Greasewood and Round Rock, is another area of *yei* weaving.

The Lukachukai *yeis* are characterized by backgrounds of dark colours: grey, black, tan, brown or red. The stylized figures appear in single or double rows, with or without a border. The Lukachukai rugs, as with those of the Shiprock region, are quite small, and large rugs are rare. The region is noted for handspun yarns and the rugs are usually coarser than the Shiprock counterparts.

Crystal
Crystal, New Mexico, due north of Window Rock, the Navajo capital, was the home of J. B. Moore, trader, from 1897 until 1911. Moore introduced production-line techniques into his rug business. Raw wool was sent east for scouring, and upon return was sent to his best spinners. Moore's wife dyed the yarn herself, using superior quality aniline dyes, and it was then issued to the best weavers. Moore pre-selected the rug designs, often taking

A contemporary Lukachukai yei rug by Irene Kayonnie. 4 ft. 5 in. × 1 ft. 5 in. (134.5 × 43 cm.).

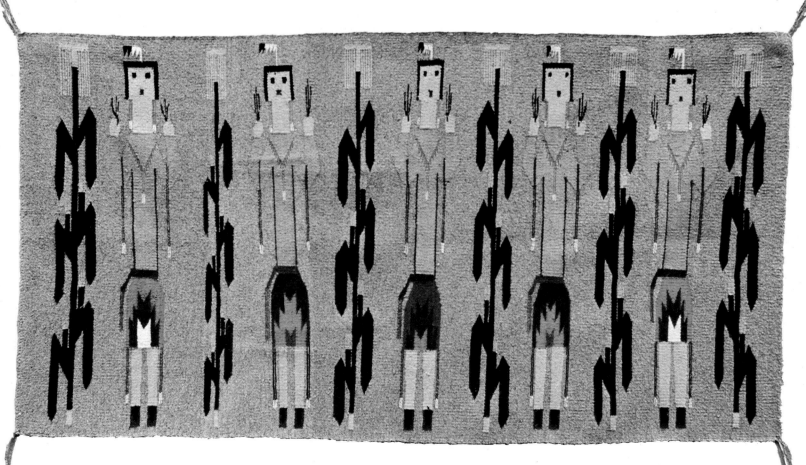

Far left: a contemporary Chinle piece by Ana Brown. Modern rugs from this region tend to be thickly textured. 7 ft. × 4 ft. 10 in. (213 × 147 cm.). Left: contemporary Crystal piece by Nellie Roan; recent Crystal weavings often use vegetal dyes. 3 ft. 10 in. × 2 ft. 7 in. (117 × 78.75 cm.).

Oriental motifs and designs from other sources. Central diamonds were set against light-coloured grounds, and within strong, complex borders. The designs were simple and direct and of particular attraction to white customers.

Moore is thought to have been the first trader to issue a mail-order catalogue of Navajo rugs, and his 1911 catalogue included the famous 'Storm Pattern rug'. Customers could order his rugs in whatever design, colour scheme, size and quality they desired.

The Moore tradition continued after his departure from the trading post, but a completely different style of rug was developed in the revival period of the 1930s and 1940s. This

Far left: contemporary Ganado rug by Alice Begay. The Ganado rugs are the most familiar of all Navajo weavings and are notable for their use of brilliant colour, especially the famous 'Ganado Red'. 5 ft. 11 in. × 4 ft. (180 × 122 cm.). Left: contemporary Ganado tapestry, also by Alice Begay. 4 ft. × 2 ft. 5 in. (122 × 73.5 cm.).

later Crystal is the most uncomplicated of all contemporary designs, featuring vegetal dyes in earthy colours in the brown-yellow-orange range. The designs are usually banded in straight unbroken patterns.

Important Crystal Weavers
Mary Arthur/Lottie Buck/Sarah Curley/Faye C. George/Laura Harvey/Ruth Moore/Helen Peshlakai/Mary Wingate

Chinle

327

The Chinle region is due north of Ganado, at the mouth of Canyon de Chelly, the Navajo holy retreat. The weaving area extends from Many Farms in the north to Nazlini in the south.

Chinle rugs were tightly woven and of good quality from the turn of the century onwards. Until the 1930s they were similar to other rugs produced throughout the reservation, with the usual black border and the large central stepped diamond in shades of red, black and grey. In the 1930s a major change took place among the Chinle weavers. L. H. 'Cozy' McSparron of the Thunderbird Ranch and Mary Wheelwright encouraged the weavers to experiment with pastel, soft hues, and abandon the bordered designs, weaving instead bands reaching from edge to edge. The Garcia Trading Post continued to encourage the weavers in the use of traditional Chinle motifs and designs, but the McSparron style eventually dominated the region.

The Chinle vegetal dyes, developed in the 1930s and 1940s, are derived from tree bark, flower petals, pine needles, leaves, lichen, berries, corn kernels, and numerous other sources, each contributing its own natural colour. Over 250 individual recipes for making vegetal dyes have been recorded.

Most of today's spinning and dyeing is done at Chinle, with a rather coarse weft creating a thick, textured rug. The earthy vegetal hues continue to dominate the region, but brighter aniline colours have also been introduced, together with an increased use of the stepped diamond motif.

Important Chinle Weavers
Mary L. Yazzie

Ganado-Klagetoh

327
330

Don Lorenzo Hubbell, who operated the Hubbell Trading Post just west of Ganado, was among the first of the traders who endeavoured to elevate the quality of Navajo weaving, and he tried to standardize designs. The trading post was established in 1876 and is still a flourishing trading post and social centre for the Indians. It is now part of the United States parks system and a National Monument.

The Ganado is the most familiar of all Navajo rugs. It is uncomplicated in design, and noted for its brilliant dark red character attributed to Hubbell urging his weavers to double the red portion in the dye formula. This colour has become known as 'Ganado Red'. The most common characteristics of the Ganado rugs are black or red borders, and a profusion of crosses, stars and, in particular, large serrate diamonds.

Klagetoh rugs have white backgrounds with one large diamond or several smaller ones, in natural grey, intensified black and aniline red.

Important Ganado-Klagetoh Weavers
Alice Begay/Louise Begay/Maggie Begay/Mary Begay/Sadie Curtis/Desbah Evans/Anna Francis/Clara Jim/Mary Jones/Rose Maloney/Esther Morgan/Grace Henderson Nez/ Nellie Roan/Stella Toadachini/Esther Whipple/Elsie Wilson/Annie Yazzie/Faye Yazzie

Gallup

Throw rugs, suitable for tables and chairs rather than floor coverings, are the primary weavings of the Gallup, New Mexico, region. These long, narrow rugs, with simple designs, are often coarsely woven on cotton warps of bright commercial yarns.

Gallup throws of better quality are made in black, white, grey and red geometric patterns, or sometimes in abstract pictorial motifs such as dancing figures and plant stalks, indicating the weavers' concern with everyday experience.

Wide Ruin/Pine Springs/Burnt Water

This is the prime vegetal dye centre of the Navajo weaving industry, and is located in the south-eastern region of the Reservation.

The traders most responsible for the vegetal revival in the late 1930s were Bill and Sallie Wagner Lippincott of the Wide Ruin Trading Post. They encouraged the weavers to return to the old design elements, and refused to accept inferior workmanship. The style omitted borders and is characterized by connected diamonds and triangles, and alternating straight lines that extend from edge to edge.

The hues most used are autumnal ochres, sepias and umber, combined with subtle areas of greys and pale blues.

Important Wide Ruin/Pine Springs/Burnt Water Weavers
Helen Bia/Nora Brown/Blanche Hale/Mabel Burnside Myers/Maggie Price/Maggie Roan/ Nellie Roan/Mary Six/Agnes Smith/Ellen Smith/Marjorie Spencer/Lottie Thompson/ Ruth Tsosie/Philomena Yazzie

Coal Mine Mesa

An unusual and interesting type of weaving was introduced at Coal Mine Mesa, south-east of Tuba City. This is the raised-outline technique in which additional weft threads accentuate the design outlines.

Dr. Ned Hatathli, Navajo educator, was largely responsible for the furtherance of raised-outline weaving which extended to twilled saddle blankets as well as two-faced rugs.

Western Reservation

The area of the Western Reservation, approximately 120 miles by 50 miles, is one of the largest of the weaving regions. The main weaving centres here are Cameron, Cedar Ridge, Chilchinbito, Coppermine, The Gap, Inscription House, Kaibito, Kerley's Trading Post, Navajo Mountain, Paiute Mesa, Shonto and Tuba City.

The characteristic styles of the Western Reservation are conventional geometrical forms with black, white, brown and grey borders, and aniline red.

The Tuba City Storm rug is the best known pattern from this region. The origins of the 'Storm pattern' are very vague. J. B. Moore of Crystal introduced 'Storm patterns' in his 1911 trading post catalogue, but it is unclear whether the design element came from Moore or another source. The typical 'Storm pattern' includes a central stepped square or diamond representing 'the centre of the world', smaller squares or rectangles in the corners ('the houses of the wind, the four sacred mountains'), and connecting zig-zag lines ('lightning') between the corner designs and central motif. Occasionally swastikas and stylized water beetles are added to the rugs.

Above left: a contemporary rug from the Burnt Water region by Philomena Yazzie. Burnt Water is one of the chief areas for the use of vegetal dyes in the Navajo weaving industry. 6 ft. 9 in. × 5 ft. 4 in. (206 × 162.5 cm.). Above centre: another centre of vegetal dyeing is Wide Ruin; this piece dates from the 1930s. 7 ft. 4 in. × 5 ft. 10 in. (223.5 × 178 cm.). Above: a contemporary piece from Wide Ruin. 4 ft. 9 in. × 2 ft. 10 in. (145 × 86 cm.).

330

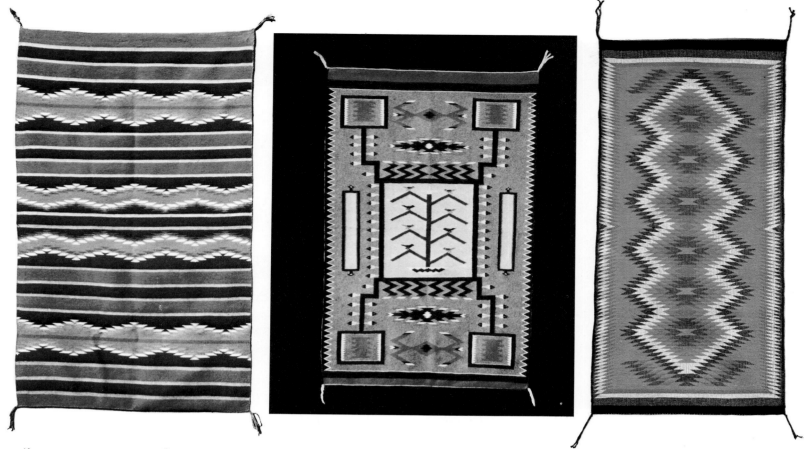

Above: a contemporary rug from Wide Ruin by Eleanor Nelson. 4 ft. 9 in. × 2 ft. 11 in. (145 × 89 cm.). Above centre: a contemporary Storm pattern rug by Lelia Featherhead; such rugs are woven mainly in the western part of the Navajo Reservation. 6 ft. 7 in. × 5 ft. 2 in. (200.5 × 157.5 cm.). Above right: a raised outline rug from the Coal Mine Mesa by an unknown contemporary weaver. 4 ft. 11 in. × 2 ft. 5 in. (150 × 73.5 cm.).

Non-regional Rugs

Twill Weaving

Twilled textiles are produced in many areas of Navajo territory. Many loom heddles are used to manipulate the vertical warp cords to allow weft threads to pass over and under unlike numbers of warps. Subtle and numerous geometric designs are achieved including diamonds, zig-zags and herring-bones. Natural wool colours are most often used.

Saddle Blankets

The only weaving currently made for Navajo use is the saddle blanket, of standard size measuring approximately 30 inches square, and about 30 inches by 60 inches for the double saddle. Many saddle blankets are extremely coarse with uneven shapes, but the best of the blankets are very finely woven. Saddle blankets are either of simple tapestry weave with striped aniline dyes, or double weave twilled for durability.

Pictorial Rugs

The earliest extant example of a pictorial motif in a Navajo weaving dates back to the late 1850s or early 1860s, but it was not until the 1880s and 1890s that the pictorial tradition began to flourish. This tradition continues today throughout the reservation.

Pictorials have always depicted, often in random fashion, day-to-day sights and scenes. Early rugs often include trains, seen by the Indians as the railroad pushed westwards, while

Right: a contemporary pictorial rug by Ella Gene from the Hubbell Trading Post. 3 ft. 6 in. × 2 ft. 7 in. (106.5 × 79 cm.). Far right: pictorial rug dating from the 1920s. 5 ft. 10 in. × 3 ft. 5 in. (178 × 104 cm.).

later rugs might include jet airplanes and helicopters. Other depicted subjects include American flags and eagles, houses and hogans, wild and domestic animals, and birds perched on cornstalks. Even Walt Disney characters, in particular Mickey and Minnie Mouse, find themselves on pictorials, as do designs from the graphic media, such as petrol company trademarks, detergent posters, and food company labels.

Important Pictorial Weavers
Sarah Begay/Julia Bryant/Linda Hadley/Virginia Ray Leonard/Ella Ninrod

Sand-painting Rugs
Sand-painting rugs depict the ceremonial paintings made of sands, minerals and organic matter that the Navajo medicine men create in the hogan for healing purposes. After ceremonial use the ritually empowered sand-paintings have to be destroyed, so there was much tribal opposition when the first sand-painting rugs were woven in the late 1890s. The weavers risked the wrath of the gods, as had the weavers of the *yei* rugs.

Hosteen Klah, a Navajo shaman and sand-painter, wove about twenty sand-painting rugs between 1905 and his death in 1938, and this did much to allay the fears of the tribe.

Today's weavings are usually slightly and subtly amended from their original designs as sand-paintings.

The 'Spirit Trail'
Many Navajo rugs include a thin line that is woven into the upper right-hand corner. The line, of a contrasting colour, extends through the outer border to the edge of the rug.

There is much speculation on the significance of this line, and the Indians themselves are uncertain of the symbolism. Some consider the trail to be an outlet for the evil spirits within the rug, while others believe it to be an intentional flaw added to the design, admitting man's imperfections to the gods. Another widely held belief is that the trail permits the exit of the weaver's spirit and energies after he has completed the rug or blanket, thus permitting them to be used in the next weaving.

The Jerga
The New Mexicans began to have carpets in their homes and churches in the late 18th century, and these weavings are known as 'jerga', after the Arabic *xerca* meaning sack cloth.

No extant example of jerga can be proven to be older than the 19th century, and most existing examples, other than pieces made with natural light and dark wool yarns, contain one or more commercial dyes.

Jerga yarns were thickly spun because of the rough treatment they received on the uneven and rocky floors. The most common jerga was made of undyed natural yarns worked into checks or, less often, plaids or stripes. The usual weave was diagonal twill, and some pieces were woven in herring-bone twill or diamond twill.

Jerga weavings coloured with indigo, logwood and vegetal yellows were probably made before 1865, before commercial dyes began to arrive in New Mexico. The later examples were woven with indigo, natural yellows and commercial red dyes.

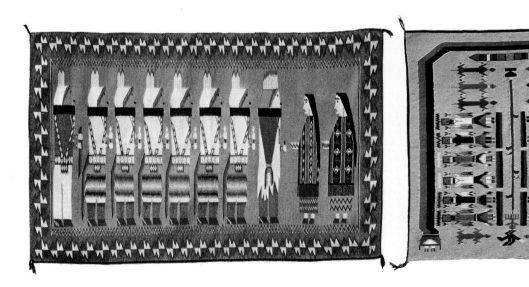

Far left: contemporary yeibichai rug by Betty Bia. *5 ft. 2 in. × 3 ft. 5 in. (157.5 × 104 cm.). Left: sand-painting rug of the 1950s by Daisy Morgan. 5 ft. 2 in. × 4 ft. 4 in. (157.5 × 132 cm.).*

Handmade American Rugs

Opposite, top: an early American embroidered rug. The Pennsylvania Dutch and German settlers brought with them a highly developed tradition of needlecraft, and many of the finest embroidered rugs came from that region. Smithsonian Institution, Washington.

Below: Nineteenth-century hooked rug. The hooking technique became popular in the United States with the introduction of Indian jute burlap. These rugs are sometimes referred to as 'drawn-in' rugs. Smithsonian Institution, Washington. Below right: a nineteenth-century knitted rug. These rugs were made up of strips of material which were cut and sewn together endwise and wound into balls of string to be knitted into floor pieces. Smithsonian Institution, Washington.

Yarn-sewn rugs

Prior to 1800 the floors in most American homes were kept bare, and it was not until about 1830 that significant amounts of finished carpeting were produced domestically.

Yarn-sewn rugs were made mostly between 1800 and 1840, and are the first examples of pictorial American floor rugs. They were usually made with two-ply yarn on a base of homespun linen or on a grain bag, and the great majority are made on burlap.

Many nineteenth-century examples show patriotic motifs, and original designs of people, ships, houses and animals replaced the more traditional English designs of balanced floral and geometric motifs.

Shirred rugs

Large-scale production of machine-made carpeting began after 1830. Braided rugs began to be made, and the appliqué technique of shirring was started at about this time. Shirring was developed because cloth strips were far thicker than yarn and could not be sewn through a woven linen or cotton fabric base. In a shirred rug the fabric lies on the top surface, and only the thread stitches show on the back of the rug.

Most shirred rugs appear to have been made between 1825 and 1860. The decline in the shirring technique seems to correspond to the rising popularity, at the end of the 1850s, of rugs hooked on burlap.

Hooked rugs

The first hooked rugs were probably made in the late 1840s with linen, tow (a coarse, flax fibre fabric), and homespun hemp as the foundation fabrics. The introduction of Indian jute burlap made the hooking technique popular as well as practical in North America.

Hooked rugs were indigenous to North America and were first made in Maine, New Hampshire, the Maritime Provinces, and other areas of eastern Canada. The making of

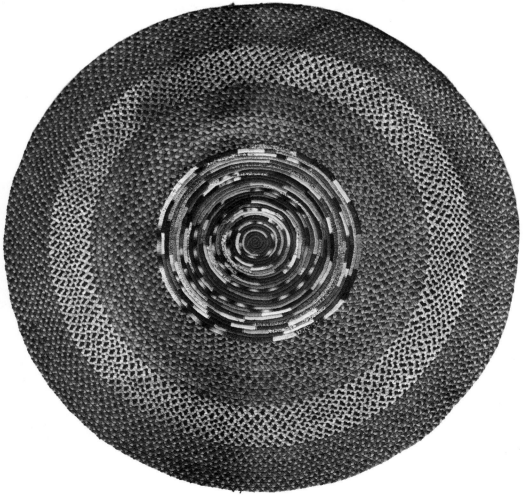

Left: The Tilton Family, *a watercolour by Joseph H. Davis, painted in 1837, showing an early American rug. Colonial Williamsburg, Williamsburg.*

Below left: among the most popular motifs among the makers of hooked rugs were floral patterns. Smithsonian Institution, Washington. Below centre: a 'fluffy' crocheted wool rug; these rugs were made in similar fashion to the knitted ones, but used strips of cut cloth in place of yarn. Smithsonian Institution, Washington. Below: an early nineteenth-century painting of Boy on a Stencilled Carpet; *the stencilled carpet would probably have been made of oilcloth or canvas. Colonial Williamsburg, Williamsburg.*

A pictorial hooked rug with lion motif. Smithsonian Institution, Washington.

hooked rugs developed into a cottage industry in the Northeast where the rigorous winter months prevented farming and fishing, and the households turned naturally to homecrafts during the evenings and snowbound winter months.

By the end of the 19th century hooked rugs were made throughout North America, though hooked rug making was still considered a country craft and the rugs were not thought to be suitable for fashionable Victorian homes.

The most popular motifs used by the rug makers were animals, houses and flowers. People, ships and landscapes required more skill and appear less frequently.

In earlier times rug makers extracted their dyes from native woods, plants and berries. Later, synthetic dyes were introduced, and this expanded their colour range.

During the 20th century hooked rug making developed into a cottage industry in many parts of the United States and Canada. The most famous of these industries was the Grenfell Mission of Labrador, while Alexander Graham Bell and his wife helped to establish the Cheticamp Hooked Rug Industry on Cape Breton Island, Nova Scotia.

The cottage industry in hooked rugs was not exclusively Canadian. In 1902 Lucy Thomson founded the Subbekakasheny Industry in Belchertown, Massachusetts, where rug designs were based on American Indian motifs. Helen Albee founded the Abenakee hooked rug community at Pequaket, New Hampshire, and these rugs were also inspired by American Indian designs. Other important centres of rug making that were founded in the 1920s and 1930s include the following: the South End Home Industry in Boston; the Society of Deerfield Industries, Massachusetts; the Pine Burr Studio in Apison, Tennessee; the Blue Ridge Weavers in Tryon, North Carolina; Rosemont Industries in Marion, Virginia; the Wooton Fireside Industries, Kentucky; the Carcassonne Community Center in Gander, Kentucky, and the Shenandoah Community workers in Bird Haven, Virginia.

American Rug Patterns

The best known of the pattern makers was Edward Sands Frost of Maine who cut designs into metal stencils, and then used them to stamp patterns on burlap for hooked rugs. Frost was a tin peddler who between 1864 and 1876 sold these hand-coloured patterns to housewives along his peddling route. Typical Frost designs are animals within floral or geometric borders, and he also used Oriental and Masonic patterns. Later, mail-order firms such as Montgomery Ward manufactured patterns that copied the early designs of Frost.

The earliest rug patterns were probably made in the 1850s by Chambers and Lealand of Lowell, Massachusetts. This company specialized in stamped embroidery patterns, and also produced large wooden printing blocks with inlaid copper designs.

BUYING AND MAINTENANCE OF RUGS AND CARPETS

Salor juval *of the 'S-group'. Probably early 19th century. Approximately 4 ft. 8 in. × 2 ft. 7 in. (142 × 78.5 cm.).*

Buying and Maintenance of Rugs and Carpets

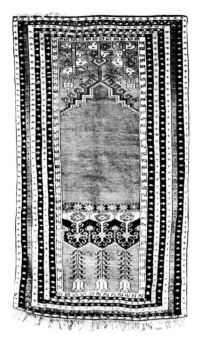

Late eighteenth- or early nineteenth-century Ladik prayer rug. 6 ft. 3 in. × 3 ft. 6 in. (190 × 106.5 cm.).

DISCUSSION ABOUT BUYING any work of art is difficult. It presumes that the writer knows better than the reader, not only from the commercial aspect, but also from the much more intangible viewpoint of taste. Also, carpets, like furniture or silver, have a functional as well as decorative use and any advice about buying must take into account the reason why a particular carpet is bought.

There are essentially two ways of buying a carpet: at auction or from a dealer. In saying this, we are deliberately ignoring private treaties between individuals, and also assuming that we are dealing with carpets and other weavings of aesthetic merit. Most department stores can provide the 'home decorator' with new carpets made in Persia, Afghanistan, Pakistan, Hong Kong and, of course, on commercial looms in Europe and the United States; some of these are of reasonable quality, but almost all are machine made, either wholly or in part, and use chemical dyes. Except for the finest Persian pieces, which in any case are very expensive and in short supply due to a very strong domestic market, it is improbable that such pieces have much life in them. From an artistic point of view, they are not worth considering when it is still possible to buy hand woven and vegetable dyed carpets of some age and beauty for the same price.

Carpets cannot properly be defined as 'antiques'. Age, of course, is of considerable importance, but fine carpets continued to be made until well into the 20th century. In certain cases (nomad carpets, kelims, Caucasian rugs, etc.), writers of saleroom and dealers' catalogues prefer, for psychological reasons, to call a piece 'late 19th century' rather than 'early 20th century', although there is little evidence to prove the matter one way or the other. Certainly the few Persian or Caucasian carpets which appear bearing dates in the early 20th century – for instance a beautiful Perepedil dated A.H. 1324 (A.D. 1906) sold at Sotheby's in November 1976 – would certainly have been dated to the late 19th century had there not been firm evidence to the contrary. Thus, the criteria for judging carpets have not to do so much with date as with quality. A Tabriz carpet (catalogued in the sale as 'Nain'), nearly fourteen feet in length, was sold by Sotheby's on 10 December 1976. Signed by Ahmed Imad Sayyid, it was vegetable dyed in fine glowing colours, well designed, being based on the sixteenth-century medallion, escutcheon and corner pattern, with cartouche and palmette borders, and was tightly knotted. Though the design was not an original concept, the piece was of superb craftsmanship, and fetched £15,400 ($26,950).

Now, £15,400 is a very high price for a modern carpet, although it has to be said that, even in the last fifteen years, pressures of commercialism have become so great that it is unlikely that a carpet of this quality could be produced today, and even if such a piece was commissioned, it would be unlikely to cost much less straight from the looms. Nevertheless, it could be argued that its price, though high, may reflect the fact that, workmanship apart, it is a modern version of a sixteenth-century design. Few medallion carpets of the Safavid period appear on the market today. In the 1960s, however, two pieces changed hands which give us some guide as to values. The Metropolitan Museum purchased the Anhalt carpet through the Kress Foundation and the Boston Museum of Fine Arts acquired the silk hunting carpet from Baron Maurice de Rothschild. Both are considered masterpieces of Safavid weaving; the prices are reported reliably to have been $1 million (£571,500) and $600,000 (£343,000) respectively. These purchases, however, were made a decade ago. In more recent years, there have been few pieces of equivalent importance. In 1976, Colnaghi's in London exhibited one of the two Doria silk Polonaise carpets (the other one being in the Metropolitan Museum); this was sold for a reputed £250,000 ($437,500). At auction, top prices today range between about £50,000 and £100,000 ($87,500 and $175,000); the newly rediscovered Shah Abbas silk medallion kelim sold at Sotheby's in 1976 made £63,800 ($111,500), despite its poor condition.

In the last two or three years, petro-dollars have had an unquestioned impact on the prices of Oriental carpets, and of Persian pieces in particular. From 1974 to 1977, prices have multiplied to an extraordinary extent. Many of the carpets dispersed in the Kevorkian sales at Sotheby's in 1969 and 1970 have reappeared in the last two years, and have, on average, increased eight-fold in price. The principal buyers are Persians who have a pre-

Nineteenth-century Herat rug with botehs *on a cream field. 6 ft. 3 in. × 4 ft. 8 in. (190 × 142 cm.).*

deliction for brightly coloured silk pieces in good condition, and it is carpets of this description which have increased the most in value. No more dramatic proof of this has been given than the $200,000 (£114,285) paid for a nineteenth-century Herez silk carpet at Sotheby Parke Bernet in New York in February 1977, the highest auction price so far recorded. It is not difficult to imagine what this piece would have been worth a few years ago. In April 1976, Sotheby's in London sold another Herez silk, woven with a large central tree-of-life motif, with animals and birds. Neither so attractive nor in such good condition as the New York piece, it made £19,800 ($34,500), having been sold at Christie's eight years previously for £2,500 ($4,375). The New York piece fetched over three times the top saleroom estimate. Its value in the late 1960s, when the pressure of Middle Eastern buying had not built up, would probably not have been more than £5,000 to £8,000.

The Persian and other Middle Eastern buyers have not been the only forces at work in the carpet market. German and American collectors have been particularly active in the field of nineteenth-century village and tribal weaving from Turkey, the Caucasus, nineteenth-century Persia and the Turkoman tribes. Prices for such pieces, although not as high as those quoted above, have probably increased by the same multiple in the equivalent period. This is also true of good late eighteenth- and nineteenth-century kelims and other flat-weaves which have, in the past five years or so (largely due to the efforts of David Black and Clive Loveless in London), become the subject of keen specialist collecting. For the finest examples of pile-knotted carpets of the types we have described, one would, in 1977, probably have been paying between £4,000 ($7,000) and £10,000 ($17,500), while the best kelims made between £2,500 ($4,375) and £3,000 ($5,250). For Baluchi rugs, which are now being collected seriously, a top price of around £2,000 ($3,500) to £2,500 ($4,375) could have been expected (although when dealing with superlatives, preconceived ideas of a top price tend to be shattered).

By normal standards of income, we admit that even £2,500 ($4,375) is a daunting sum of money. But we emphasize that the prices we have quoted above have been paid for only the finest examples, or for pieces which appeal to a particularly rich clientèle with a particular taste. Serious collectors of carpets, like serious collectors of any type of art, are prepared to pay outstanding sums for things they consider to be of exceptional rarity and importance. Their approach is essentially academic, and they are seeking features which may be of little interest to the layman. For instance, a dedicated collector of Turkoman carpets (and there are many such active today) is prepared to pay very highly for an example of the 'S-group', because he knows that these pieces are rare and crucially important to a study of Turkoman weavings. The cultured layman, however, whose eyes may be sympathetic to the colours and designs of Turkoman weavings, will not lay much store by such things, which are part of the arcane science of carpet scholarship.

Top: nineteenth-century Herez silk prayer rug. 6 ft. 2 in. × 4 ft. 8 in. (187.5 × 142 cm.). Above: nineteenth-century silk Herez rug of floral lozenge design. 10 ft. × 8 ft. 4 in. (305 × 254 cm.).

The cultured layman will seek rather to purchase a carpet of aesthetic merit at a price commensurate with his purse. He will also be hoping to use the piece in the normal domestic way – that is, as a floor covering. With this in mind, he will be aware that any carpet, no matter how finely made, will eventually show the signs of continual wear; a carpet placed in the living room of a busy family will suffer. Thus, the purchaser will have to balance the amount of money he pays for a carpet against the use to which he intends to put it. He should remember that many Oriental carpets were not intended to be placed on hard wooden floors and be walked upon by feet clad in hard leather shoes. Any carpet dealer of experience can tell stories of selling old carpets in good condition, only to see them a few years later with the pile worn down to the web. And such stories are told not only of nineteenth-century pieces, but of sixteenth-century Safavid carpets also.

Nineteenth-century Senneh rug showing European influence. 7 ft. 3 in. × 5 ft. 1 in. (210 × 155 cm.).

All this might lead the reader to suppose that it is impractical to use good carpets as floor coverings. In this respect, we emphasize that the majority of such pieces are being used under circumstances which their makers did not envisage and thus they must be treated with great care. A carpet which has a large area of pile worn away is almost irreparable, and re-piling is, even if possible, very expensive. Thus, as a general rule, carpets of real quality and some age (and we hardly need to say that this applies above all to silk pieces) should not be used in areas where they are likely to be subjected to heavy wear. They should not be kept in positions where they will be frequently and for long periods in strong, direct sunlight, and they should have a soft underlay – a fitted carpet for instance. Ideally, space permitting, they should be hung on walls. Kelims, which do not in any case make

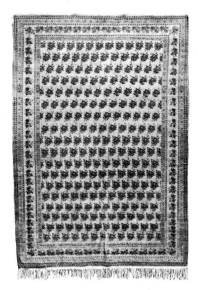

Late eighteenth- or early nineteenth-century Ladik triple-arch rug. 6 ft. 10 in. × 4 ft. 5 in. (208.5 × 134.5 cm.).

Eighteenth-century Bergama Transylvanian double-niche prayer rug. 6 ft. × 4 ft. 5 in. (183 × 134.5 cm.).

Nineteenth-century Herez silk carpet. At the time of writing, this is the most expensive carpet ever sold at auction ($200,000 at Sotheby Parke Bernet, New York, February 1977). 12 ft. 6 in. × 9 ft. (381 × 274 cm.).

very suitable floor coverings for Western homes, should be hung. We might add that it is a good idea to change the position of carpets being used on the floor. Although any marked degree of wear is regrettable, it is better to have a carpet with the pile worn low but evenly so, rather than one area of pile worn almost completely away and the rest of the surface comparatively undamaged.

For the actual purchase of a carpet, we would recommend the layman to a specialist dealer. This is not because we have anything against salerooms – far from it – but because buying a carpet is not simply a question of choosing something you like visually, and then paying for it. You have to be confident that it is in reasonable condition, that the web has not rotted (which means that it will fall to pieces within a matter of months and be irreparable), that it is free of moth holes, etc. When you buy a piece from a dealer, he will have had it cleaned and suitably repaired if necessary, or can advise you about what repairs can be done and their probable cost; he will also point out the presence of any chemical dyes and will give you, to the best of his knowledge, a guide to the piece's age and origin. If he is a good dealer, he will, in other words, tell you exactly what you are buying. As to the price, it is our experience that most serious carpet dealers, contrary to popular rumour, are very fair. They base their prices on their own estimation of the carpet's worth – both aesthetically and commercially – having regard to their costs and the generally accepted levels of similar pieces in the market place. Dealers specializing in particular types of carpets might well charge what seems an unusually high price for a piece, but they are catering to equally specialist collectors who will appreciate the reasons. This should not put off the layman because if the art market has any one rule, it is that the finest examples of any particular type of work of art, regardless of the premium they cost for *being* the finest, have little chance of decreasing in value (as long as they are well cared for). In talking of dealers, we have discussed those whose business revolves around carpets as art rather than commodities. In the last few years, hundreds of dealers have opened premises in Europe, the United States and the Middle East concerned with retailing modern, mass-produced Oriental pieces. In this respect, they are little better (and often much worse) than mini-department stores; and, in our experience, when they do have the occasional piece of some age and quality, they know less about it than the layman. Thus you must choose not only your carpet but also your dealer with care.

The attribution of many types of Oriental carpets to a particular period or place is still, in many cases, a matter of controversy. As we have seen in our section on the older types of Oriental weavings, there is no agreement about many of the most important examples of the 15th, 16th and 17th centuries, and the same holds true of nineteenth-century pieces. The dealers, like the salerooms, give the best information available, but in the case of the salerooms, *caveat emptor* is still the rule. The goods are sold as shown and catalogued and the buyer takes the risk. Thus, although many magnificent carpets come through the major salerooms of Europe and the United States every year, to make regular purchases at auction requires some considerable degree of expertise. Any dealer will, of course, be prepared to advise a private client about prospective saleroom purchases, and will act on his behalf for a commission. The salerooms will also advise clients and, if necessary, bid for them – a service they provide free of charge.

In discussing the function of the Oriental carpet in a Western domestic setting, we have given some indication of the way in which it should be treated. In terms of maintenance, carpets should be given regular cleaning; beating from the back is preferable to a Hoover, although a Hoover used on most pieces in the direction of the pile (*never* against it) is usually perfectly satisfactory. A carpet purchased from a dealer will be reasonably clean. To keep its appearance, a domestic detergent can be used by frothing it in warm water and rubbing the froth gently into the pile with a sponge or soft brush, then sponging again with a clean damp cloth (the surface of the carpet should be never more than slightly damp). However, such things as aerosol carpet foams should be avoided since many contain chemicals and artificial brighteners. Carpets which are very dirty or badly stained, or which show any signs of structural damage, should be treated professionally; most dealers offer a repair and cleaning service. Before buying a carpet with obvious damage or staining, consult an expert first to see what, if anything, can be done. Many carpets with apparently serious structural damage can be repaired, while others cannot. Also carpets may have unsightly and irremovable stains – dog urine is a particular example.

GLOSSARY

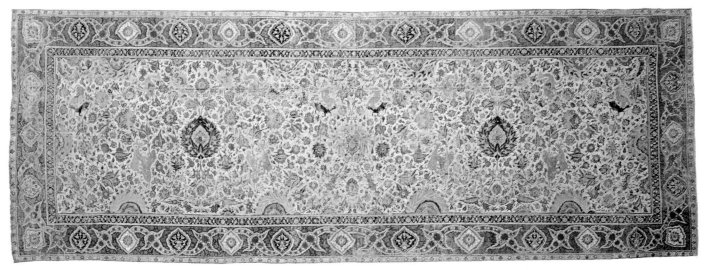

Moghul hunting carpet with white ground. First half of 17th century. Probably Jaipur.
25 ft. × 9 ft. 7 in. (760 × 292 cm.). Islamische Museum, Berlin.

Glossary

Abrash Variations of density in a colour seen in a carpet by irregular horizontal washes; caused by the wool being dyed at different times in different batches of a colour, which is of unequal density. Although an accidental and therefore arbitrary process, *abrash* can greatly enhance the beauty of a carpet.

Ainti Akbari Third part of the *Akbar Nameh*, the *Institutes of Akbar*, which contains a survey of the Moghul Empire.

Akbar Nameh Chronicle of the reign of the Emperor Akbar written by his historian Abu'l-Fazl.

Alum Double sulphate of aluminium and potassium used as a mordant.

Aniline Chemical dye, a derivative of coal-tar. First produced in the 1860s and ubiquitous in the Middle East from the 1880s. Most frequently encountered in the red-blue-purple range, the substance being named after *anil*, the indigo plant. Colours are very fugitive; a bright orange-pink, for instance, will fade at the tip to walnut-brown.

Boteh Widespread pattern of Persian origin (Persian *boteh* = cluster of leaves). Resembles a pear or pine cone, by which names it has been known in the West. Symbolic connections have also been suggested, somewhat fancifully, between it and the Flame of Zoroastra, the imprint of a fist on wet plaster, the loop in the river Jumna, etc. Best known in Europe as the principal motif of the Paisley pattern.

Boteh *motif*

Caliph Head of the Muslim community, with at one time both religious and political supremacy (Arabic, *Khalifat rasul Allah*).

Ch'ang Chinese endless knot. As the inextricable knot of destiny, the seventh of the Eight Buddhist Symbols.

Chinese endless knot

Chinese fret Pattern of interlocking swastikas. Sometimes called the *wan* pattern, *wan* being the Chinese character representing 10,000 (i.e. a swastika).

Chinese fret

Chrome dye A fast synthetic dye mordanted with potassium bichromate. This, and other more recent synthetic colours, are now used in all the major rug weaving areas of the world. Although fast, the colours are harsh and dead.

Cochineal Scarlet red similar to but more brilliant than lac. Obtained from the crushed bodies of an insect native to Mexico and the West Indies, and imported into Europe from the 16th century (but not into the Middle East until the end of the 18th century). Supposed until the 18th century to be the berry or seed of an oak.

Compound-weave Technical term for pieces made with more than one set of either warp or weft elements, or both. Form of flat-weaving.

Damascene After Damascus. Process of decorating steel by etching, inlaying gold or silver, or encrusting, so as to produce a watered effect. In old carpet literature, following European inventories of the 16th and 17th centuries, used to describe either Mamluk carpets or certain designs found on Anatolian pieces. Used either to describe the effect of the design or, as some scholars supposed, because it was believed that the carpets had originated in Damascus.

Diwan An accounts book or a collection of poems by one author. Also meant a sofa, and thus came to denote a room furnished with such pieces; thus came to mean a council chamber and eventually the council meeting itself.

Djidjim (various spellings) Refers to either a wall hanging/entrance hanging, or to a weaving technique in which flat-woven strips are joined together to form the completed piece. See the section on flat-weaving.

Ends The outer edges of the rug on the short axis often woven in the kelim technique (pile-woven ends or skirts are frequently found on Turkoman pieces); the fringes found on carpets are the free ends of the warp threads.

Escutcheon Shield-shaped medallion often found on Persian carpets as appendages on either side of a large central medallion on the long axis.

Gol Henai Pattern Floral pattern associated with Persian rugs and said to be based on the Henna shrub (*Lawsonia*); as Edwards has pointed out, more representative of the Garden Balsam, a plant of the genus *Impatiens*. Found frequently on carpets from Hamadan and environs; also found, in schematic form, on Kashgai weavings.

Hejira (or Hijra) The beginning of the Muhammedan calendar, 16 July, A.D. 622, the date of the Prophet Muhammed's flight from Mecca to Medina. Rugs dated with a year of the Hejira can be converted to the Christian equivalent. For an exact date, divide the Hejira year by 33.7, subtract the result from the original date and then add 622. For an approximate one, simply add 583 to the Hejira date.

   A number of late nineteenth- and early twentieth-century dated carpets show signs of their dates having been altered so as to make them appear earlier. It was, for instance, an easy process to change 1300 A.H. to 1200 A.H. by altering a few knots. In nineteenth- and twentieth-century dates, the character denoting 1,000 is often omitted, so that the date appears as its last three figures. However, in some instances, the 1,000 symbol is included if the last number of the date is a nought, represented by a dot, which is itself omitted. Thus 121 could equal 1121 (A.D. 1710) or 1210 (A.D. 1796). Late dated carpets, usually Caucasian, often have the Muhammedan and Christian dates woven side by side. Dated Armenian carpets usually have the Christian calendar, and the chronogram of the Gothar carpet is a unique instance. Few carpets dated after 1914 are known.

Herati Pattern Also called the *mahi* or fish pattern. As its name implies this floral pattern is supposed to have originated in east Persia. Consists of a repeat of a flower head bracketed by two serrate-edged lanceolate leaves. Probably the most frequently used of all Oriental floral designs.

Herati motif

Indigo Blue dye obtained from the leaves of the indigo plant, one of the various species of *Indigofera*, a tropical genus of *Papilionaceae*. Native to India, from whence most of the leaves used in the preparation of the dye in Persia were exported. The dye was prepared from a fermented compound of crushed indigo leaves, red clay slip, potash, grape sugar and slaked lime.

Jufti 'False' knot, either Turkish or Persian, whereby the knots are tied to four, not two, warp threads, thus coarsening the weave and halving the time involved in production. Became prevalent in Persian in the late 19th century, although for a time it was officially banned.

Kelim Also spelled kilim, khilim, kileem, gilim, ghilim, gelim, dilim, etc. Form of flat-weaving associated principally with Anatolia. See the section on flat-weaving.

Kermes	Crushed female body of an insect which gives a red similar to cochineal and lac. The insect breeds on the Kermes oak (*Quercus coccifera*). Its use in carpets has never been satisfactorily established.
Koran (Qur'an)	The sacred book of Islam. The Divine Revelations spoken by Allah to His Prophet Muhammed. After the Prophet's death in A.D. 632, the Revelations were passed on orally by *Huffaz*, those who had learned them by heart. In A.D. 633, however, following the death of a number of *Huffaz* in religious wars, it was decided to commit the Revelations to writing. The Koran was therefore compiled by the Prophet's secretary Zayd ibn Thabit and codified by the third Caliph, Uthman, in A.D. 651. This version was then produced in four identical copies which were sent to Mecca, Medina, Basra and Kufa respectively, and which formed the basis of all future manuscripts. The Koran is the literal word of God, and therefore no variations (excepting a few minor ones recognized by Ibn Mujahid and codified in A.D. 933) have ever been admitted; even vowels and accents, representing as they do the speech rhythms of God, must remain uniform.
Kufic	Form of Arabic script; its visual format is used as a decorative motif in the borders of Oriental carpets, especially those from Anatolia. Named after an erroneous ascription to Kufa(h) in Mesopotamia. The principal script of the Koran. Other Arabic or Persian scripts include *al-ma'il*, *nashki* and its variant *nastaliq*, *ta'liq*, *rihani*, *thuluth* and *shikasta*.

Typical Kufic border

Lac (or Laq)	Meaning literally 'hundreds of thousands'. Name given to a brilliant deep purple-red obtained from melting and straining the resinous excretions of the *Tachardia lacca*, a scale insect native to India which covers the twigs of certain trees in a resinous substance for the purpose of immuring the female of the species. The red dye, like that of cochineal and kermes, is the extract of the female bodies of the insect, which in this case are gathered with the resin.
Lampas	A method of weaving so that the pattern is raised in relief against the ground. A form of embroidery.
Madder	Deep red-brown dye extracted from the root of the *Rubia tinctorum* or other *Rubia* plants.
Mina Khani pattern	Floral pattern said to have been named after Mina Khan, although this is certainly apocryphal. Repeat pattern of large palmettes and small white flowers contained in a lattice of stems. Stylized geometrical versions found in certain tribal carpets, such as those of the Baluchi.

Mina khani *motif*

Mordant	Chemical substance with which the wool is treated in order to fix the dye colour. Can itself affect the eventual colour and can be corrosive.
Palas	Caucasian name for kelim.
Palmette	A flower head of heart-shape with many radiating lobes or petals.

Typical palmette

Pomegranate Rind	Gives a dull yellow dye.
Quatrefoil	Medallion with four rounded lobe sections.

Sarköy (or Sharkyoy)	Name for kelims made in Thrace.
Saph	Prayer rug with multiple mihrabs.
Selvedge	The outer warps of the rug on the long sides, which are overcast to form firm braided edges. On many tribal pieces, further strengthened with goat's hair.
Shah Abbas design	Floral design of large palmettes such as those found on the two- and three-plane lattice vase carpets.
Shah Nameh	*The Book of Kings*, an epic of pre-Islamic Persia written by Firdausi of Tus (d. 1020). Many elaborately illustrated (illuminated) copies survive from the 14th, 15th and 16th centuries.
Sileh	(Silé, Sillé, Zilé) Thought to be a corruption of a now unknown Caucasian place name. A form of Soumak, *sileh* usually refers to pieces woven with rows of large S-motifs thought to represent the dragon motif degenerated to virtual abstraction. See section on flat-weaving.
Soumak	(Sumak, Summak, Sumacq, Sumakh). Thought to be a corruption of Shemaka, town in south-east Caucasus. Technique of progressive weft wrapping. See section on flat-weaving.
Spandrels	Architectural term for the space between the curve of an arch and the enclosing mouldings. Thus the space immediately above the arch of the mihrab in a prayer rug.
Swastika	A hooked cross. Chinese symbol for 10,000 (*wan*) and happiness. In many cultures, a symbol of the sun. An extraordinarily ubiquitous symbol, found contemporaneously as far apart as Pre-Columbian America and China, which appears in the work of almost all known cultures.

 *Typical swastika designs*

Tiraz	Official weaving factory usually set up under Royal patronage.
Tchintamani	Chinese Buddhist symbol thought by some scholars to be the origin of the balls-and-stripe motif found on Ushak carpets and other Turkish weavings and textiles.
Verneh	(Verné). Thought to be a corruption of a now unknown Caucasian place name. Technically, these pieces are either Soumak or brocaded rugs (or sometimes a mixture of both), while stylistically the name usually applies to pieces woven with a design of squares, containing either geometric motifs, or a mixture of geometric and animal motifs, especially long-tailed birds.
Vine leaves	Give a yellow dye (as do autumnal apple leaves).
Waqf	The gift from a private individual to a religious institution such as a mosque.
Warp	Longitudinal threads forming part of the foundation of a carpet.
Weft	Latitudinal threads forming part of the foundation of a carpet.
Weld	Extract of the *Reselda lutuola* plant, gives a yellow dye.
Whey	Watery part of milk used in combination with madder to give a particular rose red found on certain Sultanabad carpets.
Yin-Yang	Chinese symbol of the female-male elements. Two interlocked foetal motifs in a circle.

 Yin-Yang *symbol*

Bibliography

Techniques and Materials

Emery, Irene: *The Primary Structure of Fabrics*, Textile Museum, Washington, 1965

Oriental and African Rugs and Carpets

Abbot Hall Art Gallery: *The Turkoman of Iran* (exhibition catalogue), Kendal, 1971

Allgrove, Joan, and others: *The Qashqa'i of Iran* (exhibition catalogue), Manchester, 1976

American Art Association: *The V. & L. Benguiat Private Collection of Rare Old Rugs* (sale catalogue), New York, 4–5 December 1925

Archer, Mildred: 'Gardens of Delight', in *Apollo*, September 1968

Arts Council of Great Britain exhibition at the Hayward Gallery, London: *The Arts of Islam* (exhibition catalogue), London, 1976

Azadi, Siawosch: *Turkoman Carpets*, Fishguard, 1975

Bausback, Peter: *Antike Meisterstücke Orientalischer Knupfkunst*, Mannheim, 1975 and 1976

Beattie, May: 'Background to the Turkish Rug', in *Oriental Art*, Vol. IX, no. 3, 1963

Beattie, May: 'Couple-Columned Prayer Rugs', in *Oriental Art*, Vol. XIV, no. 4, 1968

Beattie, May: *The Thyssen-Bornemisza Collection of Oriental Rugs*, Castagnola, 1972

Beattie, May: *Carpets of Central Persia* (exhibition catalogue), Sheffield, 1976

Bennett, Ian: *The Book of Oriental Carpets and Rugs*, London, 1971

Berenson, Bernard: *Lorenzo Lotto*, London, 1956

Benardout, Raymond: *Catalogue of Turkoman Weavings* (exhibition catalogue), London, 1974

Benardout, Raymond: *Turkish Rugs* (exhibition catalogue), London, 1975

Benardout, Raymond: *Tribal and Nomadic Rugs* (exhibition catalogue), London, 1976

Benardout, Raymond: 'Fashion in Rugs', in *Antique Finder*, Vol. 15, no. 11, November 1976

Bidder, Hans: *Carpets of East Turkestan*, London, 1964

Black, David: *In Praise of Allah, Prayer Kilims from the Near East* (exhibition catalogue), London, 1975

Black, David (with essays by Jon Thompson and others): *Rugs of the Wandering Baluchi* (exhibition catalogue), London, 1976

Black, David and Loveless, Clive (with essays by Yanni Petsopoulos, Jon Thompson and others): *The Undiscovered Kilim*, London, 1977

Blunt, Wilfred: *Isfahan, Pearl of Persia*, London, 1966

Bode, W. von and Kühnel, Ernst: *Antique Rugs from the Near East* (trans. Charles Grant Ellis), London, 1970

Bogolyubov, A. A.: *Carpets of Central Asia* (ed. Jon Thompson), Ramsdell, 1973

Breck, Joseph and Morris, Frances: *The James F. Ballard Collection of Oriental Rugs*, New York, 1923

Cammann, S. V. R.: 'Symbolic Meaning in Oriental Rug Patterns', in the *Textile Museum Journal*, Vol. III, Washington, 1972

Campana, M.: *Oriental Carpets*, London, 1969

Christie, Manson and Wood: *Fine Eastern Rugs and Carpets* (sale catalogue), London, 13 January 1975

Christie, Manson and Wood: *Fine Eastern Carpets and Rugs (including the property of the late Joseph V. McMullan)* (sale catalogue), London, 12 June 1975

Christie, Manson and Wood: *Important Eastern Rugs and Carpets* (sale catalogue), London, 14 April 1976

Christie, Manson and Wood: *Important Eastern Rugs and Carpets* (sale catalogue), London, 5 November 1976

Con, J. M.: *Carpets from the Orient*, New York, 1966

Denwood, P.: *The Tibetan Carpet*, London, 1974

Dickie, James: 'The Iconography of the Prayer Rug', in *Oriental Art*, Vol. XVIII, no. 4, 1973

Dilley, A. H.: *Oriental Rugs and Carpets* (revised by M. S. Dimand), New York, 1959

Dimand, M. S.: *The Ballard Collection of Oriental Rugs*, New York, 1935

Dimand, M. S.: *Peasant and Nomad Rugs of Asia*, New York, 1961

Dimand, M. S. (with an essay by Jean Mailey): *Rugs in the Metropolitan Museum, New York*, New York 1973

Dimand, M. S.: 'Persian Silk Carpets', in *The Connoisseur*, July, 1975

Edwards, A. C.: *The Persian Carpet* (revised edition), London, 1975

Eiland, Emmett and Murray: *Oriental Rugs from Western Collections* (exhibition catalogue), University of California Art Museum, 1973

Eiland, M. L.: *Oriental Rugs* (2nd edition), New York, 1976

Ellis, Charles Grant: 'Mysteries of the Misplaced Mamluks', in the *Textile Museum Journal*, Vol. II, Washington, 1967

Ellis, Charles Grant: 'The Ottoman Prayer Rug', in the *Textile Museum Journal*, Vol. II, Washington, 1969

Ellis, Charles Grant: 'The Portuguese Carpets of Gujurat', in *Islamic Art in the Metropolitan Museum* (ed. R. Ettinghausen), New York, 1972

Ellis, Charles Grant: *Early Caucasian Rugs*, Textile Museum, Washington, 1976

Enderlein, Volkmar: 'Zwei Ägyptische Gebetsteppiche im Islamischen Museum', in *Forschungen und Berichte, Staatliche Museen zu Berlin*, Band 13, 1971

Erdmann, Kurt: *Seven Hundred Years of Oriental Carpets* (trans. May Beattie and Hildegard Herzog), London, 1970

Erdmann, Kurt: *Oriental Carpets, an Account of their History* (trans. Charles Grant Ellis), Fishguard, 1976

Ettinghausen, Richard: 'New Light on Early Mamluk Carpets', in *Aus der Welt der Islamischen Kunst*; Festschrift für Ernst Kühnel, Berlin, 1962

Franses, Jack: *European and Oriental Rugs*, London, 1970

Franses, Jack: *Tribal Rugs from Afghanistan and Turkestan* (exhibition catalogue), London, 1973

Fremantle, Richard: *Florentine Gothic Painters*, London, 1975

Gardiner, Roger F. and Allen, Max: *Oriental Rugs from Canadian Collections* (exhibition catalogue), Toronto, 1975

Gascoigne, B.: *The Great Moghuls*, London, 1971

Ghirshman, R.: *Iran, from the Earliest Times to the Islamic Conquest*, Harmondsworth, 1954

Grote-Hasenbalg, W.: *Masterpieces of Oriental Rugs*, London, 1925

Grübe, E.: 'The Ottoman Empire' in the *Metropolitan Museum Bulletin*, January, 1968

Gulbenkian, Calouste: *Oriental Art, Collection of the Calouste Gulbenkian Foundation*, Lisbon, 1963

Hambly, Gavin: *Cities of Moghul India*, New York, 1968

Haskins, J. F.: *Imperial Carpets from Peking*, Pittsburg, 1975

Iten-Maritz, J.: *Turkish Carpets*, Freibourg, 1976

Jacobsen, Charles W.: *Oriental Rugs, a Complete Guide* (11th printing), New York, 1971

Jacoby, H.: *How to Know Oriental Carpets and Rugs*, London, 1967

Jones, H. McCoy and Boucher, J. W.: *Weavings of the Tribes in Afghanistan* (exhibition catalogue of the Hajji Baba Society), Washington, 1973

Jones, H. McCoy and Boucher, J. W.: *Baluchi Rugs* (exhibition catalogue of the Hajji Baba Society), Washington, 1974

Jones, H. McCoy and Boucher, J. W.: *The Ersari and their Weavings* (exhibition catalogue of the Hajji Baba Society), Washington, 1975

Kendrick, A. F. and Tattersall, C. E. C.: *Hand-woven Carpets* (reprint of the 1922 edition), New York, 1973

King, Donald: 'Industries, Merchants and Money', in *The Flowering of the Middle Ages* (ed. Joan Evans), London, 1966

King, Donald: 'Islamic Week Sale of Carpets', in *Art at Auction, the Year at Sotheby Parke Bernet 1975–6*, London, 1976

King, Donald: 'The "Doria" Polonaise Carpet', in *Persian and Moghul Art*, P. & D. Colnaghi & Co. Ltd. (exhibition catalogue), London, 1976

Kühnel, Ernst and Bellinger, L.: *The Textile Museum Catalogue Raisonné: Cairene Rugs and others technically related, 15th–17th centuries*, Washington, 1957

Kühnel, Ernst: *Islamic Art*, London, 1970

Landreau, A. N. and Pickering, W. R.: *From the Bosphorus to Samarkand. Flatwoven Rugs*, Textile Museum, Washington, 1969

Lauts, Jan: *Carpaccio*, London, 1962

Lefèvre and Partners: *Rare Oriental Carpets* (sale catalogue), London, 26 November 1976

Lefèvre and Partners: *Central Asian Carpets* (with an essay by Jon Thompson), London, 1976

Lefèvre and Partners: *Rare Oriental Carpets* (sale catalogue), London, 11 February 1977

Lefèvre and Partners: *Rural and Nomadic Carpets* (sale catalogue), London, 25 March 1977

Lefèvre and Partners: *Turkish Carpets from the 16th to the 19th Century* (with an essay by Jon Thompson), London, 1977

Lefèvre and Partners: *Central Asian Carpets (Supplement One)*, London, 1977

Lewis, G. (trans.): *The Book of Dede Korkut*, Harmondsworth, 1974

(Liberty's): *Liberty's 1875–1975* (exhibition catalogue), Victoria and Albert Museum, London, 1975

Lings, Martin and Safadi, Yasin Hamid: *The Qur'an* (exhibition catalogue), Los Angeles County Museum, 1959

Mackie, Louise W.: *The Splendor of Turkish Weaving* (exhibition catalogue), Textile Museum, Washington, 1973

Mackie, Louise W.: *The Mayer Collection of Rugs* (exhibition catalogue with essays by R. Ettinghausen and M. S. Dimand), Textile Museum, Washington, 1974

Mackie, Louis W.: *Prayer Rugs* (exhibition catalogue with essays by R. Ettinghausen and M. S. Dimand), Textile Museum, Washington, 1974

Martin, F. R.: *A History of Oriental Carpets before 1800*, Vienna, 1908

McMullan, Joseph V.: *Islamic Carpets*, New York, 1965

McMullan Joseph V.: *Islamic Carpets from the Collection of Joseph V. McMullan* (exhibition catalogue), The Arts Council of Great Britain, London, 1972

McMullan, Joseph V. and Baird, Virgil H.: 'Islamic Rugs', in *The Connoisseur*, March–April, 1973

McMullan, Joseph V. and Reichert, Donald O.: *The George Walter Vincent and Belle Townsley Smith Collection of Islamic Rugs*. Springfield, N.D.

Mills, John: *Carpets in Pictures*, National Gallery, London, 1975

Moss, H. M. Ltd.: *The World of Rugs*, London, 1973

Mumford, J. K.: *Oriental Rugs*, New York, 1900

O'Bannon, George W.: *The Turkoman Carpet*, London, 1975

Pope, A. U.: *Introduction to Persian Art*, London, 1930

Pope, A. U. and Ackermann, P. (eds.): *A Survey of Persian Art*, 6 vols., Oxford, 1938–9

Poinssot, L. and Revault, J.: *Tapis tunisiens*, 4 portfolios, Paris, 1950–7

Reed, C. D.: *Turkoman Rugs*, Cambridge, Mass., 1966

Revault, Jacques: *Designs and Patterns from North African Carpets and Textiles*, New York, 1973

Ricard, P.: *Corpus des tapis marocains*, Paris, 1923

Rice, David Talbot and Gray, Basil: *The Illustrations to the 'World History' of Rashid al-Din*, Edinburgh, 1976

Robinson, B. V. and Gray, Basil: *The Persian Art of the Book*, Oxford, 1972

(Royal Academy): *Catalogue of the International Exhibition of Persian Art*, London, 1931

Rudenko, Sergei: *Frozen Tombs of Siberia* (trans. Dr. M. W. Thompson), London, 1970

Sanghui, R., Ghirshman, R. and Minorsky, V.: *Persia, the Immortal Kingdom*, London, 1971

Sarre, F. and Trenkwald, H.: *Ancient Oriental Carpets*, (trans. A. F. Kendrick), Vienna, 1929

Schlosser, I: *The Book of Rugs, Oriental and European*, London, 1963

Schmutzler, Emil: *Altorientalische Teppiche in Siebenbürgen*, Leipzig, 1933

Schürmann, Ulrich: *Central Asian Rugs*, London, 1969

Schürmann, Ulrich: *Caucasian Rugs*, London, 1974

Smith, V. S.: *A History of Fine Art in India and Ceylon*, Oxford, 1930

Sotheby & Co.: *A Collection of Highly Important Oriental Carpets, sold by order of the Kevorkian Foundation* (sale catalogues); Part I, London, 5 December 1969; Part II, London, 11 December 1970

Sotheby Parke Bernet: *Islamic Carpets and Rugs from the 16th to the 19th Centuries*, (sale catalogue), London, 14 April 1976

Sotheby Parke Bernet: *Fine Islamic Rugs from the 16th Century* (sale catalogue), London, 18–19 November 1976

Sotheby Parke Bernet: *Fine Oriental Rugs and Carpets, etc.* (sale catalogue), London, 10 December 1976

Sotheby Parke Bernet: *Fine Caucasian, Turkoman, Baluchistan and Afghan Rugs, Carpets, Textiles, etc.* (sale catalogue), London, 11 February 1977

Sotheby Parke Bernet: *Fine Oriental Carpets and Rugs* (sale catalogue), London, 6 May 1977

Spink and Son Ltd.: *The George de Menasce Collection, Part 1* (exhibition catalogue), London, 1971

Stead, Rexford: *The Ardabil Carpets*, Los Angeles, 1974

Tanavoli, P.: *Lion Rugs from Fars* (exhibition catalogue), Washington, 1975

Thatcher, A.: *Travels in Central Asia*, London, 1864

Tiffany Studios: *Antique Chinese Rugs*, New York, 1969

Trilling, James: 'Mongol Hordes and Persian Miniatures', in *The Times Literary Supplement*, 15 April 1977

Welch, A.: *Shah Abbas and the Arts of Isfahan*, New York, 1973

Welch, S. C.: *The Art of Mughal India*, New York, 1963

Wilkinson, J. V. S.: *Mughal Painting*, London, 1948

Zick, Joanna: 'Eine Gruppe von Gebetsteppichen und ihre Datierung', in *Berliner Museen, Berichte aus den ehem. Preuss. Kunstsammlung*, N.F. Jg 11, S. 6–14, 1961

European Rugs and Carpets

Jacobs, Bertram: *Axminster Carpets*, Leigh-on-Sea, 1969

Jarry, M.: *Carpets of Aubusson*, Leigh-on-Sea, 1969

Jarry, M.: *The Carpets of the Manufacture de la Savonnerie*, Leigh-on-Sea

Mankowski, T.: 'Influences of Islamic Art in Poland', in *Ars Islamica*, Vol. II, 1935

Tattersall, C. E. C. and Reed, S.: *British Carpets*, London, 1966

Tzigara-Samurcas: *L'Art du Peuple Roumain*, Paris, 1925

Watson, J. F. B.: *The Wrightsman Collection*, Vol. II, Metropolitan Museum of Art, New York

American Rugs and Carpets

Amsden, Charles: *Navajo Weaving*, Santa Ana, 1934

Faraday, Cornelia Bateman, *European and American Carpets and Rugs*, Grand Rapids, 1929

Matthews, Washington: *Navajo Legends*, Philadelphia, 1897

Underhill, Ruth: *The Navajos*, Norman, 1958

Warner, John Anson: *The Life and Art of the North American Indian*, London, 1975

Waters, Frank: *Masked Gods: Navaho and Pueblo Ceremonialism*, Chicago, 1950

Index

Page numbers in italics refer to illustrations.

A

Abbas I, Shah 11, 44, 47, 49, 63, 66, 80, 82, *82*, 84, 86, *86*, 132, 140, 241, 362
Abbas II, Shah 44, *64*, 65
Abruzzi rugs 273, *274*
Adam, Robert 294, *294*, 296, *296*, 297
Ada-Melas prayer rugs 211
Adler Kazaks *see* Eagle Kazaks
Adraskand Valley 173, *177*
Afshars 65, 221, 243
Afshar rugs 225, 234, 241, *241*, 249
Afghanistan 33, 34, 160, 163, 168, 170–2, *170*, 174, 177
Ainabad 249
Akbar the Great 34, 122, *123*, 124, 125, *127*
Akbar II *133*
Akbar Nameh 35, 64, 108, *123*, 124, 127
Akstafa *155*, 254, 255, 256
Alaeddin Mosque 40, 41, 216
Albee, Helen 334
Alcaraz 6, 262, *264*, 265, *266*, 267
Algeria 218, 220
Alhambra 262, 265
Ali-Riza Khan 61
Allah, Nimat *see* Nimat Allah
Almeria 262
Alpujarra 267–8
Altai Mountains 7, 38, *39*
Altman, Benjamin, Bequest 55, *55*, *56*, 81
Amber garden carpets 75, 125, 129, 131, *132*
Amersfoort 262
Amin, Muhammed *see* Muhammed Amin
Anatolia 22, 33, *91*, 95, 100, 115, 140, 145, 165, 174, 197–201, 205, 208, 215, *230*, 241, 251, *251*, 265, 274, 341
Angelico, Fra 92, 93
Anhalt carpet 49, 53, 66, 336
Animal carpets *see* Motifs
Arabatchi 37, 160, 166, 168–9, *169*
Arak 221, 224, 225, 229, 231, 233–4, 239, 249, 250
Ardabil carpets 45–8, *46*, 49, 53, 65, 66, *68*, 69, 108, *214*, 223, 249
Ardabil Mosque, Shrine of Sheikh Safi 45, 47, 64, 66, *85*, 131
Armenia 138, 140, 141, 146, *150*
Armorial carpets 265, 267, *267*
Arras 261
Arshan-Chila 155
Arthur, Mary 328
Asymmetrical knot *see* Knots, Persian
Aubusson *261*, 267, 283, 284, 285, *285*, *285*, 286, *286*, *287*, 288, *289*, 292
Aufseeser, Hans 315, 317
Aurangzeb 34, 137, *137*, 245
Axminster 290, 296–7, 299, 302, 304
Aynard rug *135*, 137
Azerbaijan 33, 38, 40, 43, 65, 69, 138, 141, 144, 145, 147, 241, 250

B

Babur, Emperor 34, 122, *122*
Baghdad *26*, 28, 29, 33, 37, 41, *42*, 265
Baker carpet 70, 71, 89
Bakhtiari 41, 234–7, *237*, *239*, 243, 249
Bakshaish 224, 249
Baku 147, 155, *155*, 205

Ballard Collection 102, 104, 133, 197, 203, 208
Baltimore vase carpet 57, 61, 62, 65
Baluchi *15*, 20, 21, 40, 172–9, *174*, *177*, *178*, 186, 190, 221, 243, 249, 256, 257, 337, 342
Baluchistan 27, 173
Bartolo, Domenico di 90, *90*, 92
Bassano, Jacopo 95
Bauhaus 311–12, *312*
Bedouin 220
Begay, Alice *327*, 328
Begay, Hilda 324
Begay, Louise 328
Begay, Maggie 328
Begay, Mary 328
Begay, Sarah 331
Belgium 262
Bell, Vanessa 317
Bellanger (manufacturer) 288
Bergama 100, 102, 197, 204–5, *205*, 207, *207*, 208, *208*, 209, 211, *212*, 251, 261, *338*
Berlin crane carpet 49, *51*
Berlin dragon and phoenix carpet 7, 90, *91*, 92, 100, 140
Beshir 160, 166, 167, *167*, 168, 170, 172, *174*, *177*, 243
Bessarabia *270*, *271*, *272*, 273, *274*
Beyshehir 40, 209
Bia, Betty *331*
Bia, Helen 329
Bibikabad 249
Bidjov 153, *155*, *255*
Bigman, Lucy *325*
Bijar 15, 224, 226, *226*, *229*, 232, 233, 249
Birjand 249
Bliss kelim 84
Bokhara 34, 37, 41, 160, 163, 166, 168, 181, 257
Bordjalou 147, *147*, 149
Bordone, Paris 105
Börner, Hélène 311
Boston hunting carpet 53, 70, 125, 126–7
Boteh-Chila 155, *155*
Bowes, Benjamin 294
Bozchelu (Borchelu) 224, 249
Brahni 173, *174*
Branicki carpet 53, *55*, 66, 81
Bright, J., & Co. 300
Brintons 298, 300, 305
Brocade *see* Weaving techniques
Brown, Ana *327*
Brown, Nora 329
Bruges 261
Brummer, Eva 308
Brusa *see* Bursa
Brussels 262, 268, 293, 294, 299, 300, 304
Bryant, Julia 331
Buccleuch, Duke of, Collection 62, 105, 128
Buck, Lottie 328
Bulgaria 199
Buonaccorso, Niccolo di 92, 83
Burlap *see* Materials
Burnt Water 329, *329*
Bursa 11, 15, 17, 20, 88, *88*, 90, 103, 112, 115, 116, 117, *118*, 201, 208, 215

C

Cairene court carpets 22, 112, *117*, 197, 208, 211, 216

Cairo 17, 33, 103, 112, 115, 116, 117, 121, 208, 261
Caledon 300
Camel hair *see* Materials
Çanakkale 205, *205*
Candido, Pietro 111
Capella, Martianus 261
Carnevale, Fra 95, *95*
Carpaccio, Vittore 95, *96*, 100
Cartoons 11, 12, 49, 57, 75, 141
Cartouche *see* Motifs
Caucasian rugs 11, 15, 17, 20, 41, 61, 69, 76, 80, 88, 138–57, *138*, *142*, 168, 181, 208, *208*, 209, *212*, 220, 251–2, *254*, 255, *256*, 257, 336
Caucasus 64, 65, 85, 205, 233
Chahar bag 72, *72*, *74*, 75
Chajli 153, *153*, 155, 157
Channik 150, 151
Charshangho 170, *170*
Chaudor 37, 160, 166, *167*, 172
Chelaberd 146, 150, *150*, 153, 155
Chelsea carpet *51*, 53, 66
Cheticamp 334
Chevillon *282*, 284
Chichi 155, *155*, *156*, 157
Chief blankets 323
Ch'ien Lung, Emperor 185, 190, 192, 193
Chihil Sultan Kiosk 132, 184, 188
Chila 155, *156*, 257
China 15, 27, 34, 40, 41, 42, 43, 180, 189–95, *193*
Ch'ing Dynasty 34, 189, 190
Chinle *327*, 328
Chob-Bash 170, 172
Chondoresk 150, *150*, 151
Chosroes, Spring Carpet of 39, 75
Christus, Pietrus 95
Cloud-band Kazaks 151
Coal Mine Mesa 329, *330*
Clouet, François 111
Cohoe, Donna Marie 326
Compartment rugs *see* Motifs
Constantinople *see* Istanbul
Corcoran throne rug 59, 64, 70
Cordoba 28, 218, 261, 262
Corfu 201, *215*
Coronation rug 50
Cotton *see* Materials
Court carpets 112, 115–18, *116*, *118*
Courtrai 261
Crane, Walter 305
Crivelli, Carlo 95, *96*
Crossleys 300, 305, 319
Crystal 326–8, *327*
Cubism 313
Cuenca 262, *262*, 265
Curley, Ramon 326
Curley, Sarah 328
Curtis, Sadie 328
Czartoryski carpet 80

D

Daghestan *138*, 141, 147, 153, 155, 157, *157*, 176, 252, *254*, 255
Damascene rugs 104, 112
Damascus 28, 37, 41, 112, 141, 341
Dara-Chichi 155, 157
Da Silva Bruhns 314, 317
David, Gerard 100
Davis, Mrs. Pindar 319
Del Piombo, Sebastiano *see* Piombo
Derbend 147, 157, 252

Derghezin 224, 225, 249
Deventer *see* Royal Deventer
Doisteau kelim 84
Dokhtar-e-Ghazi 173, 174, 176
Donegal 300
Doria, Prince 83, *84*, 336
Dorn, Marion 313, *313*, 314, 317, *317*, 319
Dorukhsh (Dorosh) 249
Dragon and phoenix carpet, *see* Berlin dragon and phoenix carpet
Dragon rugs *see* Motifs
Dresser, Christopher 305
Dudley carpet 77, *78*
Duffy, Denis 294
Dulakhor 224
Dumons, Jean-Joseph 286
Dupont, Louis 281
Dupont, Pierre 279–81
Düsseldorf 262
Dyes 15, 17–18, *17*, *18*, 168, 170, 174, 177, 265, 323, 324, 326, 328, 329, 331, 334

E
Eagle Kazaks 151, 153, 165, 188
Edinburgh Weavers 315, *315*, 319
Egypt 11, 15, 27, 28, 29, 33, 37, 40, 112–21, 218
Egyptian carpets 17, *21*, *115*
Emperor's carpets 66–9
England 277–8, *277*, *278*, 290–3, *290*, *292*, 294–307, 313–19
Erivan 138, 147
Ersari 37, 160, *165*, 166–8, 169, 170, *170*, 172, 173, 174
Ersari-Beshir *see* Beshir
Eshrefoglu Mosque 40
Etsitty, Dee 324
Evans, Desbah 328
Exeter 293
Eyck, Jan van 95, *95*, 140, 197
Ezine 205, *208*

F
Fachralo 147, 149
Fars 40, 41, 65, 221, 241, 244, 245, 246–8, 250, *257*
Farsibaffs 249
Fasluyeh dynasty 41, 237
Fatamid Caliphate 28, 33, 218
Featherhead, Lelia *330*
Feke, Robert 204, 205, *207*
Feraghan 225, 229, *230*, *231*, 234, 241, 245, 246, *248*, 249
Figdor garden carpet 72, *72*, 85, *86*, 141
Finland 274–5, *276*, 308
Flat-weaves *see* Weaving techniques
Floral rugs *see* Motifs
Florence 43
Fontaine 284, 288
Fontenay, Belin de 284
Foppa, Vicenzo *98*
Fostat 33, 40, 90, 92, 158
France 152, 213–14, 279–89, 313
Francesca, Piero della 95
Franchetti, Giorgio, Baron 85, *86*
Francis, Anna 328
Fremlin carpet 128
Fringe *see* Weaving techniques
Frost, Edward Sands 334
Funstan, Anna 324

G
Gaddi, Taddeo 33
Gafsa 256

Gallen, Akseli 308
Gallup 328
Ganado *327*, 328
Garbo, Raffaelino del 96
Garden carpets *see* Motifs
Garus 61, 233
Gelder, Nicolaes van 203
Gendje 147, 152
Gene, Ella *330*
Genoa 43
George, Faye C. 328
Georgia 140, 147
Germantown 323, *323*, 324, 326
Germany 262, 311–12
Getty crane carpet 59, 66, 70
Ghengis Khan 29, *30*, 31, 37, 122, 181, 182, 241
Ghent 261
Ghiordes knot *see* Knots, Turkish
Ghiordes rugs 15, 20, 118, 197–201, *197*, *198*, *201*, 203, 209, 257
Ghirlandaio, Domenico 93, 95, *98*
Gilan 40
Gilmore, Mary 326
Girdlers' Carpet 128, *130*, 131
Goa 86, 88, 261
Goat's hair *see* Materials
Gobelins 283, *283*, 284, *284*, 288, 294
Gold thread *see* Materials
Goradiz 150, 151
Gorovan 221, 224, 249
Gothar 140, 341
Gould, Mary Joe 326
Gould, Mary Louise *325*, 326
Graf rug 141
Graham, Peter 297
Granada 218, 261, 262
Grant, Duncan 317
Grenfell Mission 334
Grierson, Ronald 313, 314, *314*, 317, *317*, 319
Grimani, Marino, Doge of Venice 82, *84*
Gujarat 86, 88
Guthries 298
Gyath u-din Jamai *44*, 45

H
Hadley, Linda 331
Hale, Blanche 329
Hamadan 17, 21, 40, 221, 223, 224–5, *226*, 249, 341
Hammersmith, 304, 305
Harun-al-Rashid, Caliph of Baghdad 33, 249
Harvey, Laura 328
Hatathli, Ned 329
Havermeyer carpet 61, *61*, 64
Havinden, Ashley *314*, 317, 319
Heal & Son 305, 314
Heckmondwike Manufacturing Co. 304
Herat 11, 42, 44, 49, 53, 60, 65, 66, *66*, *67*, *68*, 69, *69*, 70, *71*, 79, *81*, 89, 125, 128, 144, 173, 174, *248*, 250, *336*
Herat Baluchis 176
Hereke 15, 20, *88*, 89, 201, *212*, 214, 215, *215*, 216
Herez 17, 21, 221, 223, 224, *224*, 225, *226*, *232*, 233, *234*, 250, 337, *337*
Heulen, Michael 319
Hideyoshi kelim *see* Toyotomi Hideyoshi
Hogarth, Richard 293
Holbein *see* Motifs
Holland 261, 262, *275*
Hooked rugs *see* Weaving techniques
Horta, Victor 307
Hubbell, Don Lorenzo 328, *330*

Hughet, Jaime *92*, 93
Hulagu 29, 41
Humayan 34, 122
Hunting carpets *see* Motifs
Husayn Beg 140, *142*
Hutchinson, William 294

I
Iceland 274
Idhej 41, 237
Idjevan 147
Ifrikiya 218
Il-Khanid Dynasty 29, 41, 115
Imam Ali, Shrine of 84
Imam Riza Mosque 47, 249
India 11, 12, 13, 15, 17, 18, 21, 27, 33–4, 59, 64, 84, 88, 122–37, 180, 245
Ingeles 250
Ireland 293–4, 300
Isfahan 11, 41, 44, 48, 59, *61*, 62, 64, 65, 66, *68*, 69, *69*, 70, 76, 79, 80, 84, 132, 133, 184, 221, 234, *234*, 237, 249, 250, 270
Ismael I, Shah 44, 49, 50, 103, *223*, 241
Ismael II, Shah 44
Istanbul 11, 86, *88*, 103, 105, 115, 116, 117, *117*, *118*, 201, 208, *212*, 261, 274
Italy 199, 273, *274*

J
Jackson & Graham 297, 302
Jacquard 298, 300
Jacques, Maurice 284
Jaipur 8, *18*, 339
Jaipur carpet *74*, 75, *75*, 76
Jamai, Gyath u-din *see* Gyath
Japalak 224
Japan 84, 85, *86*, 261
Jehan, Shah 31, 34, 128, *129*, 131, *131*, 132, *132*
Jehangir, Emperor 125, *125*, *126*, 128, 132
Jerga 331
Jessa, William 293, 296
Jim, Clara 328
Joel, Betty *314*, 317, 319
John XXII, Pope 265, *265*
Johnson, Edith 324
Jones, Mary 328
Jones, Owen *299*, 302
Jones, Robert 297
Joshaqan 44, 48, 62, *63*, 64, 65, 76, 77, 125, 221, 234, 237, *239*, 250
Jozan 221, 250
Jufti knot *see* Knots
Jumbo, Julie 326
Jungnick, Hedwig 311
Jute *see* Materials

K
Kabul 33, 122
Kabutarhang 224, 250
Kabylie 220
Kainat 40, 249
Kairouan 218, 220, 256
Kansu 182, 184, 195
Karabagh 11, 138, 147, 150–2, *150*, *151*, 153, *153*, *156*, 157, 233, 252, 255
Karachi 172
Karadagh 152
Karagashli 155, 157
Karaja (Karadia) 224, 250

Karakalpak 160, 167, 173
Karakalpakstan 158
Karaklis 147
Karakoram 182, 189
Karatchoph 100, 147, *148*, 149
Kashan 17, 44, 45, *46*, 48, *48*, 53, *54*, 55–7, *55*, *56*, 62, 65, 66, *68*, 80, *80*, 84, 85, 86, *86*, 89, 137, 221, 223, 234, 237–9, *237*, *239*, *240*, 250, 251
Kashgai 21, 40, 177, 221, 225, 241–3, *243*, 245, 246, 250, *253*, 256, *257*, 341
Kashgar 180, 181, 182, 184, 185, 186, 188, 241
Kashmar 249
Kauffer, E. McKnight 313, *315*, 317, 319
Kayonnie, Irene *326*
Kazak 37, 138, 147, 152
Kazak rugs 20, 147–50, *147*, *148*, *150*, 208
Kazvin 48, 62, 250
Kelim 20, *20*, 21, 83, 84–6, 173, 177, 209, 220, 251, *251*, 256, *257*, *258*, 336, 337, 341
Kemareh 224
Kerman *13*, 15, 18, 20, 44, 48, *48*, 53, *58*, 60, 62, 64, 65, 66, 72, 75, 76, 77, *78*, 79, 125, 172, 221, 234, 239–41, *240*, *243*, 246, 249
Kevorkian Collection 76, 82, 108, 129, *130*, 131, *131*, 132, *132*, 137, 184, 197, *202*, 207, *211*, 212, 226, 245, 250, 336
Keyser, Thomas de 204
Kezzaz 224
Khamseh 224, 225, 244, 250
Khiva 160
Khorassan 15, 18, 37, 42, 53, 66, 173, 221, 249, 250
Khotan 144, 180, 181, 182, *183*, 184, 185, *185*, 186, *187*, 188, *191*, 193
Kidderminster carpets 289, 294, 298, 300, 304
Kildare 307
Kilkenny 293
Kirshehir 209, *210*, 214
Kis Ghiordes 201, *201*
Kizil-Ayak 160, 166, 168, 169, *169*, 170, 172, 174
Klagetoh 328
Klah, Hosteen 331
Klee, Paul 311
Knots 7, 11, 12, 13, 15, *15*, 18, *39*, 45, 53, 89, 137, 172, 199, 224
  asymmetrical *see* Persian
  Ghiordes *see* Turkish
  Jufti 15, *16*, 341
  Persian 11, 15, *16*, 20, 21, 38, 39, 40, 49, 53, 89, 115, 116, 117, 118, 120, 121, 137, 145, 170, 195, 246
  Senneh *see* Persian
  Spanish 15, *16*, 39, 40
  symmetrical *see* Turkish
  Turkish 11, 15, *16*, 20, 21, 38, 39, *39*, 40, 90, 140, 145, 164, 246, 265, 267, 274, 292, 308
Knox, Archibald 305, *306*, 307
Konagend 155, *156*, 157
Konya 33, 40, 90, 104, 209, *209*, 251
Koum Kapou 15, 20, 89, *212*, 214, 215, *215*, 216
Kuba weavings 76, 141, *141*, *143*, 144–7, *144*, *145*, 155–7, *156*, 233, 251, 252, *254*, 255
Kufic Border *see* Motifs
Kula 20, 88, 209, *210*
Kulayi 224
Kum 221, 223, 234, *237*, 250, 336
Kurdistan 33, 61, 64, 69, *75*, 76, 79, *138*, 144, 145, 225, *229*

Kurds 21, 145, 177, 226

L
Ladik 20, 118, 197, 201–4, *202*, *203*, 205, 209, 212, 251, *336*, *338*
La Hameyde de Saint-Ange *see* Saint-Ange
Lahore 128, *131*, 132, 172, 278
Lahore carpets *see* Amber garden carpets
La Mornaix, Sallandrouze de *see* Sallandrouze
Lapham, Henry 294
Lapham, Samuel 294
Lapworth, Alfred 297, 300
Lässne 274
Laver Kerman 250
Lebrun, Charles *280*, 284, 285
Lesghistan 147, 157, *157*
Le Lorrain, Louis-Joseph 288
Lenkoran 147, 153, 252
Leonard, Virginia Ray 331
Lesghi *see* Lesghistan
Liberty's 305, 307
Lilihan 225, 250
Lion carpets *see* Motifs
Lippincott, Bill Wagner 329
Long, John 294
Looms 11, 12–13
  Bunyan *see* Tabriz
  fixed 12, 13
  horizontal *10*, 12, *13*
  roller beam 12, 13
  Tabriz 12, 13
  vertical 12, *12*, *14*
Lorenzetti, Ambrogio 93, 95
Lori-Pambak 147, *147*, 149, *149*, 208
Lotto Carpets *see* Motifs
Lotto, Lorenzo 100–2, 121, 207
Lou-lan 39, 181
Lourdet, Philippe 283
Lourdet, Simon 280–1, 283
Louvre 279, 281
Lucca 43
Lukachukai *326*, *326*
Luristan 225, 250
Lwow 270, *271*, 272

M
Måas-Fjetterström, Märta 308, 310
McCreagh, William 283
McIlhenny Collection 100
Mackintosh, C. R. 305, 307, *307*
McLaren carpets 76,
McMullan Collection 49, 75, 102, 108, 121, 125, *125*, 133, *135*, *138*, *143*, 151, 170, *194*, 195, 203, 209, 211, 212, *228*, 245, 255
McSparron, L. H. 'Cozy' 328
Mahal 234, 250
Mahallet 225
Mahatschkala 157
Majanderan 40
Makri 209
Maksud 45, *46*, 47, 48, 65
Malayer 21, 221, 224, 245, 250
Maloney, Rose 328
Mamluk 22, 29, 33, 103, 112, *112*, 115, *115*, 116, *117*, 121, 205, 208, 209, 218, 341
Mansur *126*, 128
Mantegna, Andrea 93, 95
Mantes Cathedral carpet 50
Marasali *151*, 153, *153*

Marby rug 7, 90, 92
Marquand carpet 89
Materials 11, 15–17
  burlap 332, 334
  camel hair 174, 177, 192
  cotton 15, 17, 20, 21, 49, 86, 112, 117, 164, 184, 201, *201*, 323, 328
  goat's hair 121, 343
  gold thread 39, *83*, 84, *84*, 184, 185, 186
  hemp 105
  jewels 39
  jute 17
  metal thread 53, 69, *81*, *82*, 88, 188, 193, *193*, *194*, 212, 214, 216, *221*, 251
  silk 11, 15, 17, 20, 21, 45, 49, 53, 55–6, *55*, *56*, 64, 68, 81, *81*, *82*, 83, *83*, 84, *84*, 89, 112, 117, 153, 164, 170, *170*, 177, *183*, 186, *188*, 189, 193, *193*, *194*, 212, 214, 221, 224, 251
  silver thread 15, 39, 53, 68, 84, *84*, 86, 185, 186, 251
  wire 15
  wool 11, 15, 17, 18, 20, 21, 38, 45, 66, 68, 84, 85, 88, 89, 112, 117, 147, 170, 173, 174, *174*, 182, 184, 186, 189, 199, 224, 239, 323, 326
Medallion carpets *see* Motifs
Mehriban 224, 250
Mejedieh (Mejid) 212–14
Melas 209, 210–11, *210*, *211*
Memlinc, Hans 93, 96, *98*
Memmi, Lippo 93
Menasce Buddha carpet 193, *194*
Merv 160, 164, 174
Meshed 47, 65, 75, 161, 173, 174, *174*, 221, 239, 249, 250
Meshed Baluchis 176
Mesopotamia 27, 28, 33, 37
Metal thread *see* Materials
Metsu, Gabriel 69
Mielich, Hans 111
Mike, Dorothy 326
Mille-fleurs prayer rugs 244–6, *246*, *248*
Ming dynasty 34. 42, 189, *190*, 192
Mir Sayyid Ali 49, 61, 122
Moghan 138, 147, 152, *152*
Moghul carpets 7, 17, 21, 79, 122–37, *130*, *131*, *133*, *135*, *137*, 216
Moldavia 273, 274
Mongolia 27, 34, 37, 38, 39, 40, 180–2, 189, *194*, 220
Moon, Mary 324
Moore, J. B. 325, 326–7, 329
Moore, Ruth 328
Moore, Thomas 293, 296, *296*, 297
Moretto, Alessandro Bonvicino 112
Morgan, Daisy *331*
Morgan, Esther 328
Mornaix, Sallandrouze de la *see* Sallandrouze
Morocco 7, 27, 88, 218, *219*, 220, 251, 256
Morone, Domenico 93
Morris, William 59, 300, *301*, 302–5, *302*, *303*, *304*, *305*
Morton, Alastair 315
Morton, Alexander, & Co. (manufacturers) 300, 305, *306*
Morton, James 300, 315
Morton Sundour 314
Mosul 212
Motifs 12, 40, 84, 86, 104, 105, 107, 108, 112, 117, 149, 162–3, 169, 176, 189–92, 220, 324, 326, 328, 330
  animals 38, 41, 43, 48, *48*, 49, 50, 51, *51*, *52*, 53, 55–7, *55*, 59, *60*, 61, 62, *62*, 66, 67, 69, 75, 79, *79*, 80, *80*, 84–6, 89, 92, *92*, 125–8, *125*, 190, *215*, 223

arabesque 43, 47, 49, *52*, 57, 59, 60–1, *60*, 64, *66*, 69, 76, 100, *100*, 102, *103*, 104, 121, 128

balls and stripes 103, 108, *111*, 118, 197, 343

birds 41, 43, 50, *51*, 53, *66*, 69, 72, 75, 76, 84, 85, 89, 90, 92, 93, 103, 108–11, *109*, 185, 197, *231*

cartouche 43, 47, 49, 50, 51, 53, 57, 61, 62, 70, 84, 121

compartment designs 44, 102, 112, 115, 120–1

dragon 61, 76, 90, *90*, 140–4, *142*, 149, 153, 155, 157, 185, 190, *190*, 252, *253*, *254*, 255

fish 86, 190

floral 11, 22, 40, 41, 43, 45, 57, 61, *61*, 62, 65, 66–76, *67*, *68*, 70, *71*, *81*, 85, 102, *116*, 128–37, *130*, *133*, *135*, *137*, 144–7, *145*, 155, 191, 197, 223

garden 44, 57, 61, 70–6, 80, 102, 104, 132, 145, 207, *207*, 223, *223*, 237, 241

geometric 11, 40, 41, 42, 93, 95, 100, 115, *115*, 116, 155, 157, 181, 324, 329

gul 38, 41, 159–60, 162, 163–4, 174, 188, 190

Holbein 40, *93*, 95–100, *100*, 102, 115, 155, 157, 197, 205, *205*

hunting *31*, *32*, 44, *44*, 45, 49, 53, 70, 85, *125*, *138*, 241, *339*

Kufic border 96, 102, 120, 121, *141*, 145, *145*, 155, *207*, 342, *342*

lion 246–8

Lotto 40, 100–3, *100*, *103*, 104, 197, 205

medallion *frontis*, 22, 31, *32*, 43, 44, *44*, 45–53, *48*, *50*, *51*, *52*, 55–7, *55*, *56*, *60*, 61, *61*, 62, 66, *66*, 69, 80, *81*, 82, 84, 85, *87*, 102, 103, 105, 107, 108, *109*, 112, 115, *229*

stars 40, 41, 43, 85, 95, 103, 105, *106*, 108, 111, 121, 128, 132, *156*, 197

Tamerlaine, Arms of *see* balls and stripes, above

trees and shrubs 44, 50, 53, 59, *59*, 61, *64*, 65, 76–80, *77*, *80*, *126*, 128, 144, 145, 223, 241

Muche, Georg 311, *312*

Mudjur 209, *210*

Muhammed, Sultan 34, 49, 53, *54*

Muhammed Amin, of Kerman *72*, 75

Mushkabad 224, 234, 250

Mute, Elizabeth 326

Myers, Mabel Burnside 329

N

Nadir Shah 76, 173, 221

Nain 221, 223, 234, 250

Nash, Paul 317

Natoni, Mildred 326

Navajo 7, 323–31, *320*, *322*, *323*

Navajo pictorial rugs 330–1

Nelson, Alice 324

Nelson, Eleanor *330*

New Mexico 331

Nez, Grace Henderson 328

Nicholson, Ben 317

Nigde carpet *143*, 144

Nilssen, Barbra *310*

Nimat Allah *64*, 65

Ninrod, Ella *331*

Niris (Neriz) 250

Nishapur 173

Nomadic rugs 11, 12, 15, 38, 40, 44, 163, 221, 226, 336

Norway 274, 276, *399*

Norwich 105

O

Ogurjalis 164, 165, 166

Oltenian 273

Orage, Jean 313, 319

Otte, Benita 311, *311*, *312*

Ottomans 11, 17, *22*, 33

P

Pahetti, Domenico *98*

Palas 251–2, 342

Panderma 201, *201*, 209

Paolo, Giovanni di 93

Pardisah kelim 84

Parisot, Peter 290, 293, 297

Passavant 293, 296

Pazyryk 38, *39*, 40, *40*, *41*, 158, 181, 182, 197

Peacock rug 125, *126*, 127–8

Pendeh 160, *161*, 172

Pepler, Marion *313*, 314, *317*

Perepedil 155, *156*, 157, 336

Percier 284, 288

Perrot, Pierre Josse 284, 285, 288

Persia 11, 13, 15, 17, 20, 27, 28, 29, *29*, 31, 34, 37, 38, *39*, 40–3, 84, *87*, 152, 168, 180, 192

Persian knot *see* Knots

Peshlakai, Helen 328

Pietro, Sano di 83

Pile *see* Weaving techniques

Pine Springs 329

Pintoricchio, Bernardino di Betto 96, 100

Piombo, Sebastiano del 100

Pisanello, properly Antonio Pisano 92

Poland 270–2, *271*

Poldi Pezzoli carpet 45, 49, 50, *50*, 53, 66, 89

Pollaiuolo, Piero 140

Polo, Marco 11, 41, 90

Polonaise carpets 44, 49, 61, 64, 65, 80–4, *81*, *82*, *83*, *84*, 185, *221*, 336

Pondicherri 289

Portugal 44, 261

Portuguese carpets 86–9, *86*, 147, *219*, 220, *233*

Prayer rugs 88, 89, 103–4, *104*, 118, *118*, 135–7, *135*, *138*, *148*, *151*, 157, *157*, 167, *167*, 174–6, 177, *177*, *179*, 197–211, *197*, *198*, *201*, *202*, *207*, *210*, *212*, 225, 244–6, 251, *336*, *337*

Prentis, Terence *315*, *317*, 319

Price, Maggie 329

Pincket rug 137, *216*

Pueblo Indians 323

Q

Qashqai *see* Kashgai

Qazvin *see* Kazvin

Quedlinburg 261

R

Rahim Khani 173, 174

Ravar 239, 250

Reed, William 294

Rhodian carpets 115, 120–1

Riza Shah 221, *234*

Roan, Maggie 329

Roan, Nellie *327*, 328, 329

Roby 286

Romania 199, 217, *258*, 270, 272, 273

Rosenberg Castle 83, *84*

Royal Deventer Factory 262

Rukh, Shah 31, 41

Ryiji 273, 274–5, *276*, *308*

S

'S-group' 169, 170, *335*, 337

S spin *see* Weaving techniques

Sabzawar 44

Safavids 31, 33, 43, 122, 221, 223

Safavid weaving 7, 11, 15, 17, 20, 44–89, 190, 216, *219*, 220

Safi, Shah 44, 47, 82, 83

Safi, Sheikh Shrine of *see* Ardabil Mosque

Saint-Ange, La Hameyde de 284, 288

Saint Giles, Master of 100, *100*

Saliani 155

Sallandrouze de la Mornaix 288, 289

Salmon, Pierre 95

Salor 37, 100, 160, *161*, *162*, 163–4, *169*, 170, 174, *184*, *335*

Salting Carpet *frontis*, *212*, 216

Samarkand 31, 34, 41, 180, *180*, 181, 182, 184

Sand-painting rugs 331, *331*

Sanguszko carpets 20, 44, 48, *48*, 53, 59, *60*, *61*, 62, 66, 72, 75, 85

Saph 104, *107*, *135*, 186, 251, 343

Saraband 250

Sarakhs 173, 174

Sardinia 273

Sarköy 251

Saruk 221, 224, 231, *231*, *233*, 234, *234*, 250

Saryk rugs 15, 21, 159, 160, 164, 166, 169, 170, 184

Sassanian dynasty 27, 28, *28*, *29*, 39, 40

Savonnerie 267, 270, 272, 279, 280–3, *280*, *281*, *282*, 284, 285, 286, 288, 290, 314

Saxony 83, 84

Schwarzenburg, Prince of, carpet 50, 59, *59*, 66, 70

Schulaver 147, *148*

Scythians 38, *39*, 147

Seljuks 11, 29, 33, 34, 37, 40, 90, 93, 95, 115, 140, 155, 158, 173, 182, 197, 209, 220, 241

Sejshour 155, 157, 252

Senneh 21, 221, 224, 226, *226*, 229, *229*, 241, 250, 251, *337*

Senneh knot *see* Knots, Persian

Serab 224, 250

Seraband 224, 229

Sétif 220

Sewan Kazak *148*

Shah, Nadir *see* Nadir Shah

Shah Nameh 41, *42*, 33, 72, 229

Shiprock 324, 326

Shiraz *10*, 17, *31*, *32*, 41, 44, 221, 244–6

Shirvan 11, 138, *143*, 144, *145*, 145, *147*, 152, 153–5, *153*, *155*, 251, 252, *253*, *254*, 255, 256

Shosho-in Shrine 189

Shusha *143*, *145*, 150, 152, 255

Sileh 251, 252–5, *254*, 343

Silk *see* Materials

Silver thread *see* Materials

Simonetti carpet *115*

Sinkiang 180

Sistan 173, 174, *177*, *177*

Sivas 90

Six, Mary 329

Smith, Agnes 329

Smith, Alexander & Sons 300

Smith, Ellen 329

Smyrna 104, *211*, *212*, 277, 286

Sofie Amalie, Queen 83

Sotavalta, Impi 308

Souj-Boulak 250

Soumak 20, 21, *143*, 157, *177*, 251, 252, *254*, 255, *255*, 343

INDEX   349

Spain 6, 11, 17, 21, 28, 218, 262–9
Spanish knot *see* Knots
Spencer, Marjorie 329
Spring Carpet of Chosroes *see* Chosroes
Steiglitz carpet 50, 51, 65, 66
Stölzl, Gunta 311, 312
Storm pattern 327, 329, *330*
Stroganoff carpet 107
Subbekakasheny 334
Suleyman the Magnificent 103, 225
Sung dynasty 182, 189, *189*
Surahani 155
Suzanis 85
Sweden 274–5
Symmetrical knot *see* Knots, Turkish
Syria 27, 28, 33, 37

T
Tabriz 13, 17, 20, 21, 29, 31, 41, *42*, 43, 44, 47, 48, 49, 51, 53, 62, 65, 66, 76, *78*, 79, 103, 108, 115, 116, 117, 121, 138, 201, *201*, 221, 223–4, *223*, 250
Tahmasp, Shah 44, 47, 48, 49, 50, 53, *54*, 122, 225
Talish 147, 152–3, *153*, 155
Tamerlaine *see* Timur
Tamerlaine, Arms of *see* Motifs, balls and stripes
Tandy, John 314, *314*, 317, 319
T'ang Dynasty 184, 189
Taugelchee, Daisy 326
Taugelchee, Esther 326
Taugelchee, Priscilla 326
Tebily 241
Teec Nos Pos 324, *325*
Teheran 43, 221, 223, 234, *234*, 250
Tekke 37, 100, *159*, 160, 161, *162*, 163, *163*, 164, *165*, 169, 170, 172, 174, 176, 184
Templeton, James 299, *299*, 300, 302, 305, *307*
Theadore, Julie 326
Thrace 251, 256, 343
Thompson, Lottie 329
Thomson, Lucy 334
Tibet 27, 34, 195–6
Timur 31, *31*, 33, 34, 41, 122
Timuri tribe 173, 177
Timurid dynasty 11, 41, 42, 43, 66, 122, 181
Tisdall, Hans *see* Aufseeser
Todacheenie, Stella 326, 328
Tom, Mary 326
Tomkinson & Adam 300, 305, *306*, 319
Tools *see* Weaving techniques
Torback, Gerard *81*
Torbat 173
Tournai 283, 294
Toyotomi Hideyoshi carpet 84, 85, *86*

Transylvania 15, 20, 204, *207*, 212, 217, 273, *338*
Tree and shrub carpets *see* Motifs
Tsosie, Ruth 329
Tuba City Storm rug 329
Tuduc (Duduk) 217
Tuisarkhan 224
Tunisia 7, 218, 220, 251, 256
Turkestan 15, 28, 31, 34, 125
Turkestan, East 34, 38, 39, 40, 41, 144, 180–9, 192, 193, 195
Turkestan, West 11, 15, 29, 33, 34, 37
Turkey 7, 11, 13, 15, 17, 20, 27, 33, 40, 41, 42, *88*, 89, 90–111, 140, 168, 180, 197–216, 257
Turkibaffs 249
Turkish knot *see* Knots
Turkmenistan 34, 158, 166, 168, 170, 172
Turkoman carpets 7, 15, 18, 21, 38, 40, 100, 158–72, 174, 190, 192, 197, 209, *212*, 337, 341
Turkomans 34–7, *36*, 176, 221, 249, 256
Two Grey Hills 325–6, *325*

U
Ukraine *271*
Umayyad Caliphate 28, 33, 218
Ushak 11, 15, 20, 50, 76, 102, 103–11, *104*, *106*, *107*, *109*, *111*, 149, 155, 157, 197, 203, 204, *207*, 208, 209, 211, *211*, 212, 217, 233, 261, 267, 272, 277
Uzbekistan 34, 85, 158, 180, 257

V
Van der Weyden, Rogier *see* Weyden
Varda, Jean 317
Vase carpets 7, 17, 20, 21, 44, 51, 57–66, *58*, *60*, *61*, *63*, 76, 131, *131*, 132, 133, 140, 141, 144, 146, 153, 155, 223, *229*, 237
Venice 43, 104, 261
Venice carpets 81–2, *84*
Veramin 250
Verneh 251, 252, *254*, 255, *256*, 343
Veronese Paolo 80
Vienna hunting carpet 53, *54*, 70, 79
Vos, Cornelis de 204
Voysey, C. F. A. 305, *306*, 307

W
Wagner garden carpet 72–5
Warp *see* Weaving techniques
Watson, Bell & Co. 300
Weaving techniques 9–21
    brocade *20*, 21, 39, 53, *68*, 69, 84, 86, 89, 174, 177, 186, 216, 251, *254*, 256
    flat-weaves 251–6, 337

fringe 11, 17
hooked rugs 332–3, *332*, *333*, *334*
pile 11, 15, 147, 170, 176, 181, 207, 211, 218, 243
S spin 7, 17, *71*
shirring 332
tools 13–15, *13*, *15*
warp 11–12, *12*, 13, 15, 17, 18–20, 21, 86, 89, 121, 170, 184, 199, 251
weft 11–12, 13, *13*, *15*, 17, 18–20, 21, 89, 170, 181, 184, 218, 251, 252, 326, 328, 329
Z twist 17, *17*
Weft *see* Weaving techniques
Western Navajo Reservation 329
Weyden, Rogier van der *98*
Wheelwright, Mary 328
Whipple, Esther 328
Whitty, Thomas 290, 296–7
Widener carpet 125, 128
Wide Ruin 329, *329*, *330*
Williams, Esther 324
Williams tree carpet 76, 77
Wilson, Elsie 328
Wilton 293, 294, 297–8, 299, *303*, 304, *305*, *313*, 314, *314*, *315*, 319, *319*
Wingate, Mary 328
Wire *see* Materials
Wittelsbach Paradise kelim 84
Woodward Grosvenors 288
Wool *see* Materials
Wyatt, Digby 302
Wyld, Evelyn 319

Y
Yabeney, Emma 324
Yarkand 180, 181, 182, *183*, 184, 186, 188
Yates & Co. 298
Yazzie, Anny 328
Yazzie, Faye 328
Yazzie, Philomena 329, *329*
Yei rug *323*, 324, 326, *326*, 331
Yeibichai rug *323*, 324, *331*
Yerevan *see* Erivan
Yezd 44, 48, 62, 65, 66, 234, 250
Yomut 100, 157, 158, *159*, 160, *162*, 164–6, *165*, *166*, 168, 169, *169*, 170, 172, 173, 174, 184, 188, 226
Ypres 261
Yüan Dynasty 34, 182, 189
Yuruk 40, 209, *212*, 214–15

Z
Z Twist *see* Weaving techniques
Zejwa 155
Zeli Sultan *226*, 250
Zenjan 250
Ziegler's 45, 47, 221, 233–4, *234*, 239, 250

Acknowledgements

The editor and publishers would like to thank the various museums and other institutions which have provided photographs of carpets in their collections and information about them; and also Christie's in London, Sotheby Parke Bernet in London and New York, Lefèvre and Partners, Raymond Benardout and other dealers and salerooms who have, as usual, been most helpful and cooperative. Special thanks is due to the many individuals who have given us the benefit of their knowledge and experience – above all, David Black and Clive Loveless, partners in one of the most dynamic firms of carpet dealers in London, C. John, Victor Franses, Michael Franses, Jack Franses (now carpet expert at Sotheby's in London), Dr. Jon Thompson, Edmund de Unger, Jackie and Michael Pruskin, Michael Whiteway, Jay Jones of California and many others. The editor would also like to extend his thanks to his fellow authors: Isabelle Anscombe, Harmer Johnson, Gérald Schurr and John Siudmak, the last-named the carpet expert at Christie's, who has also given much help and advice in the preparation of the section on Oriental weaving, and to Anne-Marie Ehrlich for her indefatigable picture research.

The publishers and editor also wish to acknowledge their indebtedness to the owners of copyright in the short passages of quotation in the text, especially to Dr. Joan Allgrove and Dr. May Beattie, to the Metropolitan Museum of New York for permission to quote from *Rugs in the Metropolitan Museum* by M. S. Dimand, to Faber and Faber, London, and the University of California Press for permission to quote from the English-language edition of *Seven Hundred Years of Oriental Carpets* by Kurt Erdmann, and to the Arts Council of Great Britain and Donald King for permission to quote from the catalogue of the *Arts of Islam* exhibition at the Hayward Gallery, London, in 1976.

Picture Credits

(t = top; c = centre; b = bottom; l = left; r = right)

Abby Aldrich Rockefeller Folk Art Coll., Colonial Williamsburg, U.S.A. 333 (c and br); ACL Brussels 94 (b); Architectural Press, London 316; Archives Nationales, Paris 282 (t), 283, 284; Archivo Fotografico Nazionale, Rome 274 (l); Ashton Gallery, Arizona jacket back, 322–333 (all); Bayerisches Nationalmuseum, Munich 56; John Bethell 299; Biblioteca Apostolica Vaticana 95; David Black Oriental Carpets Ltd. jacket front, 139, 147 (t), 150 (r), 154, 159 (t), 163, 166, 167, 175, 187, 230 (tr), 207 (br), 208 (b), 238, 243, 254 (tr, b: l and r), 255 (t); Brighton Pavilion and Art Gallery 297, 298 (l and r); British Library 26, 30, 31 (bl), 32 (tr); Trustees of the British Museum 41, 129 (r); Collection of the Duke of Buccleuch and Queensberry 61; Christie, Manson & Woods Ltd. 77, 82 (l), 85 (l), 88 (l), 98 (tr), 99 (tl), 103, 106, 109 (b), 114 (bl), 136 (br), 147 (b), 148 (b: l, c and r), 151 (t: l and r), 152 (t), 153, 155 (t), 168 (r), 183, 185 (l), 193, 194 (b: l, c and r), 198 (r), 202 (l: t and b), 203, 205, 206 (b: l and r), 208 (t), 209, 212 (c), 214 (tl and r), 216, 225, 228 (tr), 229 (bc), 230 (tl), 231 (r: t and b), 234 (tr), 237 (l), 240 (r: t and b), 248, 251, 253 (tr), 256 (br), 271 (l); Ellio Cittone 274 (r); P. & D. Colnaghi & Co., London 83 (tr and b); Corcoran Gallery of Art, William A. Clark Collection 117 (r); Detroit Institute of Arts 56; Hotel Drouot, Paris 135 (tr); Mary Evans Picture Library 284 (t); Fogg Art Museum, Cambridge, Mass. 75; Michael Franses 6, 86 (r), 87, 111 (t), 113, 191, 196, 335, 339; The Frick Collection, New York 94 (tr); Gemäldegalerie, Dresden 94 (tl); J. Paul Getty Museum, Malibu 132; Ronald Grierson 314 (t: l and c), 317; Gulistan Museum, Teheran 66; Robert Harding & Associates 27, 28, 29 (tr), 32; Harvard Law School 206; Hispanic Society of America 266; India Office Library, London 133 (b); Iran Bastan Museum, Teheran 64; Islamisches Museum, Berlin 91, 100, 104, 107, 119, 219; Jaipur Museum, India 74 (t); C. John 258, 260, 263, 270, 273, 282 (b); Jay Jones Collection, California 231 (l), 234, 235; Kunsthistorisches Museum, Vienna 98 (tl); Kunstsammlungen zu Weimar 311, 312; Kunst und Gewerbe Museum, Hamburg 60; Mansell Collection, London 80 (r), 90, 92 (tr), 93, 96 (t and b), 98 (tr), 99, 265, 277 (br), 296, 302 (b); Manx Museum 306 (t); Foto Mas, Barcelona 92 (r); Metropolitan Museum of Art, New York 55, 61, 67 (t), 68 (tl), 69 (l), 81, 110, 114, 125, 131, 134, 138, 143, 145 (r), 280 (r); Mobilier National, Paris 281, 288; William Morris Gallery, Walthamstow 301, 304 (l and c), 305 (b), 314 (r); Musée des Gobelins, Paris 52 (br); Musée des Tissus, Lyons 126 (bl); Musée National de Malmaison 285, 286; Musée Nissim de Caimondo, Paris 280 (l); Museum of Fine Arts, Boston 126 (r); Trustees of the National Gallery, London 92 (bl), 97, 98 (b), 101; National Monuments Record of Scotland 307 (b); National Trust 278, 291, 292, 295, 302 (t); Novosti Press Agency 39, 40; Österreichisches Museum für angewandte Kunst 52 (bl), 54, 72, 86, 126 (tr); Poldi Pezzoli Museum, Milan 44; Private Collections 72, 77, 307 (t); Mrs M. D. Pruskin 314 (tr, b: l and r), 315 (b: l and r); Quarto Publishing Ltd 171, 178, 179; Röhsska Konstlogdmuseet 276, 308 (l); Rosenberg Castle, Copenhagen 83 (tl); Royal Wilton Carpet Factory 305 (t), 313 (l and r), 318; Prince Roman Sanguszko, Paris 60 (tl); H.S.H. Prince Charles of Schwarzenburg 59; Shrine Collection, Meshed 68; John Siudmak 255 (b); Courtesy of the Smithsonian Institution, Freer Gallery of Art, Washington D.C. 42; Smithsonian Institution, Washington 332, 333 (t, b: l and c), 334; Sotheby Parke Bernet 51, 58, 63 (l and r), 67 (bl), 68 (br), 69 (r), 70, 71, 78 (t and b), 79, 81 (r), 82 (r), 82 (r), 109 (t), 116, 117 (bl), 118, 120, 130 (t), 131, 132, 136 (t), 141, 144, 145 (l), 146, 148 (t: l and r), 150 (l: t and b), 151 (b), 152 (b), 155 (b), 156, 157, 158, 159 (b: l and r), 161, 165, 168 (l and c), 169, 170, 172, 185 (r), 187 (r), 197, 198 (l), 200, 201, 202 (r), 207 (bl), 210, 211, 212 (l and r), 213, 214 (bl), 215, 221, 222, 223, 224, 226, 227, 228 (tl and b: l and r), 229 (t and bl), 230 (b: l and r), 232, 233, 234 (tl, c and b), 236, 237 (r), 239, 240 (tl, c and bl), 241, 242, 244, 247, 253 (l: t and b), 254 (tl), 256 (bl), 257, 260, 275, 287 (t), 307, 314 (br), 336, 337, 338; Spink & Son Ltd 194 (t: l and r); Textile Museum, Washington 142, 264; Thyssen-Bornemisza Coll., Lugano 135 (tr); Earl of Verulam photo John Bethell 217; Victoria and Albert Museum, Crown Copyright reserved 22, 27, 29 (l and br), 31 (c and br), 32 (tl), 35, 36, 46, 51 (c), 73, 74 (b), 87, 122, 123, 124, 125, 127, 129 (l), 130 (b), 133 (t), 136 (b), 149, 162, 180, 188, 189, 190, 267, 268 (t and r), 269, 299, 303, 304 (r), 306 (l and r), 309, 310 (t and br), 315 (t); Vigo Sternberg Galleries 271 (r: t, c, and b); Trevor Wood photos 279, 286.

Special photography: *Techniques and Materials of Oriental Carpet Weaving* by Michael Freeman; *Navajo Rugs* by David Burton.
Special line illustrations: Roger Carnegie.
Special maps: QED, London.